THE USAF IN THE PERSIAN GULF WAR

Lucrative Targets

The U.S. Air Force in the Kuwaiti Theater of Operations

Perry D. Jamieson

Air Force History and Museums Program
United States Air Force
Washington, D.C., 2001

Opinions, conclusions, and recommendations expressed or implied within are solely those of the author and do not necessarily represent the views of the Air Force History and Museums Program, the U.S. Air Force, the Department of Defense, or any other U.S. government agency.

Library of Congress Cataloging-in-Publication Data

Jamieson, Perry D.
    Lucrative targets : the U.S. Air Force in the Kuwaiti Theater of Operations /
        Perry D. Jamieson.
        p. cm. — (The USAF in the Persian Gulf War)
    Includes bibliographical references and index.
     1. Persian Gulf War, 1991 — Aerial operations, American. 2. United States.
Air Force — History — Persian Gulf War, 1991. 3. Persian Gulf War, 1991 —
Campaigns — Kuwait. I. Title. II. Series.

DS79.744.A47 J36 2001
956.7044'248 — dc21

                                         2001022943

For sale by the Superintendent of Documents, U.S. Government Printing Office
Internet: bookstore.gpo.gov   Phone: (202) 512-1800   Fax: (202) 512-2250
Mail: Stop SSOP, Washington, DC 20402-0001

ISBN 0-16-050958-0

Lucrative Targets

The U.S. Air Force in the Kuwaiti Theater of Operations

Availability of Sources

The Office of the Secretary of Defense's Directorate for Freedom of Information and Security Review (OASD–PA) cleared this monograph for publication. Most of its notes cite classified documents or interviews. That OASD–PA cleared this monograph for publication does not mean its sources have been declassified or even reviewed. In many cases, they remain classified, and in some cases a document's title or the identification of an entire source remains classified.

Foreword

During the late 1970s, the United States began revitalizing its Air Force and other military services. By the close of the 1980s, America had built a force structure that stood ready for a test that, very fortunately, it never had to meet—a major war in Europe. The United States faced this dangerous possibility for more than forty years until, in 1989, the Soviet Union abruptly collapsed. Americans were still sorting out the implications of this sudden change in world affairs in August 1990, when Iraq invaded Kuwait and precipitated a crisis that led to the military conflict in the Persian Gulf. The U.S. Air Force found itself at war—although not the one it had prepared for, against the Warsaw Pact powers—but one against Saddam Hussein's heavily armed regime.

This monograph is one in a series of five works dealing with various aspects of the Air Force's participation in Desert Shield and Storm. In two other volumes, William T. Y'Blood details the Air Force's deployment to the Gulf; in a third, Diane T. Putney analyzes the planning of the air campaign; and, in a fourth, Richard G. Davis discusses the air operations against targets in Iraq.

As this monograph goes to press during the fall of 2001, the Air Force is passing through a dynamic period of reorganization and change. The era when a large USAF defended the United States against a single preeminent threat, Soviet aggression, has ended. During the years ahead, a smaller Air Force will support the interests of the nation, under diverse circumstances around the globe. While the U.S. Air Force continues to ensure that the United States has a global reach and can project global power, the service will greatly benefit from the lessons it learned during Desert Shield and Desert Storm.

RICHARD P. HALLION
Air Force Historian

Preface

During the Gulf War, Col. David Tretler was serving as acting chief of the Air Force History Program. Shortly after the conflict ended, he chose the topics for a series of monographs on the Air Force in Operations Desert Shield and Storm. He asked me to write the one on the Kuwaiti Theater of Operations, and I finished the manuscript in November 1992. This work is being published by the Air Force History and Museums Program. The former Center for Air Force History has now become the present-day Air Force History Support Office.

Many people contributed to this work and, if I fail to mention all of them here, their help is no less appreciated.

Colonel Tretler initiated the Center for Air Force History's series of works on the Gulf War, and Dr. Richard P. Hallion, who became the Air Force Historian in November 1992, supported these ongoing studies. At that time, three other CAFH historians—Jacob Neufeld, the Center's director; Herman S. Wolk, its senior historian; and Dr. Alfred M. Beck, the chief of its histories division—read my manuscript and offered many useful comments.

The enlisted historians of the Air Force History Program built a foundation for researching any topic related to the Gulf War air campaign. Before, during, and after Desert Storm, they collected thousands of feet of documents and conducted a number of valuable oral history interviews. My sincere thanks to CMSgt. John Burton and the NCOs who served with him in the Gulf. Military historians will benefit from their work for long years to come.

Dr. Wayne Thompson, a CAFH historian detailed to the Checkmate Office, did an excellent job of collecting and organizing the scores of important documents that were created or received by that organization during Desert Shield and Storm. Dr. Thompson could not have done this work without the cooperation of Col. John A. Warden III, the chief of the Checkmate Office, who assigned a high priority to preserving the historical record of the Desert Storm air campaign. Colonel Warden strongly supported the work of Dr. Thompson, myself, and other Air Force historians. In addition to Colonel Warden, Lt. Col. Ben Harvey, Lt. Col. Al Howey, and several other Checkmate officers also helped me when I worked there during the spring and summer of 1991.

I visited a number of history offices around the Air Force, and elsewhere, and I always found people who were proud of what their organizations had contributed to the Gulf War and happy to share useful information with me. Since I finished my research, some of these offices have reorganized, and a number of these people have made career moves. These contributors, and their assignments when I visited them in 1991 and 1992, included Drs. Jay H. Smith and John W. Leland, Headquarters Military Airlift Command History Office, Scott AFB, Illinois; Dr. James K. Matthews and Ms. Cora Holt, Headquarters U.S. Transportation Command History Office, Scott AFB, Illinois; Dr. Robert J. Parks, Dr. J. Todd White, Dr. Kent Beck, and Mr. Edward (Wendy) Gayle, Headquarters Strategic Air Command History Office, Offutt AFB, Nebraska; Mr. Steven L. Head, Special Assistant to the Deputy Director of Defense Research and Engineering, Tactical Warfare Programs, Under Secretary of Defense (Acquisition), the Pentagon; Mr. Grant M. Hales, Mr. George W. (Skip) Bradley III, and Dr. James M. George, Headquarters Tactical Air Command History Office, Langley AFB, Virginia; Dr. Hans Pawlisch and Col. Kenneth McGraw, Headquarters U.S. Central Command History Office, MacDill AFB, Florida; Mr. David L. Rosmer and Dr. Barry R. Barlow, Headquarters Ninth Air Force History Office, Shaw AFB, South Carolina; Drs. Frank N. (Mickey) Schubert, Theresa L. Kraus, and David W. Hogan, U.S. Army Center of Military History, Washington, D.C.; Mr. Benis M. Frank and Capt. David A. (Scotty) Dawson, U.S. Marine Corps Historical Center, Washington, D.C.; and Dr. Edward J. Marolda, U.S. Naval Historical Center, Washington, D.C.

General Charles A. Horner deserves the thanks of all military historians for his willingness to participate in interviews after the Gulf War and, moreover, for his concern for preserving the historical record during the conflict. He permitted Chief Burton to record on audiotape, each morning and afternoon throughout the conflict, his remarks to his staff in the Tactical Air Control Center (TACC). General Horner also encouraged the work of the enlisted historians who worked around the clock in the TACC: Chief Burton, MSgt. Theodore J. (Jackie) Turner, TSgt. Frederick Hosterman, TSgt. Marcus R. Walker, and TSgt. Scott A. Saluda. The CENTAF commander was personally responsible for creating one of the most important primary sources about the conduct of the air campaign: the CC/DO Logbook that the senior officers in the TACC maintained throughout the war. One colonel who served in this command center during Desert Storm remembered that when "anything…had any smack of importance," General Horner would say, "Write it in the book." This officer also recalled that the CENTAF commander "was pretty adamant" about enforcing this rule and, "You could get in trouble for not writing it in the book."

General Horner and many other officers took time from their busy schedules to give oral history interviews. I am indebted to them and to the historians who conducted these sessions. Most of the oral histories I used are listed in the List of Short Citations, and all of them appear in the endnotes. Particularly helpful to me were interviews given by General Horner, Maj. Gen. Thomas R. Olsen, Maj. Gen. Buster C. Glosson, Col. John A. Warden III, Lt. Col. David A. Deptula, and Lt. Col. Sam Baptiste.

I owe a considerable debt to two editors, Karen Fleming-Michael and Barbara Wittig. Karen Fleming-Michael improved my manuscript and, at the same time, maintained her sense of humor. I especially appreciate the time she spent on this project during 1993, when I had to set it aside while working in the Pentagon for a year. When Karen Fleming-Michael moved to another assignment, Barbara Wittig finished the project. Her long experience and common sense were invaluable.

Finally, my thanks go to the CAFH historians who worked on other Gulf War topics. Every one of them—Capt. Steven B. Michael, Mr. William T. Y'Blood, Dr. Richard G. Davis, and Dr. Diane T. Putney—shared their research and ideas with me. During trips to give presentations on the Gulf War, and at other times, I learned much from these colleagues and friends.

The Author

Perry D. Jamieson earned a B.A. from Michigan State University and an M.A. and a Ph.D. from Wayne State University. Dr. Jamieson taught American military history at the University of Texas at El Paso and has worked for the Air Force History Program since 1980. He has contributed to the annual histories of the Strategic Air Command, Air Force Systems Command, Air Force Space Command, and Headquarters United States Air Force, and to many special projects. Dr. Jamieson is also the author of three books on the U.S. Army during and after the Civil War.

Contents

Illustrations

Chapter One

This Will Not Stand:
A Crisis in the Persian Gulf

In early August 1990, Iraq attacked Kuwait, its small neighbor to the south, with overwhelming forces. U.S. Army General H. Norman Schwarzkopf, Commander in Chief, United States Central Command (USCENTCOM), later recalled how the sudden Iraqi mobilization during late July had misled some U.S. military leaders. "Iraq had used the desert near Basra for training before," he explained, "and at first we thought this might be merely another exercise…. But by the end of July, the Iraqis were no longer confined to the exercise area; they had fanned out southeast and southwest of Basra and pointed themselves toward the Kuwaiti border." On August 2, heavy units of the Republican Guard Forces Command plunged across that frontier, leading a brutally swift assault. These elite troops quickly overran Kuwait, seized Kuwait City, and, on the second day of the invasion, moved rapidly toward the Saudi Arabian border. By August 6, elements of eleven divisions were either in or entering the small kingdom south of Iraq. These powerful forces firmly occupied Kuwait and stood poised to invade Saudi Arabia.[1]

Kuwait, a nation of fewer than two million people and seven thousand square miles, had neither the military strength to resist this overpowering assault nor the room to retreat while fighting for time. Iraqi infantrymen and armor quickly killed or put to flight most of the small kingdom's army of approximately twenty thousand soldiers. No more than one-third of Kuwait's troops—and only forty of its tanks—escaped the disaster. A year after the invasion, one young resident of Kuwait City recalled, "For us, August 2 marks the time we lost our children, our families and our country."[2]

Saddam Hussein, Iraq's dictator, voiced two major grievances against Kuwait before seizing it. He alleged that the Kuwaitis had stolen oil from fields that straddled the border between the two countries and that the Kuwaitis had disregarded the production limits set by the Organization of Petroleum Exporting Countries

Lucrative Targets

(OPEC). Saddam charged that Kuwait's violation of these cartel ceilings had driven down the price of oil, and he accordingly demanded billions of dollars in compensation to Iraq. As a pretext for invading his neighbor, the Iraqi autocrat claimed that revolutionaries had overthrown the Kuwaiti government and asked him to intervene.[3]

None of these contentions carried any weight with the president of the United States, George H. W. Bush, who immediately denounced Iraq's attack on its neighbor as "naked aggression." The president promptly banned nearly all imports from Iraq and froze its assets in the United States. A few days later he told reporters, "This will not stand. This will not stand, this aggression against Kuwait."[4]

The United States had several reasons for its interest in the fate of a remote sheikdom on the Persian Gulf. First, Americans fundamentally objected to any nation destroying the sovereignty of another, particularly in cases in which the conqueror was so much stronger than its opponent. Iraq, which fielded the world's fourth-largest army, had abruptly overrun a neighbor roughly the size of New Jersey.[5] Second, the United States was gravely concerned about the future designs of Saddam Hussein, a truculent, unpredictable dictator who had doggedly waged an eight-year war against another bordering nation, Iran, and had brutally repressed his own countrymen. If Saddam's conquest of Kuwait went unchallenged, he might become the dominant figure in the Middle East.[6] Third, the Iraqi autocrat held in Iraq and Kuwait more than three thousand American civilians who he could use as "human shields" for cities and military installations.[7] Fourth, the United States, which in 1990 drew approximately half of its oil from foreign sources, had a compelling economic interest in the region. If Iraq absorbed Kuwait, Baghdad would roughly double the petroleum supply under its control. Its oil reserves then would stand at about 195 billion barrels, second in the world only to Saudi Arabia.[8]

America's immediate concern was that Saddam Hussein might invade Saudi Arabia. After overrunning Kuwait, the Iraqi dictator controlled almost 20 percent of the world's petroleum supplies, and his forces stood poised within a half-day's tank ride of the oilfields of Saudi Arabia and the United Arab Emirates, which held another 37 percent. Saddam also might have seized some of the military installations on the Arabian peninsula, denying their use by the United States and other nations. In August 1991, Brig. Gen. Patrick P. Caruana, the Strategic Air Command Strategic Force (STRATFOR) Commander, recalled how tenuous the circumstances had been a year earlier, when the Iraqis might well have invaded Saudi Arabia. "If [Saddam Hussein] had been smart," General Caruana suggested, "he would have done that. That would have complicated things tremendously for us.... How effective we would have been with B–52s against an armored column was marginal, at best." A captain from the 668th Bombardment Squadron later recalled: "With the exception of Langley's [AFB] F–15s which were in Saudi, [our

B–52s] were it…. For the first two or three weeks we were pretty nervous and just kept hoping that Saddam would hold off."[9]

Senior American leaders were as concerned as this company-grade officer. General Schwarzkopf later described the opening days of the crisis: "My main worry was that a ground war would come to us…. I knew that the Iraqis could overrun the Saudi oil region in a week. Our soldiers knew it too: paratroopers from the 82d Airborne Division at Dhahran nicknamed themselves 'Iraqi speed-bumps.'" In late March 1991, Lt. Gen. Charles A. Horner, Commander, U.S. Air Force, Central Command (CENTAF), reminded an interviewer how uncertain the situation had been during early August 1990. "During that time," General Horner pointed out, "we never knew whether the Iraqis were going to attack Saudi Arabia or not…. In reality, if Iraq had attacked during [those] first few days, there really was very little to stop them other than air power. So, we would have had to trade distance." General Horner's deputy, Maj. Gen. Thomas Olsen, said dryly, "Personally, I never unpacked my suitcase."[10]

Although Iraq did not invade Saudi Arabia, it announced the annexation of Kuwait on the eighth of August, and it held that country with powerful military units. As one official American assessment tersely stated on August 10, "Iraqi forces in Kuwait far exceed occupation requirements." On that day, five Republican Guard divisions held the small sheikdom, with one of them deployed along the Saudi border. By then the Iraqis also had established air defenses, repaired airfields in Kuwait, and based in southern Iraq and its conquered neighbor a variety of aircraft, including MiG–21 Fishbeds, MiG–23 Floggers, MiG–25 Foxbats, MiG–29 Fulcrums, and Mirage F–1Es. Saddam Hussein's arsenal further included Scud-B, Frog–7, and CSSC–3 Silkworm missiles and chemical weapons, which he had used not only against the Iranians but also against rebels within his own country.[11]

With these Iraqi forces deployed near their border, the Saudis were willing to receive help from the United States. During a meeting at Camp David, Maryland, on August 4, President Bush told his senior defense advisers that he wanted a firm agreement with Saudi Arabia before committing any American military forces to that country.[12] Two days later, King Fahd bin Abd al-Aziz met in Jidda with a high-ranking American delegation that included Secretary of Defense Richard Cheney, General Schwarzkopf, and General Horner. At this meeting, for the first time in Saudi history, the head of state agreed to accept the deployment of foreign troops into his country. King Fahd also affirmed that the Saudis would cut the Iraqi oil pipeline, which originated in Basra (the second largest city in Iraq) and ran across Saudi Arabia to Yanbu, on the Red Sea.[13]

In addition to this firm agreement with Saudi Arabia, President Bush also wanted the support of an international Coalition to avoid a unilateral American intervention in behalf of the Saudis or any appearance that non-Arab countries from outside the Middle East were combining against a lone Islamic state. The president built against Iraq a diplomatic alliance that included many Arab countries that were opposed to the occupation of Kuwait. On August 6, the United Nations (UN) Security Council imposed a trade embargo on Iraq. Thirteen delegates voted for the measure and none opposed it; however, Yemen and Cuba abstained. Saudi

*CENTAF Commander
Lt. Gen. Charles A. Horner.*

Arabia, Egypt, and other Arab nations endorsed the resolution, as did the Soviet Union.[14] After the United States announced on August 9 that it would begin a blockade of Iraqi commerce, Great Britain, France, Canada, and other countries supported that effort. Eventually, thirty-nine countries joined the Coalition that confronted Iraq, contributing either military forces or combat support units to the alliance.[15] After the Gulf War, an Iraqi general acknowledged that this mobilization of international opinion had affected the morale of his troops, prompting some of them to question whether so many nations could be wrong and Iraq, alone, right.[16]

The recent, dramatic change in its relations with the Soviet Union aided the United States enormously. For decades during the Cold War, this massive Eurasian country had been a persistent antagonist to American interests, always ready to support any leader who, like Saddam Hussein, challenged the United States. During the late 1980s, however, severe internal problems crippled the Soviet Union and ended its rivalry with the West. By August 1990, the once-powerful opponent of the United States was in no condition to aid Saddam Hussein; instead, it was struggling for its own survival. Within ten months of the end of the Gulf War, the Soviet Union would no longer exist.

It was in this new context of world affairs that, on August 6, President Bush directed U.S. military forces to deploy to the Persian Gulf. Within twenty-four hours, F–15C/D Eagles of the 1st Tactical Fighter Wing launched from Langley AFB, Virginia, for Saudi Arabia, and seven B–52s of the 42d Bombardment Wing were ordered to deploy from Loring AFB, Maine, to the Indian Ocean island of Diego Garcia. Less than forty-eight hours after their arrival in Southwest Asia, the

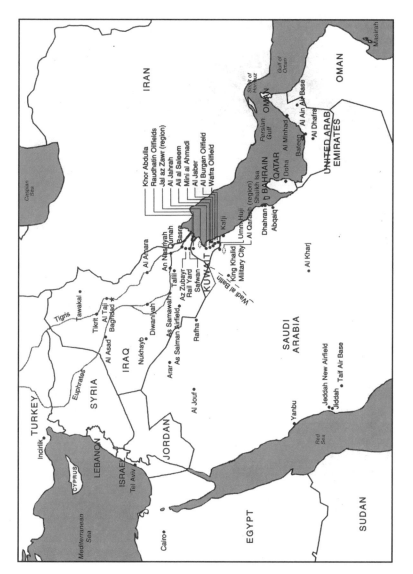

The Persian Gulf region.

F–15s were flying defensive patrols, seven thousand miles from their base in the United States. Within eight days of President Bush's directive, twenty B–52s were on Diego Garcia, fully loaded with weapons and ready to fly missions. These

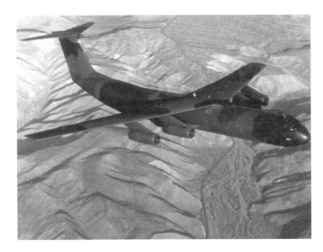

A Military Airlift Command C–141B, a workhorse during the Gulf War, flies over arid terrain typical of the Middle East.

fighters and bombers represented the first combat aircraft to participate in what soon would be called Operation Desert Shield, an enormous deployment of forces to defend Saudi Arabia from further Iraqi aggression.[17]

Saudi Arabia was among the eighteen countries of Southwest Asia and northeastern Africa that fell within the area of responsibility (AOR) of USCENTCOM, also known as CENTCOM, the unified command that had replaced the Rapid Deployment Joint Task Force in 1983.[18] General Schwarzkopf had commanded USCENTCOM since November 1988, and General Horner had been his air component commander since March 1987. These two general officers conferred with Secretary of Defense Cheney during the morning of August 7. On that Tuesday, the three men were still in Jidda, following their meeting with King Fahd. They quickly decided that General Schwarzkopf would return to the States and initiate the Desert Shield deployment, while General Horner would remain in Saudi Arabia and receive the forces for him. "[General Schwarzkopf] had to go home," General Horner later explained. "A major job was which units would come first. That was his decision to make, and he would do that.... I took over at CINCCENT [Commander-in-Chief, Central Command] Forward when General Schwarzkopf left the country the morning after our meeting with the King."[19]

The following deployment was unprecedented in size and rate. Saudi Arabia's enormous oil wealth and vast expanses of open land had allowed the development, since the 1970s, of a military infrastructure that could receive an enormous and rapid infusion of American materiel. Without this foundation, there could have been no buildup as large and as swift as Desert Shield.[20] The United States Transportation Command (USTRANSCOM)—a unified command whose components were the Military Airlift Command, Military Sealift Command, and Military Traffic Management Command—moved unprecedented personnel and supplies during Desert Shield. Within the first five days of the deployment, five fighter squadrons, an airborne warning and control system (AWACS) contingent, and a brigade of the 82d Airborne Division arrived in Saudi Arabia.[21] By the end of the third week, USTRANSCOM had moved more passengers and equipment to the Persian Gulf than the United States had transported to Korea during the first three months of the Korean War. During the sixth week, the total tonnage deployed by air surpassed that of the Berlin Airlift, which had lasted a year and three months. Eventually, in about seven months, the Desert Shield transporters moved 500,000 passengers and nearly 3,700,000 tons of dry cargo—roughly the equivalent of the population of Denver, Colorado, with their possessions—a third of the way around the world.[22]

This massive movement of personnel and supplies continued into the fall of 1990 and remained unaffected by a change in command at the highest level of the Air Force. On September 16, the *Washington Post* quoted Air Force Chief of Staff General Michael J. Dugan as saying that the Joint Chiefs of Staff (JCS) had concluded that, if war erupted in the Gulf, air power would be the only effective means to force the Iraqis from Kuwait. The paper also reported General Dugan as saying that this airpower strategy would include a massive bombing campaign against Baghdad specifically targeting Saddam Hussein, that the Iraqi Air Force had "very limited military capability," and that Israel recently had provided the United States with approximately two dozen Have Nap missiles. On the following day, Secretary Cheney fired General Dugan, who expressed regret for "any embarrassment my comments may have caused the administration" and noted that his remarks to the press represented only his "personal views." On October 30, General Merrill A. McPeak succeeded General Dugan as chief of staff. Shortly after the Gulf War, when General Horner was asked about the change of command, he emphasized that it had no effect on Desert Shield or on that autumn's planning. "It didn't make my job more difficult," he stated. "I think we did the job in an appropriate way."[23]

By early November, U.S. forces in Saudi Arabia had spent three months adjusting to the country's Islamic culture. It was particularly important that the Americans respect the religious sensibilities of their hosts as well as of other Moslem members of the Coalition, who held deep convictions about the status of women, public conduct, dress, and other social issues. Islamic law included firm strictures against alcohol, gambling, and pornography. Both General Horner and General Schwarzkopf (who had returned to the theater on August 28) issued directives insisting that all USCENTCOM personnel respect the religious and social views of their Moslem host and allies.[24]

Besides cultural differences, the Americans also had to cope with Saudi Arabia's desert temperatures. From August into the early autumn, the heat was stifling. With the temperatures reaching daily highs of 115 to 120 degrees Fahrenheit, medics advised the American troops to drink at least six gallons of water a day. In mid-August, a Saudi Arabian sergeant remarked about his Western allies: "God willing, they will get used to the heat soon." By November, the weather

Women soldiers on their way to a nuclear/biological/chemical training session at Dhahran.

moderated to an average high of seventy degrees. In addition to temperature extremes, the region's average ceilings and visibility were of keen interest to Air Force units. These conditions were generally good, exceeding ten thousand feet and five miles, respectively. Coastal fog, haze, and sandstorms carried the greatest potential for trouble.[25]

The terrain of Saudi Arabia, Kuwait, and southern Iraq would be a critical factor in any military operations in the region. The entire area was flat and open, with three noteworthy exceptions: the Jal az Zawr escarpment northwest of Kuwait City, some saltflats near the Kuwaiti coast, and the networks of aboveground oil pipelines that were common around the Persian Gulf. Outside these few places, the level and sandy terrain favored ground operations, including off-road maneuvers. "Cover and concealment is virtually nonexistent," one US-CENTCOM source declared, "except in the urban areas and in the wadis" in the extreme north of Kuwait, where some havens might be found.[26]

This open, desert terrain strongly favored the use of air power, particularly the high-technology version that the United States and its allies could bring to bear. General Horner articulated this point soon after the invasion of Kuwait. On August 4, Secretary Cheney asked General Horner if an air campaign would succeed in this case where it had not "in the past." The Air Force general replied that the Iraqis offered a target-rich environment, with many targets out in the open. Improvements in the technology of air warfare since the Vietnam War strongly supported Horner's point of view. As one military historian predicted during the Desert Shield deployment, air power would perform much differently over the deserts of the Persian Gulf than it had over the jungles of Southeast Asia, or during any earlier conflict. "The one major change from past wars," he pointed out, "is that modern sensors allow aircraft to attack by day and night, denying the Iraqi forces the historic nighttime lull that gave armies a chance to regroup and resupply."[27]

The use of air power was among the possibilities available to President Bush as Iraq's occupation of Kuwait continued through the autumn of 1990. By late October, the president had concluded that Saddam Hussein did not intend to leave Kuwait and that the UN embargo alone might not force the autocrat's hand. President Bush decided that more American military units were needed in the Gulf, to give the Coalition forces the option of taking the offensive and expelling the Iraqis from occupied Kuwait. On October 26, Secretary Cheney announced that as many as 100,000 additional troops might be sent to Southwest Asia. On November 9, President Bush reinforced the secretary's statement, telling the press that the United States would more than double its strength in the Gulf. General Schwarzkopf later commented that this increase had been made necessary by the large number of Iraqi troops that had entered Kuwait.[28]

General Schwarzkopf also explained that, as these additional troops arrived in the AOR, "we made a very deliberate decision to align all of those forces within the boundary looking north towards Kuwait" and to deploy all of them east of the western boundary of Kuwait. When the first U.S. Army Central Command (ARCENT) forces, commanded by Lt. Gen. John Yeosock, had arrived in the Gulf in August 1990, their mission had been to defend Saudi Arabia from an attack by the Iraqi units in Kuwait.[29] They had been aligned in positions running roughly east to west across Saudi Arabia, facing north toward Kuwait. Their assignment remained unchanged throughout September, but, in the middle of that month, ARCENT officers began planning for the time when the Coalition would have enough strength to undertake an offensive.[30] When the additional troops arrived in November and an Allied initiative became a possibility, the new units continued to deploy in the same pattern as those already in place. General Schwarzkopf gave the Iraqis no hint that any of his ground forces might operate west of Kuwait's western boundary. "So we aligned those forces [in November]," the USCENTCOM commander later explained, "so it very much looked like they were all aligned directly on the Iraqi position."[31]

While these additional troops were arriving in the Gulf during November, the United States moved to strengthen its diplomatic as well as its military position. Throughout that month, the American delegation chaired the UN Security Council, a position it would yield in December to Yemen, which was sympathetic to Iraq. During late November, Secretary of State James A. Baker III, UN Ambassador Thomas Pickering, and other U.S. diplomats garnered support for Resolution 678, which stated that, if Iraq failed to leave Kuwait before January 15, 1991, UN members might "use all necessary means…to restore international peace and security in the area." On November 29, just before rotating out of the Security

Lucrative Targets

Council presidency, the American delegation called for a vote on this authorization of the use of force against Iraq. Yemen and Cuba voted no, China abstained, and the other twelve members supported the resolution. General Horner was emphatic about the significance of this diplomacy: "Obviously the important battle in November was getting the UN to come to some sort of agreement for [a] resolution that led to the 15 January deadline." The Coalition members had put themselves on a forty-seven-day countdown to war.[32]

It remained for the U.S. Congress to take a similar position. President Bush wrote to the nation's legislative leaders on January 8, 1991, and asked them to endorse the use of force to drive Iraq from Kuwait. During the next three days, Congress debated House Joint Resolution 77, the "Authorization for Use of Military Force Against Iraq Resolution." Only once before had the nation's lawmakers been more closely divided over the issue of war and peace: the vote in June 1812 to declare hostilities with Great Britain. Saddam Hussein had announced on December 7 that he would release all foreign nationals who remained in Iraq and Kuwait, which was a surprising concession that made some members of the Congress and public think that war was less urgent. Many of the opponents of House Joint Resolution 77 argued that the United States should give the embargo against Iraq more time to succeed before adopting the riskier course of offensive military operations. This point of view was articulated by Senator Sam Nunn, the Georgia Democrat and Chairman of the Senate Armed Services Committee, who stated, "We are playing a winning hand. I see no compelling reason to rush to military action."[33]

Proponents of the resolution countered that economic sanctions alone would not force the Iraqis from Kuwait and that Congress should support President Bush in his efforts against Saddam Hussein. Robert A. Michel, the House Minority Leader, contended, "President Bush has openly and forthrightly asked for our help. How can we turn our backs on him?" Like many Americans, Congressman Stephen J. Solarz, a Democrat from Brooklyn, drew a sharp contrast between the country's past experience in Southeast Asia and the need to use force in the Persian Gulf. Solarz had begun his political career as a Vietnam War critic, but he believed that the circumstances in the Gulf were fundamentally different. The New York congressman played a leading role in writing and sponsoring House Joint Resolution 77. "If we prevail," Solarz urged, "we will have prevented a brutal dictator from getting his hands on the economic jugular of the world." On January 12, the House voted for the resolution, 250 to 183, as did the Senate, 52 to 47.[34]

While these political and diplomatic developments were taking place, Saddam Hussein had strengthened his forces in Kuwait and southern Iraq. On the eve of the conflict, Headquarters USCENTCOM intelligence officers concluded that at least forty-three Iraqi divisions defended the Kuwaiti theater of operations (KTO), formally defined as the area south of 31° N, west of the Persian Gulf and the Iraq-Iran border, north of the Kuwait-Saudi Arabia and Iraq-Saudi Arabia borders, and east of 45° E.[35] They believed that these forty-three divisions represented roughly 546,700 personnel with about 4,280 tanks, 2,880 armored personnel carriers, and 3,100 artillery pieces. (Later evidence showed that these numbers were high.)[36] Soon after the Iraqis secured Kuwait, the highly mobile Republican Guard divisions withdrew to southern Iraq and formed a theater reserve. From this

An airman practices wearing his chemical protection hood.

new position, these elite units could either mobilize for an invasion of Saudi Arabia or quickly counterattack against any Coalition offensive.[37]

Although postwar evidence suggested that these Iraqi divisions stood at less than full strength and suffered from low morale,[38] CENTAF planners dared not risk such assumptions. Instead, they prudently prepared for war against a large, well-armed, and strongly entrenched enemy. Soon after seizing Kuwait,[39] the Iraqis had begun fortifying its border with Saudi Arabia and creating the "Saddam Line," a military frontier running for approximately 150 miles. By mid-January, this defensive line consisted of a formidable series of obstacles, beginning with long expanses of barbed wire and enormous numbers of mines. Beyond these minefields, advancing Coalition forces would confront a berm, or sand ridge, backed by an antitank ditch, which could be filled with oil. The next set of obstacles typically included another line of barbed wire and more minefields. American intelligence officers estimated that the Iraqis had laid as many as 2,500,000 mines along the Saddam Line. Beyond this final barrier, the enemy's infantry, tanks, and artillery waited in their fortifications. Shortly after the war, an Iraqi brigade commander told his captors that his unit had prepared defenses typical of those along the front: his infantrymen not only had dug in, but also protected themselves with camouflage and overhead cover.[40] General Schwarzkopf credited the skills of the Iraqi field engineers and said of the Saddam Line, "The nightmare scenario for all of us would have been to…get hung up in [the Iraqi defenses], and then have the enemy artillery rain chemical weapons down on troops that were in a gaggle in the breach…. That was the nightmare scenario." From behind these defenses, Saddam Hussein threatened, he would win a "great victory in the mother of all battles."[41]

Soldiers of the 179th Infantry Brigade in an evacuation exercise during Desert Shield; the exercise was conducted by the 1st Aeromedical Evacuation Squadron using a C–130E of the 63d TAS.

In addition to his ground defenses, the Iraqi dictator also fielded the world's sixth-largest air force. At the time of the January 15 deadline, operations officers at Headquarters CENTAF credited him with 1,761 aircraft, roughly 40 percent of which were fighters. The Soviet Union heavily influenced the Iraqi military, both in its system of centralized control and also in its force structure. The Soviets had delivered 47 percent of all the new arms that Iraq received between 1980 and 1987. Most of the aircraft in the Iraqi inventory in 1991 were Soviet imports, including 208 MiG–21 Fishbeds, the most widely exported Russian fighter; 123 MiG–23 Floggers, interceptors that formed the backbone of their own country's tactical air forces and air defenses; and 119 Su–20 Fitters, the basic single-seat attack aircraft of the Red air force. The Iraqis also had acquired 17 bombers from the same source, and these planes comprised nine Tu–22 Blinders (the first Soviet bombers capable of any supersonic performance) and eight Tu–16 Badger-Bs (strategic jets carrying two antiship missiles as well as conventional ordnance). Nor could Coalition planners ignore the threat posed by Saddam Hussein's 601 helicopters. The Iraqi Mi–8 Hip and Mi–24 Hind machines, again of Soviet origin, could deliver chemical weapons against the ground troops in Saudi Arabia, from bases within 250 miles of the Saddam Line.[42]

Iraq's helicopters and fixed-wing aircraft enjoyed extensive facilities at twenty main airfields, thirteen dispersal fields, and another nineteen potential support sites. These fifty-two airfields extended from Al Jaber in Kuwait to Tall Kayf in northern Iraq, and from Kuwait International Airport in the east to a site that Americans designated as Airfield H–3 South West, in western Iraq. "The size of the Iraqi Air Force is bolstered by its modern and extensive airfield network," a

STRATFOR intelligence report observed, "that can house the entire fighter force in hardened aircraft shelters. This will make a single, quick[,] knock-out blow against Iraqi aircraft difficult to achieve."[43]

In addition to his ground and air forces, Saddam Hussein held other arrows in his quiver. His scientists were improving Iraq's ability to produce, store, and deliver nuclear weapons. Intelligence analysts believed that, although Saddam lacked any viable nuclear device, he could mount a crash program that would produce a crude explosive within a matter of months.[44] Iraqi chemical weapons posed a more immediate threat. Iraq sustained the largest program of this kind in the Third World, and this program was able to manufacture blister, mustard, and nerve gases, as well as other gaseous agents. Iraq also had an advanced biological weapons program that could produce anthrax, botulinum, and other toxins. The Defense Intelligence Agency (DIA) concluded that Hussein was storing his chemical munitions in S-shaped bunkers. The Iraqis could deliver these weapons in aerial bombs from Fitters and Floggers, in rockets or aerosol sprays from helicopters, in artillery shells, or from Scud missiles.[45]

Saddam Hussein had previously used chemicals not only against the Iranians but also against the Kurds within his own country, forcing the Coalition to prepare for the possibility that he would employ the same agents against it. One Army historian described the attention given to chemical combat training by the XVIII Corps, the first of the two ARCENT corps to arrive in the theater. The soldiers, he wrote, "placed considerable emphasis on chemical warfare instruction, including detection, quick changes into protective suits, and use of antidotes. Second only to breaching training, the sight of American soldiers rushing to don gas masks became a common sight on American television screens." Coalition leaders remained wary about the possibility of chemical warfare until the end of the war. During the early-morning hours of February 24, when units of the 1st Marine Division began advancing into southern Kuwait at the opening of the ground campaign, a Headquarters CENTAF historian entered in his logbook: "There is reported to be an Iraqi Brigade moving north from this area [away from the Marines]. It is feared that they might be clearing the area for the Iraqi use of chemicals." Taking notes on an intelligence briefing given shortly after 0900 that morning, General Horner wrote, "Expect to see CW [chemical weapons] employed today—Troops in Kuwait City told to put on gear." After the war, General Schwarzkopf candidly admitted, "We had a lot of questions about why the Iraqis didn't use chemical weapons, and I don't know the answer. I just thank God that they didn't."[46]

In addition to chemical warfare, Coalition leaders also faced the threat of Iraqi terrorism. "We worried about it," General Olsen, CENTAF Vice Commander, acknowledged after the war. An American intelligence source predicted in December 1990, "Terrorism attacks are virtually certain both in-theater and worldwide if hostilities begin or if Saddam perceives that war imminent." A week into the Gulf War, General Horner warned his CENTAF staff against three unhappy possibilities: terrorism, sabotage, and air attacks.[47]

Lucrative Targets

Several factors, though, discouraged Saddam Hussein from undertaking a terrorist campaign. Coalition forces were alert to the possibility and took measures to protect themselves. Saudi Arabian internal security officials, unfettered by Western notions of civil liberties, moved quickly against suspected Iraqi agents. "The Saudis have a very good internal security system, as do most of the Islamic countries," General Olsen pointed out after the war. "There were some [Iraqi] agents but I just don't think they had an opportunity,…the internal security was so high that they really couldn't move and they really couldn't make any preparations." Once the allies began Operation Desert Storm, the intensity of their air operations and the destruction of Iraqi communications prevented Saddam from directing any well-organized, sustained terrorist campaign.[48]

Although the Iraqi dictator did not undertake the anticipated terrorist activities, he did direct bizarre acts of environmental terrorism. During the war, the Iraqis deliberately released an estimated seven to nine million barrels of petroleum from tankers berthed at Mina al Ahmadi, Kuwait, and from the country's Sea Island supertanker terminal. On January 26, CENTAF countered the enormous oil spill with an airpower operation that demonstrated the value of precision-guided munitions (PGMs). F–111Fs of the 48th Tactical Fighter Wing (TFW) delivered GBU–15s, electro-optical guided bombs, against the inland complex of pipes and valves that controlled the flow of petroleum to the Sea Island terminal and effectively resolved the problem at its "spigot."[49] In other acts of environmental terrorism, the Iraqis set fire to nearly 600 oil wells in Kuwait, 365 of them concentrated in three fields, and left more than 80 others flowing freely. Rough estimates made immediately after the war suggested it would cost $200 million in U.S. currency to clean up the oil spills alone. The total damage that Saddam had inflicted on the environment of Southwest Asia was far too great to calculate.[50]

In addition to terrorism and other threats, the Iraqis maintained an air defense that, as General Horner pointed out after the war, was twice as dense as that of Eastern Europe during the Cold War. Saddam Hussein's regime was protected by an extensive radar network, roughly 6,000 pieces of antiaircraft artillery (AAA), more than 700 fixed-site surface-to-air missiles (SAMs), and about 550 aircraft, including 75 French F–1 Mirages and 41 Soviet MiG–29 Fulcrums. The Mirage already had demonstrated its effectiveness when an F–1EQ had delivered the two Exocet missiles that hit the USS *Stark* in May 1987. For its part, the MiG–29 also is a very capable air defense fighter.[51] The air defenses around Basra, the densest in the KTO, included 118 missiles and 167 AAA sites with 442 guns. AAA posed the main threat to Coalition air operations, if only by sheer volume of fire.[52]

The redundant Kari (Iraq spelled backwards in French) command-and-control (C^2) system integrated Iraq's multilayered air defenses. Less than ten years old, this C^2 network capitalized on recent French technology. Highly centralized, the Kari system united Iraq's four air defense sectors, each with its own Sector Operations Center (SOC). Well-hardened facilities, these centers reported the air situation, analyzed threats, and coordinated responses to intrusions of their sector.

The centers communicated with SAM sites and with the Interceptor Operations Centers (IOCs), which directed fighters to intercept intruding aircraft. These SOCs were very capable facilities and could correlate as many as 120 aircraft tracks and direct SAM targeting. An Air Defense Operations Center in Baghdad centralized all of the information from the four SOCs and from a fifth center that operated from a command bunker to cover the airspace of occupied Kuwait.[53]

Saddam Hussein also had acquired a diverse collection of electronic warfare (EW) systems from Soviet, Japanese, and European sources. These included radars and other sophisticated equipment that could determine the direction of Coalition communications and then intercept or jam them. Saddam Hussein had refined his deployments of these devices[54] and other systems, as the Kuwaiti crisis dragged on through the autumn of 1990. The more than five months between the August 2 invasion and the January 15 deadline, as one Headquarters Strategic Air Command (SAC) report later pointed out, gave Iraq plenty of time to play "shell games" with its aircraft, Scuds, AAA, and SAMs.[55]

During the same period, the United States and its thirty-eight allies had countered Saddam Hussein with an impressive mobilization of their own. By January 16, USCENTCOM's total strength in the theater stood at more than 426,000 personnel, roughly 47,700 of which were assigned to CENTAF. General Yeosock's ARCENT troops, consisting of Lt. Gen. Frederick Franks, Jr.'s VII Corps and Lt. Gen. Gary E. Luck's XVIII Airborne Corps,[56] were deployed behind the Syrian, French, Saudi, Egyptian, and Kuwaiti forces that faced north along the Saddam Line, from Kuwait's western border to its heel.[57] East of the XVIII Airborne Corps, Lt. Gen. Walter E. Boomer's I Marine Expeditionary Force (I MEF), Marine Corps Central Command (MARCENT), held the Saudi coast.[58] The Navy had been well represented in the theater since the beginning of the Desert Shield deployment, when the USS *Eisenhower* and *Saratoga* carrier battle groups and other surface ships had contributed to the blockade of Iraq. On the eve of Desert Storm, Vice Admiral Stanley P. Arthur's Naval Central Command (NAVCENT) had six carriers and their escorts in the AOR. The *America*, *Saratoga*, and *Kennedy* were on station in the Red Sea; the *Ranger* and *Midway* were operating in the Persian Gulf; and the *Theodore Roosevelt* was steaming from the Red Sea into the Gulf.[59]

General Horner's CENTAF units stood ready for combat, at twenty-six bases extending from Cairo West, Egypt, to Masirah, off the coast of Oman. From Incirlik Air Base, Turkey, Joint Task Force (JTF) Proven Force would operate against targets in northern Iraq. Composed of F–15s, F–16s, F–111s, KC–135s, and E–3s from United States Air Forces in Europe (USAFE) units, JTF Proven Force would give the Air Force combat experience with the composite-wing organization and prevent the Iraqis from concentrating their attention on the KTO.[60] On the eve of the air campaign, CENTAF had 1,131 combat and support aircraft. General Horner could call on 492 fighters—including 42 F–117 stealth fighters, 154 F–15s, and 234 F–16s—and on a force of B–52s based on Diego Garcia in the Indian Ocean, and elsewhere. The CENTAF commander also had 243 tankers, KC–10s and KC–135s, at bases from Cairo West to Diego Garcia; 51 reconnaissance aircraft, including 30 RF–4Cs that would operate from Shaikh Isa, on the Saudi Gulf Coast, and 10 E–3As from Riyadh; 129 cargo carriers, 120 of them C–130s, stationed from Al Kharj, southeast of Riyadh, to Masirah; 33 special operations aircraft, 28 of them based at King Fahd, in eastern Saudi Arabia; and 31 electronic warfare airplanes, including 18 EF–111s at Taif, east of Mecca, and 5 EC–130s at Bateen, in the United Arab Emirates.[61]

For the first time ever, space satellites would support wartime operations. A crew member at each Defense Support Program (DSP) ground station dedicated his time solely to monitoring the theater. This satellite network and a tracker radar would alert the allies to Iraqi missile attacks and give targeting information to the ARCENT Patriot batteries. Spacecraft of the global positioning system would provide navigation and positioning data; the Defense Meteorological Support Program, weather information; and the Defense Satellite Communications System, secure communications.[62]

With these assets in place, the United States could conduct a devastating air campaign against Iraq. If Saddam Hussein defied the January 15 deadline, President Bush would direct the use of American air power before turning to ground operations. Several reasons justified this order of battle, and one prominent military historian later summarized them: "the size and deployment pattern of the Iraqi armed forces, the threat of Iraqi weapons of mass and indiscriminate destruction, favorable weather and terrain, the estimated effect of PGMs, and the fragility of the Iraqi air defense system. In addition, CENTCOM would not have its [ground] offensive force, principally VII Corps from Germany and two mechanized divisions from the United States, in place until well into February." Each of these considerations favored the use of air power, and employing it before undertaking a ground campaign would save allied lives. As General Olsen later said, "We were going to limit friendly casualties.... When we went into combat operations, the air forces would carry the brunt of the operation and ground-force operations would be delayed until such a point that the enemy had been beaten down and could not generate an effective defense."[63] Air Force officers had long embraced the wisdom of General Olsen's thinking and, for months, had prepared accordingly.

Chapter Two

Jump Start and Concentric Rings: Preparing for an Air Campaign

The Ninth Air Force was the numbered air force that provided its service's component of CENTCOM. Officers in the Ninth's headquarters at Shaw AFB, in the pinetree country near Sumter, South Carolina, had been planning and exercising many years for a contingency in Southwest Asia. During the early 1980s, the large staff at Headquarters Ninth Air Force's Directorate of Operational Plans reflected an emphasis on preparing concepts of operations and operations plans. In those years, the directorate accounted for half of the personnel assigned to the entire DCS/Operations.[1]

"Dual-hatted" as both Ninth Air Force and CENTAF planners, these officers performed as a Combat Operations Planning Staff (COPS). By the late 1980s, they had refined an effective process for producing an air tasking order (ATO), the complex document that was vital to any deployment's flight operations and that detailed all the sorties that would be flown, by location, time, and altitude, and taking into account airspace management, combat air patrol (CAP) operations, electronic warfare coordination, AWACS coverage, tanker support, and other factors.[2] The COPS had trained and exercised to deploy to Southwest Asia and quickly began preparing daily ATOs, exactly as they were to do in Riyadh after Saddam Hussein's invasion of Kuwait.[3]

The Ninth Air Force planners deepened their experience at Blue Flags, the C^2 battle-management exercises held by the Tactical Air Command (TAC) since December 1976. By the late 1980s, CENTAF officers were able to prepare, within the first twenty-four hours of a Blue Flag, an ATO so detailed that it could be flown. This level of detail demanded many specifics, including tanker radio frequencies, altitudes, and offloads; fighter routes; and deconflicted call signs and identification–friend-or-foe (IFF) "squawks." In contrast to CENTAF, planners from other commands might work several days of a Blue Flag, before they arrived at a "flyable" ATO.[4]

Lucrative Targets

In late July 1990, on the eve of the invasion of Kuwait, the COPS planners practiced preparing ATOs during Internal Look, a CENTCOM command-post exercise at Eglin AFB, Florida. "During that exercise," one Ninth Air Force officer recalled, "we started getting the initial 'real-world' intel on Iraq massing forces at the Kuwaiti border. Then shortly after returning from that exercise, the invasion took place and a week later we found ourselves in Riyadh." During Internal Look, the planners from Shaw AFB developed contingency target lists and worked out procedures for parceling out those targets among the services, for integrating CENTAF's air defense system with that of the Saudis, and for managing the theater's airspace. At General Horner's suggestion and with General Yeosock's concurrence, the exercise participants practiced using Patriot missiles to counter Iraqi Scuds, a possibility that was soon to become a reality. Internal Look, General Horner summarized, gave CENTAF a "jump start" toward accomplishing its mission in Saudi Arabia.[5]

In addition to Ninth Air Force's many years of contingency planning, a change in personnel policy during the late 1980s also brought the advantage of continuity to its efforts. Forced to save money by keeping people at Shaw for longer tours, the headquarters gained a group of officers with a long experience together preparing operations plans, building ATOs, and refining the other skills that would be demanded by a major deployment. In August 1990, General Horner had commanded the Ninth Air Force for approximately three and a half years and participated in its Blue Flag exercises, and he directed a seasoned, closely knit staff. "If Hussein had waited two years," one officer in the headquarters reflected in March 1992, "it would have been totally different, because by then, another year from now, all these people will be gone." This continuity in experience—and the five months of preparation time during Desert Shield—proved greatly to the advantage of Headquarters CENTAF during Desert Storm.[6]

Ninth Air Force first became involved in the crisis as early as August 3, the day after Saddam Hussein began his aggression. That Friday, General Horner flew to MacDill AFB, Florida, where Headquarters CENTCOM J–3 (Operations Directorate) and J–5 (Strategic Plans and Policy Directorate) officers already were developing options for responding to the crisis. These ranged from executing CENTAF Plan 1307, which would deploy a "force package" of electronic reconnaissance and surveillance aircraft, fighters, and tankers to the AOR, to executing the most recent draft of Operations Plan 1002-90, which governed a major deployment of CENTCOM forces to "counter an intraregional attack on the Arabian Peninsula."[7] Also on August 3, Headquarters CENTCOM planners already were preparing a briefing for President Bush to be given the next morning at Camp David. "We listened to their briefing," General Horner recalled, "and it was terrible. So General Schwarzkopf was upset about that." The CENTCOM commander thought that the section of the briefing dealing with ground operations was passable, but that the portion addressing air operations lacked the per-

Jump Start and Concentric Rings: Preparing for an Air Campaign

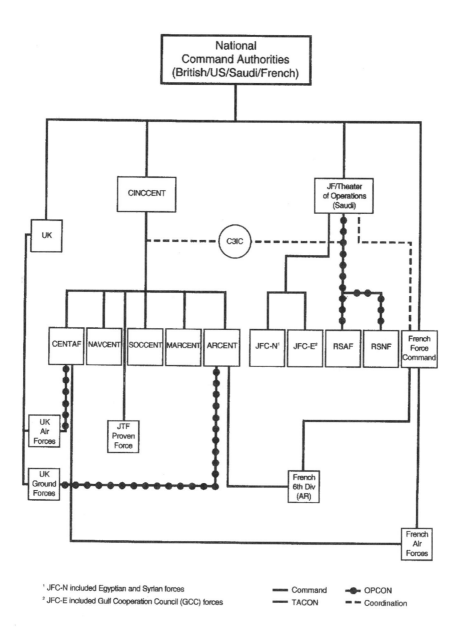

The Coalition command structure of Operation Desert Storm.

spective of a professional airman. He accepted an offer from General Horner to prepare the air campaign part of the briefing.[8]

The CENTAF commander worked through the night of August 3, drawing on sortie statistics and other facts he recalled from the recent Internal Look exercise and from a briefing his staff had prepared the preceding spring. General Horner also used information sent by fax from his COPS planners at Shaw AFB. "We worked until about three in the morning," he remembered, "the slides were still dripping wet when we got on a C–21 and flew to Washington. I think I paid thirty bucks to spend one night in the VOQ [visiting officer quarters] at Fort Myer." General Horner took a quick nap, joined several other senior officers and defense advisers at the Pentagon, and then went on to the Camp David meeting with President Bush about 8:30 that morning. After General Schwarzkopf briefed the Commander in Chief on the possibilities of ground operations to defend Saudi Arabia or liberate Kuwait, the CENTAF commander discussed the options for an air campaign. "I talked about what we could do from the air side," General Horner later said, "how we would repel an invasion, how we would use air [assets] to secure control of the air, and how we would conduct a strategic campaign against Iraq should it be decided to do that because [of] their using things like Scuds and chemical weapons." It was at this conference that, after these briefings, President Bush told his advisers he wanted a firm agreement with the Saudis, before sending any American forces to the Gulf.[9]

Following the meeting at Camp David, General Horner flew to Saudi Arabia, attended the meeting with King Fahd, and remained there to act as CINCCENT Forward while General Schwarzkopf returned to the United States. On August 9, General Olsen, CENTAF Deputy, officially established Headquarters CENTAF Forward in the headquarters building of the Royal Saudi Air Force (RSAF) in downtown Riyadh. During the hectic days that followed, Operation Desert Shield gained momentum, and scores of long-experienced officers and airmen deployed from Headquarters Ninth Air Force to the theater. On the 14th, the personnel and hardware needed to establish a Tactical Air Control Center (TACC) began arriving in Riyadh from Shaw AFB. During the initial deployment, the TACC had to be housed in "the bubble," an inflated module in the parking lot of the RSAF headquarters. Later, when more space became available, the staff and their computers moved indoors to the building's basement, where they would oversee the execution of CENTAF's combat plans during Desert Storm.[10]

The planners deploying to Riyadh quickly began work on the ATOs that would be needed if Saddam Hussein continued his aggression from Kuwait into Saudi Arabia. Col. James C. Crigger, Jr., CENTAF Forward's Director of Operations, arrived in the theater on August 8. Assisted by approximately ten officers, he immediately started developing a D-day, or defensive, plan. Colonel Crigger's planners, whose numbers doubled during the early weeks of Desert Shield, arrived at a plan for air power to impede Saddam's advance into Saudi Arabia, emphasizing air attacks on Iraqi logistics while available ground forces waged a war of maneuver.[11]

While these officers developed a D-day plan, other members of CENTAF's COPS prepared the daily ATOs that were required for each day's operations, in-

Generals Powell and Schwarzkopf.

cluding defensive CAPs, cargo shipments, and tanker refuelings. The daily ATO also included training sorties, which were critically important in preparing for future operations. CENTAF planners practiced "force packaging" various groups of aircraft and positioning tankers for them, while aircrews practiced flying CAPs and combat scenarios. As forces continued to arrive in the AOR throughout the fall, these daily and training ATOs became enormous, complex documents, foreshadowing the ones Desert Storm would later demand. Whereas a large Blue Flag exercise might require preparing an ATO for a thousand sorties per day, by the end of Desert Shield the training and defensive ATOs had to account for two thousand sorties per day.[12]

The daily and training ATOs helped immensely in smoothing the integration of CENTAF and Saudi air defenses and in strengthening the cooperation between the Americans and their hosts. CENTAF adopted, with only slight modifications, the Saudi air defenses that were already in place. The resulting system required an ATO to manage the flights of USAF F–15s, AWACS, RC–135s (Rivet Joint signals-intelligence aircraft), Royal Air Force Air Defense variant Tornados, and other aircraft. CENTAF combined these air defense operations with F–16, A–10, and other training sorties in a single ATO. The Saudis embraced that arrangement, General Horner pointed out, because the training ATO gave them some control over flights over their own country. General Olsen observed that the RSAF gained valuable experience in helping to build the daily and training ATOs, for it had never worked on tasking orders that large. "It was beneficial to the Saudis," he said, "because it was an avenue for us to bring them in and make them feel that they were a part of the operation.... They were part of the planning process, from the very beginning."[13]

The daily and training ATOs also strengthened cooperation between the Americans and Saudis and among the U.S. military services. To ensure unity of

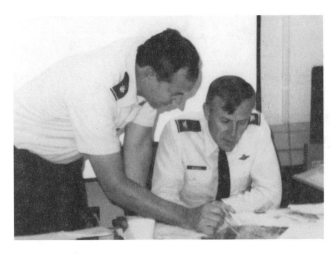

Lt. Col. David Deptula, SECAF's Staff Group, and Col. John Warden, Director for Warfighting Concepts.

effort and safety of flight throughout the theater, the CENTAF commander also served as the Joint Force Air Component Commander (JFACC), deriving his authority from the Joint Force Commander (JFC), in this case CINCCENT. In his role as JFACC, General Horner recommended to General Schwarzkopf how air sorties might be best apportioned within the theater. Based on the JFC's guidance, the JFACC planned, coordinated, allocated, and tasked all of the Coalition's air operations in the AOR and acted as Airspace Control Authority and as Area Air Defense Commander. Consistent with the military principle of unity of effort, the JFACC sent a single ATO to the units that conducted the operations in the theater, a procedure that proved invaluable. Gen. George L. Butler, Commander in Chief, Strategic Air Command (CINCSAC), stressed this point shortly after the war: "The integration of all coalition air power aimed at Iraq and Kuwait prior to the start of the ground campaign into a single ATO was, without a doubt, a major reason for the success of the air war." General Horner equated his authority as JFACC with the fact that every sortie flown in the theater had to appear in this one tasking order. "The ATO is the Joint Force Air Component Commander," he emphasized. "That's the whole thing. Without the ATO, you don't have the JFACC. With the ATO, you don't have anything but a JFACC.... If you're going to fly, it's got to be in the ATO. So that really was the key thing in...making the Navy come on board, for example, and the Marine Corps come on board."[14]

While the JFACC's staff put in long hours in Riyadh, a group of Air Staff officers did the same in Washington. These Pentagon planners began work at the request of General Schwarzkopf, who had decided early in August that he needed "a series of options" to deal with the Kuwaiti crisis, including an air plan to retaliate if Saddam Hussein committed a "heinous act" against the U.S. Embassy personnel in Kuwait City or against the American hostages he held.[15] "If the Iraqis started executing U.S. embassy employees, say," the CENTCOM commander later wrote, "and the President wanted to retaliate, Central Command had little to offer short of a nuclear strike on Baghdad."[16]

General Schwarzkopf discussed this concern with Gen. Colin L. Powell, the Chairman of the Joint Chiefs of Staff. The CENTCOM commander remembered well from the Vietnam War the problems that resulted when planning was done in Washington rather than in the theater. General Schwarzkopf, however, also faced a pressing need for air options to deal with the immediate crisis, and he concluded that General Horner, then in Saudi Arabia and acting as CINCCENT Forward, had "his hands full, working the deployment." Therefore, the CENTCOM commander thought it best to ask Headquarters USAF to initiate his air planning. General Powell agreed and advised General Dugan that CINCCENT would call the Air Staff with this request.[17]

General Schwarzkopf telephoned Headquarters U.S. Air Force (USAF) on August 8, a day when neither General Dugan nor Lt. Gen. Jimmie V. Adams, DCS/Plans and Operations, were in the Pentagon. In General Dugan's absence, the CENTCOM commander spoke with Vice Chief of Staff Gen. John M. Loh, asking Headquarters USAF to develop some air operations that might be conducted if Saddam Hussein committed some atrocity, making it necessary to retaliate against Iraq. General Loh gave General Schwarzkopf's tasking to the Deputy Directorate for Warfighting Concepts, whose officers already had done some preliminary thinking about the possibility of an air campaign against Iraq.[18]

In 1988, General Dugan, then DCS/Plans and Operations, and Maj. Gen. Charles G. Boyd, Director of Plans, had approved establishing the Deputy Directorate for Warfighting Concepts, a successor to the Deputy Directorate for Planning Integration. The office drew its personnel from a wide diversity of backgrounds and became a hothouse for germinating airpower ideas and doctrine. Its director was Col. John A. Warden III, author of *The Air Campaign: Planning for Combat*.[19]

On August 8, officers from the Warfighting Concepts directorate—joined the next day by planners from Headquarters SAC and the Air Force Intelligence Agency—began work on a briefing that would answer the CENTCOM commander's tasking. They met in a Pentagon basement facility belonging to the recently redesignated Checkmate division. The Checkmate sign was still on the door, and so these planners—and those who later joined them—were referred to as the Checkmate planning group or Checkmate office.[20]

The Checkmate officers used a concept that Colonel Warden had described in *The Air Campaign*: a war planner should identify his enemy's "centers of gravity," the critical points at which a successful attack would be decisive. Warden depicted these centers of gravity as a series of five concentric rings, with the enemy's leadership as the central ring and then moving outward through key production facilities, transportation infrastructure, population, and fielded military forces. In this construction, the closer that an element was to the central ring, the more vital a target it offered. Leadership was the most important because without it, for example, the population and military forces would lack direction. Fielded military forces, on the other hand, stood on the peripheral ring because their defeat would be less decisive than the loss of the other centers of gravity. A nation might suffer casualties to its units in the field and yet continue to wage war. Using this concept, the Checkmate planners established ten sets of targets, such as electrical facilities, railroads, and strategic air defenses. They put each set into one of the five rings: electrical facilities, for example, went under key production; railroads, under infrastructure; and strategic air defenses, fielded forces. Eighty-four targets accompanied the ten sets. "Using [Colonel John] Warden's 'five rings' construct, which generically describes the make-up of a modern nation state," one of the planners recalled, "we identified the centers of gravity" that would affect Saddam Hussein.[21]

Colonel Warden named the resulting plan "Instant Thunder," to underscore its sharp contrast with the Rolling Thunder campaign of the Vietnam War. "We wanted to make it clear to people," he emphasized, "that this was the antithesis of Rolling Thunder." The Air Staff planners stressed that the Persian Gulf operation would not be, as the Southeast Asian one had been, "a graduated, long-term campaign…designed to provide escalation options to counter [enemy] moves." Instead, Instant Thunder called for a "focused, intense air campaign, designed to incapacitate Iraqi leadership and destroy key Iraqi military capability, in a short period of time," while leaving Iraq's fundamental infrastructure intact.[22] The plan envisioned a rapid destruction of the enemy's warfighting capability before any ground campaign took place. "This air campaign was scheduled to be completed within six days," one of its planners pointed out, "with the crucial objectives (the first three) achieved by day one."[23]

On August 10, Colonel Warden flew to MacDill AFB and briefed the Instant Thunder plan to General Schwarzkopf, who responded favorably. "I was leery of Warden," the CENTCOM commander later acknowledged, "who was from the Curtis LeMay school of Air Force planners—guys who think strategic bombing can do it all and that armies are obsolete…. But to my delight he turned out to be a flexible thinker who was just as knowledgeable about close air support—the kind of air strike used to support soldiers on the battlefield—as he was about strategic bombing." General Schwarzkopf directed the Air Staff planners to flesh out their briefing to a more detailed plan that CENTAF could execute. Specifically, he asked them to add a section on logistics and to take into account the possibility of operations from Turkish bases. The Checkmate briefers then were to return to the CENTCOM commander with this revised plan.[24]

General Schwarzkopf had asked the Air Staff to prepare the Instant Thunder presentation, but arrangements had to be made to permit a functional office of a military service headquarters, the Warfighting Concepts directorate of the Air Staff, to brief a plan in the "joint arena" or to a unified command, such as CENT-COM. On August 11, Lt. Gen. Thomas W. Kelly, the JCS J–3, temporarily designated General Adams as the J–3 for air operations. (Maj. Gen. James W. Meier, an Air Force general then assigned to JCS J–3, later would sponsor the Air Staff's Instant Thunder briefing to Headquarters CENTCOM on August 17.)[25]

On August 11, the same day General Adams was designated J–3 for air operations, Colonel Warden presented the Instant Thunder plan to General Powell. Commenting on the briefing, the chairman of the JCS stressed that he did not want the air operations to end with Saddam Hussein withdrawing from Kuwait, yet keeping his Republican Guard divisions and their tanks intact, remaining able to raise some threat elsewhere in the region. Destroying these Iraqi units might require a ground campaign, and so General Powell directed that the planning for the air campaign be a joint services effort.[26]

While these presentations were being made, the Checkmate team was expanding the Instant Thunder briefing, as General Schwarzkopf had requested, in a multiservice effort that now required additional planners. More than forty officers representing the Navy, Marine Corps, Army, and TAC joined the group already at work in the Pentagon basement. The Checkmate planners kept Generals Dugan and Loh informed of their progress and finished their work promptly. On August 17, Colonel Warden presented the results to General Schwarzkopf at Headquarters CENTCOM, and Secretary of the Air Force Donald B. Rice and General Dugan were debriefed that evening on the details of the Air Staff team's presentation to the CINC.[27]

These senior leaders responded favorably to the expanded Checkmate plan. Secretary Rice was impressed with the group's effort and pointed out that, depending upon Saddam Hussein's actions, the Coalition might have to execute an air campaign within a matter of days. General Dugan endorsed Colonel Warden's briefing, with the qualifications that air operations might be necessary against the KTO as well as Iraq and that the overall campaign would last longer than six days.[28]

In addition to these reactions, Colonel Warden's briefing of August 17 stimulated General Schwarzkopf's thinking about an air campaign. The CENTCOM commander later recalled this exchange with the Air Staff planner: "What would you have to do if we wanted our airplanes to operate freely over the battlefield in Kuwait?' 'Immediately destroy their air defenses,' Warden replied, adding that doing so in Kuwait would be tough." General Schwarzkopf told the Air Staff planner that he would need 50 percent of the Iraqi occupying forces destroyed before he attempted any ground offensive. At the time of his session with Colonel Warden on August 17, the CINC already had his Combat Analysis Group studying concepts for a possible ground campaign to drive the Iraqis from the KTO. These CENTCOM planners based their work on the assumption—consistent with Army doctrine—that for a Coalition offensive by just a single corps to succeed, an air campaign first would have to achieve an attrition of 50 percent of the enemy's forces in the Kuwaiti theater. For several months before the Gulf War, J–5 planners had been using this same criterion. They had been developing computer models that assumed that, to successfully defend the relatively small number of ground troops that could deploy rapidly to Southwest Asia, air attacks would have

U.S. forces' leaders: front row, JCS Chairman General Colin Powell; Secretary of Defense Richard Cheney; CENTCOM CINC General Norman Schwarzkopf; Deputy CINC CENTCOM Lt. Gen. Calvin Waller; back row, MARCENT Commander Lt. Gen. Walter Boomer; CENTAF Commander Lt. Gen. Charles A. Horner; ARCENT Commander Lt. Gen. John Yeosock; NAVCENT Commander Vice Adm. Stanley P. Arthur; SOCCENT Commander Col. Jesse Johnson.

to destroy 50 percent of the enemy's assaulting forces.[29] General Schwarzkopf saw that Instant Thunder had the virtue of being compatible with the planning for ground operations which his own staff had been doing.[30]

The CENTCOM commander reacted to the briefing of August 17 immediately after hearing it, and also later that evening. Right after the Air Staff presentation, General Schwarzkopf directed Colonel Warden and his team to take the Instant Thunder plan to General Horner at CENTAF Forward.[31] That evening, the CINC gave further thought to the air campaign that might take place in his theater. During his session with Colonel Warden earlier on the 17th, General Schwarzkopf had made notes that described the potential elements of such an undertaking: "1. Instant Thunder. 2. Suppression of air defenses over Kuwait. 3. Attrition of enemy force by fifty percent. 4. Ground attack. (?)." That evening the CENTCOM commander's thinking crystallized on this framework for an air campaign made up of four phases.[32]

Jump Start and Concentric Rings: Preparing for an Air Campaign

For his part, Colonel Warden carried out General Schwarzkopf's instruction to take the Instant Thunder briefing to Headquarters CENTAF. Accompanied by two other members of the Checkmate planning group—Lt. Cols. Ben Harvey and Ron Stanfill—and by Lt. Col. David A. Deptula from the Secretary of the Air Force's staff group, Colonel Warden flew to Riyadh aboard an RC–135 from Andrews AFB. On the afternoon of the 20th, he gave General Horner the Instant Thunder briefing, and the CENTAF commander later credited the Pentagon team for bringing together "a lot of information" on strategic targets, some of it not previously available in the theater. "They had excellent target materials," General Horner commented several months later, "and they gave us [a] full range of things" on targets, including facilities for producing and storing munitions, research and development, and command and control. "It was a good effort," General Olsen believed, "on developing a targeting plan…. We took many ingredients from that original plan." Colonel Crigger acknowledged that the Air Staff planners "had gone into more depth…and made a larger target set than we had, and they had gone into much more detail because of the time they had had to spend on how you would actually go about executing that [plan]."[33]

Although granting that the Instant Thunder briefing was strong in its treatment of strategic targets, the CENTAF commander and his staff were disappointed that it did not address immediate air operations to defend Saudi Arabia if Saddam Hussein continued his offensive. General Horner questioned Colonel Warden on this and other points, and, the Air Staff planner later acknowledged, "We got into a couple of sharp exchanges." Shortly after the war, General Horner recalled his initial reaction to Instant Thunder: "In terms of execution, it was very poor. It failed to bring into account protection of the [Coalition] force [in Saudi Arabia], and what we would do in the event of [Iraqi] military forces in the KTO coming into play." General Caruana considered the briefing a good starting point but believed it lacked the perspective of the people in the theater, the viewpoint of those who faced Saddam Hussein "across the line" from day to day.[34] Brig. Gen. Buster C. Glosson, who soon was to become the director of Headquarters CENTAF's special planning group, commented after the war that the Instant Thunder plan had represented "a very narrow view of the situation." Various sources, General Glosson recalled, each day provided photographs of Iraqi brutalities in Kuwait to the senior officers in the theater, giving them a "totally different mindset" than the Air Staff briefers' emphasis on strategic targets.[35]

Some of the CENTAF officers who heard the Air Staff briefing interpreted it as an effort to impose Washington's direction upon the officers in the theater in a situation that was analogous to what had occurred during the Air Force's last war, Vietnam. This perception was extremely unfortunate: no officers would have opposed such a course more strongly than Colonel Warden and his staff. General Schwarzkopf had assured General Horner about precisely this concern, as had General Adams, in a telephone call to the theater commander shortly before the Pentagon briefers arrived. General Horner later recalled their conversation: "Jimmie Adams called me and [said], 'We're not picking the targets in Washington, and I [said], 'I know that, Jimmie. Don't worry about it.'"[36]

Despite these assurances to their commander, some of the CENTAF staff perceived an unhappy similarity to Vietnam. One officer later characterized the tone of the briefing: "It was kind of like, 'Here's this plan that we developed for you guys to execute.' And of course the first thing in most of our minds was, 'This is Vietnam all over again, with forces sent over there that have no say in anything that's going on. All the targets are picked back in Washington, and we're told how to do it.'" Another officer said he believed that although "98 percent" of the decisions were made in the theater during the war, "There were factions back in Washington that were trying to run things, just like in Vietnam."[37]

Another reaction of some CENTAF officers was that the Air Staff plan, although sound, was not particularly innovative. This assessment emphasized the similarities between the briefing prepared at Checkmate and the work done at Headquarters Ninth Air Force. Lt. Col. David L. Waterstreet, Ninth Air Force's Chief of Combat Plans Automation, who later helped write ATOs in the theater, saw close parallels between the two efforts. He pointed out that, during the week between Internal Look and the invasion of Kuwait, officers at Shaw AFB had planned for the possibility of "punishing Iraq," if Saddam Hussein undertook a campaign of aggression, and had sent the results of their efforts to the Air Staff. Colonel Waterstreet described the reaction of many CENTAF staff members to the briefing as "We've seen all that before." Another of General Horner's officers said he considered the Instant Thunder briefing a "confirmation" of the planning done by the Ninth Air Force. Working as they had along parallel lines, it is perhaps unremarkable that the planners in the basement of the Pentagon and in the headquarters at Shaw had arrived at similar results. "If you look at Iraq," Colonel Crigger later explained, "there's only so many targets up there…. Anybody that's looking at a map and starts to identify targets will identify the same targets. So it's not unusual that [Checkmate's] targets were the same [as Ninth Air Force's]."[38]

On August 21, the day after Colonel Warden's controversial briefing to General Horner, the chief Checkmate planner returned to the Pentagon; Colonels Harvey and Stanfill followed a week and a half later. The Instant Thunder plan remained in Riyadh, as did Colonel Deptula, the one officer in the Air Staff party whom General Horner knew before its arrival. Colonel Deptula then became the only Air Force officer with experience in the Directorate of Warfighting Concepts in the theater. He eventually shared this distinction with Maj. Mark "Buck" Rogers, a Checkmate planner who later became his night officer in Riyadh, and with Lt. Col. William Lucyshin and Capt. Christopher Hines.[39]

A number of the participants concluded that the division of talent between the Pentagon and the theater proved advantageous. Colonel Warden believed the arrangement "worked out well" and that "a symbiotic relationship" developed between the officers in Riyadh and Headquarters USAF. Drawing an analogy with the World War II cooperation between the military leaders in Washington, D.C., and in the theaters, Warden stated, "We did not tell them how to run the war. We provided information." One contemporary observer noted that, although General Glosson and Colonel Deptula in Riyadh had entrée to the intelligence community, the Checkmate officers in the Pentagon were able to supply additional information

Secretary of the Air Force Donald Rice.

from a wide range of government, contractor, and academic sources. Lt. Col. Jeffery Feinstein, a Headquarters CENTAF planner, made a similar point, emphasizing the importance of Checkmate's access to the DIA and other intelligence agencies. Colonel Deptula credited the Air Staff office with important contributions both before and during the Gulf War. Prior to the conflict, the Checkmate office gathered data from a variety of sources and acted as a "fusion center." After the war began, its role shifted from being a source of information to providing "feedback" and analysis of the effects of the air campaign. General Glosson described his relationship with the office: "All I had to do was call [Checkmate] and say, I need this analysis done; I need you to contact this country, this contractor, I don't know enough about this…. I could not have dreamed of such support."[40]

Commenting after the war, Colonel Deptula stressed the significance of General Glosson's ability to use Checkmate material in concert with information gained through the general's "vital" relationship with Rear Adm. J. M. McConnell, DIA's director for joint staff intelligence. When General Glosson visited Washington in December 1990, he toured the Joint Intelligence Center in the Pentagon basement and saw its hundreds of intelligence analysts, coordinators, photo interpreters, and other experts. "If you need anything," Admiral McConnell told him during that visit, "I've got two thousand guys waiting to do it for you." The general readily accepted the admiral's offer. "If there was anything we needed immediately," Colonel Deptula recalled, "General Glosson picked up the phone and called Admiral McConnell." Colonel Deptula pointed to the example of General Glosson's asking the admiral for a particular intelligence photograph and receiving it within two hours, when other sources took a day or two to produce the same item. General Glosson recalled that during the war he talked by telephone with Admiral McConnell two, three, or more times a day. He emphasized that the admiral was the senior officer who "went in and told the Sec Def, the chairman, and the presi-

Brig. Gen. Buster Glosson,
Director of the Headquarters
Special Planning Group.

dent, 'This is what's happening.' So it was a very irrefutable source I had [in Admiral McConnell]."[41]

After Colonel Warden returned to Checkmate on the 21st and while Colonel Crigger's officers continued their work on the D-day plan, CENTAF Forward's special planning group began preparing an offensive air campaign plan. General Glosson became available, by chance, to direct the efforts. He was serving on the staff of the Joint Task Force Middle East and, when that organization was dissolved as a joint command, General Horner secured his assignment as director of the special planning group.[42]

These planners initially worked in a small conference room next door to General Horner's office on the third floor of the RSAF headquarters building. Intense security measures protected the early efforts of the special planning group, and this security was the source of its nickname, "the Black Hole." Target lists that had been classified "Secret" at Shaw AFB became "Top Secret/Special Compartmented Information" in Riyadh. At the time the Black Hole planners started their work, the Bush administration had affirmed that the United States would defend Saudi Arabia but had not stated any intention to attack Iraq. Thus, planning for an offensive campaign against strategic targets in Iraq was an extremely sensitive activity protected by high-level security. Further, as more allies joined the Coalition, the need to protect sources of intelligence information only increased.[43]

The Black Hole planners, like all of the CENTAF personnel in Riyadh that August, put in long hours under crowded conditions. General Olsen later recalled the original, cramped offices in the headquarters, when "the loggies, the operators, the planners, the COPS, and the administrators" all worked in two rooms, each about twenty by twenty-five feet. One Black Hole planner remembered that officers commonly served thirty-six- to forty-eight-hour shifts, catnapping when they could and sleeping under conference tables.[44] As the Desert Shield deployment continued and the RSAF headquarters became even more crowded, tents and portable shelters were set up around the building and used for offices. The parking lot was the only available space that was large enough to accommodate the heavy generators that powered the TACC's computers.[45]

Working space was scarce, and so were computers in the early headquarters. The demand for automatic data-processing hardware was so intense that General Glosson gave his staff his own credit card to purchase a Macintosh and a printer in Riyadh. Some officers who reported to CENTAF Forward in late August complained that the headquarters personnel who had arrived ahead of them would not share their computers. In fact, many of the first personnel to deploy to Riyadh did not bring personal computers with them and were reluctant to loan the later arrivals the few pieces of hardware they had.[46]

Constrained by this lack of processors, the Black Hole planners worked to meet the crucial tasking that General Horner had given them on August 21: prepare "an executable ATO" within five days for a strategic air campaign.[47] Time was a compelling factor. Secretary of the Air Force Donald Rice had alerted the CENTAF planners that it could become necessary to execute an air offensive soon, perhaps as early as September 6, and that an even earlier date was possible because Hussein might attack Saudi Arabia at any time. In that contingency, CENTAF could be asked to conduct offensive as well as defensive air operations.[48] General Horner wanted his combat units to begin their mission planning as quickly as possible. When target-planning materials later became available, the unit planners could factor these into their plans, without loss of time.[49] Given these circumstances, the officers at CENTAF Forward in late August were working eighteen to twenty hours a day.[50]

If the planners in the Black Hole had followed traditional methods, they first would have developed a list of targets and put them in priority order. Intelligence officers and targeteers then would have determined the level of damage, stated as a percentage, that was needed for a successful attack on each target. A goal, for example, might be to destroy 80 percent of a target. Finally, specialists of particular aircraft and ordnance would have planned the "packages" of weapons that were required to gain these desired levels of damage. This traditional approach contained two fundamental working assumptions. The first was that the attackers would work their way from top to bottom through a list of targets, ranked in the order of their importance. The second was that the success of an attack would be measured by stating, as a percentage, the level of damage it had achieved and comparing this to the desired level of damage. A target, for example, might be 30 percent destroyed, yet the goal remained 80 percent destruction.[51]

Lucrative Targets

Some of the Black Hole officers concluded that this traditional approach was inadequate for the task they faced. Colonel Deptula, the group's chief planner, had two concerns: First, the conventional planning method assumed the availability of rapid and accurate bomb-damage assessment (BDA) information, which was necessary to measure the success of air operations and determine after an initial strike whether follow-on attacks were needed.[52]

The ability of the intelligence agencies to supply planners and operators with BDA soon enough for it to be useful—and the larger question of how well the "IN [intelligence] community" performed—became controversial subjects during the Gulf War.[53] Although participants reached no consensus regarding these issues, a number of them agreed that intelligence support improved during Desert Shield and Storm, and that it was weakest early in the deployment, at the very time when the Black Hole planners were beginning their efforts. Col. Christopher Christon, Headquarters CENTAF's DCS/Intelligence, said that the "structure [of intelligence] evolved over time, but was evolutionary and had many fits and starts and was particularly ineffective, early on." He explained this in part by pointing to the Ninth Air Force's lack of interactive computers, access to the Defense Data Network, and other information-processing and -transferring capabilities. Colonel Christon also pointed out that, although the deployed units of the United States Air Forces in Europe and Pacific Air Forces enjoyed these high-technology assets, the numbered air forces that were the components of the unified commands did not. He noted that Ninth Air Force intelligence officers had deployed for Desert Shield with nothing more than a limited fax capability.[54] The early shortage of communications might have been reduced sooner, but General Schwarzkopf put a priority on sending combat assets to the theater, ahead of support ones.[55] "The decision was made to get the 'shooters' over there first," Colonel Christon reflected. "It was absolutely the right [decision], but what happened was that, without communications, intelligence is awfully difficult to do…. Theater air intelligence was not ready to support…the full range of combat functions, until around the middle of October."[56]

General Olsen agreed that intelligence support improved during Desert Shield. "Intelligence…took a long time to grow," he believed, "because it is so compartmented. It took a while to get the intelligence process moving out of the national level down to the tactical level, [in] a timely manner [so] that it could be used for planning." The agencies involved had to focus their assets on the AOR, to shift their analysts to the theater, and to establish communications with them. These steps were taken, General Olsen observed, and intelligence support to CENTAF eventually improved.[57]

General Horner made a similar assessment soon after the war. The CENTAF commander indicated that the national effort to collect information on fixed targets was extensive, surpassing that to gain information about Iraqi field forces and their tactical capabilities. Like General Olsen, General Horner connected the shifting of assets to the AOR to an improvement in theater intelligence. He noted that the IN community always develops information about the adversary's tactical forces and capabilities as a war progresses. "In this case," General Horner said, "that's what we did, and that's why we started getting better and better about what we were doing to the [enemy's] forces in the field and [about] where his Scuds were going."[58] The consensus was that intelligence support improved over time and was at its lowest point when the Black Hole planners began their work.[59]

In addition to the availability of intelligence, Colonel Deptula's second concern about applying traditional planning methods to the task at hand was that CENTAF lacked enough assets to generate in one mission all the sorties needed to achieve an 80 percent level of damage against all of its targets. The conventional answer to this was that the attackers would move through the prioritized list as far as possible, then resume the next day against whatever target now had reached the top of the roll. Deptula concluded that this methodology was not acceptable. He acknowledged that some targets (such as leadership, air defense facilities, and Scud missiles) "come up front," but, beyond them, "You can't prioritize [our targets]—they were all number one."[60]

Colonel Deptula, General Glosson, and others believed that the fundamental problem with the conventional approach was that it evaluated success by the amount of damage, rather than by the effect of the attack. These two measures were distinctly different, as General Schwarzkopf illustrated with a hypothetical example: "You have got a four-span bridge. You knock out two complete spans, and you are...told the bridge is [only] 50 percent destroyed. Nothing can go across the bridge, but it is only 50 percent destroyed." General Glosson drew the same distinction between quantified destruction and effective results, when he affirmed after the war that he had not been "interested in seeing how much rubble" could be created in Iraq, but rather in making it impossible for Saddam's regime to function, getting his army out of Kuwait, and destroying his weapons of mass destruction. Pursuing this contrast between damage and effects, Colonel Deptula argued that level of damage was a less useful measure of success than effects achieved. He pointed to the example of a Headquarters CENTCOM/J–2 (Joint Intelligence Directorate) assessment that, as of mid-February 1991, the air campaign had not met its objectives against electrical targets—as measured by level of damage. But, when the operations were evaluated in terms of effects achieved, the results were a complete success. At the time of this report, no electricity had moved through the entire Iraqi powergrid for more than a week.[61]

Once the planners decided to measure success by effects rather than levels of damage, they resolved the problem of running out of assets and having to stop at some point down a list of prioritized targets. It took fewer weapons, for example, to strike an air-defense site and stop its functioning than it did to destroy 80 or 90 percent of the facility. This meant that resources became available to cause disruption and confusion across the entire spectrum of target sets, an approach to warfare that Colonel Deptula called "simultaneity."[62]

Lucrative Targets

This concept was well suited to the weapons available to CENTAF in August 1990, particularly the F–117A stealth fighter and PGMs, which were ideal systems for an air campaign aimed at achieving effects rather than levels of damage. The stealth qualities of the F–117 gave the aircraft a certain amount of "built-in" air superiority. This high-technology fighter needed little "force packaging"; that is, it required fewer accompanying aircraft to help it accomplish a mission than did other strike aircraft, thereby freeing assets for other operations. PGMs, which produced precise effects rather than piles of rubble, also were highly compatible with the concept of simultaneity. "Stealth and PGMs," Colonel Deptula summarized, "[made] simultaneity possible."[63]

Using the simultaneity concept, the special planning group arrived at a plan in time to meet General Horner's five-day deadline. Working through the night of August 25/26, they completed a master attack plan (MAP) that delineated the sequence of attacks for the first twenty-four hours of an offensive air campaign and identified targets, the numbers and type of aircraft that would strike them, and the times that they would attack.[64] The MAP served a vital role as the starting point in the planning process. "The master attack plan," General Olsen said, "was the document that…set down the philosophy of how the ATO would be built and how we would allocate resources." The plan also served an important purpose after combat began, giving senior officers a concise summary of the operations underway at any given time. As Colonel Deptula pointed out, this document not only "drove the planning process," but also "was used during the execution of the war as well[,] since it provided a clear 'script' of what was to occur, when, and by whom."[65]

Whereas the MAP provided a brief summary of a day's air operations, the ATO delineated the thousands of specific details that were necessary to execute them. Each document served its own essential purposes. The MAP document was invaluable to planners and senior officers, the ATO to aircrews. General Horner explained: "The master attack plan is…the outline, the thing that you fleshed out [to make] the ATO. The ATO had all the details…. You start out with the master attack plan, [and] translate it into an ATO…. The people who do the actual execution need all those details, but somebody conceptualizing what you're doing the next day just needs the master attack plan." General Olsen explained the difference between the two documents by making an analogy to planning a trip. A traveler first needs a MAP, a broad decision that he intends to go from one city to another. Then he also must have an ATO, giving the details of his specific route between the two points.[66]

By the morning of August 26, General Glosson and his officers had arrived at a MAP for the first day of an air campaign as well as an extensively revised version of the Instant Thunder plan. The CENTAF planner briefed these results to a small audience, which included General Horner, General Caruana, Brig. Gen. Larry L. Henry (Headquarters CENTAF's director of electronic combat), and Colonel Crigger. The CENTAF commander directed that this briefing be revised to a format using maps and overlays and discussing the theater air offensive as a series of time-sequenced events. "After General Glosson briefed General Horner," Colonel Deptula recalled, "the briefing was then adjusted. We then put together the real specifics of the first attacks, with acetate overlays that [could] take someone through the [form-up for the] initial attack…all the way through the first twenty-four hours."[67]

Like General Schwarzkopf, General Horner favored describing the air campaign as a series of phases, a framework that audiences beyond the Air Force would understand readily. "You had to have [phases]," the CENTAF commander later explained, "because you knew you've got to brief it up to the president, so it's got to be understandable, it's got to make sense, and it's got to be complete." Shortly after General Glosson's presentation on August 26, General Horner decided on a framework that embraced General Schwarzkopf's four phases and that remained unchanged throughout the Gulf War.[68]

CENTAF briefings described Phase I as a "strategic air campaign", Phase II as an effort to gain "air supremacy" in the KTO, Phase III to "destroy enemy ground forces" in the KTO or "battlefield preparation", and Phase IV as "air support of the ground campaign."[69] Phase II was called "air supremacy in the KTO," because General Schwarzkopf used this phrase and other Army officers were well familiar with it. CENTAF briefers sometimes labeled Phase III "battlefield preparation" because, again, ARCENT and MARCENT planners readily understood the term.[70] It is significant that Air Staff briefings, prepared for Air Force audiences, identified the four phases slightly differently. Headquarters USAF briefers commonly used the following labels: Phase I—strategic air campaign; Phase II—suppression of enemy air defenses (SEAD); Phase III—operations in the KTO; and Phase IV—ground campaign.[71]

In early September, CENTAF officers briefed the four-phase air campaign in follow-on presentations to General Horner, Maj. Gen. Royal N. Moore, Jr. (the commander of the 3d Marine Air Wing), the Headquarters CENTCOM staff, and General Schwarzkopf. The CENTCOM commander later praised the work of the Riyadh officers: "Brig. Gen. Buster Glosson, Chuck Horner's top planner, had expanded the retaliatory scheme of the Pentagon Air Staff into the best air campaign I'd ever seen. It gave us a broad range of attack options and could be conducted as a stand-alone operation or as part of a larger war." On September 12, General Powell heard and approved the CENTAF plan. From that date on, as General Glosson later said, General Schwarzkopf "really could provide President Bush with an option" for an offensive air campaign against Iraq.[72]

The 24th Mechanized Infantry Division arrived in the theater during September, giving CENTCOM planners confidence that they had enough soldiers and armor to stop an Iraqi incursion into Saudi Arabia. As the autumn progressed, CENTAF's offensive air plan eventually assumed greater importance than its defensive D-day plan, which had been so vital in early August. By October, General

Lucrative Targets

Horner believed that the latter was no longer needed: if Saddam attempted an advance into Saudi Arabia, CENTAF could respond by using its offensive plan.[73]

The offensive air plan continued to evolve during the fall, adding, for example, the Republican Guard as a major target set. From the earliest planning, American senior officers emphasized the importance of air operations against these elite Iraqi units. When Colonel Warden had briefed General Powell on the Instant Thunder plan on August 11, the chairman commented that he did not want Saddam Hussein to withdraw from Kuwait with the Republican Guard and their tanks intact.[74] General Schwarzkopf held the same apprehension: one Air Force senior officer recalled the CENTCOM commander's ongoing concern "that the Republican Guards were going to escape, that they were going to get up and run." In mid-August, General Schwarzkopf had emphasized that, if it came to an air campaign, "I want the Republican Guard bombed the very first day, and I want them bombed every day after that."[75] General Glosson, who characterized these elite forces as the Iraqis' "only real tough-fighting unit," recalled that General Horner stressed the same point to his staff during the earliest stages of their planning. On September 2, after a meeting between General Schwarzkopf and General Glosson, the officers in the Black Hole added the Republican Guard as a target set in their plan.[76]

During October, the air planners in Washington also gave more attention to the Republican Guard in particular, and to Phase III in general, producing a diversity of ideas. At the request of General Alexander, the Air Force Center for Studies and Analyses studied the KTO portion of the air plan and suggested using modeling techniques to gain a more realistic estimate of how long it would take to destroy the targets in the Kuwaiti theater.[77] On October 9, representatives from the RAND Corporation briefed Colonel Warden on their recommendation that CENTAF should follow its Instant Thunder operations in Iraq with weeks of bombing of enemy forces in Kuwait before Coalition ground forces undertook an offensive. The Air Staff planner was skeptical of this presentation, believing it underestimated what air attacks against strategic targets in Iraq could achieve. For their part, RAND analysts contended that Checkmate's planning was based on overly optimistic assumptions.[78]

At the suggestion of Secretary Rice and General Adams, the Checkmate office in mid-October began a thorough study of Phase III of the air campaign. Their initial planning concentrated on operations against the regular Iraqi divisions that were deployed along the Saddam Line and elsewhere in Kuwait.[79] Generals McPeak and Glosson both pointed out that General Schwarzkopf would put a priority on attacking the Republican Guard.[80] In late October, the Checkmate staff developed and sent to Riyadh a briefing that highlighted the importance of striking these elite units. This Air Staff presentation emphasized the Republican Guard, devoting to them an entire segment of the Phase III KTO operations. The Checkmate planners divided Phase III into two parts: attacks on the Republican Guard and strikes against all other targets in the theater.[81]

Jump Start and Concentric Rings: Preparing for an Air Campaign

Making use of this Checkmate briefing and other sources,[82] the Black Hole officers completed their planning for Phase III, including the Republican Guard, and their results were well received. On October 10 and 11, General Glosson and Maj. Gen. Robert B. Johnston (USMC), the CENTCOM Chief of Staff, briefed President Bush, Secretary Cheney, and the Joint Staff on the planning for the air and ground campaigns. Although these audiences criticized the plans for the land operations, they commended those from CENTAF.[83] One strong point of the Phase III planning was that it reinforced the crucial feature of the eventual plan for the ground campaign, the "shift west" of the XVIII Airborne and VII Corps.[84] By this move to their left, the ARCENT forces would avoid an attack into the teeth of the Saddam Line, and they would be able to encircle the Iraqis in the KTO. In late November, General Schwarzkopf heard General Glosson's briefing on Phase III and the Republican Guard and saw how these air attacks would contribute to the "shift west."[85]

In addition to the Republican Guard, the CENTAF planners added another target set—highway bridges—to the original Air Staff plan. As General Glosson later pointed out, the Instant Thunder briefing had considered only railroad bridges, categorizing them with marshalling yards. The rail network had military significance; for example, the Iraqis used it to move tanks from Baghdad to the KTO. The importance of railroads to the general economy, however, was modest. The Iraqi economy, like that of most developing nations, depended more on moving goods by road than by rail. Although roadways had this economic significance, the officers in the Black Hole at first thought that attacking them would be a poor use of Coalition resources. Many Iraqi "highways" were little more than sandy tracks immune to bomb craters. The more-substantial roads often had little value as targets, because trucks could operate easily across the desert, independent of any defined roadway. However, the highway bridges over the Tigris and Euphrates Rivers represented a different case. Like railroad bridges, they were important "choke points" whose destruction would block the movement of supplies and troops into the KTO.[86] Moreover, the Tigris and Euphrates bridges were significant because the Republican Guard could use them to flee the KTO, an ongoing concern of General Schwarzkopf and other American senior officers.[87] General Glosson directed that his planners identify every bridge in Iraq that could support a single automobile. There proved to be fifty-four, thirty-two of which were of critical military value. The Black Hole officers included all of them in their planning.[88]

The addition of the bridges was only one factor in the continuing increase, through the autumn and early winter, in the number of targets in the air campaign plan. The Instant Thunder briefing on August 8 contained eighty-four strategic targets. In September, the Headquarters CENTAF special planning group added the Republican Guard and other Iraqi army targets in the KTO, bringing the number first to 127 and then 178, where it remained into October. As intelligence sources provided the Black Hole planners with more and better information, the figure increased in November to 218 and in December to 238. By January 1991, more than 350 strategic targets were included in the air campaign plan.[89]

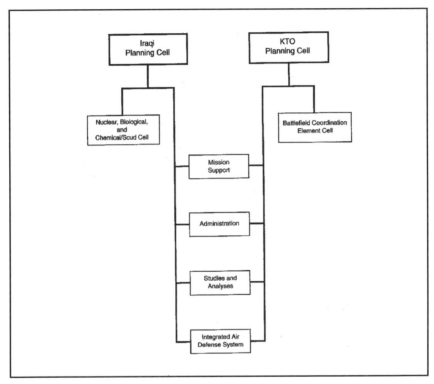

The GAT division.

As the air plan expanded, as the Coalition forces increased, and as Headquarters CENTAF grew larger, a reorganization of General Glosson's Directorate of Campaign Plans became necessary in December. The Special Planning Group, or Black Hole, merged with the COPS to form a Guidance, Apportionment, and Targeting (GAT) division. The GAT division consisted of two primary cells: the Iraqi planning cell (the former Black Hole), with Colonel Deptula serving as its chief; and the KTO planning cell, with Lt. Col. Sam Baptiste as its chief. Six other cells aided these two primary ones. The Nuclear, Biological, and Chemical/Scud cell exclusively supported the Iraqi planning cell, and the Battlefield Coordination Element (BCE) cell did the same for the KTO planning cell. Comprising personnel from Fort Bragg, the BCE cell provided the KTO planners with current information on both enemy and friendly orders of battle. The Army had identified these staffers long in advance of Desert Shield, and they had participated in Ninth Air

Force exercises, thus gaining an advantage in experience over the liaison officers from other services. The other four GAT cells—Mission Support, Administration, Studies and Analysis, and the Integrated Air Defense System cell, which tracked information on enemy airfields and SAMs—supported both the Iraqi and the KTO cell. While the Black Hole and COPS merged to form the GAT division, Col. Rick Bennett's ATO division maintained its same place in the directorate organization and continued to report, like the new GAT division, directly to General Glosson.[90]

At least two major considerations influenced this reorganization. General Horner commented afterward that the shift in the emphasis of the planning, from the defensive plan that had been critically needed in early August to the offensive option that was developed later, made it desirable to merge the daily planners with the Black Hole officers. With the Bush administration's decision to double the size of the force and to prepare to take the initiative against Iraq, the CENTAF commander said, "the Black Hole became the plans function, as we shifted from defense to offense." Initially there had been a pressing need to have the Ninth Air Force planners, with their years of experience developing ATOs, working on the D-day and training tasking orders. That situation changed over time, and, by December, the question became whether to shift some of this expertise to the Black Hole. The solution was to merge them, while at the same time keeping the Iraqi and KTO cells distinct. This separation maintained two coherent pools of expertise: the KTO planning cell drew heavily on the daily planners, who were Ninth Air Force officers with long experience developing ATOs; and the Iraqi planning cell represented a continuation of the Black Hole, with a larger percentage of augmentees to the numbered air force personnel. The second major consideration in the reorganization was that it could not be carried out until the Saudis made available more space in the RSAF headquarters. In August, all of the Headquarters CENTAF officers had worked under extremely crowded conditions. "There was no way to pull [the planners] together," General Olsen explained, "because we just didn't have the space." In December, the Saudis made available three large work areas on the building's lowest floor. "Once we got those three big rooms in the basement," General Olsen recalled, "then we could consolidate."[91]

Complementing this headquarters organization was one in the field in which four provisional air divisions exercised operational control of CENTAF's aircraft, grouped by aircraft type. Headquarters SAC and Military Airlift Command (MAC) had activated two of these units earlier during Desert Shield: the 17th Provisional Air Division on September 21, and the 1610th Provisional Air Lift Division on October 15. The former, commanded by General Caruana, had operational control of SAC/Strategic Force tankers and bombers. The 1610th—led initially by Brig. Gen. Frederic N. Buckingham and, after November 11, by Brig. Gen. Edwin E. Tenoso—had the same responsibility for MAC/Commander Airlift Forces (COMALF) cargo aircraft. "The provisional air division structure is working well," General Olsen observed in late November, "and we would like to apply a similar concept to the rest of the operational forces." The provisional air division organization indeed had worked well and, moreover, Generals Olsen and Horner recognized that the administration's decision to double the size of the force would bring so many aircraft and units to the theater that the CENTAF commander's span of control would become unwieldy. On December 5, at the request of CENT-AF Forward, CENTAF Rear and USAFE activated the 14th and 15th Provisional Air Divisions. The 15th, commanded by Brig. Gen. Glenn A. Profitt II, provided operational control over CENTAF's electronic combat, reconnaissance, and C^2 aircraft. The 14th, assigned to General Glosson, had the same authority over the command's tactical fighter wings. At the same time, General Glosson continued in his role as director of campaign plans, wearing "two hats," as chief of both planners and "shooters."[92]

Airmen in both the headquarters and the field units were keenly aware of the approaching deadline of January 15, 1991. On January 8, General Powell passed a warning order to General Schwarzkopf for launching an air campaign against Iraq at 0300 January 17. On January 9, Secretary Baker met with Iraqi Foreign Minister Tariq Aziz at the International Hotel in Geneva, but the two diplomats reached no compromise. After their session, the Secretary of State told reporters, "Regrettably, I heard nothing today that suggested to me any Iraqi flexibility." Mr. Aziz commented, at a separate press conference, that Iraq was now "preparing for the worst." On the eve of the deadline, Secretary General of the United Nations Javier Perez de Cuellar went to Baghdad and spent two-and-a-half hours with Saddam Hussein in a fruitless effort to convince him to withdraw from Kuwait. After these diplomatic efforts failed and the deadline passed, the American chief executive gave the Iraqi leader a one-day grace. Then, as President Bush later reported to Congress, "pursuant to my authority as Commander in Chief, I directed U.S. Armed Forces to commence combat operations on 16 January 1991, against Iraqi forces and military targets in Iraq and Kuwait." Desert Shield, the defensive deployment to protect Saudi Arabia, gave way to Desert Storm, an offensive operation to expel the Iraqis from Kuwait.[93]

When the president ordered the Gulf operations to begin, morale among American forces in the theater stood high. A maintenance officer of the 363d Provisional Tactical Fighter Wing [TFW(P)] noted in his logbook for January 17: "At 0300 hrs the message from General Schwarzkopf came down announcing the onset of Desert Storm and giving us a shot in the arm.... There was plenty of turn time the first day and with the amount of adrenaline flowing things went perfectly and smoothly." Another maintenance officer, stationed at Seeb, Oman, believed that morale "got better and better as the January 15 deadline got nearer. Once the major holidays had passed, and once we knew that a final resolution was going to take place, people drew even closer together and morale got better." "I remember the first night," a B–52 crewmember recalled, "when we launched eighteen bombers and eleven or twelve tankers. We were all pumped, and we were even more pumped as we took off and saw all the maintenance troops lining the runways cheering and waving flags." Operation Desert Storm was underway.[94]

Chapter Three

No Place to Hide:
Phases I, II, and the Shift to III

During the early morning hours of January 17, more than 160 tankers circled south of the Iraqi border in cells five deep, following the same tracks they had used since August.[1] Accompanied by their F–15 escorts, three E–3 AWACS Sentrys looked into Iraq, keeping track of the enemy's air forces. They, too, flew routes familiar to their enemy. The Iraqis watching their radar screens saw only these reassuring patterns of aircraft. "They were seeing a situation," General Mc-Peak later remarked, "that we had been showing them since August." The Iraqis did not see the aircraft behind the tankers: the stealth F–117s, the vanguard of the covert, stunningly successful air attack that would open the Gulf War. At twenty-five minutes before "H-hour" (0300)—the time designated for the attack to begin—ten of these low-observable aircraft dropped from their tankers. Four minutes later, a task force of Special Operations Forces MH–53 Pave Low and AR-CENT AH–64 Apache helicopters destroyed two electronic warfare sites in western Iraq, opening a corridor for F–15Es to strike Scud sites in Iraq.[2]

The Gulf War opened with CENTAF aircraft attacking SEAD targets in both Iraq and the KTO, "blinding" Saddam Hussein by knocking out his air defenses, and at the same time hitting crucial Phase I targets in Baghdad and across the enemy's homeland. The first night's attack came in two waves. The initial, covert one achieved tactical surprise, with F–117s destroying vital C^2 centers and the Navy's Tomahawk Land Attack Missiles (TLAMs) hitting electrical powerplants, the presidential palace, the Ba'ath Party headquarters, and other targets in Baghdad. These strikes caused confusion throughout Iraq, beginning in the first minutes of the war. The Iraqis took half an hour to black out Baghdad, and their pilots managed to fly only a few air defense sorties.[3]

Lucrative Targets

During these initial attacks, the F–117s and their PGMs demonstrated their inherent air superiority, while carrying out the "simultaneity" strategy. The stealth aircraft flew only 8 percent of the first night's sorties, yet they covered 65 percent of the target base. General McPeak later asserted, "They did all the work—they and the TLAMs did all the work in the heavily defended downtown Baghdad area. They also attacked key parts of the air defense system throughout Iraq."[4]

Overwhelming the Iraqi air defenses, these initial covert strikes purchased thirty to forty minutes for the second wave of the attack, comprising the Coalition's non-stealthy aircraft, to join the combat. At 0340, this enormous force of F–111s, F–4Gs, F–15Es, B–52s, and other aircraft—"the gorilla," in Air Force slang—began attacking Iraqi air-defense facilities, airfields, Scud fixed launchers, chemical munitions storage areas, and other vital targets in Baghdad, around Basra, and throughout the country. General Caruana later commented on the rationale behind these wide-ranging attacks: "Airpower was essentially going to beat [Saddam Hussein] down and take away his ability…not just to command and control, but to execute. You have to remember we had a concern with biological weapons and chemical weapons and our charter was to not let that guy have any avenue through which he could execute that, either through the Scuds or his aircraft."[5]

The initial Coalition operations stunned the enemy. "Every mission went as fragged," General Glosson later said. "It followed the script so close, it was eerie." General McPeak characterized the beginning of the air campaign: "It was a very heavy attack, very precisely delivered." The first CENTAF strikes shut down Baghdad's electrical power, knocking out television, telephone, and radio communications. General Horner later said that he knew exactly when the F–117s hit their target: at precisely the time planned for destroying the Iraqi capital's main communications link, the Cable News Network (CNN) broadcast from Baghdad disappeared from his television screen. An Iraqi businessman from Diwaniyah, south of Baghdad, told a reporter, "The Americans inflicted more damage on our country in the first two hours of the war than the Iranians did in eight years."[6]

At the beginning of the war, CENTAF sorties also devastated the C^2 facilities that integrated the Iraqi air defenses. Within the opening minutes of the conflict, Iraq no longer had a nationally coordinated air defense system. Coalition air strikes quickly knocked out the National Air Defense Center and Baghdad's two communications centers. Other attacks ended all communications from the SOCs to the SAM sites or the IOCs, and reduced the connectivity between the IOCs and Iraqi's air defense fighters. From the first minutes of the war until its close, all of the enemy's air defense operations were autonomous.[7]

Overwhelmed by these initial Coalition attacks, the Iraqi air defenses never regained their effectiveness. This was largely due, as General Glosson later pointed out, to the destruction of enemy radars by AGM–88A high-speed antiradiation missiles (HARMs) during the first three hours of the war. F–4G Wild Weasels detected the emissions from a radar site, locked on to the emitter, and launched a HARM which homed on it. Their frequent successes discouraged the Iraqis from turning on their radars, whether to guide SAMs or AAA. Colonel Baptiste, chief

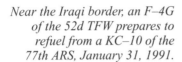

Near the Iraqi border, an F–4G of the 52d TFW prepares to refuel from a KC–10 of the 77th ARS, January 31, 1991.

of the KTO planning cell, recalled how the advanced radars and other electronic warfare equipment of the F–4G Wild Weasels intimidated enemy air defenders. "The Iraqi SAM operators respected the F–4Gs," he said, "because they quickly learned that whenever an F–4G radar was up in the air, they'd better not even come up with their tracking radar, otherwise they'd be eating a HARM shortly thereafter."[8] Wary of turning on their hardware, the Iraqi air defenders were reduced to unguided, ballistic SAM firings, which, as General Glosson later noted, explained "why they were so ineffective for the remainder of the war." Iraqi SAM launches, from both Iraq and the KTO, dropped dramatically after the first day of the war. On February 7, the enemy fired forty SAMs, which was they most they launched on any day between January 18 and the start of the ground campaign. On just three days—January 17 and February 25 and 26—did the Iraqis muster more than sixty SAM firings. The overwhelming majority of the launches, even on these three days, were unguided, ballistic efforts.[9]

Some CENTAF officers wondered why the Iraqis had no contingency plans for continuing operations after their air defense system was attacked and its subordinate elements were rendered autonomous. One KTO planner expressed surprise that "those individual [Iraqi] commanders didn't have autonomous plans.... Any sound military commander would have an autonomous plan, if he's cut off from his command and control, that he would immediately execute—some launching of fighters, launching strikes against targets that's already pre-planned, launching a defense CAP,...that's just sound military strategy, and we didn't see that happen."[10] This Air Force officer's comments suggested what the Iraqis needed to respond to this devastating attack on their air defenses: contingency plans laid in advance, flexible options that they could readily implement, and individual initiative from their commanders. The Iraqi Air Force, modeled on the Soviet pattern of rigid centralization in the hands of a ruthless dictator, suffered

An F–15C of the 36th TFW refuels during a Desert Storm mission on January 20, 1991.

from the inflexibility that is common to all totalitarian military systems. The Iraqi Air Force's inability to reply effectively to the Coalition's attack on its air defenses, as General Horner told one reporter, showed the "horrible" weakness inherent in "a one-man show."[11]

These opening Coalition attacks against Iraq and its air defenses represented simultaneous operations against Phase I and II targets. Before and during the Gulf War, planners sometimes referred to a framework of four phases, and, after the conflict, historians adopted the same convention.[12] The air campaign was a complex event, and the four phases offered a simple way of delineating its major elements. The air operation in the Gulf, General Glosson commented shortly after the war, "was initially portrayed as four specific phases" to provide "an easy way to explain how this [conflict] could go from an air campaign to a ground campaign, which was always the mindset of both the CINC and Chairman. There had to be a logical-step process or logical sequence that would lead you from the first bomb drop in the strategic air campaign and culminate with the ground forces liberating Kuwait City." Colonel Crigger explained that the phases were adopted as an effective way "to present the thing…so that people could get a better idea of when things were going to happen," and General Horner emphasized that the framework was particularly helpful to audiences outside the Air Force.[13]

Although the concept had its utility, it could be misleading. The four phases were not separate entities that followed each other in neat chronological order, with Phase II SEAD operations over the KTO ending on one day and Phase III ones beginning the next. The officers in the Black Hole did not plan an air campaign composed of four distinct phases, nor did the Coalition aircrews execute it in that way. Colonel Baptiste later commented, "We really didn't 'think phases' so much, I don't think, as we were actually executing the war or planning [it].... We were just trying to follow the guidance and get the job done." The air campaign plan did not provide for four distinct phases but, rather, for simultaneous attacks on targets across all of the target sets. "The initial strikes were designed to attack the entire target base," Colonel Deptula explained, "to achieve simultaneous impact against all the target sets as opposed to striking one target set at a time." After the war, General Horner told a congressional committee, "Actually, all phases were going on simultaneously from the first day we started attacking the Iraqi armed forces in the vicinity of the front lines and through the last day we were bombing targets in Baghdad." Although the emphasis of the air campaign shifted among the four phases, it never settled exclusively on any one of them.[14]

The phases of CENTAF's offensive plan overlapped as early as the MAP covering the first twenty-four hours of the war, which called for attacks on targets representing Phase I, II, and III. "Phase I consumed Phase II very quickly," General Glosson pointed out. The two were actually inseparable: it was essential that the Coalition destroy the enemy's integrated air defense system in Iraq (Phase I) and also in the KTO (Phase II). The MAP, therefore, provided for SEAD sorties in both Kuwait and the enemy's homeland. Among the very earliest targets, in fact, were two electronic warfare sites not far north of the Saudi border.[15] The same plan addressed Phase III KTO targets, as well: it included strikes against the Republican Guard and their escape routes to Iraq. The first day's MAP provided for several F–15E and F–111 attacks on highway and railroad bridges across the Tigris and Euphrates Rivers, crucial crossing points for supplies entering—or troops leaving—the Kuwaiti theater. Both of these aircraft were well suited for night operations. The F–111s had terrain-following radar, an internal navigation system, and a radar bombing system, and the F–15Es were equipped with low-altitude navigation and targeting infrared for night (LANTIRN) pods.[16] The MAP also called for twenty-four F–16s, during the first afternoon of the war, to strike the Medina Division, one of the two such armored Republican Guard units in the KTO. Further, within the first twenty-four hours of the conflict, three B–52s would attack the mechanized Tawakalna Division, conducting the first of a relentless series of sorties against Hussein's elite units. These bombers were scheduled to hit the Republican Guard in the KTO every hour, twenty-four hours a day, until the end of the war.[17]

During the first hours of the war, Coalition aircrews successfully attacked targets representing all three phases, in an operation that demanded precise execution. At the beginning of the conflict, more than 160 tankers orbited in intricate patterns, with four to six airplanes refueling from each of them. One CENTAF planner recalled these initial hours, when hundreds of Coalition aircraft were "airborne all at the same time, covering the same field.... And, as they pressed north, they had their lights out and most of their radiating radars down, so as to avoid detection. So the potential for a mid-air [collision], with that number of planes out there, was actually very high."[18]

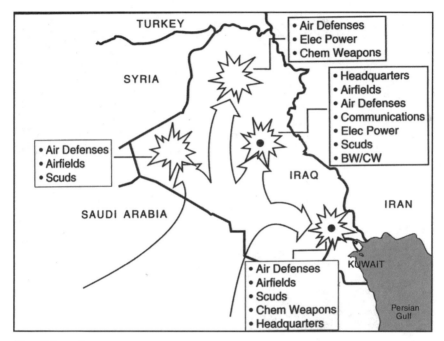

Day 1 targets.

"This whole thing hadn't been practiced all together," another officer pointed out. "It had been practiced in elements but not as a whole." Although CENTAF aircrews had begun small-scale practices for the offensive air campaign in late November, it was not until mid-December that they flew any sizeable force packages for it. "We had practiced parts of it," General Horner told a congressional committee after the war, "but the first time—opening night, the opening show—was the first time we did it, and it went off without a hitch. And those were some of the most nervous moments of my life."[19]

In spite of the fact that this enormous, complex attack had never been fully rehearsed, the first night passed without an accident. Although some planners were concerned that the Coalition might lose as many as thirty or more aircraft that first night, only three were lost during the first twenty-four hours: an F/A–18 from the *Saratoga*, a Royal Air Force Tornado, and a Kuwaiti A–4. Two weeks later, Coalition losses still remained remarkably low: on January 31, allied combat casualties totaled forty-two personnel and twenty aircraft.[20]

The initial air operations achieved so much, so quickly, that the Coalition airmen had to guard against overconfidence. After the successes during the early morning hours of January 17, at 0730 General Horner held the first of his wartime meetings in the TACC. The CENTAF commander strongly warned against complacency. "Your job is to worry," General Horner told his staff. "Your job is to

*Air Force Chief of Staff
General Merrill "Tony" McPeak.*

work very hard and make sure that we understand we're in for a long haul." Later the same day, a fighter maintenance officer wrote in his log: "Things look too good at this point.... I had to fight the urge to become too elated, too early."[21] That evening, General Horner again counseled his staff against overconfidence, adding a prescient remark: "We're on day one of probably a thirty- or forty-day war."[22]

The planners in the Black Hole, who had been reorganized in early January from the CENTAF special planning group into the Iraq strategic-target planning cell, had little time for self-congratulation. They now had to perform what Colonel Deptula called "a dynamic planning process." The Black Hole planners had devoted months to the first MAP; now they had to prepare one every twenty-four hours, for the duration of the war.[23] At any given time, they had three ATOs in front of them. Three "wars," Colonel Deptula explained, "were ongoing each day—the execution war of 'today,' the ATO processing of tomorrow's war, and the planning of the war for the day after tomorrow."[24]

Coalition aircrews sustained their initial successes during the days that followed. By the end of January, they had destroyed four of Baghdad's six major communications centers, as well as the Ministry of Defense's computer center. The city's telephone system remained out of service, as did Iraqi television and radio. CENTAF attacks had destroyed Baghdad's two major powerplants and had shut down the country's electrical powergrid. Air strikes also had damaged eleven of Iraq's twelve major oil refineries and had reduced refining by 87 percent. Coalition sorties left the Baghdad Nuclear Research Facility "largely demolished," destroyed other similar facilities, and cut both Iraq's chemical and biological warfare production by 40 to 50 percent.[25]

The operations early in the air campaign, which emphasized attacks on Phase I and II targets, were not a tale of unbroken successes. CENTAF won its initial

On January 21, 1991, an explosive ordnance disposal team assigned to the 4409th Combat Support Group, stationed at Riyadh, recovered the remains of a Scud missile found north-west of Riyadh.

achievements, as General Horner pointed out at the time, "with one hand tied behind our back because of weather and chasing Scuds." These two factors, both beyond the control of Coalition airmen, lengthened the air campaign and forced Headquarters CENTAF to adjust its plans. Adopting a football analogy, General McPeak compared the air planners' flexible reaction to poor weather and Iraqi Scud attacks to a quarterback calling an "audible," changing the plan for the next play after his team had left its huddle and lined up for the snap of the ball.[26]

The need for flexibility came partly because low clouds settled over the Arabian peninsula soon after the war began. Ceilings held at 20,000 to 25,000 feet during the opening morning of the conflict but, by the end of day, lowered to 10,000 to 15,000 feet. This sudden change of cloud levels was particularly vexing, because the Coalition airmen had enjoyed good flying weather throughout most of the Desert Shield deployment and had every reason to assume that the favorable conditions would continue. One Headquarters CENTAF officer recalled that it was very frustrating "to be in Riyadh and look up in the sky, and for five months you do not see a cloud, not a cloud in the sky. And then [when] we start [the war], we had the worst weather in fourteen years." Ten days of fog, low clouds, drizzle, and downpours followed the opening of the conflict.[27]

"The weather is irrefutably very consistent until about December," General Glosson later pointed out, but the conditions during the first three months of the year are much harder to predict. Meteorological records proved of little value for prognosticating the weather of January and February 1991, which proved atypically bad. In the fourteen years of records that were available to CENTAF weather officers, northern Saudi Arabia had averaged one major storm each January. In 1991, however, it had seven, all within the first two weeks of the air campaign. A winter frontal system usually moved on after twenty-four to thirty-six hours, but, here again, the wartime storms proved irregular, lingering a day longer than the norm. Weather records suggested that low clouds would cover the region 18 percent of the time, but the actual percentage during the first ten days of the war proved double that figure.[28]

Good flying weather returned on January 28, which was the first day in ten when no sorties were lost to the weather. At 1700 that Monday, a senior NCO in the TACC gladly entered in his log, "No weather aborts!" Two-and-a-half hours later, when the weather officer predicted clear skies through the night across the theater, the TACC staff raised a collective cheer.[29]

In addition to the dismal weather, the other development that caused General McPeak's imaginary quarterback to call an audible was Hussein's Scud attacks. These short-range ballistic missiles (SRBMs) gained sudden prominence when, on the second day of the war, Iraq launched seven of the weapons against Israel. Largely inaccurate and prone to breaking up during flight, the Scuds posed greater political and diplomatic, rather than military, dangers to the Coalition. Saddam Hussein owned three models of the weapon: the original Soviet Scud-B and two Iraqi derivatives, the Al Hussein and the Al Abbas. Among these, only the Al Abbas with its modified airframe could reach as far as 560 miles. The Al Hussein's range was limited to approximately 400 miles and the Scud-B's to roughly 190. The modifications that increased the range of the Al Abbas proved deficient and probably contributed to its poor accuracy and its tendency to break up in flight.[30]

Although these limitations hindered the Scuds, the Iraqi missiles nonetheless posed serious threats. They were formidable military systems that could carry chemical and biological agents, and they also were dangerous political weapons with the potential to influence public opinion in America. If the usually inaccurate missiles somehow managed to inflict large numbers of U.S. casualties, then Americans—and their representatives in Congress—might clamor either for a precipitous ground campaign, or, at the other extreme of policy, a withdrawal from the theater. One Scud attack did result in high losses, striking a warehouse near Dhahran that was used for ARCENT housing; twenty-eight soldiers were killed and more than ninety others were wounded. A series of such tragedies might have affected American public opinion, but this missile proved to be the last to land in Saudi Arabia. Furthermore, this single calamity did not occur until February 25, when the Coalition's successful ground campaign already had gained momentum, and it did not influence the course of the war.[31]

In addition to this political danger, the Scuds posed a diplomatic one also when the Iraqis used these weapons against Israel. Saddam Hussein launched forty of the missiles against the only non-Arab state in the region, undoubtedly in an effort to provoke a retaliation that would destroy the alliance that President

Lucrative Targets

Bush painstakingly had constructed. On January 18, within hours after the first Scud attacks, General Olsen, CENTAF Vice Commander, began a seven-day mission to Tel Aviv, delineating for the Israelis the Coalition's plans and operations to counter the Iraqi missiles. Israeli forbearance defeated Saddam's strategy of provocation. Israel publicly took the position that, given the intensity of the CENTAF air campaign against Iraq, its own retaliation was unnecessary; privately, Israel accepted the argument that its intervention would unravel the Coalition.[32]

CENTAF intelligence officers believed the Iraqis to have twenty-eight Scud fixed launchers deployed in nine complexes in western Iraq, and these facilities came under attack beginning with the F–15E strikes at the opening of the war. Later, some postwar analysts raised this fixed-missile arsenal to thirty.[33] Original intelligence estimates also credit the Iraqis with thirty-six mobile Scud launchers, rating thirty-three of them operational; again studies conducted after the conflict increased this number.[34] The mobile Scuds, essentially eight-wheeled heavy trucks modified to carry the missiles, proved particularly troublesome: they could move at night, stop and launch, and then go into hiding in storage facilities, highway culverts, or elsewhere.[35]

During the course of the war, the Iraqis launched eighty-six Scuds: forty-six against Saudi Arabia and forty against Israel. Before the conflict began, ARCENT had deployed dozens of Patriot missile batteries to meet this threat and soon began using these counterweapons. As early as the morning of January 18, a Patriot intercepted a Scud over Dhahran. Three nights later, these ARCENT missiles shot down five of the Iraqi weapons in the same area, four of which were heading towards Riyadh. Space Command (SPACECOM) assets, as their commander noted after the war, enhanced the effectiveness of the Coalition's missile defense.[36]

The Patriot batteries and SPACECOM crews did not provide the only heroes and heroines in the effort against the Iraqi missiles. A–10s scoured the roads that the mobile Scuds were likely to travel from their storage areas to launch sites. "In the daytime we're looking for [them] with A–10s," General Horner stated on January 20, "and in the nighttime we're looking for [them] with the AC–130s." CENTAF planners knew the ranges of the enemy's weapons and could determine the "launch boxes," the clearly defined areas from which Scuds must be fired, if they were to reach, for example, Tel Aviv, Riyadh, or Dhahran, and F–15Es flew CAPs directly over these launch boxes. Two Joint Surveillance Target Attack Radar System (J–STARS) E–8As, although still in development, had deployed to the theater on January 12. These aircraft were derived from the Boeing 707 and featured radars in a long fairing beneath the nose that could detect and track both stationary and moving targets. The J–STARS located mobile Scuds and directed CAP fighters against them.[37]

"The Scuds are priority targets, if anyone has any doubts," General Horner told his staff on the fourth morning of the air campaign. "The way we are handling it is we attempt to do preplanned targeting—hitting the Scud production, hitting the Scud storage, hitting the Scud [launch] sites, and hitting the Scud repair yard." As soon as CENTAF began Scud hunting, the percentage of the missiles that hit targets dropped dramatically, and it remained low throughout the remainder of the war. The Scud launch rate also declined sharply: during the first ten days of the

F–15Cs of the 33d TFW, based at Tabuk, Saudi Arabia, escort a Royal Saudi Air Force F–5E on a mission early in Desert Storm.

conflict, the Iraqis fired an average of five a day; during the remaining thirty-three days, the average was one a day. Coalition aircrews gained results against the Iraqi SRBMs, but their Scud hunting required sorties that could have been flown against other targets. General McPeak acknowledged after the war that "we put about three times the effort that we thought we would on this job."[38]

Despite the Scud-hunting diversions and weather delays, CENTAF had rapidly gained air superiority in the theater. The Iraqi Air Force, which in General Mc-Peak's opinion "never recovered" from the war's opening attack, proved no match for its opponents. Without a single loss of their own, Coalition aircraft scored forty-one air-to-air kills.[39] After the third day of the conflict, the Iraqi Air Force never generated more than sixty sorties within a day. "There was a plan for [our aircraft] to support us," one Iraqi brigade commander stated shortly after the war. Each day he and his men looked for their airborne comrades but, he lamented, "there was nothing." Never a vigorous night-flying air force, the Iraqi Air Force stopped nighttime operations by late January.[40]

Among the forty-one total air-to-air victories that helped the Coalition win air superiority, the first in the KTO was on January 24 by an RSAF F–15C. This Saudi fighter used AIM–9M missile fire to down two F–1 Mirages over the Persian Gulf.[41] It proved fitting that an F–15C achieved the first KTO air-to-air kills, because these air-superiority fighters, which flew about 5,900 offensive and defensive counterair sorties during the war, scored thirty-six of the Coalition's forty-one air-to-air victories.[42] In another KTO air-to-air success, A–10 pilot Capt.

Lucrative Targets

Robert R. Swain destroyed an Iraqi helicopter west of Ali al Saleem, over central Kuwait on February 6, the first aerial victory in the history of this aircraft, which was designed primarily for ground attack. On February 15, another Warthog pilot,

On March 2, 1991, a U.S. soldier inspects the interior of a supposedly indestructible Iraqi hardened aircraft shelter that proved highly destructible by U.S. Air Force PGMs.

Capt. Todd K. Sheehy, scored a similar kill against another helicopter, an Mi–8 Hip, west of the KTO near Nukhayb, Iraq.[43]

The Coalition won air superiority over an opponent who had a large inventory of fighters and who tried to resist the allied attacks. "The Iraqi Air Force tried to fight," Colonel Christon said after the war: "It isn't a case of them not being motivated, not capable, not having the machines." One KTO planner reflected, "A lot of people say, 'Why didn't the Iraqi Air Force fight?' Well, they did fight.... Look at the kills in the first three days." In December 1991, General Horner remarked that commentators on the war had overlooked "the intensity of the air-to-air battle."[44]

The Coalition gained air superiority not because the Iraqis failed to resist, but in large part because the allies succeeded in their attacks against Phase II targets. During the first hours of the conflict, CENTAF air strikes had made a shambles of the Iraqi C^2 facilities in the KTO. An enemy pilot leaving an airfield had no way of knowing if there were Coalition aircraft in the air around him. A veteran of thirty-eight F–15E missions with the 335th Tactical Fighter Squadron recalled that "after the first week we had taken out all their EW radar, so they didn't know we were there until [we] started dropping bombs on them." General Glosson wryly pointed out that, when F–15s intercepted and destroyed the first or second Iraqi aircraft to leave an airbase, the remaining enemy aircrews rarely showed much enthusiasm for combat. He recalled one such occasion when the "first two [Iraqi] airplanes took off and the lead airplane blew up at about eight to nine thousand feet. The other guy immediately went back to [the base] and the other six airplanes sitting on the ground all developed 'maintenance problems.'" Another CENTAF officer described how the Coalition's Phase II attacks crippled the Iraqi Air Force: "We hurt them so bad, they didn't have that [IFF] system still in place. So when they launched, they got shot down." If you were the Iraqis, he asked rhetorically, "How long do you keep doing that?"[45]

The single-seat "C" model of the F–15, credited with the great majority of the Coalition's air-to-air kills, greatly contributed to winning air supremacy at the opening of the war. One hundred and eighteen of these fighters served in the theater, flying sweep, CAP, and escort assignments. When Iraqi aircraft tried to flee to Iran, the F–15Cs flew intercept missions as well. Not one of these fighters was lost in combat, and only one suffered battle damage: it was struck by Scud debris while on the ground and was repaired within a day. One pilot said of the fighter reliability: "Seven months and 500 hours without a ground abort, now that's amazing."[46]

After the F–15Cs and other Coalition aircraft gained air superiority, the Iraqis tried to hide their airplanes in the nearly six hundred hardened shelters constructed of concrete and reinforced with steel that were available countrywide. CENTAF quickly countered this strategy, waging a "Battle of the Shelters," which began on the war's first day and intensified after its first week.[47] By January 29, Coalition air strikes with 2,000-pound bombs had destroyed at least twenty-six of these hardened aircraft shelters and inflicted major damage on another sixty-seven, including ten hits on one airfield alone—As Salman—in central-southern Iraq.[48] On January 30, General Schwarzkopf told the press, "Quite frankly, the Iraqi aircraft are running out of places to hide." By the end of the war, Coalition attacks had destroyed or damaged 375 of the 594 Iraqi aircraft shelters. CENT-COM intelligence analysts estimated that at least 117—and perhaps as many as 203—enemy fighters had been destroyed while sitting in these hardened bunkers. One Air Force officer visited the KTO soon after the war, surveyed this damage, and quipped: "Hardened aircraft shelters—aren't."[49]

The Coalition victory in the "Battle of the Shelters" led to one of the most curious episodes of the Gulf War, the flight of the Iraqi Air Force to haven in Iran. This was a surprising development, because Iraq had been at war with this country only two years earlier. The two Islamic neighbors had waged a bloody and protracted struggle from September 1980 until March 1989. Colonel Christon, Headquarters CENTAF's Director of Intelligence, said after the war, "The only thing that surprised me about the Iraqi Air Force was [its] pushing the aircraft over to Iran. I did not anticipate that." Iran's deputy foreign minister claimed at the time that the arriving Iraqi flights were a surprise to his own government. The Iraqi pilots, he affirmed, were not deserting but carrying out a deliberate plan to save their aircraft. Shortly after the war, General McPeak offered this assessment of the unexpected exodus: "I think [the Iraqis] made a decision that since they were no longer safe in shelters, that they would have to leave. Then they started out to Iran." CENTCOM intelligence officers believed that the Coalition strikes that wreaked havoc with the Iraqi air defenses also motivated the flights to Iran. One Air Staff officer summarized the dilemma of the Iraqi Air Force at the end of January: "[It] can't hide, can't fight, [it] can only run away."[50]

The Iraqi wartime exodus began as early as the first day of the war, when eighteen aircraft fled to Iran. The first of two large waves of escapes occurred between January 26 and 29. By the end of these four days, the DIA estimated that more than a hundred airplanes had taken Iranian refuge, including most of Iraq's transports and many of its best fighters—EQ5 and EQ6 models of F–1 Mirages, Su–24 Fencers (the Iraqi's main attack aircraft), and MiG–29 Fulcrums.[51] CENT-AF deployed F–15s on CAPs northeast and southeast of Baghdad to halt these flights to the east. No Iraqi aircraft escaped to Iran for five days, but when the Coalition stopped its patrols, a second wave of escapes occurred from February 5 to 7. General McPeak commented after the war that the Iraqis "were playing kind of a cat-and-mouse game here." Intercepting these flights proved difficult, given that the Iraqi-Iranian border extended seven hundred miles and that fleeing pilots needed only five to ten minutes to make good their escape. By the end of the war, nearly 140 enemy aircraft had fled to Iran. Humorist Dave Barry sarcastically assigned the Iraqi Air Force a new motto: "We're Out of Here."[52]

This comedian's quip, though, pointed to a serious truth: the Coalition airmen had knocked the Iraqi Air Force virtually out of the war. Having won air superiority, they could shift the emphasis of their attacks to Phase III—targets in the KTO—sooner than had been expected. General Olsen pointed out that the rapid defeat of the Iraqi air defenses meant that "we could start moving to take out the ground forces, the Republican Guard, working on their fixed locations, earlier than we had thought." Colonel Baptiste recalled that the emphasis shifted to Phase III "quicker than I thought it would…. Within the first week of the war,…they had pretty much 'done a job' on that target set in the Iraqi cell, and then it would be a matter of mop-up targets, going back and refragging those that needed to be [hit again]. Within the first week, the emphasis had already shifted to…the KTO cell." As early as January 24, CENTAF crews flew more than 450 combat sorties in the KTO.[53]

The Coalition shifted the emphasis of its attacks to the KTO gradually, not abruptly, a development that was consistent with the planners' original conception of the air campaign. Briefers had described the operation as a series of phases because this motif would help outsiders understand it, not because they envisioned the phases as rigidly defined segments. General Olsen later said that CENTAF's senior officers recognized, with the early successes against Phase I and II targets, that the air campaign "was all going to flow together." Colonel Baptiste made the same point: "Those phases became hazy…. We did some effort in all the first three phases, from day one on." Although the attacks against targets in Iraq continued until the end of the war, their numbers declined gradually during late January. At the same time, missions against the KTO increased. January 25 was the first day of the war on which the allies flew more combat sorties against Phase III than against Phase I targets.[54]

CENTAF's shift in emphasis to targets in the KTO followed the guidance of senior officers in the theater. General Schwarzkopf long had been concerned about the Republican Guard, deployed north and northwest of Kuwait, and wanted a strenuous air effort against them as soon as possible.[55] "After two weeks of war," he later said, "my instincts and experience told me that we'd bombed most of our strategic targets enough to accomplish our campaign objectives. It was now time, I thought, to shift most of our air power onto the army we were about to face in battle." As early as the fourth morning of the war, after the initial successes against Phase I and II targets, General Horner told his staff: "Now we're going to be doing other things, like attacking forces in the KTO." On February 4, Maj. Gen. John A. Corder, Headquarters CENTAF's DCS/Operations, made some specific recommendations about operations against Phase III targets. He called attention to the F–111Fs, which were equipped with Pave Tack forward-looking infrared (FLIR) pods that allowed them to attack point targets at night with laser-guided weapons. The other Desert Storm Aardvarks, the "E" models, did not have this capability. General Corder recommended that the F–111Fs attack armor, vehicles, and artillery in the KTO with GBU–12s, essentially the concept that emerged a few days later as "tank plinking." He also suggested that the Aardvarks "buddy lase" for F–16s: in this proposal, the F–111s would use their Pave Tack systems to designate ground targets for the Fighting Falcons to attack with their own laser-guided PGMs, an idea that General Glosson and his planners already had anticipated.[56]

As the weight of the Coalition's attacks shifted down to southern Iraq and Kuwait, the tempo of work increased for the dozen or so personnel assigned to the KTO planning cell. The GAT division, to which it belonged, totaled about 100 officers and airmen. The manning of the neighboring ATO division, also under General Glosson's Directorate of Campaign Plans, varied between 200 and 250 personnel. Current Operations, a separate directorate under Col. Al Doman, accounted for another staff of roughly 200.[57]

Each of these three functional offices—the GAT division, ATO division, and Current Operations directorate—performed essential roles in the ATO process. The GAT division worked up an initial "gameplan" for each ATO, including selecting targets and the "force packages" to be sent against them. The GAT division then sent this information to the ATO division, where specialists representing each type of aircraft prepared fragmentary ("frag") orders and provided deconflicted mission numbers, call signs, targeting data, the details of CAP and EW support, and other mission and target details. The ATO division planners also wrote special instructions (SPINS), which included all of the essential, specific information not found in the tasking order's mission lines: all of the particulars of airspace management such as IFF squawks; ingress and egress routes (including all of their legs, or parts); restricted areas; low-level approaches; reconnaissance,

Lucrative Targets

AWACS, and tanker coordination, including tanker tracks, radio frequencies, altitudes, and offloads; combat search-and-rescue arrangements; and other specific considerations.[58] They then put this enormous compilation of data into a format compatible with the Computer Assisted Force Management System (CAFMS), the electronic system brought to the theater on August 14 to transmit the ATO from Headquarters CENTAF to remote terminals at the units in the field. Some commands could not receive the ATO electronically, and the ATO division sent it to them by secure telephone or fax, or by Air Force C–21 or Navy S–3 courier flights.[59] The field units received the tasking order and "broke out" their portion of the enormous document, and, while they flew their missions, the Current Operations directorate oversaw their execution of the ATO.[60]

These three functional offices—the GAT and ATO divisions and the Current Operations directorate—worked simultaneously on three ATOs. At any given time, the GAT division was developing the day-after-tomorrow's ATO while the ATO division was producing and distributing the next day's document. Simultaneously, the Current Operations directorate was executing the current day's ATO from the TACC and its airborne elements.[61]

The senior officers in the theater provided the guidance for preparing the ATO. Each evening at 1900 Generals Horner and Glosson attended Schwarzkopf's CENTCOM staff meeting. General Glosson briefed the CENTCOM commander on the progress of the air campaign and on the planning for the next operations. General Schwarzkopf, who retained the authority to apportion sorties in the theater, then gave Generals Horner and Glosson his guidance for their efforts. The CENTAF commander's notes on the February 15 meeting, for example, quoted the CINC as directing, "We must keep on hitting [the] Republican Guard—that's the quickest way to get through to [Saddam Hussein]." General Glosson, who kept a daily log of these conferences, added this refinement, in his entry on the same session: "Watch units [less than] 50% [strength]." After this meeting, General Glosson took any immediate guidance to Maj. John D. Sweeney, night-shift director of the GAT division. These examples from February 15 contained very broad directions; on other occasions, the 1900 conference produced specific, last-minute changes in the ATO, which had already left the GAT division and gone on to the ATO "shop."[62]

Senior officers also provided guidance at other times. General Horner routinely visited the GAT division each morning and afternoon. He later recalled: "About nine o'clock in the morning, I'd wander down and I'd stop and talk to Deptula and say, 'Okay, now what do you think [we should do] two days from now?' And [then I would] go see Sam Baptiste and say,…'What are you looking at?'" Using a large map, Colonel Baptiste reviewed with General Horner the plans for air operations on the next day and the day after that, and gained the commander's comments. General Horner also said of his daily routine: "Maybe I'd go back again in the afternoon and see if they had changed anything, and if I had any objections, but normally I didn't." In his role as chief planner, General Glosson was usually in the GAT division all day and late into the night. General Corder also occasionally came in from the Current Operations directorate and passed on guidance.[63]

All of these directives were summarized in the Commander, USCENTAF (COMUSCENTAF) Air Guidance Letter, which was signed by General Glosson and issued daily. This document, preliminary to the ATO process, listed each day's overall priorities for the air campaign and stated guidelines for the use of assets within broad categories such as targeting, collection management, and electronic combat. A further example of the guidance given at the CINCCENT meeting on February 15 is General Schwarzkopf's directive about the Republican Guard as reflected in the daily Air Guidance Letter. One section of the document routinely stated: "Emphasis will be on the elimination of the Republican Guard, armor, artillery and chemical/biological weapons in the KTO."[64]

This guidance from senior officers was one element that shaped the KTO planning cell's daily work, which began each morning between 0600 and 0630 when the day shift replaced the night crew. Arriving personnel invariably found that the night shift had made changes in the ATO for the next day's operation. The day shift's first task was to make those alterations in the ATO for tomorrow. About midmorning, the KTO planners turned their attention to the ATO for the day after next, a process that began when Colonels Baptiste and Deptula, chief of the Iraqi planning cell, developed a shell, or outline, of a MAP.[65]

With the shift of emphasis to the KTO, the MAP lost some of the importance that it had held before the war and during its first phase, when the burden of effort had been on strategic targets in Iraq. Nonetheless, the MAP continued to perform several valuable functions. It remained the air planners' essential starting point. "The MAP was the key JFACC internal planning document," one official postwar report declared, "which consolidated all inputs into a single, concise plan.... The MAP drove the process." Second, the MAP served as a helpful aid to senior officers, giving them a quick overview of current and planned air operations and answering broad questions, without having to sift through the specifics of an enormous ATO. Further, the MAP proved useful in dealing with the alterations inevitably made to the ATO. When a switch of targets or other modification was suggested, planners often turned first to the MAP to learn quickly what other operations were scheduled at the time of the proposed change. The MAP, Colonel Baptiste commented, "was very useful for any changes and deconflictions."[66]

After the MAP shell was completed, the Joint Target Coordination Board (JTCB) convened at 1230 each afternoon. Comprising representatives of ARCENT, MARCENT, NAVCENT, and the Coalition members, including Kuwait, and chaired by a member of the JFACC's staff, the JTCB provided the forum for the service components to nominate targets. The board nominated and prioritized a list of targets almost exclusively in the KTO, rather than in Iraq, which remained the responsibility of the Iraqi planning cell. The JTCB recessed its daily meeting early each afternoon, compiled a Joint Combined Prioritized Target List,

Day 1

AM
At the GAT Division, KTO planners make changes to next day's ATO

Mid AM
KTO planners begin day-after-next's ATO with Iraqi Planning Cell. Develop MAP with use of the Air Guidance Letter—a list of daily priorities and guidelines for use of assets (targeting, collection management, electronic combat)

Noon
Joint Target Coordination Board nominates targets and compiles a Joint Combined Prioritized Target List.

Evening
Joint Combined Prioritized Target List is revised and sent to the KTO Planning Cell.

Final target list is developed. Fragmentary orders are prepared for force packages that will fly against targets.

Lt. Gen. Horner and Brig. Gen. Glosson attend CENTCOM staff meeting and receive guidance on air campaign from Gen. Schwarzkopf.

Day 2

Early AM
Target Planning Worksheet, which has essential information for each force package and target, is forwarded to the ATO division.

AM
ATO Division takes GAT's day-after-tomorrow's ATO and makes it tomorrow's ATO. Fraggers for each aircraft type coordinate assets that will fly, or support, every sortie on the Target Planning Worksheet. They also provide deconflicted mission numbers, call signs, targeting data, details of CAP and EW support, etc.
ATO specifics are refined.
Details of tanker support are fixed. Special Instructions (SPINS) are prepared to resolve conflicts in airspace management (IFF squawks, ingress and egress routes, and low-level approaches); reconnaissance; AWACS and tanker coordination including tanker tracks, radio frequencies, altitudes, offloads; and CSAR arrangements.

Mid Afternoon
ATO given to the CAFMS Cell to be put into a computer format. Information is transmitted electronically or, in some cases, brought to the units by C-21 or Navy S-3 courier.

Deadline to have ATO to field where individual units break out their sections of the ATO

Day 3

Early AM
Flight crews receive mission briefings and reach their first TOTs at 0400.

Current Operations Directorate oversees the execution of today's ATO via the TACC, the EC-130E ABCCC and AWACS aircraft.

The life of an ATO.

updated that list at 1700, and sent it on to the KTO planning cell, where it arrived shortly after the day's shift change.[67]

The JTCB members, like all CENTAF planners, paid close attention to the issue of collateral damage. "Civilian casualties and collateral damages," one piece of command guidance enjoined, "will be kept to a minimum. The target is Saddam Hussein's regime, not the Iraqi populace." Headquarters CENTAF's Office of the Judge Advocate General reviewed all potential targets in both Kuwait and Iraq against the strictures of international law, and Headquarters CENTCOM's intelligence analysts prepared a "joint no-fire target list," again covering both countries, listing mosques and other holy places; hospitals; dams; cultural, historical, and archaeological sites; and other locations that Coalition forces were not to attack. Although in most instances it was obvious whether a potential target belonged on the "no-fire" list or not, a few cases required particularly close review.[68]

These rules of engagement were taken into account in preparing the Joint Combined Prioritized Target List which, along with the day's COMUSCENTAF Air Guidance Letter and MAP shell, Major Sweeney's night crew inherited when they arrived at work, between 1800 and 1830. Using these pieces of guidance, they developed a final target list and began "fragging"—preparing fragmentary orders for the force packages that would fly the missions. The KTO-cell night shift set aside some sorties that had no predetermined, specific objectives. For examples, the two E–8A J–STARS aircraft assigned some targets offered by circumstances, and F–16s on "Killer Scout" operations looked for opportunities of their own. In most cases, however, the KTO planners fragged sorties against designated objectives. They worked through the night, helped by intelligence targeteers who answered their specific questions about targets and weapons. By 0430, the officers in the KTO cell had compiled the essential information for each force package and target, entering it on target-planning worksheets that they sent to Colonel Bennett's ATO division.[69]

The second morning in the planning cycle had arrived, and by now the document that the GAT division had initiated as the day-after-tomorrow's ATO had gone on to the ATO division, which developed it as tomorrow's ATO. In Colonel Bennett's ATO division, fraggers representing each individual type of aircraft coordinated all of the assets that would fly, or support, every sortie on the target-planning worksheets. These planners spent the morning and early afternoon refining the specifics of the ATO, fixing the details of its tanker support and preparing the SPINS needed to resolve any conflicts in airspace management, communications, or other problems. They completed their work by 1400 and dispatched it to the ATO division's CAFMS cell, which put it into a computer format. These officers printed out a preliminary version of the ATO, reviewed and corrected this enormous proofsheet, and then sent the ATO to the forces in the field, before the daily deadline of 1800.[70]

Each evening, mission-planning cells at every unit headquarters "broke out" their section of the enormous ATO. In late January, at the time when the emphasis of the air campaign shifted to the KTO, the ATO provided the details for more than two thousand sorties a day; before the end of the war, this total would exceed three thousand sorties. This was vastly more information than any given squadron needed, and, while the aircrews who would fly early the next day were asleep, their mission planners extracted the information that they required from the immense ATO. One STRATFOR officer noted after the war that "crews never saw" the "massive ATO." Instead, he explained, Headquarters CENTAF sent the operations planning teams at each of the B–52 wings the "essential mission information," such as targets, times, numbers of aircraft, air refueling details, poststrike data, and axis of attack, via KY–68 cryptographic communication, later followed by a two- or three-page summary message, and still later by the full ATO, which was several hundred—and sometimes a thousand—pages long. Unit planners refined the details of the mission, such as the lines of approach to the target and bombing tracks, taking into account wind conditions, battlefield or oilfield smoke, enemy defenses, and other considerations.[71]

During the early morning hours, the flight crews received their mission briefings. The ATO cycle now had entered its third morning: the document that the GAT had initiated for the day after tomorrow and that the ATO division had developed for tomorrow, now had become the present day's ATO. Aircrews would fly this ATO that morning, reaching their first times over targets (TOTs) at 0400.[72]

Colonel Doman's Current Operations directorate would oversee their execution of the ATO, working from the TACC and its airborne elements, the EC–130E Airborne Battlefield Command and Control Center (ABCCC) and AWACS aircraft. Six ABCCCs were stationed at Riyadh, with one on orbit at all times. These modified C–130s provided C^2 for the Coalition aircraft flying battlefield air interdiction (BAI) sorties, and, after the ground campaign began, they could do the same for the close air support (CAS) sorties. The ABCCC performed the first of these two roles by controlling the air traffic into individual "kill boxes," the precisely defined areas that were used to ensure the safe and efficient management of airspace. After the war, General Corder commented on how the EC–130s performed their CAS and BAI roles. "ABCCC controls the close-in fight," he explained. "When there is a [ground] war going on, they control the close air support sorties, and they keep track of what's going on in the battle…to make sure that everybody [among the ground forces] had airplanes to fight with…. Before the land war started, we used [ABCCC] to keep track of airplanes going into these kill boxes we had, starting at the border and going north, making sure we had the right number of airplanes in the right box."[73]

While the ABCCCs served as air traffic-control authorities, the AWACS provided advisories, updating pilots on the air situation, alerting them to the locations of enemy aircraft, and directing them to tankers. The E–3 Sentrys flew in their orbits for about fifteen hours: twelve-hour missions bracketed by the one and a half to two hours typically needed to get on-station plus the hour usually taken to come off an assignment. If problems developed during the changeover to the new shift, aircrews might well be airborne longer than the usual fifteen hours. Nineteen-hour missions were not unknown. The airborne command element (ACE) battle staff, usually headed by a colonel, sat in the back of each Sentry. In Air Force slang, the ACE had "the hammer"—the responsibility of making difficult command decisions.[74] The ACEs "were key, especially early in the war," General Corder explained, "because sometimes you had eight fighters and one tanker. Who is going to get the gas?…Who is going to go find the other tankers and get them up there, or who is going to tell the fighters to divert because you've only got one tanker? Those kind of airborne command decisions are made by the ACE bunch, and they did an outstanding job."[75]

Working with the AWACS and ABCCC, Colonel Doman's Current Operations staff played a dynamic role in the ATO process because, once the field units received the ATO through the CAFMS, it became the responsibility of the Current Operations directorate to make any further changes in the tasking order, based on how the day's battle developed. As the directorate staff entered its changes, another day shift reported to the KTO cell at 0600, reviewed the directorate's last-minute changes in the ATO, and then began planning—again—for operations two days hence. The ATO sequence had completed one full cycle.[76]

By late January, this ATO process was operating against an enemy who had been badly damaged. Coalition aircrews had destroyed many strategic targets in Iraq, made a shambles of Saddam Hussein's air defenses, and knocked the Iraqi Air Force virtually out of the war. On the eve of the conflict, CENTAF had credited its opponent with approximately seventeen bombers and more than seven hundred fighters. By January 31, the allies had destroyed seven of these bombers and more than thirty of the fighters. Moreover, in excess of eighty additional fighters and transports had fled to Iran, and scores of other aircraft remained in shelters, intimidated against joining the battle. CENTAF had won the dominant position that came with gaining air superiority, and, as Colonel Warden, General Horner, and other airmen said of that advantage: everything is possible if you have it; little is possible if you lose it.[77] The Coalition would continue to capitalize on this dominance when the emphasis of its air campaign shifted to the Kuwaiti Theater of Operations.

Chapter Four

Destroying the Battlefield: Phase III Operations in the KTO

When the emphasis of the air campaign shifted to the KTO in late January, the Iraqis had lost air superiority; yet Coalition leaders believed they remained a dangerous foe. CENTCOM J–2 officers estimated that as of January 31, elements of forty enemy divisions occupied the Kuwaiti theater: twenty-three of them committed, nine held ready to reinforce them, and eight others in theater reserve. Eight of these units were heavy divisions, either mechanized or armored, only one of which—the 6th Armored Division—was believed to have been significantly reduced by the air campaign. On the first of February, the Iraqis had approximately 3,800 tanks, 2,600 armored personnel carriers (APCs), and 2,700 artillery pieces in the KTO.[1]

The forty enemy divisions in the theater included eight belonging to the Republican Guard: four infantry, two armored, one mechanized, and one special forces. In late January, these elite components remained strong, in contrast to the Iraqi regular units, which were beginning to show evidence of deteriorating morale. As one Checkmate assessment underscored at the time, the Republican Guard stood ready for combat and their corps and division command posts continued to operate, largely unaffected by the air campaign. A CENTCOM intelligence briefer credited the Republican Guard in the KTO, as of the thirty-first of that month, with approximately 990 tanks, more than 630 pieces of artillery, and nearly 600 armored vehicles.[2]

This elite force was originally a single unit, the Republican Guard Brigade, which had become Saddam Hussein's personal bodyguard after he seized power in 1979. Recruiting many of its officers from his native village of Tikrit, Saddam expanded this command and rewarded it with better pay, promotions, food, and equipment than those that the Iraqi army's regular divisions received. By the opening of the Iran-Iraq War in September 1980, the Iraqi dictator had increased his elite force to two brigades of palace guards, and during this long, bloody conflict he expanded it to a corps-sized formation. By the August 1990 invasion of Kuwait, the organization had grown to an overly large corps, designated the Republican Guard Forces Command.[3]

The names of these Republican Guard divisions, many of them drawn from Iraq's military and cultural history, reflected their elite status. The Al Faw Division gained its designation from the port city on the Shatt al-Arab River and the peninsula of the same name, which lay between its waters and those of the Khor Abdulla. In this strategic area along the Iranian border, Iraqi troops—including Republican Guard units—had won a decisive victory over the Iranians in April 1988. The Hammurabi Division was named for the king who had united all of Mesopotamia during the eighteenth century B.C. and had given his citizens a famous code of laws.[4] The Nebuchadnezzar Division received its appellation from a Babylonian monarch said to be among Saddam Hussein's heroes, Nebuchadnezzar II, who conquered Jerusalem, built the fabled Hanging Gardens, and surrounded his capital with a double wall ten miles long.[5] The Medina armored unit was named for the city second only to Mecca as the holiest in the Islamic world.[6] The capital of Iraq gave its name to one division, and Tawakal, a city in the northern part of the country, to another. The designation of the Adnan Division had perhaps the most interesting origin: it was named after one of Saddam Hussein's cousins.[7]

In late January 1991, eight of these large Republican Guard units were deployed in the KTO. Having spearheaded the invasion of Kuwait, these divisions had pulled back to form a strategic reserve, north and west of Kuwait. Five of them held a long semicircle extending through southern Iraq near the Kuwaiti border. From west to east, these forces were the mechanized Tawakalna Division, the armored Medina and Hammurabi Divisions, the Republican Guard Special Forces Division, and an infantry unit, the Baghdad Division. North were three more foot formations: from west to east, the Nebuchadnezzar, Al Faw, and Adnan Divisions.[8]

CENTAF intelligence officers believed that Republican Guard infantry divisions typically consisted of four brigades. They described the Baghdad Division, for example, as being composed of three brigades, each with approximately 3,300 AK–47 assault rifles, and a commando brigade with roughly 1,900 of them. The armored Hammurabi and Medina Divisions operated the T–72, an advanced tank they had acquired from the Soviet Union. One CENTAF assessment credited the Medina Division with one armored brigade with 220 T–72s, another with 165, a mechanized brigade with 110, and an infantry brigade. The three armored brigades of the Hammurabi Division were believed to be operating 440 of the advanced Soviet tanks. The Republican Guard units also drove hundreds of APCs and other reconnaissance and infantry-fighting vehicles. These vehicles included the Soviet-made BRDM–2 scout car and the very capable BMP–2, an armored carrier that had been battle-tested in Afghanistan.[9]

Destroying the Battlefield: Phase III Operations in the KTO

The Republican Guard, from the beginning of the Kuwaiti crisis, raised great concern among American military leaders. After General Powell had heard the Instant Thunder briefing in August, he stressed that he did not want Saddam Hussein to be able to withdraw from Kuwait with his elite infantry and tanks intact. During October meetings of the JCS, General Powell pressed General Loh, then the Air Force Chief of Staff's representative in "the tank," about the Air Force's plans for operations against the Republican Guard. General Glosson characterized these Iraqi elite forces as the enemy's "only real tough-fighting unit." Checkmate briefers, beginning in early November 1990, highlighted the significance of the Republican Guard by separating Phase III into two parts that distinguished the attacks against these elite forces from those against regular infantry divisions.[10]

No American officer was more convinced of the threat posed by the Republican Guard than General Schwarzkopf. In an interview after the war, General Horner stressed that the CENTCOM commander's concerns about the Iraqi elite forces were long-standing, dating back to the earliest theater planning, preceding even the invasion of Kuwait. General Schwarzkopf "identified the Republican Guard as a center of the enemy's gravity," General Horner recalled, as early as April 1990. The CENTCOM commander had been concerned about the Republican Guard "from the beginning, I mean from whenever, from before Desert Shield." For his own part, General Schwarzkopf included in his "commander's intent" the statement that offensive operations would end with these elite enemy units "destroyed and major U.S. forces controlling critical [lines of communication] in the Kuwaiti Theater of Operations." He drove the point home to his corps and division commanders during a meeting in Dhahran on November 14: "We need to destroy—not attack, not damage, not surround—I want you to destroy the Republican Guard. When you're done with them, I don't want them to be an effective fighting force anymore."[11]

CENTAF began its first operations against the Republican Guard as early as the first afternoon of the war, when twenty-four F–16s flew against several of their command facilities. It was also within the first day of the conflict that three B–52s attacked the mechanized Tawakalna Division, the onset of an unrelenting series of sorties against the Iraqi elite units, as at least three of these bombers were to strike at the Republican Guard every hour, around the clock, until the close of the war. Thirty-seven percent of all of the BUFF (slang for a B–52: rendered politely, "Big, Ugly, Fat Fellow") sorties flown during the conflict—and 40 percent of all of their missions—went against these elite units.[12] After a single, highly classified mission flown from Barksdale AFB, Louisiana, to Iraq during the first night of the war, these bombers operated from Diego Garcia in the Indian Ocean, Moron AB in Spain, and elsewhere.[13]

On the second day of combat, the Coalition increased the pressure on the Republican Guard's three heavy divisions. B–52s and F/A–18 Hornets, Marine Corps strike fighters, attacked the Tawakalna and Medina units. Eight F/A–18s began bombing the Hammurabi Division, the enemy's other elite armored force in the theater. The Coalition continued this effort against the Republican Guard on the third day of the war (D+2, or January 19), with the Hammurabi unit receiving the heaviest attention: thirty-two F–16s, six F/A–18s, eight F–15Es, and twelve B–52s flew against it.[14]

As the war continued, CENTAF aircrews sustained this high level of operations against these premier Iraqi forces. On January 25, or D+8, the daily total of sorties against the Republican Guard exceeded 200 for the first time. On January 29 and February 4, Coalition aircraft flew more than 350 daily sorties against the elite units. On only one day, February 14—which was marred by bad weather—did the total number of sorties against the Republican Guard drop significantly below 200.[15] The following day, General Schwarzkopf exhorted his staff to "keep on hitting the Republican Guard" as "the quickest way to get through to [Saddam Hussein]."[16] His commanders took this guidance to heart. Of the roughly 35,000 sorties that Coalition aircraft flew in the KTO, more than 5,600 (or approximately 16 percent) went against these forces.[17]

The official history of the 363d TFW(P) showed how one F–16 unit made the transition from Phase I operations against strategic targets in Iraq to Phase III ones against the Republican Guard in the KTO. On January 28, the organization's historian reported, the wing's targets included the Basra missile production facilities, regular artillery battalions, logistics sites, infantry battalions, ground-controlled intercept sites, and Scud missile launchers. A transition began the following day: "Switching to hitting ground forces, the wing [flies] 73 of 73 scheduled sorties. Arty [battalions], Republican Guard command posts, Armored and Mech [battalions] are targeted." On January 31, the unit historian wrote: "During 63 of 64 scheduled sorties, the 363 [TFW(P)] and Hahn [Air Base]'s 10 [Tactical Fighter Squadron (TFS)] pound the Hammurabi's tanks and mech assets." The transition was completed by the first of February: "Medinah Republican Guard's Armor, Command Posts, and Ammo Storage Areas are bombed by 363 TFW(P) F–16 pilots. Road networks leading to the front are mined by the wing. Sixty-four sorties are flown, against 64 scheduled. Clear weather helps the allied cause."[18]

A major who flew with the 335th TFS described a typical F–15E mission against the Republican Guard, conducted in mid-February. "On the evening of the 12th," he recalled, "we were sent up against a Republican Guard division [the Medina] which was in the northwest corner of Kuwait. By that time we had placed a lot of emphasis on the Republican Guard. General Schwarzkopf was very worried about the Republican Guard." This pilot explained how a typical night operation was coordinated with ABCCC or J–STARS: "When we took off, we contacted the J–STARS and were given a very lucrative target. It was 200 vehicles in a bivouac area, and that's what we hit. We hit the target about two in the morning. When we left, there were numerous fires burning and several large secondaries."[19]

As with BDA in other instances, it proved difficult to learn the results of missions against the Republican Guard. One postwar official study acknowledged that in "most cases the effects of the B–52 attacks on the Iraqi forces in the KTO were not observed," and the same might have been said of other aircraft missions in the theater. Yet some evidence of the bombing's effectiveness emerged early in the air campaign. On January 22, photography showed the effects of cluster bombs on a howitzer battalion of the Hammurabi Division and, two days later, damage to twenty or more trucks of the Tawakalna. Intelligence sources also had evidence on January 28 that air attacks had destroyed sixty large and one hundred small revetments around a Republican Guard ammunition dump. The following day, Headquarters SAC intelligence officers concluded that CENTAF sorties probably had forced the Tawakalna Division to move its command post.[20]

Evidence of damage suffered by the Republican Guard continued to emerge in late January and early February. On January 30, photography of an armored brigade and a division support area showed two command posts damaged and eighteen revetments destroyed. The following day, CENTAF/IN reported evidence of extensive bombing and that "secondary explosions were observed in two logistics areas" of the Medina Division and that three battalion-size command posts of the same unit had "also sustained bomb damage."[21] On February 3, CENTCOM intelligence officers affirmed that 138 of the Tawakalna Division's 222 tanks had been destroyed and the unit reduced to 60 percent of its original combat strength. They reported that the Adnan Division had been reduced to 84 percent of its initial strength and the Nebuchadnezzar to 88 percent.[22]

Although planners and operators doubtless would have liked to have additional, and more rapid, BDA of Republican Guard and other targets in the KTO, intelligence was not as large an issue in this theater as it was in Iraq. In the case of Phase I targets such as nuclear, chemical, and biological sites, photographs were important in evaluating results and planning follow-on strikes. However, the Kuwaiti theater, where Coalition aircrews flew against maneuvering units and targets of opportunity, presented a different situation. It was, Colonel Baptiste explained, "a much more dynamic environment. And so when it came to photography, it wasn't as critical in the KTO as it was in the Iraqi cell." Furthermore, the large number of sorties flown across the relatively small theater also reduced the comparative significance of intelligence. General Corder commented, "When you are running 900 to 1,400 [sorties] a day across there—who cares—in the overall scheme of things? The cost of trying to do that better is horrendous, and who cares? So, in that context I thought intelligence was good."[23]

Closely related to these operations against the Republican Guard were those against the bridges over the Tigris and Euphrates Rivers, important choke points for supplies entering the KTO. Moreover, these crossing points were crucial because the Iraqi elite units would need them if, as General Schwarzkopf and other senior officers apprehended, they tried to retreat from the theater with their tanks and heavy equipment. "When we talk about 'isolating the battlefield,'" General Horner stressed, "we're not talking about supplies getting *in*. We're talking about the Republican Guard *leaving*." The MAP for the first twenty hours of operations addressed this same consideration: after listing four bridges to be attacked by F–15Es, it labeled them "Republican Guard escape routes." "The initial intent of the bridge campaign," a CENTAF intelligence officer later explained, "was to fix the Republican Guard, and block them from flowing back to Baghdad." General Glosson noted that the sorties against the Tigris and Euphrates bridges made it impossible for the Iraqi elite units to resupply or, he added significantly, to retreat. Two days before the ground campaign began, one of General Glosson's subordinates underscored the same point. This GAT officer, who helped plan the attacks on the bridges, said he hoped that, if the Iraqis left the KTO, they had to walk out and leave behind "everything bigger than five-ton trucks."[24]

Crucial to any escape by the Republican Guard, the river crossings also presented vulnerable choke points for materiel entering the KTO. Across the Tigris and Euphrates bridges, as General Glosson put it, ran "the lifeline of the battle-field." Before the opening of the Gulf War, the Iraqis had positioned large quantities of ammunition and other supplies in the theater, but Coalition leaders knew that the Iraqis still needed an ongoing resupply effort to sustain offensive, or even defensive, operations.[25] The main lines of supply between Baghdad and the KTO were one four-lane highway along the Tigris River, another along the Euphrates, and a single-track railroad that ran from the capital to Basra.[26]

"The bombing of those bridges," General Olsen reflected after the war, represented an effort so extensive that it "was almost a separate campaign." Before the war, General Glosson's planners had identified fifty-four bridges in Iraq that could support an automobile; thirty-two of these were of critical military value.[27] The planners assigned most of the sorties against these spans to F–111Fs, long-range air interdiction aircraft whose Pave Tack FLIR allowed them to attack point targets at night with laser-guided bombs (LGBs). The Aardvarks also proved durable: during the entire war, they flew more than 4,000 sorties and turned in an 85 percent mission-capable rate, with no aircraft lost and only one suffering battle damage.[28] The F–111s flew their first bridge attacks on January 24 and their largest number of strikes on these targets within twenty-four hours, twelve, on January 29.[29] General Glosson visited the Aardvark crews at Taif Air Base, Saudi Arabia, in early February and reported them "upbeat, especially [about] destroying bridges and hardened aircraft shelters." Tornados, F–117s, and F–15Es augmented the numerous F–111 sorties against bridges, and A–6s, F/A–18s, F–16s, and F–1s also contributed to the campaign.[30]

The overwhelming majority of F–111F bridge missions were flown at night, with the pilot and weapons system officer relying on their Pave Tack FLIR and laser-guided munitions. In a typical attack, the Aardvarks flew in at medium altitude, delivered their ordnance during level flight, and left at medium altitude. "They are avid mid-altitude fighters," General Glosson commented after his visit to Taif. "Low altitude is fading from their minds." The F–111 and F–15E crews conducted their night operations with considerable flexibility. They patrolled stretches of a river, and if they found the Iraqis installing a pontoon bridge, they attacked it. If not, they could fly on to an alternate target.[31]

Understandably, the first concern of the aircrews that flew against the bridges was the strength of the Iraqi air defenses. Given the Coalition's early success against Phase II targets, this consideration proved less a problem than did some other factors, which General Olsen enumerated: "the number of bridges, the hardness of the bridges, and ability of the Iraqis to put [in] alternate bypasses, through pontoon bridges." After the war, General Horner commented on the frustrations accompanying any operation of this sort. "Anybody who does a campaign against a transportation system," he advised, "had better beware. It looks deceptively easy. It is a tough nut to crack."[32]

One specific problem was the durability of the bridges. "Bridges are tough targets," General Horner emphasized. "We had to hit them with 2,000-pound bombs, and then hit them again." "Even with our most accurate weapons," General Olsen acknowledged, "we would only damage, say, one half of a bridge span." To prevent the Iraqis from rapidly repairing a structure damaged in this way, he added, "We had to take down the bridge in two or three places." On the eve of the ground campaign, one CENTAF officer reported on several bridges that had proven their durability. Among these were the Nasiriyah canal span, that "was damaged, but not down"; an earthen bypass over Basra's Canal Number One, "attacked and made inoperable, but has been rebuilt"; and the Qurnah highway bridge over the Euphrates, with "no bridge spans actually down, . . . could possibly be reconstituted, and should have two spans dropped."[33]

This officer's request for additional attacks against the Qurnah bridge was a common occurrence. Such strikes often were needed because the Iraqis proved, as General Horner put it, "very ingenious and industrious" at making repairs. If bombs blew out just one point on a bridge, the enemy could lay boards or steel plates over the damaged area and continue to use the route. An officer in the GAT division described one such case to General Glosson on February 20, when RF–4C imagery showed that one span of a railroad bridge at Qurnah had been partially repaired. "We have imagery of this span being severed," this planner reported. "I suspect the Iraqis have laid a piece of bridging equipment over the gap. It is open to one lane of traffic."[34]

CENTAF endured a particularly frustrating experience with the canals near Basra. After Coalition airmen bombed these waterways, the Iraqis filled them in with dirt and drove across the resulting embankments. "We'd bomb the dirt," General Horner recalled, "[and] they'd just put more dirt in." The same officer who informed General Glosson about the Qurnah bridge on February 20 also reported the same day: "RR64 [bridge], the dirt bypass built over the Basra canal just north of the highway bridge RR15 has been rebuilt. Recommendation: This area must be revisited every couple of days. Mk 82/84 LGB, Mk 82 [destructors], and Gator [mines] in this area are all appropriate." Four days later, another planner recommended reattacking this same earthen bypass, along with others around the Basra canals.[35]

Another problem Coalition airmen confronted was that, after they destroyed permanent bridges, the Iraqis substituted pontoons for them and developed other skillful workarounds. A DIA assessment in mid-February found that "the Iraqis are bypassing destroyed highway bridges by using alternate routes, pontoon bridges, and newly constructed causeways." "I've never seen so many pontoon bridges," the CENTAF commander commented after war. "I don't know where they came from. A pontoon bridge, you bomb it, you sink fourteen, fifteen boats, [but] it's easily repaired." General Olsen recalled this same problem and also pointed out that the Iraqis developed numerous alternate routes.[36]

Despite these problems, the CENTAF aircrews steadily made progress in their campaign against the bridges. By January 28, air strikes had shut down the Euphrates crossing point of the single rail line between Baghdad and Basra and had severed four tracks in the Az Zubayr railroad yard, the railhead connecting southeastern Iraq with the rest of the country. As the allies destroyed bridges, Iraqi trucks began to back up, offering choice targets. On January 30, CENTAF aircrews took one such opportunity, striking a stalled convoy near Basra.[37] By February 6, when Secretary Cheney visited the Checkmate office during the middle of the day, Colonel Warden was able to brief him that the attacks on the bridges had greatly reduced the Iraqis' ability to resupply the KTO. With the single rail line to the theater cut, the enemy had lost its prewar railroad capacity and its highway volume had been reduced.[38] By February 19, SAC intelligence officers reported that Coalition attacks had taken thirty-four Iraqi highway bridges out of operation.[39]

The air campaign against the bridges made an important contribution to the Coalition's victory in the Gulf War. By the end of the conflict, CENTAF attacks had knocked down forty-one major bridges and thirty-one pontoon bridges. Of the fifty-four bridges identified by General Glosson's planners, only five survived the war undamaged.[40] The enemy's ability to resupply the KTO dropped sharply in late January and continued to decline in February until, by the eve of the ground campaign, it was negligible.[41] Perhaps the most dramatic evidence of the Coalition's success against the bridges came at the close of the war, when, as General Schwarzkopf and others had foreseen, the destruction of the river crossings hindered the Iraqis' retreat from the theater. One Headquarters CENTAF augmentee who helped plan the bridges campaign and also flew two missions, later claimed: "The beauty of the thing was the campaign against the lines of communication worked. . . . We had destroyed their lines of communication so effectively that they didn't even know the roads and bridges were out. And then they started to run, they get to where the bridges were out and they can't go anywhere."[42]

PGMs made a vital contribution to the success against the bridges. "If we hadn't had laser-guided bombs," General Horner asserted, "it would have been terrible. The LGBs did wonderful work." The PGMs, in General Olsen's view, "really paid off." Reporting on the "impressive" results that GBU–10s and GBU–24s scored against the river spans, Colonel Deptula pointed out, "Before we put PGMs against bridges, over 200 sorties with F–16s, F–18s, and A–6s were flown with no dropped spans—once we put F–117s and F–111s against bridges, I would estimate a dropped span for every 2 sorties."[43]

With these weapons in their inventory, the Gulf War pilots were able to avoid a recurrence of the Vietnam War's frustrating episode of the Thanh Hoa bridge. During the early years of the conflict, hundreds of Air Force and Navy aircraft repeatedly bombed this structure, losing many aircrews but failing to close it permanently. Not until late in the war, when precision-guided ordnance became available, were American airmen finally able to destroy the Thanh Hoa bridge.[44]

In addition to the KTO's bridges and the Republican Guard, the Iraqi regular divisions that were deployed in the theater were given close attention by General Horner and his subordinates. In late January, CENTCOM intelligence officers believed that elements of forty enemy divisions were deployed in the KTO. The Republican Guard accounted for only eight of these: the other thirty-two were regular units. These divisions belonged to four corps—the II, III, IV, and VII. CENTAF intelligence officers described the status of these troops on February 3: "Iraqi forces remain in a defensive crouch as the [Multinational Coalition Forces'] bombing campaign in the Kuwait Theater of Operations continues. Ground forces are occupying static, well fortified positions with little or no movement detected."[45]

After the war, evidence emerged that some of these Iraqi regular divisions mustered less than full strength and suffered low morale, even before the air campaign began. Shortly after the ceasefire, interrogators at the Joint Debriefing Center interviewed nine enemy senior officers from frontline and second-echelon units. Synthesizing the answers, these debriefers reported "that the Iraqi army deployed to the KTO at considerably less than full strength, and that, by the time the 39-day air offensive commenced, army morale was already extremely low, and descending. . . . From figures provided to us by our sources, it appears that the average frontline and second echelon division deployed at no more than 80 percent strength, in some cases as low as 50 percent."[46]

Before and during the war, however, simple prudence dictated that CENTCOM officers plan against worst-case assumptions. ARCENT and MARCENT commanders understandably were concerned about the Iraqi frontline units, as these were the enemy troops nearest their own. Air Staff briefers identified these forces, running from east to west along the Saddam Line, from the Iraqi left to right flank, as follows: the 18th, 8th, 42d, 29th, 14th, 7th, 36th, 16th, 30th, 20th, 27th, 28th, 25th, and 48th Infantry Divisions. In the second echelon were the 5th Mechanized, 3d Armored, 1st Mechanized, and 21st, 47th, and 31st Infantry Divisions.[47]

The planners in the KTO cell directed an unrelenting effort against these Iraqi units throughout the air campaign. On February 7, for example, they scheduled

Lucrative Targets

172 A–10 missions, including operations against three of these enemy divisions in the first and second echelons and against the 6th and 10th Armored Divisions farther to the rear.[48] Another 237 aircraft would fly sorties, on road reconnaissance, against Iraqi artillery concentrations, and against the 36th Infantry Division (a frontline unit at the left-center of the Saddam Line), and two other armored divisions. Three days later, the KTO planners intended to send 182 A–10 missions, emphasizing three infantry divisions near the front and an armored division. On the eve of the ground campaign, they scheduled 180 A–10 sorties, directing most of them against artillery positions and the 26th Infantry Division, a second-line unit on the crucial Iraqi right flank. Other aircraft were to conduct 650 more missions, with the burden falling on other regular Iraqi infantry and armored formations.[49]

Like that of other targets, the BDA of Iraqi regular units was never as complete or available as rapidly as all of its users wished, but analysts presented enough evidence that planners and aircrews could discern the results of their efforts. As early as January 29, CENTAF intelligence officers reported an appreciable decline in the combat strength of three Iraqi regular divisions: the 1st Mechanized and the 10th and 12th Armored. Two mornings later, a CENTCOM J–2 briefer told General Schwarzkopf that the 10th Armored Division, whose losses included twelve tanks, twenty armored vehicles, and twenty-two artillery pieces, had been reduced to 88 percent of its original combat strength and that the 6th Armored Division had been reduced to 80 percent. "Most of the heavy divisions in the KTO theater," CENTAF/IN reported on February 3, "have probably sustained significant damage." In mid-February, Headquarters SAC intelligence officers offered a guarded assessment: "The air campaign is methodically reducing the capabilities of the Iraqi ground forces in the KTO. The frontline infantry divisions, several heavy divisions, and some elements of the Republican Guard have suffered the most damage. The Iraqis remain capable of limited offensive operations though their counterattack capability has been degraded."[50]

Postwar interviews with prisoners of war provided dramatic evidence of how the air campaign affected the Iraqi regulars. Having reported that many of the enemy's divisions deployed to the KTO at half strength or less, the officers at the Joint Debriefing Center went on to point out that these formations "then lost 50% of [their] already depleted numbers through desertions, AWOL, and casualties." After questioning prisoners from seven different Iraqi divisions, these debriefers concluded that "in some units the genuine foot race north really commenced when the bombs began to fall."[51]

Coalition leaders did not define "crushing" the Iraqi regular and Republican Guard divisions in terms of inflicting personnel casualties, but rather in terms of destroying their tanks and equipment. "When you went to the KTO," one veteran of thirty-eight missions said, "you're looking for tanks and artillery, Republican Guard." On February 1, about a week after the emphasis of the air campaign had settled on Phase III targets, ARCENT analysts believed that the Iraqis still maintained an imposing amount of materiel in the KTO: approximately 3,800 tanks, 2,600 APCs, and 2,700 artillery pieces.[52]

These three types of equipment were so valuable to the enemy that according to Army doctrine they formed the basis for measuring the combat effectiveness of its units.[53] Because ARCENT's combat units had an enormous stake in the success of the air campaign, General Schwarzkopf assigned the command the responsibility for estimating the aerial attrition of the Iraqi ground forces in the KTO.[54] The Army G–2 officers who took on this task adopted the criterion that, when air operations had destroyed more than 50 percent of the equipment—tanks, APCs, and artillery pieces—of any enemy division, regular or Republican Guard, that unit was rendered ineffective. This standard was supported by Army doctrine: General Schwarzkopf had drawn on it in his discussions with Colonel Warden in August 1990, and the CINC's special planning cell had used it during their work that autumn. ARCENT planners believed that when air operations had met this 50 percent criterion, the Coalition could undertake a ground offensive with confidence.[55]

The allied senior officers regarded tanks and artillery as particularly important—and difficult—targets. Shortly after the war, General Horner emphasized the significance of General Schwarzkopf's "directions to us to take out armor and artillery. I think that was the key to [the ground forces'] low casualties." To underscore the importance of tanks, one senior officer in the TACC developed a running joke throughout the war, adopting the pose that the enemy's armor was so vital that he had no interest in any other subject. When someone approached with news of a successful operation against a Scud site, enemy aircraft, or other target, he facetiously dismissed the messenger: "All I want to hear about are tanks. Tanks get me home!"[56]

In addition to the Iraqi armor, Coalition planners also remained concerned about the enemy's artillery, knowing that Saddam Hussein had relied heavily on this weapon during the Iran-Iraq war and expecting him to use it to deliver deadly conventional, or even chemical, weapons against the advancing allies. Further, the officers who were old enough to remember the Vietnam War recalled all too vividly how difficult it had been to destroy field guns from the air. A "successful" bombing run might throw a howitzer into the air, and yet within minutes gun crews could right it and have it firing again. Generals Olsen and Corder, and doubtless others, contended that it was more effective to bomb artillery-ammunition storage sites, which were relatively vulnerable, than to attack the field guns themselves.[57]

The enemy's artillery, APCs, and tanks received considerable attention from F–16s, which flew the largest number of combat sorties during the Gulf War.[58] The Fighting Falcon was the Air Force's primary multirole aircraft, and the 251 that served during Desert Storm flew missions ranging from strategic attack to close air support. The F–16s operated from Al Dhafra and Al Minhad, United Arab Emirates; Doha, Qatar; Al Kharj, Saudi Arabia; and, in the case of the

Lucrative Targets

Proven Force assets, Incirlik, Turkey.[59] Seven Falcons were lost during the war, five of them in combat.[60]

Whereas the LANTIRN-equipped F–16Ls flew at night, contributing to the Scud and other missions, the F–16s in the KTO operated in the daylight. These

An F–16A of the 138th TFS (174th TFW, New York Air National Guard) prepares to taxi from its Al Kharj parking slot for the first daylight mission of Desert Storm.

fighters were closely associated with Killer Scout operations, a role that called for them to fly armed reconnaissance and to coordinate air strikes against Iraqi tanks, artillery, APCs, and other assets.[61] The ATO assigned an F–16 a precisely defined area, a "kill box," where it would locate and attack targets of opportunity. Whenever possible, planners gave a pilot the same assignment repeatedly, allowing him to become familiar with its terrain and targets. After flying over the same kill box a number of times, an F–16 pilot could readily detect changes, a shifting of armor or vehicles, an attempt at camouflage or deception, or the arrival of new units in the area. "The Iraqis couldn't make a move," a veteran of the 4th TFS asserted, "without the Killer Scouts knowing about it."[62]

The Killer Scouts originated from a blend of historical experience, Air Force doctrine, and "operator" initiative. The concept had its antecedents in the Fast Forward Air Controller (or "Fast FAC") F–4 and F–100 operations of the Vietnam War. One Air National Guard officer, old enough to remember the Southeast Asian conflict, reported that the Guard's F–16s operating out of Al Kharj were finding more primary and secondary targets in mid-February, a success he credited to the Fast FAC concept. This tactic, he noted, was "called Killer Scout in the AOR. But it's pure SEA [South East Asia] Fast FAC."[63]

Although the Killer Scouts had their historical antecedents in Vietnam, the concept of the kill box, used by F–16s and other aircraft during Desert Storm, was based on a system that the Air Force had developed long before the Gulf War. This grid pattern of boxes met an obvious and essential need, as one KTO planner explained, for "some method, either geographically or with lat-longs [latitude and longitude lines], . . . to designate a piece of airspace." With AWACS and ABCCC aircraft providing command and control of the kill boxes, a pilot could operate in his assigned area and remain confident that he had that area to himself. A B–52

An F–16A of the 4th TFS (388th TFW) carrying a load of AIM–9L/M (on wingtips) and AIM–9P–2/3 Sidewinder missiles, a pair of MK–84 2,000-pound bombs, two 370-gallon drop tanks, and an ALQ–119 (V)–15 ECM pod. The 388th converted to the F–16C in 1989, flying this version during the Gulf War.

captain explained how the system accommodated a variety of attackers: "Each aircraft had a particular box or several particular boxes to hit (B–52s, with their tremendous bomb loads, usually had several boxes to drop on[,] while smaller fighter-bombers usually hit one such box), and we were in line to get at our target. The waiting line consisted of a B–52 cell, an F–16 cell, another B–52 cell, a cell of A–10s, and finally our cell of B–52s."[64]

The Killer Scouts using these kill boxes drew on standard Air Force practice and Vietnam War precedents, yet some conditions were unique to the Gulf War. These F–16 operations, Colonel Baptiste emphasized, were "a prime example of flexibility" that "originated right at the units. . . . The Killer Scout option . . . was an excellent plan that came right from the units." By late January, many Coalition airmen had concluded that a better means of locating and validating targets in the KTO was needed, and General Schwarzkopf embraced their point of view. The enormous number of sorties being generated in the relatively small theater ruled out any kind of loitering tactics, which would have allowed strike aircraft long TOTs. "We were sending anywhere from 900 to 1,400 sorties" over the KTO, General Corder pointed out, and pilots "didn't have time to wander around and find [their] target." Another significant factor was that, early in the war, the F–16s were attacking from altitudes of approximately 25,000 feet. Operating at those levels, combined with the poor weather that hindered the air campaign in January and with the lack of local-unit overhead photography, meant that the aircrews received very limited BDA. "Accurate BDA was impossible," a lieutenant colonel at one F–16 squadron recalled after the war, "making it very difficult for us to say we had reached the goal of 50 percent attrition [of Iraqi strength in the KTO]."[65]

It was under these circumstances that General Schwarzkopf decided to evaluate the Killer Scout concept, a task that General Horner gave to the 388th TFW. This unit's F–16Cs, based at Al Minhad, successfully tested these operations during early February. One veteran of the evaluation later recounted: "The first day [February 4] was our best day." Eight F–16s "went back and forth all day" over their assigned kill boxes, this pilot recalled, locating and destroying ground targets. The successes of that first day, he believed, ensured that the Killer Scout mission would continue. At approximately the same time, General Glosson, who was not satisfied with the results that F–16s were achieving against Iraqi tanks from higher altitudes, brought into the theater a group of instructors from the Air Force Fighter Weapons Center at Nellis AFB, Nevada, to consult on fighter weapons and tactics. They recommended that two F–16s operate together, one at low altitude and one high, one locating a target and the other attacking it. Their proposal was very similar to the Killer Scout concept that many officers at the units had suggested: the instructors from the Fighter Weapons Center and the pilots in the field had independently arrived at much the same idea. Their ideas, as General Glosson later said, "were in the same ballpark," and after the war both the consultants and many squadron officers could claim a role in the origin of the Killer Scouts.[66]

The basic concept was that the aircraft worked in pairs, one to find and evaluate the target, and then point the other to attack it. The F–16 Killer Scout usually operated at medium altitude and, relying on his high degree of training and cumulative experience over the same kill box, identified targets both by radar reconnaissance and sight. Flying on autopilot in a slow curve, the "pointer" pilot could evaluate with binoculars dug-in tanks or camouflaged areas. He then directed the "Killer Bee," another F–16 or other attacker, down from his high altitude, to the target.[67]

This concept of aircraft operating in pairs was compatible with a larger trend that had emerged in Coalition air planning by early February, when the Killer Scout mission began. At the opening of the war, large attack packages had been the norm, but with the reduction of enemy air defenses, flights of four or even two aircraft became practical. This was another instance when the Coalition's success against Phase II targets represented a turning point in the air campaign. By early February, as the Killer Scout missions got underway, operations by pairs of strike aircraft were desirable and, more important, feasible.[68]

Destroying the Battlefield: Phase III Operations in the KTO

The kill boxes used by the F–16 Killer Scouts and other Coalition aircraft were based on a system that the Saudis already had in place, a gridwork defined by latitude and longitude lines. CENTAF planners expanded this framework to cover the KTO and the rest of the AOR. A kill box was one-half degree latitude by one-half degree longitude, or roughly thirty miles on a side. Each was divided further into four quadrants, fifteen miles on a side.[69]

Coalition aircrews were sometimes moved from one kill box to another, based on information from J–STARS about the movements and concentrations of Iraqi forces. The E–8A's side-looking radar could locate stationary targets such as parked tanks or APCs or, operating in its moving-target indicator mode, the aircraft could detect slow-moving objects such as convoys.[70]

As on the AWACS, an ACE headed by a senior colonel sat at the back of the J–STARS aircraft. Unlike the E–3 ACE, the E–8 battle staff was composed of both Air Force and Army officers. The J–STARS radars could rapidly identify targets on the ground and communicate them to the ABCCC, which had the authority to control the airspace used by the Coalition's strike aircraft.[71] Working either through the EC–130 C^2 aircraft or in direct communication with the "shooters," the E–8s supported the F–16 Killer Scouts, F–15Es, F–111s, and—communicating through the U.S. Marine Corps Direct Air Support Center (DASC)—Marine Corps aircraft.[72] The J–STARS and AWACS therefore differed both in roles and authority. The AWACS found enemy aircraft and used its airspace-control authority to direct Coalition strikers against them, and the J–STARS identified enemy ground targets and, lacking the same authority, worked through the ABCCC or DASC to send attackers over them.[73]

The J–STARS therefore worked closely with the ABCCC and with the Killer Scouts, who flew under the call sign "Pointer" and received their kill boxes from the ATO. When a Coalition strike aircraft entered a kill box, it checked in with the ABCCC for targeting information and with the Killer Scout working that box to learn about any targets of opportunity. If the incoming "shooter" failed to make contact with a "Pointer," it continued with its assigned mission.[74]

The evidence mounted that the Killer Scouts were making a significant contribution to the air campaign. As early as February 6, General Glosson offered General Horner his opinion that the new concept was "producing desired results" and quoted a commander who told him that there had been an "order of magnitude increase in effectiveness compared to one week ago." With the reduction of the Iraqi air defenses, the F–16s were able to make systematic, multiple passes over their kill boxes and find "lucrative targets." One Killer Scout commander told General Glosson, "Most of my guys are smiling now." On February 14, the Fighter Weapons Center consultants strongly endorsed these operations. "Maximize the use of kill zones in conjunction with the Killer Scout program," they urged. "Targets should be selected by [the] scout to maximize the capability of the type of ordnance to be delivered." A day later, General Glosson commented that the F–16 scouts had more than doubled the amount of BDA information available each day.

Lucrative Targets

Shortly after Desert Storm ended, operations officers at Headquarters TAC studied these wartime operations and concluded they had been particularly effective in "locating dug-in targets for attack aircraft operating from medium altitude." They recommended institutionalizing the Killer Scout concept and developing further its doctrine, training, tactics, and equipment.[75]

The F–16s and A–10s, General Horner told a reporter after the war, "did a lot of work that was really not heralded. They basically kept pressure on Saddam during the daytime. He could not move his forces. He just had to sit there and absorb punishment during the daytime." The A–10A Thunderbolt II, the Air Force's primary CAS aircraft, may have increased its reputation more than any other aircraft during the Gulf War. On the eve of Desert Storm, the Air Force had been pursuing its plans to phase out the Warthog (as it was affectionately nicknamed for its ugly appearance) in favor of an F–16 version designed for CAS. Yet during the war the A–10 proved a durable workhorse, well suited to attacking Iraqi tanks and artillery and able to contribute thousands of sorties to other missions as well.[76]

During Desert Shield, the Air Force deployed 135 A–10s and 12 O/A–10s, the airborne-control version of the aircraft. Arriving in Saudi Arabia in their tricolor woodland camouflage, the Warthogs assembled at King Fahd International Airport—the largest concentration at one base in their history—and later operated also from forward locations at King Khalid Military City and Al Jouf.[77] Assigned to the 10th, 23d, and 354th TFWs, to the 926th Tactical Fighter Group, and to the 602d Tactical Air Control Wing, these aircraft flew more than 8,000 combat sorties, a total second only to that of the F–16s,[78] and maintained an 87.7 percent mission-capable rate.[79]

The A–10s served almost exclusively in the KTO, with the notable exception of their contribution to the Scud hunt. The Warthogs joined this search as early as the second day of the war and flew patrols against the Iraqi missiles until the end of the conflict. Unit records credited the A–10s with destroying fifty-one Scud-related targets,[80] and the aircraft gained another nickname: Scudhog.[81]

When the A–10 performed in its Scud-hunting and BAI roles, it operated at ceilings far higher than the low altitudes that were required for its intended CAS mission. The Warthog had been designed—and its pilots trained—for operating at less than 1,000 feet and at low speeds, destroying artillery and tanks with its 30-mm armor-piercing cannon shells and relying on its durable airframe to survive enemy ground fire.[82] At the outset of the war, the A–10 began flying BAI missions at medium altitudes. In a typical operation, the controller in the ABCCC cleared one or two Warthogs into a kill box, where they hunted targets for thirty minutes. When weather conditions were dicey, an A–10 weather scout would search for an area clear enough for operations, and the airborne center would base its assignments on his report.[83]

The CAS-designed A–10 not only hunted Scuds and performed BAI, it also contributed to the SEAD mission. The Warthogs took on this role because, early in the air campaign, the Iraqis became reluctant to turn on their seeking radars or other emitters because they were intimidated by the likelihood of F–4Gs launching HARMs at them. To break down this reticence, A–10s throughout the war accompanied the Wild Weasels in attacks on air defenses. The Warthogs used their multiple weapons to engage an Iraqi SAM site, and, if the enemy responded by

A 355th Tactical Training Wing A–10 from Davis-Monthan AFB, Arizona. In 1991, the wing's designation was changed to the 355th Fighter Wing.

homing in on the attacking formation, the F–4Gs launched their standoff missiles. As one senior officer in the TACC put it, the Gulf War saw "the birth of the 'wart weasel.'"[84]

The A–10 units could point to a number of successes in this new role. The aircraft's first operation against the Republican Guard, flown against the Tawakalna Division on January 29, was a Wart Weasel mission. A pilot from the 76th TFS led a four-aircraft attack that destroyed SA–2 and SA–6 sites protecting this unit deployed west of Kuwait. A Wart Weasel mission on February 8 was credited with eliminating one or more SA–9s, and an even more successful operation was completed six days later, against some of the air defenses of the Medina Division. Smoke from oil-well fires in northern Kuwait covered the target area on that day, February 14, when another 76th TFS pilot led a mixed force of Warthogs and Wild Weasels that destroyed five SA–6s. When one KTO planner praised the A–10's contribution to the "SAM removal teams," he was speaking of a role that had not been anticipated for the CAS aircraft.[85] "If Fairchild-Republic had known that we were going to be flying strike missions against SAM and radar sites," one pilot said, "they would have designed the A–10 a lot differently."[86]

Serving in these diverse roles and enjoying a flexible weapons load, the A–10 used a variety of ordnance. The Warthogs launched approximately 4,800 Mavericks, which is more than 90 percent of the total delivered during the war. They expended more than 17,000 MK–82s, approximately 2,600 MK–84s, and roughly another 2,600 CBU–58s, while also using several other types of ordnance, as well as their 30-mm cannon. Every category of A–10 weapon—bombs, rockets, Maverick missiles, and cannon—scored high reliability rates.[87]

Perhaps above all, the Warthog proved a durable combat aircraft. Its extremely rugged airframe shielded the pilot, who sat encased within a titanium tub, while the fuselage protected the high-mounted twin engines. Eight A–10s suffered minor battle damage, and all were repaired and flying at the end of the war. Five of the six that received major battle damage also returned to combat.[88]

Even the story of this sixth, irreparable A–10 testified to the aircraft's durability. This Warthog, piloted by Capt. Rich Biley of the 76th TFS, flew its last mis-

A pair of 48th TFW F–111Fs roar over barren Saudi soil during Desert Shield. The leading aircraft is named "Miss Liberty II."

sion on February 22. In preparation for the ground campaign, Captain Biley's mission was to set fire to oil trenches in southern Kuwait. After he launched white phosphorus rockets at his target, a SAM struck the tail of his aircraft. His A–10 lost hydraulic power and might have gone down then, but the Warthog's manual-reversion system was designed for just such a contingency. When the hydraulic system went out, the flight-control linkages shifted to allow manual flight. Manipulating the throttle, Biley recovered his A–10 and returned to base. Using emergency trim, he was able to attempt a landing (although he remained virtually without brakes or rudder control), and his aircraft skidded off the runway. Captain Biley made an emergency egress and escaped unharmed, and his aircraft proved to be the only A–10 lost to major battle damage during the war.[89]

Other cases, in which not only the pilot but also the aircraft survived major battle damage, were equally dramatic. On February 6, Capt. Paul Johnson's A–10, assigned to the 353d TFW, was heavily damaged during an unsuccessful attack on a SAM battery. The aircraft was hit at approximately 7,500 feet as it climbed away from the target. As the last attacker to leave the area, the A–10 was probably struck by a shoulder-fired missile. Captain Johnson recounted that his aircraft "rolled about 120 degrees to the right with the nose slicing downward." He was preparing to eject when he regained control and leveled off at about 6,000 feet. The enemy missile had hit near one of the aircraft's Mavericks and blasted a huge hole in Johnson's right wing. His engine on that side lost power, but only briefly. At first Johnson hoped only to reach Saudi airspace and eject there, but, after crossing the border and jettisoning his remaining ordnance, he raised his aspirations. After refueling from a KC–10, the fortunate pilot landed safely at King Fahd International Airport. His aircraft was among the five A–10s that suffered major battle damage, were repaired, and returned to combat.[90]

Nine days later, a similar episode occurred that gained considerable attention, because the pilot in this instance was the wing commander of the 23d TFW. On February 15, a day when two A–10s were lost in combat, Col. David A. Sawyer returned in an aircraft that had suffered a partial loss of its hydraulics and extensive damage to its tail. He wrote this account the following day: "I took what we believe was an SA–13 EO [enemy ordnance] proximity-fused explosion over the top of my right empennage. . . . My aircraft's hydraulics and engines remained sound and I was able to recover with available elevator and rudder control surfaces." Adding a touch of pilot humor, the wing commander reflected, "Loneliness is climbing at 200 kts [knots] with the nearest friendlies 55 miles away." The morning of Colonel Sawyer's return, Col. Al Doman made this entry in the TACC log: "354th [TFW] reports another case of badly damaged A–10 recovering safely. Incident occurred at 0530Z today, [call sign] Gatling 41 [mission number] MSN 5041A attacking Medina [Division] armor took either an airburst or SAM in the tail. Right elevator blown off, right rudder bowed, major damage to tail area aft of engines. Pilot was one-each Col. Dave Sawyer."[91]

While the A–10s demonstrated their durability attacking ground targets, the F–111F Aardvarks, F–15E Strike Eagles, and Navy A–6E Intruders made a specialty of what came to be known as tank plinking. These operations, another Gulf War "first," began when CENTAF aircrews realized that aircraft with thermal imaging or infrared (IR) seekers could locate and destroy individual pieces of armor. The enemy typically buried his tanks to make them harder to locate, but, in early February, F–111 crews learned that their FLIR sensors could detect the hidden armor. The desert sun heated the surface metal of the Iraqi tanks, and, at day's end, the armor cooled more slowly than did the surrounding sand. Aircraft with IR capability could detect this contrast, identify individual targets, and attack them with 500-pound bombs. The Iraqis, General Corder recalled, put their tanks "in the sand, push[ed] berms up around [them], thinking they would hide. But you can't hide from infrared. When you disturb the sand, you change the character of how the dirt absorbs the heat, and, in fact, [it] makes it look like a bull's-eye." F–111Fs with Pave Tack and F–15Es with LANTIRN were well equipped for tank plinking. One Strike Eagle pilot offered this basic definition of the tactic: "When you're at 15 or 20,000 feet with a laser-guided bomb and you put one 500-pounder through every tank, that's tank plinking."[92] "We used Joint–STARS for cuing," General Corder explained. "We would go around at night and put a bomb on top of a tank. . . . And a 500-pound bomb on top of a tank will get it every time."[93]

These attacks on individual tanks were another example of an initiative that originated from the units in the field. General Horner acknowledged after the war that he had not foreseen any such use for 500-pound LGBs and readily credited

81

his Aardvark pilots with the innovation. "The –111 guys," he offered, "were really the guys that started that." Enthusiastic about an early demonstration by the F–111 of its capabilities against armor, General Horner made this entry in the TACC's logbook: "Just returned from watching video of F–111/Pave Tack/500-lb LGB blowing up tanks in Kuwait that ought to be required reading at Army War College and A–10 Fighter Weapons School—classic of how to do the job right." The tank-plinking tactic was tried on February 5, when a single F–111 sortie carried GBU–12s (500-pound LGBs) against individual Republican Guard tanks.[94] A concerted effort began on February 11, with the Aardvarks focusing on the two armored Republican Guard divisions, the Hammurabi and Medina. During the war's fourth week, tank plinking accounted for well over half of all F–111 strikes.[95]

While the F–111 scored its successes against enemy armor, General Corder announced on February 11 that the F–15E had been cleared to use the same ordnance and tactics, and it, too, would begin night tank-plinking operations. The two-seat, dual-role "E" model was relatively new, having entered the inventory in 1988, and the two F–15E squadrons that served in the Gulf attained operational readiness just before deploying. To begin effective tank plinking, they needed to complete operational test and evaluation with the LANTIRN system, which consisted of a navigation and a targeting pod both mounted under the fighter's fuselage. The navigation pod featured a wide-field FLIR sensor and a terrain-following radar that displayed its returns on a monitor in the cockpit. The targeting pod FLIR had both wide and narrow fields of view and a laser designator, each of which were able to track targets either manually or automatically. The Strike Eagles conducted the operational test and evaluation with the night-targeting pods, after receiving sixteen of them in the theater.[96] F–15E tank plinking also required certification with the GBU–12. In earlier tests, this fighter had encountered problems with this munition, but pilots found that they could overcome them if they limited their maneuvers, reduced their "G" loads, and restricted their angles of attack. Col. Hal M. Hornburg, Commander of the 4th TFW(P), commented shortly after the war: "The laser-guided bomb capability proved to be an extremely valuable commodity. Even though they were introduced ten days into the air war and no training had been accomplished, the 4 TFW(P) delivered over 1700 Paveway II LGBs with a very good success rate."[97]

Using 500-pound LGBs for this mission was an unexpected turn of events. General Horner remembered an incident a few years before the Gulf War, when he had watched workcrews unload a ship holding thousands of these weapons. The CENTAF commander chuckled to himself as he recalled his thoughts at the time: "I said, 'We'll never use those things. Who is the fool that bought those?'" The common wisdom before the war was that 500-pound bombs were too light for attacking bunkers or armored units. During Desert Storm, however, once aircrews determined that IR seekers could locate individual tanks, the relatively light ordnance proved more than adequate for the job. A 500-pound LGB could totally destroy a tank, or, failing that, the weapon was powerful enough to damage the vehicle's treads, gun tubes, or any of its ranging, optical, or targeting systems so badly that it became useless for battle.[98]

The tank-plinking operations had no more than been introduced when officers in the TACC learned that the CENTCOM commander disliked the term. "At first," General Horner later recalled, "General Schwarzkopf asked us to name it something more 'combat,' like 'tank busting.' Of course, whenever you tell fighter pilots to do something, they do exactly the opposite. 'Tank plinking' became the preferred term."[99]

In addition to tank plinking, the F–15Es performed a number of other missions, primarily at night. Able to deliver twelve tons of munitions long distances from their base at Al Kharj, Saudi Arabia, these fighters operated against strategic targets in Iraq and contributed to the Scud hunt, while in the KTO they flew both air interdiction and antitank sorties. The F–15Es used their buddy-lasing tactics against Iraqi tanks as well as artillery. A relatively new aircraft, the Strike Eagle proved its flexibility during Desert Storm. With understandable pride, one veteran of twenty F–15E missions said, "We could change coordinates, change bombs, change where we're going and very effectively, quicker than any other weapons system, and they knew that in Riyadh." "The F–15E's flexibility was the key," one weapons system officer stated. "The entire weapons system was so flexible it enabled us to do our job—effectively and efficiently."[100]

The F–15Es and other aircraft scored devastating successes against the Iraqi tanks, littering the Kuwaiti desert with their ruins. One official postwar report stated that, on several occasions, pairs of Strike Eagles, each armed with eight GBU–12s, destroyed sixteen armored vehicles during a single sortie. During the course of the war, F–111s were credited with destroying approximately 1,000 tanks with GBU–12s, and A–10s using Maverick missiles were credited with about the same number.[101]

Night operations contributed much to the Coalition's success. Desert Storm, as one postwar study correctly asserted, "was the first war in which air power was truly effective at night." As many had predicted before the conflict began, Coalition aircrews were able to pressure the Iraqis around the clock, allowing them no respite from combat. Some of CENTAF's aircraft were able to navigate and attack at night nearly as effectively as during the day. Nighttime technologies including FLIR, LANTIRN, and radars—and aircrew trained in night tactics—gave the Coalition an enormous advantage.[102]

Although the night aircraft perhaps best known to the press and public, the stealth F–117A, flew almost exclusively over Iraq, it also performed a few KTO missions. On the opening night of the war, a stealth fighter attacked an air defense sector headquarters,[103] and, on February 15, fourteen F–117s attacked the pumping station, distribution points, and T junctions that controlled the flow of oil to the Saddam Line's fire trenches. The Nighthawks destroyed these facilities within twenty minutes, ending the possibility that advancing Coalition troops would encounter the daunting obstacle of flaming trenches.[104] During the early morning hours of February 23, ten F–117s flew against the Iraqi intelligence and special operations headquarters in Kuwait. Nine reached their target areas and scored fifteen direct hits.[105]

The F–111, however, saw far more service in the KTO than did the stealth fighter. It deserved great credit for its night operations in the theater, for its effective work against the bridges and Republican Guard, and particularly for its innovation of tank plinking. The two F–15E squadrons received their LANTIRN equipment in the theater and rapidly moved—during combat—through the learning curve with their night-targeting pods and buddy-lasing tactics. One Strike Eagle pilot later recalled, "When we first got there, not many of us had even seen the [night-targeting pods]. So it was a real maturing process that occurred there. The good news was that we were able to effectively employ them from day one."[106] Other Coalition aircraft, including the A–6E and F–16L, also contributed to the night operations, and two A–10 squadrons, the 74th and 355th TFSs, had limited nighttime capabilities and were restricted to firing Mavericks or dropping flares for conventional bombs.[107]

The value of even the most limited of CENTAF's nocturnal capabilities was magnified by the enemy's vulnerabilities in nighttime operations. Night flying was never the long suit of the Iraqi Air Force, and the Coalition's intense attacks at the opening of the war further discouraged the enemy from this option. From late January until the end of the war, the Iraqis flew only in the daylight. Also, the enemy's air defenses were weaker at night than they were during the day.[108]

Both night and day operations produced growing evidence of CENTAF's success with its Phase III operations against armor, APCs, and artillery. On January 29, CENTAF intelligence officers offered the assessment that air attacks had destroyed 80 Iraqi tanks, 86 APCs, and 308 pieces of artillery. During an evening presentation to General Horner on February 15, the command's operations briefer reported that F–15Es had killed 10 tanks the previous night, A–6s had killed 28, and F–111s 55. ARCENT officers verified that the F–111s of the 48th TFW, operating out of Taif, killed 673 pieces of armor between February 7 and the opening of the ground campaign.[109] By the eve of the ground campaign, Coalition air attacks had destroyed almost one-third of the Iraqi APCs in the KTO, approximately 40 percent of the tanks, and nearly half of the artillery pieces.[110]

Phase III of the Coalition's air campaign was deemed an overwhelming success. RSAF Commander Lt. Gen. Ahmad Ibrahim Behery emphasized that it destroyed the Iraqis' will to fight. Col. Mike Reavey, the director of nighttime operations in the TACC, described the Coalition's achievement in the skies over the KTO as a blend of successful Phase II, tank plinking, and Killer Scout operations. "We went in and took out all the fixed SAM sites, and then we went and started plinking tanks. We instituted a Fast FAC program in the daytime to go out and find this stuff, because they were pretty well embedded and hard to see." A sign hanging over Colonel Deptula's desk summarized CENTAF's understanding of its mission in the KTO: "We are not preparing the battlefield—we are destroying it." Another officer, a veteran of twenty missions, later elaborated on this same motto: "We didn't prepare the battlefield, we destroyed it. We didn't soften the Republican Guard, we decimated it. We were killing, between the F–111s and F–15Es, between 100 and 120 tanks a night for seven nights in a row, before we went into the land battle, the 100-hour dash through Kuwait."[111]

Chapter Five

An Intricate Ballet:
Some KTO Issues

The history of warfare records no easy victories. "Everything is very simple in War," Carl von Clausewitz, the famous Prussian military theorist, wrote with deliberate irony, "but the simplest thing is difficult."[1] The Gulf War proved this maxim. CENTAF's officers and airmen won an overwhelming victory over Saddam Hussein, but only after they contended with issues of bombing accuracy and precision, adjustments in tactics and operations, problems in gaining timely and accurate BDA, confusion posed by Iraqi deceptions and operations, limitations of poor flying weather, changes in ATOs, stresses to the ATO process, and other dilemmas.

B–52 bombing accuracy provided one example of an issue that Coalition airmen encountered during the Gulf War. The subject was particularly important in the KTO, because these bombers delivered almost 70 percent of their total Desert Storm munitions either in attacks against Republican Guard or Iraqi regular divisions, or in breaching efforts against the minefields of the Saddam Line. With their large payloads, the B–52s were well suited to strikes against dispersed and dug-in infantry and armor, precisely the targets the enemy offered in the KTO.[2]

The B–52 delivered conventional, gravity weapons: "dumb" bombs in contrast to "smart" bombs (the jargon for PGMs). The M117C—a 750-pound, blast/fragmentation, general-purpose bomb—was far and away the most commonly used ordnance against the Republican Guard, Iraqi regulars, and minefields. B–52 aircrews dropped approximately 14,000 of these weapons against the enemy's elite units, almost 11,000 against his other ground forces in the KTO, and roughly 4,600 in breaching operations. The bomber's next weapon of choice against these targets was the MK–82, using more than 13,000 against the three target sets combined. The BUFFs also delivered more than 3,000 CBU–58s against the Republican Guard and more than 1,000 of them against the Iraqi regulars, although none went against the minefields.[3]

Lucrative Targets

Limited to conventional weapons, some of the STRATFOR bombers began the war flying low-level, radar-evading approaches, for which they had trained during the more than fifteen years since the Vietnam War.[4] On the opening night of the war, for example, twelve B–52s from the 4300th Provisional Bombardment

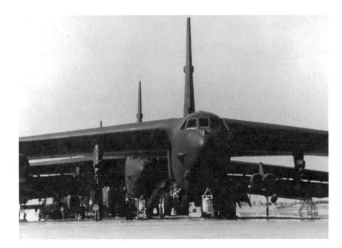

B–52Gs of the 1708th BMW(P) are lined up on the Jeddah flightline on February 26.

Wing [BW(P)] entered Iraq at low altitude. A STRATFOR after-action report explained why: "The primary reason the 4300 BW(P) wanted to go low on night one against AAA-only, point-defended targets was HQ SAC [had] directed peacetime training in the low level environment."[5]

IR-directed SAMs and barrage-fired AAA and SAMs forced the B–52s, like other Coalition aircraft, to higher altitudes. On January 22, an enemy SAM struck the tail of one of the 4300th's bombers, inflicting major battle damage. Other B–52s suffered minor damage from AAA fire. "It quickly became clear," one senior officer stated dryly, "the high altitude environment was [the] most survivable." A colonel of the 806th Provisional Bombardment Wing put it even more tersely when he stated, "We rediscovered high-level bombing." One B–52 captain later recalled how the bomber crews grew wiser about the details of ingress routes: "For the first two weeks of the war we flew our missions low level through Turkey until we reached the Iraqi border, at which time we climbed to avoid AA fire. But this meant we were climbing right into the fire and we were endangering ourselves, we all learned things like this."[6]

Shifting to higher altitudes naturally affected the bombing accuracy of the B–52s. Other factors also contributed, because bombing from this aircraft was not as smooth as the uninitiated might imagine. As one B–52 navigator described it: "Dropping real bombs is like driving over a railroad track. The bumps are amazing. You sort of feel it in the pit of your stomach." Wind effects and, specifically, the inability of the software in the B–52's avionics to account precisely for them, were important considerations. At about the time that the breaching operations began, General Caruana told an interviewer that, although the B–52 bombing had "gone well," overall, its accuracy left "something to be desired," largely because of this problem with gauging the wind effects on the ordnance. STRATFOR officers studied this issue further and learned that Air Force intelligence and operations officers were sending target coordinates to their radar vans in degrees, minutes, and seconds, the contractors in the vehicles were entering them into their computer in degrees, minutes, and hundredths of minutes. This discrepancy—which was caught and corrected on the second day of the breaching operations—eliminated some, although not all, of the accuracy error.[7]

It was reasonable to question why the B–52 accuracy problem was not discovered (and addressed) sooner. The first part of the answer was that SAC had historically trained for low-altitude operations and had little experience with high-altitude bombing and the issues that might accompany it. "With timely BDA," one Headquarters SAC study contended after the war, "STRATFOR could have quickly determine[d] that the bombers had an accuracy problem and then directed an adjustment, even though the precise cause of the problem was unknown. Instead, a month into the air war, STRATFOR discovered a 600–700-foot ballistic error at the same time STRATFOR saw...the results of our early breaching efforts."[8] Demands on the B–52 aircrews were doubtless another factor. In mid-February, a group of intelligence and operations officers from Headquarters Eighth Air Force and Headquarters SAC visited the theater and concluded, after discussions with flight crews and planners, that "a minimum of two missions were required before the crews were able to adjust to the combat environment." Bomber target changes were common, particularly in the KTO,[9] and three different authorities—the ABCCC, AWACS, and TACC—could issue these changes independently to a B–52.[10] Finally, a 600-foot error from altitude was masked easily in a 1,000- to 2,000-foot train of bombs. It was not surprising that the problem came into sharp relief only when the B–52s began the breaching operations, which was a mission that emphasized accuracy.[11]

When the B–52 crews had enough BDA information, they addressed the dead-short error. Usually they simply adjusted their desired mean points of impact by 600 feet to accommodate for it.[12] The bomber crews were content to let peacetime analysts determine all of the diverse factors that caused the error.[13]

It would be misleading, however, to make too much of the issue of B–52 accuracy. Many of the targets assigned to the BUFFs, particularly in Iraq, were so large that accuracy was not terribly important to the success of their operations. B–52s delivered, for example, approximately 3,000 bombs against Al Taji, an enormous military-industrial complex just northwest of Baghdad, which covered more than seven square miles—roughly double the combined areas of the USAF's Ogden, Oklahoma City, and Sacramento Air Logistics Centers. When the STRATFOR bombers delivered high tonnages of 500-pound MK–82 and 750-pound M117 bombs against targets this large, a 600-foot error carried no great consequence.[14]

Lucrative Targets

Further, the primary contribution of the B–52 to the air campaign may well have been its effect on the morale of the Iraqis, and this effect was a result of the bomber's massive payload rather than its accuracy. The enormous firepower of this aircraft placed it in a unique category and made it an ideal weapon for psy-

Debris litters the ground around an Iraqi APC of the Republican Guard after the vehicle was hit by U.S. forces.

chological operations. Coalition leaders recognized this and developed standard procedures for such B–52 missions. Planners targeted a specific Iraqi division, and aircrews dropped leaflets on it that warned that a massive strike would follow. The next day, B–52s (and sometimes other strike aircraft) concentrated their attacks on this unit. The final sortie delivered another leaflet, warning that the bombing would continue. In one example, on a single day in early February, B–52s made an intense attack on the Iraqi 16th Division, a regular unit near the center of the Saddam Line. The next day Special Operations MC–130s distributed leaflets over the enemy infantrymen. The leaflet read: "We told you that you were to be bombed and you were…we are telling you again that you will be bombed tomorrow…leave now—flee south or die." The commander of another Iraqi frontline division told his captors after the war that these warnings led many of his junior officers and men to desert. The leaflets damaged the morale of his troops more than anything except the bombings themselves.[15]

Although the evidence from Iraqi prisoners of war was limited and impressionistic, it left no doubt that the B–52 attacks helped crush the enemy's morale. General Corder commented: "I have heard reports that many if not most of the [Iraqi] troops had broken ear drums, terrible sinus problems,…associated with concussion and blast…. They never got to sleep. We were always on them." "Equipment losses exceeded personnel losses," POW debriefers explained shortly after the war, "due to the fact that Iraqi forces either heeded Coalition psyops [psychological operations] leaflets warning them to stay away from their vehicles, or because the Iraqi soldier quickly figured out that his tanks and APCs were not safe places to sleep."[16] Coalition intelligence officers concluded: "Leaflets depicting the B–52 aircraft, and the actual appearance of the B–52s over the Iraqi positions had a significant effect, instilling great fear in the soldiers. Even though the A–10 would win the award as the aircraft that hurt them the most, Iraqi soldiers would no doubt confess to greater fear of the B–52."[17]

The B–52's effectiveness as a psychological weapon was not impaired by its accuracy, nor was this bomber the only Coalition aircraft to experience problems with delivering ordnance from high altitudes. It followed as a matter of course that when the BUFFs, the F–16s, and other attackers moved to higher ceilings, it became more difficult for any of them to put conventional bombs on target. The need to operate at high altitudes increased the premium on "smart" weapons. "The biggest lesson learned so far for the F–16 community," the Fighter Weapons Center consultants reported on February 14, "is the need to incorporate the capability of delivering Precision Guided Munitions beyond just the AGM–65 [Maverick]." One fighter pilot asserted after the war that "when you're up there and you're in your airplane and trying to drop your bombs and all that stuff is coming up at you, and you have a 100-knot crosswind, the probability of hitting your target is pretty low." But, he added, "when we went back up against those targets with PGMs, we killed them." A postwar Headquarters TAC study noted that the Desert Storm fighters with long-range and precision-guided weapons, the F–117s, F–15Es, and F–111s, were (in an implied contrast with the short-legged and conventionally armed F–16s) "very effective." The same evaluators recommended improving the "precision weapons capability on all fighters and [matching] the accuracy of platform and weapon to the target set." A similar argument was made for "smart" weapons for the B–52, which also had demonstrated difficulties with high-altitude accuracy. One STRATFOR after-action report first pointed out that the "ground-to-air threat (primarily AAA) drove the B–52 to the high altitude role," and then it advocated, "Precision-guided, standoff weapons are an absolute must."[18]

Although improved munitions doubtless would help future aircrews, commanders had to make decisions during Desert Storm based on the resources at hand. In the case of the F–16, General Glosson explained that he deliberately accepted a tradeoff of some of the fighter's accuracy in exchange for safer operations. "I put [the F–16s] at an altitude where they didn't have the technology to be very effective," he conceded. "Had I been willing to tolerate the losses and to have let them drop two or three thousand feet, then I'm sure they would have been significantly more effective." This policy would have been costly, and, in a war in which the American homeland was secure and CENTAF's leaders were confident of ultimate victory, risky tactics were unnecessary. General Glosson estimated that he "would have had to tolerate, in my own opinion, losing thirty or forty...F–16s. There was just no way I was going to walk down that road." General McPeak made the same point in some remarks shortly after the war. "The bombing accuracy at '17-5' [17,500 feet altitude]," the chief of staff noted, "ain't what it is at lower altitudes.... But then, the tradeoff is, well, look at our losses. We lost only one airplane every three days." It also was true that, in late February, when more of the Iraqi AAA had been suppressed, the F–16s operated at lower altitudes, and their accuracy improved accordingly.[19]

General McPeak referred to a tradeoff that affected not only F–16s but other aircraft as well. Although aircrews had done some high-altitude training during Desert Shield, they had not concentrated on it. Planners and commanders had instead emphasized training for the kind of operations that the Air Force might have conducted had there been a conventional war in Europe or Korea during the 1980s. The Coalition's successes early in the air campaign established that aircrews would be operating at higher altitudes than expected before the conflict began. By January 19, the third day of the war, it became clear that Iraqi AAA posed the chief surface-to-air threat and that this threat was also far greater than even enemy fighters. The Coalition's rapid success against the enemy's air defenses meant that low-level evasion tactics would not be needed, and Headquarters CENTAF shifted from low-level operations to medium and medium-high ones. "That was some surprise there," an officer of the 4th TFW commented, "medium-altitude stuff. We all thought we'd be at 200 feet at two in the morning to avoid the air-to-air threat.... Fight our way in, fight our way out." Instead, he reflected, it "turned out that we could avoid that triple-A stuff and stay above 10,000 feet and kick hell out of anything in that country." Drawing on his experience as a Vietnam War F–4D pilot, General Corder reflected: "I'm a medium-altitude guy, anyway. I got shot down at low altitude."[20]

Although this change in tactics required flexibility, aircrews hardly needed to be convinced of its wisdom. Units that began the war operating at low altitudes gladly shifted to higher ones. An F–15E pilot recalled his first Gulf War mission, which was flown at low level and had encountered "very heavy AAA from about ten to fifteen miles out from the target all the way to the target area, and then for about ten miles past, it was just streams of triple-A coming up, some SAMs were being fired." Faced with this fire, he flew through it as fast as possible: "But that's very, very memorable to do that when you're down at 300 feet. It's pretty impressive to see all those bullets flying over the canopy." Units that began the war at high altitudes were happy to stay there. The B–52Gs of the 97th Bombardment Wing at RAF Fairford, for example, flew all of their sorties at high level—35,000 feet or higher—and were more than content to do so. The unit's operations officer reported after the war that "reducing altitude from the mid 30s to mid 20s doesn't help bombing accuracy and exposes the cell to more threats. Keep the B–52 at high altitude." At least one Iraqi officer commented on the wisdom of CENTAF's shift to higher altitudes. He told his captors that his command had been well equipped for air defense, with twin 57-mm antiaircraft guns, antiaircraft machine guns, and SA–7 missiles, but that the Coalition's aircraft flew too high for any of these weapons to be effective. His unit's heavy guns tried to engage the allied attackers, but each time it did, "Coalition aircraft would identify their positions and attack."[21]

Many of the allied strike aircraft made the shift to medium and medium-high ceilings, but the A–10s changed their area of operation as well as their altitudes. From the onset of the war, Iraqi AAA and small-arms fire forced the Warthog pilots to fly their air interdiction missions at 4,000 to 6,000 feet, significantly higher than the levels for their traditional CAS sorties. Writing on February 3, the commanders of the 23d and 354th TFWs described the difficulty of identifying targets while flying over hundreds of Iraqi revetments at these relatively high altitudes. "It's nearly impossible," they reported, "to tell what's in them. Pilots (including ourselves) describe them as deep, tarp or dirt covered, oil darkened, contain boxlike containers or old trucks, etc." Nor was dropping altitude the answer. "The lower we fly to check," the commanders pointed out, "the more AAA/small arms we take without a systematic payoff. [The enemy is] dug in so deep we probably couldn't tell much more from lower anyhow." Visiting these units at about the time of this report, General Glosson agreed that targets were "hard to find and ID [identify] at any altitude." In an effort to improve their target identification, the A–10s began flying at lower altitudes in early February, a time when many other strike aircraft were moving up to higher altitudes.[22]

In a mid-February report, Colonel Sawyer, the 23d TFW commander, pointed out that, in addition to working at lower altitudes, the A–10s also were flying farther into enemy territory than expected at the opening of the war. Vulnerable at its relatively slow speed, the aircraft was operating against SAM sites and fixed structures far into Iraq, as well as looking for "elusive high-value armor among the hundreds of dug-in revetments in the dirt below us." The A–10 pilots expressed frustration when, after they had planned and studied their assigned targets, the ABCCC diverted them to what their commanders described as "suspected active armor/artillery revetments—literally thousands of them—that can't be distinguished from surrounding decoys and/or empty revetments."[23] Colonel Sawyer also noted that, after the A–10s' successes in their Scud hunting and Wart Weasel roles, they began to receive "even higher threat tasking," both in the ATO and from the ABCCC.[24]

February 15, a day when the A–10s launched 216 sorties,[25] proved to be their most difficult of the war. Operating against the Tawakalna Division and, for the first time, the Medina, the Warthogs flew into some of the heaviest defenses in the KTO.[26] "After weeks of holding their fire," Colonel Sawyer reported to General Horner the next day, "the Iraqis launched eight IR SAMs at us yesterday, bagging two and damaging one, which I happened to be flying." Colonel Sawyer managed to return his aircraft to base. The other two A–10s were shot down: 1st Lt. Robert J. Sweet was captured and repatriated shortly after the war, and Capt. Stephen R. Phillis was killed in action.[27]

These losses produced an immediate change in the A–10's mission profile. General Horner directed that these aircraft be pulled back from the heavily defended northern KTO where the Republican Guard was deployed, and that the Warthogs operate at safer altitudes of 7,000 feet or higher. After the war, the CENTAF commander commented, "I had fourteen airplanes sitting on the ramp having battle damage repaired, and I lost two A–10s in one day [February 15], and I said, 'I've had enough of this.'" Col. Charles R. Harr entered in the TACC's logbook that afternoon, "CENTAF/CC guidance: A–10s are restricted to within 20 nm [nautical miles] of the southern border within the KTO." The next morning Colonel Doman made a follow-on entry stating, "Refinement of CENTAF/CC guidance on A–10 tasking in KTO: A–10s restricted to the kill zone adjacent to the southern border of Kuwait (including [kill box] AG5, threat permitting)."[28]

This change of operating areas and altitudes gave the A–10 a safer mission profile. Colonel Sawyer praised the CENTAF guidance as "timely and appropriate." After February 15, with few exceptions, the A–10s also stopped daytime strafing, and the O/A–10s made their reconnaissance passes over Iraqi armor as speedily as their engines would allow. "We'll save the gun (and our aircraft)," Colonel Sawyer commented on February 16, "for the ground offensive." Moving the A–10s south from the heavily defended Iraqi elite units and concentrating their efforts against the enemy's frontline divisions proved a viable strategy because, as General Horner noted, "we had F–16s to go after the Republican Guard."[29]

These changes in the A–10's mission profile proved beneficial, but another KTO issue proved much harder to resolve: the difficulty in obtaining timely and accurate BDA of the theater's air operations. General Schwarzkopf assigned AR-CENT the responsibility for reporting on the air campaign's results in destroying the Iraqi ground forces in the KTO. The senior Air Force officers in the theater, who well remembered the "body counts" and other efforts to quantify military progress during the Vietnam War, were well satisfied to have another service assume this task. General Caruana remained wary of the criterion that destroying 50 percent of a division's tanks and APCs rendered it ineffective. "I would be reluctant to say that anybody in [our planning] cell," he stated after the war, "would have pointed to a hard percentage of attrition. Now, we very much wanted to get to 40 to 50 percent before we saw any ground action, but I don't think I would characterize it that strongly, to say that we were going to guarantee a given percentage by a given time." General Horner emphasized that all the senior officers in the theater were sensitive to the possibility that counting tanks during the Gulf War could become analogous to counting bodies during Vietnam. "I was not going to get involved," he stressed, "in keeping track of the decimation of the Iraqi army in the field." The CENTAF commander characterized his attitude toward the ARCENT officers and their responsibility for BDA of the air campaign: "You guys have got it. Just tell me how we're doing."[30]

Army G–2 (intelligence) officers soon found their BDA responsibility a vexing one. Brig. Gen. John F. Stewart, Jr., ARCENT G–2, acknowledged this during the war: "Battle-damage assessment is one of our biggest challenges. Our method is sound—the results frustrating…. BDA is an art, not a science." General Stewart found he did not always receive rapid and useful information on the results of air attacks against the equipment of frontline Iraqi units. DIA's BDA took four or five days to reach ARCENT officers, and it often had limited value.[31]

Whereas ARCENT G–2 found that DIA did not always provide it with timely and useful data, CENTAF officers criticized the Army intelligence briefers for presenting General Schwarzkopf and his staff with BDA statistics that were too low and therefore underestimated the progress of the air campaign. On January 31, for example, ARCENT's BDA for the CENTCOM commander stated that the Republican Guard stood at 99 percent of its prewar strength: 98 percent of its tanks remained, as did 99 percent of its armored vehicles and 99 percent of its artillery. Air Force officers found this hardly credible, because 300 F–16 and 24 B–52 sorties had been flown against these Iraqi elite units during the fifteen days since the war had started.[32]

The ARCENT and CENTAF staffs fundamentally disagreed on how the strength of Iraqi units should be measured. The G–2 briefers adopted the criterion that was endorsed by General Schwarzkopf's ground campaign planners: a unit was ineffective when 50 percent of its equipment was destroyed. They defined "equipment" as being three categories: tanks, artillery, and APCs. CENTAF officers, however, advocated a broader definition to include ammunition depots, supply concentrations, command posts, and food, water, and other stores that were essential for keeping any unit operational.[33]

Air Force critics of ARCENT's BDA briefings also believed that the G–2 analysts contributed to their own frustrations by refusing to accept pilot reports as a source of information on the results of air attacks. CENTAF officers, including General Horner, readily acknowledged that these accounts sometimes were exaggerated, but they believed it would have been wiser to use them judiciously than to reject them altogether. On February 3, they learned that ARCENT G–2 drew on A–10 pilot reports of damage to Iraqi units while it ignored those from F–16s, B–52s, and all other Coalition aircraft. When General Horner questioned an AR-CENT senior officer about this practice during a CENTCOM meeting, he received an answer that damaged the credibility of the Army's BDA briefings. As the CENTAF commander later recalled the exchange: "I said, 'Why do you use A–10 pilot reports?' He said, 'Well, it's got two people in the airplane—you got two sets of eyes.'…I didn't say anything. I just let that fall on the floor, like a mighty drop of putty."[34]

ARCENT analysts eventually accepted F–111 videotape recordings as BDA evidence, but only reluctantly. General Glosson cited an instance at a CENTCOM staff meeting when, after ARCENT briefers reported only eleven tanks had been destroyed the night before, he played a videotape of Aardvark operations during the same period, which showed more than thirty tanks being blown up. Yet the G–2 analysts remained reluctant to credit the F–111 Pave Tack videotapes. When CENTAF video and other sources showed that the Aardvarks had destroyed over 100 Iraqi armored vehicles on February 9, G–2 officers rejected each of these claims. Only after several days of screening videotapes taken by the F–111s did ARCENT officers agree to accept these kills, and then only if the Ground Liaison Officer with the unit verified them and documented each one in a separate report. Later in February, the G–2 analysts reluctantly agreed to credit this source as a routine part of their BDA process.[35]

The ARCENT evaluators also began accepting pilot reports, but only after receiving guidance from General Schwarzkopf to do so, and only with certain restrictions. The G–2 officers accepted this source only from A–10s. Furthermore, to "offset the uncertainties" accompanying this evidence, they counted as one-third of a kill each target that a Warthog mission report stated was destroyed, and they credited as one-half of a kill each target that an F–111 videotape recorded as destroyed. Air Force personnel contended that this procedure still overestimated the remaining strength of the Iraqi divisions and led to additional, unnecessary sorties against some of them.[36]

CENTAF officers also charged that the ARCENT analysts failed to establish a consistent standard for measuring the progress of the air campaign against the enemy's regular and Republican Guard divisions. The G–2 officers developed this credibility problem because they reevaluated the status of Iraqi units. When ARCENT's BDA showed that an enemy division had been reduced to 49 percent effectiveness, the Army evaluators "froze" the assessment at that level while high-resolution imagery was used to reevaluate it. This created situations in the G–2 briefings in which the Iraqi forces sometimes dropped in strength, and later—despite the continuing air attacks over the KTO—were posited to have gained in effectiveness. On February 19, for example, ARCENT briefers assessed the Iraqi 20th Infantry Division as 49 percent effective; earlier, they had reported that it had been rendered completely ineffective. On the same day, they evaluated the 35th and the 30th Infantry Divisions as 49 percent effective; previously, they had assessed them at 5 and 9 percent, respectively. The G–2 officers similarly reassessed a number of other Iraqi units in this presentation. Nor did their difficulties end after the ground campaign began: on February 26, they credited the enemy with more artillery pieces than he had possessed on the preceding day.[37]

The inconsistencies of these briefings bemused the CENTAF officers in their audience. "We saw their enemy unit strengths go down," one KTO planner recounted, "and then come back up, down, and then back up." "It almost got to be a humorous part of the briefing," another CENTAF officer recalled, "when they'd throw those slides up, trying to tell General Horner what the combat effectiveness of the frontline [Iraqi] divisions were, and the Republican Guard units. He'd chuckle every now and then, because they'd changed how they'd figured it; the numbers would change." The CENTAF commander remembered "the little pie charts, these little circles" used by the ARCENT briefers to illustrate what percentage of an enemy division remained operational. "They would run them down on the Iraqi army," General Horner explained, until they recognized that a unit was 20 percent destroyed. Then, he continued, "they would crank them back up to

80 percent. If you took their BDA as it progressed and didn't crank it back up, then they should have started the ground war two weeks before they did."[38]

General Schwarzkopf sympathized with a number of CENTAF's views about BDA. On January 29, he commented on the lack of BDA information on the Republican Guard, recommended the use of pilot reports, and indicated that CENT-COM J–2 was overly conservative in evaluating the number of destroyed Iraqi vehicles. On February 11, ARCENT officers briefed General Schwarzkopf that the average strength of the enemy's frontline divisions, for the first time, had fallen below 50 percent. The following day, in a significant piece of guidance that strongly endorsed CENTAF's point of view, the CENTCOM commander directed that Coalition aircraft were not to bomb any Iraqi units that were evaluated as under 50 percent strength.[39]

CENTAF officers welcomed General Schwarzkopf's guidance, and they acknowledged that ARCENT's intelligence officers faced a daunting task. General Corder reflected after the war that the use of pilot reports had improved the BDA, "but it still was not a clear picture. I'm not sure a clear picture in the numeric terms they wanted was ever going to be possible. I don't know how you keep track of that stuff." Iraqi deception tactics further compounded the problem. One CENTAF planner commented sympathetically on the Army's task: "How do you tell the live [Iraqi vehicles] from the dead ones, and the decoys? It's very tough. … You just do the best you can."[40]

In one dramatic instance, the Iraqis moved beyond these passive deceptions and actively seized the initiative, waging what was called the Battle of Khafji but was actually a series of engagements along the Kuwaiti-Saudi border between January 29 and 31. Without Iraqi sources, it was impossible to know what Saddam Hussein intended to accomplish by these attacks. The consensus of Coalition leaders was that the Iraqi dictator hoped to draw his enemy's forces—American units in particular—into a bloody combat, spur them to begin a precipitous ground campaign, and inflict losses on them so high that congressional and public opinion would turn against the war. "The Iraqi objective," SAC intelligence officers reported shortly after the battle began, "is probably to force Coalition forces to begin a premature ground offensive."[41] Allied commanders also suggested that Saddam Hussein took the initiative at Khafji in an effort to capture prisoners and gain badly needed intelligence about the Coalition forces.[42]

Hussein chose for his offensive the eastern flank of the Coalition, near Ras al Khafji, Saudi Arabia. This oil and resort town was just south of the Kuwaiti border on the strategically important route from Kuwait City to Dhahran. The coastal road ran south from Kuwait, passing through marshland and climbing onto the rising terrain around Khafji. On January 29, this town was abandoned; its roughly 35,000 residents had begun evacuating the region on the first day of the war.[43]

This section of the Coalition front was held by troops from three nations: Saudi Arabia, Qatar, and the United States. Units of the I Marine Expeditionary Force (I MEF) had defended the area at the opening of the war, but, with the massive redeployment that followed the start of the air campaign, the Joint Forces Command–East (JFC–E) now had the primary responsibility for the coastal sector. One battalion of the Saudi Arabian National Guard (SANG) and a Qatari tank battalion covered the road south from Khafji, supported by other JFC–E units.[44] In late January, small Marine Corps units were reconnoitering the area, staging artillery raids and screening along the Kuwaiti-Saudi border.[45] Task Force Taro, composed of the 3d Marine Regiment of the 1st Marine Division, was patrolling near Khafji.[46] The 2d Marine Light Armored Infantry (LAI) Battalion, which belonged to the 2d Marine Division, was moving through the area about thirty miles west of the town and due south of the Wafra oilfield, which lay behind the Saddam Line in Kuwait.[47] Another thirty miles west, two other Marine units—the 1st Marine Division's Task Force Sheperd, made up of the 1st LAI Battalion, and Company D of the 3d LAI Battalion—were screening the region south of the heel of Kuwait.[48]

The Iraqis struck into Saudi Arabia in three columns, battalion-sized or larger, representing elements of two III Corps divisions, the 5th Mechanized and the 3d Armored. They also intended to attack Khafji with two small naval contingents, but Coalition helicopters, A–6s, and RAF Jaguars broke up these convoys well offshore.[49] Among the three ground columns, the farthest west was a mechanized task force, consisting of a T–62 tank battalion, reinforced with APCs, BMP–2s, and BTR–60s. This force advanced southwest out of the heel of Kuwait, moving toward the region of Al Qaraah and putting itself on a collision course with Task Force Sheperd.[50] The enemy's central column, consisting of roughly fifty tanks and twenty-nine APCs, moved south from the Wafra oilfield and encountered the 2d LAI Battalion.[51] The eastern contingent took the coastal road directly toward Khafji. Marine sources originally estimated this force at forty-one vehicles, and it gained strength as it moved south.[52] The Iraqis also massed artillery pieces from at least three batteries near the Kuwaiti-Saudi border in support of the operation.[53] What the enemy vitally lacked, however, was air support—another testimony to the Coalition's early success against the Iraqi Air Force.[54]

The Battle of Khafji began at approximately 2030 local time on January 29, when a Marine Corps patrol reported seeing thirty-five vehicles of the enemy's western column approaching Outpost 4 (OP–4), which was held by Task Force Sheperd.[55] Under other circumstances, J–STARS doubtless would have alerted theater commanders to this Iraqi attack, but, at the time the enemy was moving south, one E–8A was "down" while the second was operating far west of Kuwait, serving in the Scud hunt. Thus it was that the Checkmate office initially alerted Headquarters CENTAF at about 1900 that national intelligence sources indicated preparations for an Iraqi offensive.[56] About a half hour after Checkmate's 1900 alert to the theater, Marine pilots reported Iraqi vehicles heading south toward the rear of the enemy's western column in an apparent effort to reinforce it. The

TACC directed twenty A–10 sorties against these units, breaking up the reserve force before the main body began its attack south.[57]

At approximately 2030, the Iraqi western column advanced from the heel of Kuwait, crossed the berm that ran in front of the Saddam Line along the border, and encountered Task Force Sheperd at OP–4, near an abandoned Saudi police post at Umm Hjul. The Marines picked up the images of the advancing Iraqi tanks on their thermal sights, began defending themselves with fire from their light armored vehicles (LAVs), and soon received air support.[58] Shortly after 2300, Task Force Sheperd reported being heavily engaged, and three Special Operations AC–130H Spectre gunships, two F–15Es, two F–16Ls, and four A–10s joined the battle. Two more Warthogs went on alert at King Fahd International Airport, ready if needed.[59]

Marine firepower and CENTAF air power defeated the Iraqis at OP–4. While one of the AC–130s from the 1st Special Operations Wing met the oncoming enemy formation with cannon fire, the A–10s fired Maverick missiles and the F–16Ls delivered CBU–87 munitions against it. The Marines initially reported that seven Iraqi tanks were destroyed: three by their antitank missiles and four by CENTAF aircraft.[60] The fighting continued for several hours and ended with the Iraqis retreating north from OP–4 into the heel of Kuwait. After daylight on the thirtieth, aerial reconnaissance showed that the enemy's losses were larger than first thought: twenty-two tanks and vehicles were burning in the desert near the abandoned Umm Hjul police post.[61] Mopping up the next morning, the Coalition forces captured seventeen Iraqis after 1000. "It appeared to us," a Marine platoon commander later wrote, "that these Iraqis surrendered after fleeing their vehicles because of the presence of A–10s on the battlefield in the morning hours."[62]

However, a tragedy marred this victory at OP–4. The first Coalition fratricide of the war occurred when an A–10 launched a Maverick that killed eleven Marines. At 2148, the pilot fired at a target identified by a forward air controller's ground flare. His missile, instead of following its IR guidance, went straight down like a conventional gravity weapon, hitting a LAV below his A–10. The Marine captain who commanded Company D of the 3d LAI Battalion later described the rapid sequence of events from his perspective on the ground, during the combat. The A–10, he recounted, "dropped a ground flare on our right flank. We didn't know initially where it came from and 1st Platoon dismounted a scout to bury the flare." Company D's executive officer alerted the Marines that this had been "a friendly mark and asked for an azimuth and range" from the LAV "closest to the flare to a group of enemy vehicles. Just as the XO [executive officer] was receiving this information, Red 2 exploded in a ball of flames." The Marine company commander at first assumed that the Iraqis had flanked his unit, and he had his LAVs sweep the area with their thermal detectors. When they found no enemy tanks, he radioed the nearest Marine company to see if they had mistakenly fired on his vehicles. "The report was negative," he stated, "as they were still 12 klicks

Lucrative Targets

[kilometers] away. The XO on the company tactical net then said he thought it was friendly air."[63]

This tragedy did not halt the fighting near Umm Hjul or the other Iraqi advances into Saudi Arabia. As these enemy probes continued during the night of the twenty-ninth, General Horner asked the J–STARS shortly after 2230 to observe the border areas where the Iraqis were marshalling. The E–8A aircraft identified three breaks in the tank obstacles along the Saddam Line, as well as columns of enemy vehicles moving south. Maj. Gen. Burton R. Moore, CENT-COM J–3, suggested that the J–STARS also move north and investigate the possibility that the Iraqis intended to follow up their initial probes with an attack by the Republican Guard. Of course, the Marine commanders were interested in the same information: they had assessed the size of the forces that they had engaged so far, but they wanted the E–8A aircraft to determine if their opponents would be reinforced. J–STARS carried out this mission and found that the Republican Guard had put some individual vehicles—but no convoys—on the road. The E–8A surveillance thus confirmed that the Iraqi elite units did not intend to join the Battle of Khafji.[64]

Soon after the Battle of Khafji had begun with the 2030 attack by the Iraqi western column, the central one advanced from the Wafra oilfield, just north of the Saddam Line, to attack the 2d LAI Battalion's OP–1. At approximately 2100, Headquarters 2d Marine Division received the first of several reports of enemy armor and APCs moving south in this sector. The Marines opened fire with their antitank missiles and the automatic cannons mounted on their LAVs and, like their comrades farther west, received air support. Before 2240, General Horner received word at the TACC that fifty tanks were approaching the 2d LAI Battalion. He itemized the aircraft then available to join the battle rapidly: the Marine Corps assets were one OV–10D, an EA–6, two A–6s, two A–6Es, two AV–8s, two F/A–18Ds, and three AH–1 and three AH–1E Cobra gunships; Air Force assets included two A–10s, two LANTIRN-equipped F–16Ls, and two F–15Es. While the Strike Eagles checked in with the ABCCC to learn where they could serve best, the Warthogs, Falcons, and Marine aircraft flew to the aid of the 2d LAI Battalion.[65] At 2250, the Marine battalion reported to its division that it was engaging twenty-nine APCs. For about three hours, A–10s, F–16Ls, A–6s, and AV–8s struck at the enemy vehicles in front of the 2d LAI Battalion.[66] By 0220 on the thirtieth, the Iraqis had abandoned their effort and retreated back toward Wafra. Later that morning, at 1000, the Marines reported that only enemy stragglers remained north of OP–1.[67]

The Iraqis posed no further threat to the 2d LAI Battalion, but farther west they remained troublesome. Coalition aircrews continued through the night to attack tanks and APCs that marshalled in an apparent effort to renew the advance from the heel of Kuwait. At 0235 on the thirtieth, Task Force Sheperd reported that air strikes had destroyed ten to fifteen enemy tanks north of OP–4. At 0350, the TACC directed twenty A–10s against two concentrations of Iraqi armor: one west of the heel of Kuwait, doubtless mobilizing to renew the attack in the Umm Hjul sector; and the other convoy gathered in the central part of the country, possibly intending to move south.[68]

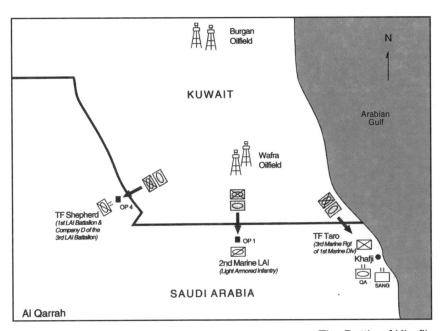

The Battle of Khafji.

While Coalition forces stopped the Iraqi western and central columns during the night of January 29/30, the eastern one proved more successful. Moving down the coastal road, the enemy tankers approached Khafji with their gun turrets reversed, signaling to Western armored combatants an intention to surrender. The Saudi and Qatari defenders south of the town hesitated, and the Iraqis ran their T–55s into the abandoned community, seizing their objective.[69] Two six-member teams from Task Force Taro were reconnoitering in Khafji when the enemy arrived. One of these Marine patrols took cover in a culvert along the town's main street, the other on the roof of a building, and began calling in air support.[70]

Brig. Gen. Prince Ahmed bin Musaid al-Sudairy, the RSAF's deputy chief of staff for operations who was coordinating the operations of his country's F–5s with the USAF's A–10s, called the TACC at 0130 on January 30 with the report that Iraqi tanks had entered Khafji. Col. John Robbin, the MARCENT liaison officer in the TACC, rapidly confirmed that four or five pieces of enemy armor and five or six APCs had entered the town and that a CENTAF AC–130 also had been on the scene for the past thirty to forty minutes. This gunship continued to operate through the early morning hours of the thirtieth, in one instance catching out in the open several Iraqi vehicles and their personnel. A second AC–130 relieved it before dawn. Through the night of January 29/30, Marine OV–10 Broncos worked as FACs of the air operations around Khafji, and A–10s and an accompanying O/A–10 joined the battle the next day.[71]

As early as 0415 on the thirtieth, the Saudis expressed their willingness to recapture Khafji. General Schwarzkopf and other senior Coalition leaders recognized that the American press and public might assign an exaggerated significance to the Iraqis' ability to hold the town for several days, but they otherwise felt no urgency about retaking a collection of abandoned buildings that had no military value. Nor was there any immediate concern about the two reconnaissance teams: the commander of Task Force Taro estimated that these twelve Marines could remain undetected for thirty-six to forty-eight hours. Finally, and most significantly, CENTAF aircrews had the skies over Khafji to themselves, making a precipitous ground attack unnecessary. General Schwarzkopf later acknowledged that he had been "so satisfied" with the tactical position at Khafji that he "ignored Saudi sensibilities" about allowing the enemy to continue occupying one of their towns.[72]

The battle continued during the morning of January 30, with the Iraqis mounting another attack in the west, against Task Force Sheperd. At 0750, Headquarters I MEF reported that forty enemy tanks were attacking OP–4. They were abruptly repulsed, and, at 0930, after air strikes destroyed an estimated fifteen pieces of Iraqi armor, the Iraqis retreated. At 1000, the Marines confirmed that the surviving enemy tanks were back north of the border, and the main action of the battle shifted back east, to Khafji.[73]

With the return of daylight on the thirtieth, Marine Cobra gunships began patrolling the area around the enemy-occupied town, flying north along the coastal road above Khafji to the border. Although these helicopter crews saw no Iraqi soldiers or active vehicles, the enemy reopened the battle with other weapons. At 1000, three artillery batteries posted north of the town began firing on the allies. A–10s and Marine aircraft immediately attacked these field guns and the vehicles near them.[74]

Early in the afternoon some of the Iraqis in Khafji indicated a willingness to surrender. Their offer proved to be another ruse: when a SANG negotiating team came out in the open, the enemy fired on them. The Saudis and Qataris renewed the battle, supported by A–10s and Marine AV–8Bs and A–6s. Bad weather hindered the afternoon's air operations, imposing a 4,000-foot ceiling.[75]

During the second night of the Battle of Khafji (January 30/31), senior Marine officers, including MARCENT commander Lt. Gen. Walter Boomer, asked the TACC for B–52 strikes into Kuwait. Concerned that the Iraqis were massing tanks that would move south to Khafji or against the Marine outposts along the border, the Marine commanders specifically requested BUFF sorties. At least one CENTAF senior officer pointed out that the B–52s were not the aircraft best suited to close air support,[76] and another recommended that these bombers continue to hit the elite Republican Guard and not be diverted against the enemy's probing forces. But General Horner understood the psychology behind the Marine request. He later reflected, with some humor in his tone, "[Ground guys] always ask for B–52s. Ground guys always ask for B–52s first."[77] The CENTAF commander later directed the heavy bombers to join the battle.

At approximately 2000, J–STARS imagery had shown a convoy of about seventy Iraqi armored vehicles, which divided into two columns as it reached a road junction in central Kuwait. Roughly two-thirds of the main body took the fork to the southwest, toward the tri-border area of Kuwait, Saudi Arabia, and Iraq. The remaining one-third of the vehicles branched off to the southeast, heading for the coast and Khafji.[78]

The Marine commanders understandably were interested in both of these formations. Just before the Iraqi attack, Lt. Gen. Prince Khalid bin Sultan bin Abd al-Aziz had arrived in the area to inspect the Saudi troops. He found himself with the SANG battalion during the battle and so was concerned, even more than the Marines, about any Iraqi armor that might attack Khafji.[79] After talking to General Boomer at 2200, General Horner directed B–52s, F–15Es, and F–16Ls against the southwestern Iraqi column.[80]

The fighters checked in with the ABCCC and began attacking enemy vehicles along their assigned stretch of the road to the tri-border region. Four B–52s began orbiting over the road intersection where the two Iraqi columns diverged. The bombers waited for an F–4G that would deal with the SA–6s defending the area. Their orbiting also gave the J–STARS time to update the imagery of the Iraqi convoys. When the TACC learned that the F–4G already had passed through the area, the B–52s attacked without it, delivering their M117s from altitudes high enough to avoid the enemy SAMs.[81]

At the same time that General Horner directed the aircraft against the southwestern Iraqi column, he also sent A–10s and AC–130s against the southeastern one. While the F–16Ls and F–15Es worked the road to the tri-border region, the Warthogs and gunships operated along the coastal road to Khafji. Marine A–6s covered the area between these two roads, patrolling along the Kuwaiti border.[82]

Working closely with the ABCCC, the A–10s maintained a continuous flow over the coastal road throughout the night of January 30/31, and the AC–130s concentrated on the area north of Khafji.[83] Three gunships contributed to this mission: the first began operations at approximately 2200, a second launched at 2303 to give constant coverage during refuelings, and a third went on ground alert at the same time.[84] The first AC–130 on station spent an effective twenty minutes between 2330 and 2350 in an attack on the Iraqis along the coastal road north of Khafji, assisted by an Air Naval Gunfire Liaison Company (ANGLICO) team that helped direct its fire. At 0040 on the thirty-first, this gunship radioed that it had attacked "various vehicles, trucks, and personnel" along the route north of the town and had destroyed three AAA sites and a radar van. The crew reported that they had "cleaned off" the coastal road south of the border and now were working north of it. They remained on station until they had exhausted their ammunition.[85]

At 0230, the Saudis and Qataris entered Khafji from the south and, supported by Marine fire teams, began their attack to recapture the town. At 0445, the SANG battalion reported that it had destroyed one Iraqi tank and also had established radio contact with the Marines in Khafji. The fighting among the buildings continued into the daylight.[86]

As dawn approached on the thirty-first, the second AC–130 to operate north of Khafji—call sign Spirit 03—was due to end its station time at 0600. As it began to get light, the gunship's fourteen crew members turned their attention to a mobile Frog–7 battery, which, left undisturbed, could have fired its ground-to-ground missiles into Khafji. Spirit 03 successfully attacked this target, but the mission left the AC–130, accustomed to the cover of darkness, operating in the vulnerability of daylight. At 0635, an AWACS received the crew's last radio communication: "Mayday."[87] An AWACS officer recalled, "We heard the Mayday call, which was short. Then we tried to vector people in [to search for Spirit 03]....They were trying to see if the wreckage was on the shore. It's hard to tell when you're just looking at a blip on the scope." Bad weather and battle smoke hindered the CENTAF pilots who searched for Spirit 03, and it was not until the morning of March 4 that an HC–130 Combat Shadow found the wreckage in the Persian Gulf.[88]

In spite of this tragic loss, Coalition forces brought the Battle of Khafji to a successful conclusion on January 31. During the morning, the allies continued to regain control of the town and the isolated vigil of the two Marine patrols ended at approximately 1200. During the afternoon, the number of surrendering Iraqi soldiers began to mount. At 1400, Headquarters JFC–E reported that Khafji had been liberated, with a few remaining pockets of resistance being cleared in building-to-building fighting.[89] JFC–E noted that 160 Iraqis had been captured (a figure that later grew to more than 600) and also that Coalition forces were moving north from the town to establish a defensive line closer to the border. At 1415, elements of two Iraqi tank companies moved south from Kuwait, apparently making a belated effort to aid their countrymen in Khafji. Saudi forces moving north from the town met this enemy armor and, supported by ten A–10s, forced it to retreat north along the coast road.[90]

The Iraqis who escaped capture in Khafji made their way north. Into the evening of the thirty-first, Coalition aircrews struck at these retreating forces. Headquarters I MEF reported at 1800 that air attacks north of Khafji had destroyed eleven tanks, six APCs, five trucks, and a mobile SAM unit. Pilots reported that so many burning vehicles lay along the coastal road between the town and the border that they had difficulty identifying any more targets. "The 5th Mechanized Division," General Schwarzkopf later pointed out, "which had been rated one of their finest armored units,...was almost totally destroyed—we monitored Iraqi reports afterward that indicated that only twenty percent of that division made it back." The Coalition estimated that it had destroyed more than ninety

Iraqi tanks and APCs during the battle. During the days after January 31, there were small actions in northern Saudi Arabia, but the Battle of Khafji—the only major Iraqi ground offensive of the war—was over.[91]

In this engagement, the enemy had seized the initiative, gained what General Horner later acknowledged was something of a tactical surprise, and forced the Coalition to react. Yet the Battle of Khafji created no problems that CENTAF could not promptly resolve. Perhaps the largest mistake the allies could have made—as General Corder and others pointed out at the time—would have been to overreact to the Iraqi probes along the border and to divert air resources away from the Republican Guard and other important Phase III targets.[92]

The Battle of Khafji proved to be the only significant initiative taken by Hussein's ground forces. The Coalition commanders correctly assessed the Iraqi probing attacks and refused to be drawn prematurely into a major engagement. Unruffled by the enemy's initiative, General Schwarzkopf dismissed Saddam Hussein's initial claims of success: "Moving into an unoccupied village when there's no opposition, I don't call that a military victory." On the morning of January 30, General Boomer assured his staff: "Other than our loss[es], I am not unhappy with last night.... I think our air [power] probably stopped them; so whatever it was they were trying to do, [it] wasn't very successful." After the battle's second night at Khafji, the Marine commander was even more confident. "In my view," he asserted, "[Saddam Hussein is] playing into our hands.... I think if he decides to come across...the same thing will happen to him that happened to him night before last. [Our] divisions are in a good position.... If he wants to come across, fine."[93]

The Battle of Khafji sharpened the perception that the Iraqi troops were in poor condition. By late January, the air campaign had taken its toll on the enemy. Saddam Hussein undoubtedly selected some of his best regular units to undertake this important offensive, and yet even these forces were ill supplied. On January 29, Saudi officers at an observation post on the border reported that the Iraqi soldiers were eating whatever forage they could find and were carrying off the rest. Enemy troops west of Khafji, General Horner noted on the same day, were looking for food and supplies. After the border battle of late January, a Marine regimental commander said, "We concluded that the Iraqi Army had no resolve." General Schwarzkopf agreed: "I concluded with great relief that the Iraqi army wasn't half as skilled or highly trained as it had been portrayed, and all we should really worry about in the future was their use of unconventional weapons."[94]

Most telling of all, CENTAF aircrews controlled the skies throughout the engagement. Immediately after the action ended, CENTCOM intelligence officers pointed out that "lack of air cover [had] severely inhibited the Iraqi ground forces' ability to operate" during the battle. The attack at Khafji, Colonel Warden later asserted, "just plain got smashed" by air power. General Horner recounted CENTAF's reply to the Iraqi initiative: "We found LANTIRNs, gunships, B–52s, and just kept air pouring in there. Air broke up that attack, I'm absolutely convinced of it."[95] In several areas—the sound judgment of the allied leaders, the poor condition of the Iraqi troops, and, most significantly, the complete dominance of the air by the Coalition—Khafji proved a harbinger of the ground campaign to come.

Unfortunately, the victory also carried a dark underlining. With the tragedy of the Maverick destroying the Marine LAV, the issue of fratricide surfaced in the press. Before the Battle of Khafji, few Americans had given much thought to the possibility of casualties by fire from friendly forces, but military professionals were long familiar with this ancient problem. At the Battle of Zama in 202 B.C. Hannibal's elephants, terrified by the blasts from Roman trumpets, stampeded into his own cavalrymen. During battles from ancient times, when troops deployed in phalanx, through the nineteenth century, when infantry fought in close-ordered line formations, soldiers sometimes mistakenly attacked their comrades. During the Revolutionary War, one American unit volleyed into another on the foggy Pennsylvania battlefield at Germantown, on October 4, 1777. A more famous episode occurred during the Civil War, on May 2, 1863, during the Battle of Chancellorsville in Virginia. That night Lt. Gen. Thomas Jonathan Jackson and his staff rode out to scout the Union positions along the Orange Turnpike. As these Confederate horsemen returned to their own lines, some Southern infantrymen mistook them in the moonlight for Federal cavalrymen, fired on them, and mortally wounded Gen. "Stonewall" Jackson, one of the most famous Civil War commanders. During the century after the Civil War, as weapons became more lethal and as tactics emphasized rapid, flexible maneuvers by small units, the danger of fratricide increased. Bitter experiences during the two world wars and in Korea and Vietnam underscored this horrible problem.[96]

By the 1990s, troops fought fast-paced combats, maneuvering rapidly across nonlinear battlefields, using high-technology weapons, navigating by satellite, communicating with other units by radio, and often waging simultaneous ground and air actions. These conditions increased enormously the risks of firing on friendly forces. In the specific case of the Gulf War, much of the combat occurred at night or under conditions of poor visibility, and Coalition units conducted the war's major ground campaign rapidly and over vast distances. Tanks delivered lethal fire across ranges of two miles, and artillery pieces operated against targets twenty miles distant. Each of these factors contributed to the likelihood of fratricide.[97]

Coalition leaders were keenly aware of this terrible problem and took preventive measures before Desert Storm (many of them still classified) to avoid such tragedies. In spite of these efforts, however, allied units sometimes fired on friendly forces. After the conflict, Department of Defense investigators identified twenty-eight such instances involving U.S. servicemen in which thirty-five Americans were killed and seventy-two others wounded.[98] Some of these cases involved air-to-ground fratricide, but, given the pace and stress of combat, the aircraft involved could not always be identified. It was known that an A–10 delivered the Maverick that killed eleven Marines at Umm Hjul, and another such aircraft launched an AGM–65 that resulted in the death of nine British soldiers, on February 26, during the ground campaign.[99]

During the war, Coalition leaders continued to emphasize the danger of fratricide and undertook a number of initiatives to prevent it. "All aircrews," General Olsen directed on February 3, "will be briefed on the extreme importance of ensuring that they have the proper target coordinates and are following proper procedures, especially when supporting troops in contact.... Some important items to discuss with your aircrews are target identification, forward air controller procedures, munitions effects and delivery accuracy." In mid-February, the allied units of JFC–E and JFC–N adopted CENTCOM's use of the inverted V marking to identify Coalition vehicles. The number of these conveyances soon exceeded the quantity of VS–17 panels in stock. Headquarters MARCENT met this contingency by allotting the available panels first to LAVs and amphibious assault vehicles, then to tanks, and finally to trucks. When convoys took the road, only the first and last units within a column, rather than all of them, displayed the markers on their roofs. At least one vehicle in every tactical formation was required to display a marking panel, as were all armored vehicles operating in forward areas during the daylight.[100]

On the eve of the ground campaign, General Moore, the CENTCOM J–3, provided some important guidance on measures to prevent fratricide. Among several other issues, he reviewed with the component commands the procedures for establishing and coordinating the fire support coordination line (FSCL). This demarcation played a crucial role in the effort to prevent fratricide. Between the front line and the FSCL, all aircraft sorties were under the positive control either of the ground forces or of airborne FACs who were in communication with them. Beyond the FSCL, attack aircraft were free to strike at any targets that they believed hostile.[101]

The difficulty in coordinating the FSCL while addressing other fire-control issues was compounded by the fact that Coalition aircraft and ground units often operated at night. After the war, General McPeak identified the common elements in the cases in which CENTAF aircraft mistakenly had made fatal attacks on their allies below them. "These mistakes were made," the chief of staff pointed out, "in the fog of combat, [during] heavy fighting on the ground. They were both done at night." Discussing the Umm Hjul tragedy in a postwar interview, Maj. Gen. J. M. Myatt, commander of the 1st Marine Division, emphasized the large number of vehicles on the battlefield that night.[102]

In view of the difficulties involved, it was remarkable that CENTAF aircrews were as successful as they were in minimizing fratricide. Whereas they mistakenly hit two Coalition vehicles, General McPeak pointed out that they probably attacked more than 10,000 such targets over the course of the war. General Corder expanded on this point, estimating that Coalition aircrews had "probably had 45 or 50,000 different occasions to shoot highly accurate, very deadly ordnance in the vicinity of our own people." It was equally remarkable that an air campaign that eventually generated 3,000 sorties a day ended unmarred by a single case of air-to-air fratricide.[103]

Given the realities on the battlefields of the late twentieth century, fratricide remains virtually inevitable. General Olsen pointed to an obvious truth about the dizzying pace of contemporary warfare: "People just get disoriented." In 1990, two analysts of the Iran-Iraq War offered some stark comments that applied to the Gulf War and other conflicts as well. "War kills," they wrote, "and it does not kill wisely or fairly. Nothing is ultimately more predictable than the fact that war will produce unpredictable losses."[104]

Although Coalition leaders could take steps to prevent fratricide, they could do little about another issue: the weather. Poor flying conditions had prevailed for ten days at the opening of the war, and they returned, in places, during mid-February. "Weather, heavy smoke and haze," an Air National Guard officer wrote on February 12, "have been ongoing problems in the AOR. Having to work at the higher altitudes and not being able to get under lower overcast…have hindered operations." During the next day, ceilings dropped as low as 8,000 feet, and pilots saw smoke plumes over southern Kuwait from the oilfields torched by the Iraqis. Early the same morning, weather officers told the TACC's nighttime director of combat operations that they expected a front to move in that afternoon. "Well," he replied facetiously, "you've got six to eight hours to fix it."[105] On February 14, the weather proved fair over most of the theater, but a morning fog covered the Kuwaiti coast and winds of more than twenty miles per hour blew dust across southern Iraq. This turned out to be the only day, after January 24, when CENTAF flew fewer than 150 sorties against the Republican Guard.[106] Perhaps the worst weather of the period came on February 17, when rain fell across Kuwait and southeastern Iraq, followed by an evening fog that kept visibility low. CENTAF aircrews aborted 300 sorties and scored only thirteen confirmed tank kills for the day.[107]

The spotty weather of mid-February proved less troublesome than the more widespread bad conditions of January had been. Aircrews found the later period less frustrating than the initial one, which had come at the opening of the war. Further, weather was a greater consideration in operations over Iraq, where the F–117s and PGMs played so large a role, than it was over the KTO. "Regardless of the weather," Colonel Baptiste emphasized, "we pretty much tried to get the job done, and, if we lost a sortie, we had so many sorties going in the KTO—it was just a continuous flow of strikers in there—that regardless of what the weather was, we were going to press on." Planners in the KTO cell had more options than did those in the Iraqi cell to "work around" bad flying conditions. A TACC logbook entry made at 0800 on February 20, when the weather was "doggy" in the KTO, illustrated one such case: "Expect to lose many KTO & Basrah missions. A–10s on [weather] hold. F–16s being sent west to better weather."[108] Colonel Baptiste also pointed out that "down in the KTO, we didn't have to worry so much [as the Iraqi cell did] about collateral damage and what might happen if you missed a target. Most of our maneuver-unit targets were out away from Kuwait City and [the] inhabited areas, and those that were close to Kuwait City, obviously we were very conservative on."[109]

Weather was one of several factors that necessitated changes in the ATO. The Scud attacks, fraught with diplomatic implications, forced rapid changes in the ATO. Col. Mark A. Winstel, who directed the AWACS ACE effort, commented, "We did some real dancing with the ATO, trying to kill Scuds and trying to make sure that we were knocking them out at an incredible rate." New reconnaissance or BDA information about targets also led to changes in the ATO for the next day's operations, or even the one for that same day on which the new data was gained. Recently gained intelligence created the majority of the changes in the ATO.[110] Movements by friendly forces were another source: if a shift by a ground unit introduced the slightest possibility for fratricide, planners had to amend the tasking order. Feedback from weapons specialists provided yet another source of changes. "Some of these mission specialists would run in," Colonel Deptula recalled, "and say, well, we don't have this munition...or they would have suggestions, we don't want to hit that target because of this or that or the other thing, or this would be a better [target]. Those kind of changes occurred all the time."[111]

CENTAF officers accepted some of these changes in the ATO as inevitable, the result of variables beyond their control. Colonel Baptiste pointed to the weather as an obvious source of unavoidable alterations in the ATO. General Horner considered some alterations to the ATO as a favorable development, in that they indicated that his command was gaining useful intelligence and acting promptly on it. On February 6, he told his staff not to hope for changes in the ATO "to go away, because if they do, that just means our intelligence is getting worse and worse." After the war, General Olsen commented that the "dual hatting" of General Glosson as Headquarters CENTAF's chief planner and 14th Provisional Air Division commander had proven helpful, because it allowed Glosson to expedite changes in the ATO based on recent intelligence. Colonel Deptula characterized the arrangement as "a stroke of genius," because it authorized General Glosson to telephone directly the unit commanders and discuss changes and other guidance.[112]

Although CENTAF planners acknowledged that alterations in the tasking order were inevitable, they shared the hope expressed by General Horner on February 4 that "our changes will become fewer and fewer as we learn to build a reacting force that will accommodate good intelligence [which] we get on very short notice."[113] The CENTAF commander was keenly aware of this issue, and, as early as the third day of the war, he directed that any ATO alterations proposed in the TACC be submitted in writing to Colonel Doman. General Corder later listed the "mechanics of getting out the ATO" and "managing the [ATO] change process inside the TACC" as two of his most significant day-to-day problems during Desert Storm. Officers in the KTO cell developed a standardized form, which helped them process more smoothly the amendments made to the ATO. Colonel Baptiste remained concerned that his planners were obliged to make immediately some changes that could have waited a day or been processed through the normal seventy-two-hour ATO cycle. Major Sweeney pointed out that the shifts in ARCENT's BDA statistics sometimes created changes in the ATO. "That created problems," he stated shortly after the war, "for the targeting in [the KTO cell] at night.... Based on those [BDA] statistics, [ARCENT] would say 'Do this,' or 'Don't do this,' and that would turn into a change in direction, and very frequently that occurred during the night, which delayed the process of getting the ATO done." Other CENTAF officers contended that the Checkmate and Black Hole planners also had to accept responsibility for some of the rapid changes in the ATO, because they often urged acting quickly on new intelligence, rather than waiting to fold it into the normal ATO cycle. Finally, some observers believed that the dual-hatting of the director of campaign plans and 14th Air Division commander also contributed to the number of late alterations in the tasking order.[114]

Changing the ATO was a significant issue because the tasking order was an enormous document, consisting of thousands of individual pieces of interrelated information. A single substitution created a "ripple effect," requiring a series of alterations throughout the ATO. If an aircraft was moved from one ingress route to another, for example, it might become necessary to shift other airplanes already planned for that path. This, in turn, might create what one planner called "cascading changes," in tanker support, frequencies available, search and rescue arrangements, and other considerations, for any number of aircrews, as one alteration of the ATO multiplied into others. "You really have a ripple effect," Colonel Baptiste explained, "when you change something. You have to make sure that all the support assets know about it, make sure that all the tankers know about it, so you don't end up with a refueling programmed without tankers."[115]

Changes made late in the tasking order process raised a particularly sensitive issue because they introduced delays, made it difficult to keep the MAP current, diverted planners from their ongoing work, and, above all, adversely affected aircrews. Early in Desert Storm, according to one E–3 officer, the ATO "was changing so fast that on AWACS we couldn't even keep up with the changes, and at times you would kind of lose grip of where people were going and what they were supposed to be doing.... Not just from the AWACS standpoint, but from the TACC viewpoint also, and the wings. We were jerking aircrews around seriously." As early as January 19, General Horner directed his staff: "Do not make a change to that ATO without getting it in writing.... And remember, the people that we are really hurting are the crews in the field."[116] "If [an aircrew member] doesn't get the word [of an ATO change] until he's almost ready to step," Colonel Baptiste said, "then that's putting him in a tough situation—to change his mission on him, just as he's ready to step.... We need to be more sensitive to the effect of [ATO] changes to the guy walking out to the cockpit, the guy in the field, and keep those changes to the absolute minimum that are necessary."[117]

Another collection of ATO issues centered on the contentions of Navy officers, Marine Corps leaders, and others that the ATO process was "inflexible," that the CAFMS system was too slow, and that the JTCB should have been chaired by a member of the CENTCOM commander's staff. The critics of the tasking order system argued that its tightly defined seventy-two-hour cycle was too rigid to respond to the contingencies of rapid combat. In an interview in November 1991, Lt. Gen. Royal N. Moore, Jr., USMC, argued this point of view. "If you're trying to build a war for the next 72 to 96 hours," he asserted, "you can probably build a pretty good war. But if you're trying to fight [on] a fluid battlefield like we were on, then you need a system that can react." As for the CAFMS, the fundamental complaint of Navy and Marine Corps officers was that it was incompatible with their own command, control, and communications (C^3) architecture.[118] The issue of the JTCB chair was more wide-ranging, involving larger criticisms of the JFACC process. During the Gulf War, Navy and Marine Corps aircraft by no means always attacked the targets that their representatives nominated to the JTCB. Usually, the board gave priority to Air Force F–16s and A–10s for daytime operations and to F–111s and F–15Es for nighttime ones. To gain more sorties of their own, Marine planners cited the Corps' need to control the airspace over its own area of responsibility. The ABCCC coordinated with the TACC requests from the Marines for high-density airspace control zones over their forces, and, when the JFACC approved the dimensions of these zones, the ABCCC monitored the activity within them. Navy as well as USMC planners tried to gain more ATO sorties against tanks, but the Navy was generally less successful than the Marine Corps in its efforts.[119] Following these experiences, a Navy and Marine Corps "lessons learned" study published shortly after the war advocated that a member of the staff of the Joint Forces commander, rather than the JFACC, chair the JTCB.[120]

Acknowledging that no process was perfect, Air Force officers answered these criticisms. They contended that the final responsibility for prioritizing targets should remain with the JFACC. "We feel it should be at the JFACC level," Colonel Baptiste explained, "because he's staffed to do it and has the expertise to do it. And he's probably going to be the one that exercises during peacetime to do it." During the war, General Schwarzkopf strongly endorsed the authority of the JFACC. In a message on February 1 that commended to General Boomer "the contribution made by Marine air to date," the CINC also gave this guidance: "As we begin to shift attention to the KTO and battlefield preparation, I want you and Chuck Horner to work together to ensure that we strike key Iraqi targets in southeastern Kuwait. We must continue to utilize the JFACC concept to integrate all available air assets[,] while giving you maximum flexibility to shape the battlefield in your assigned sector."[121] After the war, Air Force officers pointed out that the ABCCC had been willing to delegate airspace to Marine Corps aircraft during Desert Storm, but it had done so only because the Marine Corps' DASC and its forward air controllers had been able to maintain communication with the Air

Force C^3 aircraft, and different circumstances might prevail during the next conflict.[122]

As for the Navy's inability to receive the ATO through CAFMS, this problem was addressed by having daily couriers fly a hard copy of the document to the ships. "This proved to be," one Navy captain wrote, "the fastest and most reliable method of getting them the ATO information they needed to support the air war…. The bottom line is that there were many problems in getting the ATO to the Navy ships, but it was accomplished and to my knowledge, there were no Navy missions canceled because it was not available."[123] After the war, the Navy began equipping its ships with the hardware needed to receive the ATO. By January 1992, three carriers and six other ships had added the CAFMS capability.[124]

The criticism that the ATO process was inflexible was valid, in a narrow way, in that it was true that the enormous document had to be produced within a fixed cycle of seventy-two hours. Air Force officers conceded that the system had its inefficiencies. After the war, General McPeak characterized the ATO's fixed cycle as "World War I stuff." During the conflict, in late January, another senior officer acknowledged that, if CENTAF were to prioritize all of the component commands' target requests, both preplanned and immediate, "we need to make some adjustments in our daily planning cycle." After Desert Storm, General Corder suggested that the TACC needed a more formal process for making ATO changes.[125] Such acknowledgments that procedures could be improved, however, did not mean that Air Force officers favored shortening the seventy-two hours of the tasking order cycle. They remained more inclined to retain the fixed, three-day period and to develop improved computer software to help prepare the ATO more efficiently.[126]

The critics may have scored their best point when they recommended that the Air Force study the responsiveness of the tasking order process. In a future conflict against an able air strategist who conducted dynamic offensives, the flexibility of the ATO system might prove a large consideration. The criticism that the ATO was "inflexible," however, had little bearing on the circumstances of Desert Storm, which put a greater premium on safe and efficient air operations than on rapid response to enemy initiatives. Judged on these terms, the prevailing conditions of the conflict, the ATO process was enormously successful, generating at its peak more than 3,000 sorties a day and concluding the war without an instance of air-to-air fratricide. "That we had no blue-on-blue air engagements," General Moore himself acknowledged, "and no mid-air collisions attest to the [success of the] coordination aspect of the process." "I don't know how we were able to pull it off," one TACC officer marveled, "without having mid-airs, and missed tankers, and air aborts because they didn't get lined up with their flight properly, and things like that. If you have been in a few mass gaggles in your life, you understand that this is a pretty intricate ballet that we do."[127]

It would be misleading to overemphasize these ATO, and other, issues that surfaced during the Gulf War, for they were far outweighed by CENTAF's advantages in its high-technology weapons, the time it had during Desert Shield to prepare for combat, its ample resources, and the mistakes of its opponent. The Coalition's strengths were great enough that its leaders never had to make some of the brutally harsh choices that combat can demand. As General Horner gratefully acknowledged after the war, "We never had to make a decision as to whether the French brigade died, or the Marine brigade died, or the Saudi brigade died."[128]

Although the leaders in the theater, most fortunately, never had to make decisions of that magnitude, they did have to face obstacles to their victory: issues of bombing accuracy, adjustments in tactics, problems in gaining timely and useful BDA, confusion introduced by the enemy, sorties canceled by weather, and stresses on the ATO process, among others. Such difficulties are inherent in all large military operations. The Gulf War verified Napoleon's belief that experienced commanders always expect problems in war and that only "the ignorant suspect no difficulties."[129]

Chapter Six

Jedi Knights and Push CAS:
Preparing for a Ground Campaign

Given the achievements of the first three phases of the air campaign, many CENTAF officers wanted to continue those efforts rather than move to Phase IV, the ground campaign against the Iraqis in the KTO. General Corder's views represented those of many airmen: "I told them from the first,…There's nothing wrong with the air war going for three months. Why attack? As long as [Saddam Hussein] doesn't pick up his stuff and try to get away, as long as he sits there and doesn't attack us, what's the big rush?" A year after Desert Storm, General Horner commented on the Air Force's hope that the air campaign alone would gain the victory. The CENTAF commander characterized the service's thinking: "We weren't so stupid as to think we were going to win it all on our own, but if we had, we were going to be happy…. It would have been great if it had happened that way and would have saved a lot of lives."[1]

On February 11, Air Staff planners, hoping to give the air campaign every chance to conclude the war before undertaking a ground offensive, recommended an "immediate surge effort to maximize air sorties and other firepower assets to concentrate on Iraqi forces in [the] KTO…. We must conduct a maximum effort over the next 2–3 weeks to achieve victory." A few days later, a Checkmate briefing drew on the precedent of World War II's "Big Week" air offensive of late February 1944 and called for a "Big Week II," an intensive, three-day operation that would have included 1,400 sorties a day against the Republican Guard and sixty F–117 sorties a day against targets in Iraq. These Air Staff planners believed that a "Big Week II" would hasten the end of the war by encouraging mass desertions and surrenders, might provoke a coup against Saddam Hussein, and would help prepare the battlefield for a ground campaign, should one prove necessary. If the "Big Week II" effort did not end the war, the Coalition still would have the option of refocusing its air efforts on the KTO and invading Kuwait, "if required."[2]

Lucrative Targets

Although airmen hoped to give their campaign every chance to end the war without a ground offensive, their very successes ironically hindered that intent. The more the air campaign achieved, the more the Coalition's ground commanders pressed to begin their own offensive. Colonel Warden believed that the success in the air strengthened the momentum to begin the land operations, and he concluded it was "only human" that the CENTCOM Deputy Commander (Lt. Gen. Calvin A. H. Waller) and the ARCENT Corps Commanders (Lt. Gen. Frederick Franks, Jr., and Lt. Gen. Gary E. Luck) wanted to start the ground offensive as soon as possible.[3] Although CENTAF planners preferred to continue "destroying" the battlefield rather than to begin "preparing" for a ground campaign, they assumed that such an operation was inevitable. The ground offensive, General Glosson said after the war, "was almost one of those things that had a life of its own. After it got to a certain stage and you had so many people over there, how do you say 'I don't need a land [campaign]'?" On February 3, one Black Hole planner confided to another, "The reality [is] this conflict will require a final Arab-Allied forces occupation—that will be measured in how well we prepare or destroy the area…. What must be necessarily done is a tactically valid clearing to maximize our ground troops' effectiveness so that all they have to do is take prisoners and reclaim Kuwait."[4]

The Coalition's senior leaders concluded much the same thing: that, however successful the air campaign, a ground offensive would be required to force the Iraqis from Kuwait. On February 5, President Bush commented to reporters that he was "skeptical" that air power alone could win the war. When General Schwarzkopf was asked, approximately fourteen months after Desert Storm, if he always had believed a ground war would be necessary, he replied emphatically, "Always." General Powell, at least as early as his comments in August 1990 on the "Instant Thunder" briefing, had indicated that a land campaign might be needed to destroy the Iraqi units in Kuwait.[5] On February 4, General McPeak told journalists that it was "very likely it will take the Army and Marines to deliver the 'two' punch," after air power delivered the "one" punch to Iraq. By late February, most members of Congress had concluded that a ground campaign was inevitable.[6]

A series of meetings among senior Coalition leaders in Riyadh during early February provided a forum on whether—and when—there would be a land offensive. Following his remarks to the press on February 5, President Bush sent Secretary Cheney and General Powell to confer with General Schwarzkopf and his component commanders. A White House official briefed journalists that the secretary and the chairman would "take a final look…[at] when the ground attack should begin." On February 9, the second of three days of meetings,[7] General Powell strongly advocated a ground offensive, expressing concern that the enemy's units would crumble and retreat before the Coalition forces could destroy them. General Schwarzkopf agreed with the chairman and recommended beginning the attack on February 21, with a window of three or four days to take into account the weather.[8] General Glosson, who attended the meeting on February 9, later recalled, "The only question that would be answered was when would the ground war start. All the 'ground guys' were ready for it to start." After Secretary Cheney returned to the Pentagon, Washington reporters noted that he "began to say 'when,' not 'if,' in his discussions of land and amphibious battle."[9]

At the beginning of the prewar crisis, inadequate forces had precluded any thought of a Coalition ground offensive. The initial question had been whether the first Americans to enter the theater would be able to defend themselves if the Iraqis continued into Saudi Arabia. During the early days of August, they stood virtually defenseless. General Horner recalled, "One night I said to [General Yeosock], 'Jack, what have you got to defend us?' He pulled out his pocketknife. That was it." The Desert Shield deployment rapidly increased the Coalition forces beyond the ARCENT commander's pocket arsenal, but their ground units remained modest in comparison with Saddam Hussein's. It was not until the 24th Mechanized Infantry Division arrived during September that CENTCOM leaders became confident that they had enough troops and armor to defend Saudi Arabia.[10] ARCENT did not have a full corps until October 30, the day General Luck's XVIII Airborne Corps, a light formation, first could report that its entire force was in the theater. Throughout the autumn, the Coalition ground forces remained heavily outnumbered and on the defensive.[11]

Given these force-structure realities that prevailed that fall, Headquarters CENTAF's special planning group gave little attention to Phase IV of the air campaign. The Black Hole planners had no way of knowing when the Coalition might be able to undertake a ground campaign, and they devoted their long days to the more pressing work of developing the first three phases of the air plan. During late August, Colonel Deptula later recalled, Air Force officers did not "talk about Phase IV. [We] were focusing on a three-phase air campaign." A Headquarters CENTAF operations order published on September second bore out his remarks. This document addressed the first three phases of the air campaign, dealing with Phase I in particular depth but containing nothing about Phase IV. As late as November 30, a Checkmate summary paper delineated in some detail the results that were optimistically expected from Phases I through III, but it did little more than acknowledge the possibility of a land invasion.[12]

CENTCOM planners, of course, had a different perspective and were quicker to turn their attention to the possibility of a ground campaign. With the 24th Mechanized Infantry Division arriving during September and alleviating the immediate threat of an Iraqi strike into Saudi Arabia, General Schwarzkopf could look ahead to the future possibility of an offensive of his own. He asked Army Chief of Staff General Carl E. Vuono to provide Headquarters CENTCOM with four graduates of the School of Advanced Military Studies of the Command and General Staff College. Army slang labeled such officers "Jedi Knights," a reference to the heroic figures in the popular *Star Wars* films. Lt. Col. Joseph H.

Lucrative Targets

Purvis, then at Headquarters Pacific Command J–5, and three other recent graduates of the Fort Leavenworth school arrived in Riyadh on September 16 and were assigned to Headquarters CENTCOM J–5. General Schwarzkopf gave them their initial guidance two days later, directing them to plan how the single corps currently in the theater would conduct a ground campaign. The CENTCOM commander made it clear that an indirect approach was to be preferred over a frontal assault against the Saddam Line. His preliminary concept of the campaign envisioned a drive across the Kuwaiti frontier to the Raudhatin oilfields, cutting the primary north-south route from Kuwait City to Iraq. General Schwarzkopf later acknowledged that he himself had reservations about this single-corps option, even as he outlined it for his planners. The work of the Jedi Knights, like that of the Black Hole officers, was to be highly classified and tightly compartmented.[13]

The Jedi Knights rapidly began their task. CENTCOM J–5 already had done some offensive planning and immediately made its work available to Colonel Purvis's cell. Within a week, the Jedi Knights had developed a set of fundamental considerations for an offensive plan. The most significant of these, from CENT-AF's perspective, concurred with General Schwarzkopf's view that the air campaign would have to reduce the Iraqi forces in the KTO by 50 percent before the Coalition would undertake a ground offensive.[14]

On October 6, the CENTCOM planning cell briefed General Schwarzkopf and his staff on their initial recommendations for a course of action. Their presentation called for the XVIII Airborne Corps to advance from Saudi Arabia between the tri-border area and the heel of Kuwait and to drive northeast to Al Jahrah, cutting the road north from Kuwait City. From here, General Luck's forces might continue the attack north to the Raudhatin oilfields and the Iraqi border beyond. After hearing this presentation, General Schwarzkopf made two specific suggestions: the attack would move from west of the heel of Kuwait to a point nearly forty miles north of Al Jahrah or Kuwait City, and the option of continuing on to the Raudhatin oilfields and the border would be included as a formal part of the plan.[15]

More important than these individual recommendations was the CENTCOM commander's fundamental conclusion that the enemy's advantage in numbers would put the mission of the XVIII Airborne Corps at risk.[16] General Schwarzkopf later said that, assuming his force was limited to a single corps, this approach was the best possible, but that the Jedi Knights' presentation reinforced his own original reservations about the concept. The CENTCOM commander went on to describe the operation as "a straight-up-the-middle charge right into the teeth of the Iraqi defenses." General Horner, who attended this briefing on October 6, was equally candid about the concept: "I mean, you just cringed…. The idea was, the ground war would start at the same time the air war started, and we would attack into the strength of the enemy."[17]

On October 10 and 11, General Glosson and Maj. Gen. Robert B. Johnston (USMC), CENTCOM Chief of Staff, briefed the Joint Staff, Secretary Cheney, and President Bush on the plans for the air and ground campaigns. General Glosson's presentation was well received, but there were many reservations, similar to General Horner's, about the concept of a single-corps breaching attack through the Saddam Line into north-central Kuwait. "The White House is very comfortable with the air plan," General Powell told General Schwarzkopf, soon after these briefings, "but there was a lot of criticism of the ground attack." The CENTCOM briefers acknowledged that it would be better to shift forces to the left, begin the attack from points farther west, and avoid the enemy's strength. When they pointed out that the command lacked the forces for this option, they were told to develop their concepts further and ask for more resources, if needed.[18]

General Schwarzkopf accordingly directed his Jedi Knights on October 15 that, while the single-corps concept remained an option, they were to begin work on a second one, which assumed the availability of an additional, heavy corps. Three days later, Colonel Purvis and his planners briefed Rear Adm. William M. Fogarty, CENTCOM J–5, on three different courses of action for a two-corps offensive. The preferred option among these provided for the two large units to attack abreast, beginning their advance from the region west of the tri-border area (which, in fact, was where the VII Corps alone jumped off for the actual campaign). In this scheme, the main mission of the two corps was to strike into Kuwait, with a follow-on possibility of destroying the Republican Guard.[19]

On October 21, the Jedi Knights briefed this concept to General Schwarzkopf. The CENTCOM commander approved the plan and emphasized that, once behind the Saddam Line, the two corps must continue their attack and destroy the Republican Guard. Pointing into Kuwait on the briefing map, General Schwarzkopf said, "I've got forces here…. I've threatened his Republican Guard; now, I'll destroy it!"[20]

During the next two days, the CENTCOM planners briefed General Powell in Riyadh on both the single- and two-corps concepts. The same reservations remained about the former: it meant an attack into the enemy's strength and with insufficient force to move west of the Kuwaiti border. The chairman agreed to support CENTCOM's request for a second corps. "If we go to war, we will not do it halfway," General Powell assured General Schwarzkopf. "The United States military will give you whatever you need to do it right."[21]

On October 26, the planning for the ground campaign shifted from CENTCOM to ARCENT. Colonel Purvis and the other Knights moved into the headquarters of the Army component command, where more ARCENT and other green-suit officers joined them.[22] The expanded staff briefly considered a third option to the one- and two-corps ones, an offensive to seize the western Iraq airfields H–2 and H–3 and their surrounding Scud sites. Briefed on this alternative, General Schwarzkopf concluded that these objectives lay too far from the Coalition's logistical bases, and he directed his planners to focus on the two-corps concept.[23]

Lucrative Targets

The ARCENT team vigorously pursued this guidance. On November 2, they briefed General Yeosock on a two-corps attack that would begin west of the Wadi al Batin, which ran along the western Kuwaiti border. Accompanied by the I MEF,

Kuwait and the surrounding region.

these units would turn the main Iraqi defenses and destroy the Republican Guard in the rear of the Saddam Line. General Yeosock questioned the wisdom of using the Marines so far west, where their logistics and air operations would be more difficult. The ARCENT commander made some other suggestions and approved the plan.[24]

Four days later, General Schwarzkopf and his component commanders received the same briefing. The CENTCOM commander agreed with General Yeosock that the Marine divisions could serve better in the east than with the ARCENT corps in the west. Most important from CENTAF's point of view, General Schwarzkopf counted on the air campaign, which would precede the ground offensive, to "blind" the Iraqis and allow the ARCENT units to move undetected to their jump-off positions west of the Wadi al Batin. Above all, he stressed that deception would be essential to distract the enemy from the intentions of Coalition ground forces.[25]

On November 9, President Bush announced the decision that eventually would make the two-corps plan an operational reality: the United States would more than double its strength in the Gulf.[26] When the VII Corps reached the theater, the Coalition forces would become strong enough for the option of a ground offensive. It would take this heavy formation considerable time, however, to arrive from Europe. Although the corps began moving in November, on Christmas Eve, the 2d Armored Cavalry Regiment represented its only combat unit in place within the AOR. When the war began on January 17, 1991, most of the VII Corps was at sea,[27] and it was not until February 18 that the last of its equipment left Europe.[28]

On November 11, General Glosson briefed General Yeosock and his staff on CENTAF's plans for Phases I through III of the air campaign. The ARCENT officers expressed concern that their ideas on the KTO phase of the plan had not been solicited, and they wanted more influence over the prioritizing of targets in front of their troops. Other issues included the alleged rigidity of the ATO cycle and the details of how the FSCL would function.[29] The CENTAF officers rejoined that the entire air campaign plan, including Phase III, met General Schwarzkopf's approval. The Air Force briefers assured the ground component commanders that their requirements would eventually be incorporated into the planning for air operations over the KTO.[30]

This exchange of views did not close these issues, however. Later, after General Glosson had been dual-hatted, he reassured the ground commanders that their requirements would be met.[31] CENTAF, ARCENT, and MARCENT officers continued to discuss target prioritization, the ATO cycle, the FSCL, and other related issues until the end of the war and, indeed, even after it.[32]

While the discussion of these questions continued, the president's decision to double the force had made possible a "shift west" strategy. On November 14, General Schwarzkopf unveiled this concept to his component, corps, and division commanders, briefing them at a conference in Dhahran. The CENTCOM commander described how the XVIII Airborne Corps would move far to its left and attack through As Salman to As Samawah, on the Euphrates. From there, this light formation would move rapidly downriver along Highway 8 and seize An Nasiriyah. To the right of XVIII Corps, the VII Corps would drive northeast from the Wadi al Batin. This heavier formation would execute the crucial mission of destroying the Republican Guard.[33] Farther east, JFC–N, I MEF, and JFC–E would breach the Saddam Line and encircle the Iraqis in Kuwait City and the heel of the country. General Schwarzkopf later stated that one "inviolable principle" of his planning was that "Arab forces must be the ones to liberate Kuwait City."[34] Naval forces and Marines afloat would offer an amphibious feint, providing the deception that the CENTCOM commander considered essential to the plan's success.[35]

Following this conference on November 14, General Glosson briefed General Schwarzkopf on the first three phases of the air campaign, and his presentation strongly reinforced the CENTCOM commander's plans for the shift west. CENTAF's attacks against Iraq, its air defenses, and the Republican Guard and other targets in the KTO would blind the enemy and give the ARCENT forces time to move to their jump-off positions.[36] Also following the conference, the ARCENT planners reconsidered the possibility of a ground offensive against airfields H–2 and H–3, but, unlike the plans for the air campaign, this idea was not compatible with the shift-west strategy. General Schwarzkopf's earlier reservations about it remained as strong as ever, and, after December 11, the Jedi Knights dropped this option.[37]

On December 18, Colonel Purvis and his group reported to Headquarters CENTCOM, ending their work at ARCENT. Two days later, Secretary Cheney and General Powell heard much the same briefing that the ground commanders had received on November 14. The fundamental plan now was in place, and, although CENTCOM would make many changes in its details, only two major modifications would occur before G-day, the first day of the ground offensive.[38]

These alterations, made at an ARCENT briefing to General Schwarzkopf on January 8, addressed two of the plan's riskiest elements. Answering the CENT-COM commander's concerns about logistical support for the XVIII Corps, the planners moved this unit's line of attack back to the east, closer to that of the VII Corps. The second change, which responded to General Schwarzkopf's guidance that ARCENT was not to put any force at risk to block Highway 8, provided for helicopter strikes, rather than ground units, to cut this important route along the Euphrates.[39]

In late January, after Coalition air operations were underway, General Corder directed that Headquarters CENTAF sponsor a meeting "to prepare for the transition in emphasis from a strategic to a tactical air campaign." On January 30, sixty representatives of the five component commands that were CENTAF's "customers" (ARCENT, NAVCENT, MARCENT, JFC–E, and JFC–N) met for a four-hour conference that was chaired by Brig. Gen. Mike Hall, CENTAF's chief air liaison officer to all of the ground units in the theater. General Hall reviewed the first three phases of the air campaign and discussed the transition to the fourth, advising the component commands to state their requirements and let CENTAF match its capabilities to them. Representatives of each of the ground forces briefed the other conferees on their objectives, schemes of maneuver, and requirements from CENTAF.[40]

On the heels of this meeting came the conference of senior leaders in Riyadh on February 9. ARCENT planners briefed Secretary Cheney and General Powell on the plan of January 8, which they since had improved with a few refinements in arrangements for logistics and C^2. General Horner gave a presentation on the air campaign's progress to date, covering both Phases I and III. After an optimistic summary of the achievements of the strategic phase, the CENTAF commander turned to the KTO, emphasizing the successes in gaining air superiority, reducing the Republican Guard, and shaping the battlefield. General Horner detailed in particular the process of distributing CAS and air interdiction (AI) sorties among the ground components and described the tactical air support system already in place.[41] Three days after this meeting, General Schwarzkopf advised General Horner and his other component commanders, "Effective immediately, the emphasis of combat operations must shift to preparing the battlefield for a ground offensive.... All commanders must orient their targeting priorities on those Iraqi units which pose the greatest threat to Coalition forces as they attack. Of greatest significance is the elimination of Republican Guards, armor, artillery, and chemical/biological weapons."[42]

An important element in the Coalition's preparations for Phase IV was its deception efforts, some of which predated the air campaign. During November 15–21, CENTCOM had conducted Imminent Thunder, its first joint and combined exercise in Saudi Arabia. CENTAF aircrews had flown approximately 1,580 sorties, and NAVCENT ships and MARCENT units had practiced an amphibious operation near the Kuwaiti coast. Imminent Thunder had served as both a ploy to encourage belief in just such a Marine Corps assault and a realistic exercise to train for it should the need arise.[43] The Marines had made ship-to-shore landings during America's three most recent wars—major ones during World War II and the Korean War—and it was quite believable that they would do so again in this conflict. Press coverage of Imminent Thunder added to the credibility of an amphibious attack. The *Los Angeles Times* reported, for example, that the exercise would "simulate a tactic likely to be used in any actual U.S. military offensive."[44]

Some evidence suggests that the Iraqis took the deception seriously. At least seven enemy divisions deployed along the Kuwaiti coast, two of them near Kuwait City and still others within supporting distance of it. An Iraqi sandtable battle map captured in Kuwait City during the ground campaign showed that the defenders expected Coalition forces to attack from the south, out of Saudi Arabia, and to attempt amphibious assaults.[45]

Aided by deception, General Schwarzkopf's plan required 270,000 troops to travel considerable distances across the desert, under the greatest possible secrecy. The VII Corps would have to move more than 330 miles west to its attack position.[46] The XVIII Airborne Corps would turn over its defensive sector to MARCENT, cross the VII Corps, and cover approximately 500 miles to reach its line of departure near Rafha.[47] The airborne corps' crossing of the heavy corps demanded particularly close planning, a fact keenly appreciated by Lt. Gen. William G. Pagonis, ARCENT's chief logistics officer. "Somewhere out there in the desert, far from the nearest stoplight," General Pagonis said, "we would have to create the Mother of All Intersections." Achieving surprise was also a vital part of the plan. At his 1900 staff meeting on February 22, General Schwarzkopf stressed the importance of shrouding these movements in secrecy. General Horner's notes on that conference read: "Do not discuss XVIII [Airborne Corps] or [6th] French [Armored Division] in [the] West—Do not draw attention to anything West—til several days further." A few hours after the ground campaign had begun, he told his staff, "Our goal is to keep the operation in the west out of the press—out of anybody's view. We think that [Saddam's] communications are so bad that he may not even know what's going on out there. We'd like it to be a surprise when the Republican Guard gets attacked in their positions."[48]

The shift west would put ARCENT forces far beyond the right flank of the Saddam Line, in position to execute a strategic envelopment of the Iraqi forces in the KTO. General Schwarzkopf later called it a "giant lateral movement of combat forces and supplies." The CENTCOM commander also drew an analogy that compared the move of the two ARCENT corps to the "Hail Mary" play in football, a high and very long pass into, or near, the opponent's end zone.[49] Yet, in one significant regard, the "shift west" was not at all like a Hail Mary pass, which teams usually attempted in desperation, when far from their opponent's goal line with time running out. Given the success of the first three phases of the air campaign, General Schwarzkopf directed the shift west with confidence, not despair.[50]

ARCENT forces began moving soon after the opening of the air campaign. By the early dawn of January 20, truck convoys were shipping personnel and equipment westward. While units of the VII Corps gathered in their tactical assembly areas, the XVIII Airborne Corps started its shift from the region around King Fahd Air Base to its attack positions near Rafha.[51] Bad weather at first hindered the troop movements, but the operation gained momentum. The ARCENT forces moved twenty-four hours a day and completed their deployment without a serious setback.[52] By February 20, General Pagonis could later claim, the two corps "were in place, fully equipped with all classes of supply, and ready to go on the offensive."[53]

CENTAF contributed to the shift west in two vital ways. First, the early successes of the air campaign were fundamental to the execution of the ground plan. The Coalition airmen prevented the Iraqis from detecting the movement of large numbers of troops across long distances, and they restricted the ability of the enemy to react to the deployment, even if he had learned of it. "We knew [the enemy] had very, very limited reconnaissance means," General Schwarzkopf later explained. "Therefore, when we took out his air force, for all intents and purposes, we took out his ability to see what we were doing down here in Saudi Arabia." Col. John R. Wingfield III, Commander of the 1630th Provisional Tactical Airlift Wing, which supported the XVIII Airborne Corps, expanded on this same point. "A very deliberate decision was made," Colonel Wingfield pointed out, "to not move troops into their pre-attack positions until the air war began…. The first strikes took out their C^3I [command, control, communications, and intelligence]…and blinded them to where our units were moving." Another of the wing's senior officers emphasized, "What was really important here was to keep the move classified, to get the XVIII Airborne Corps moved to the area of Rafha…and we couldn't let the Iraqis know that this was in progress. We had to keep it just as low profile and quiet as possible." Their success was strongly evidenced after the war, when Coalition interrogators questioned captured Iraqi commanders. One debriefing team reported, "None of our sources had seen the reality of the Coalition deployment of the XVIII [Airborne] Corps to their far right flank; all believed firmly in the inevitability of a Coalition amphibious assault

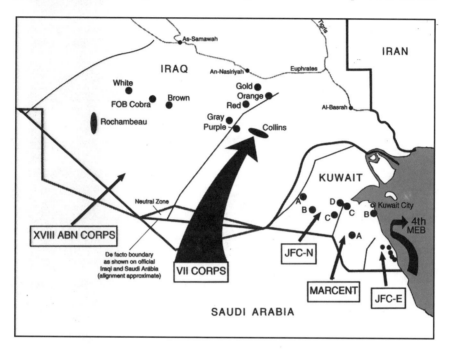

Ground tactical plan.

against Kuwait City, supported by an attack in the Wadi al Batin. One source, when the plan was finally explained to him, shook his head and remarked ruefully that it would not have mattered if the Iraqi army had had good intelligence to detect the XVIII Corps' move, because they could not move their forces after 16 January due to the air campaign." During the shift west, thousands of Coalition vehicles crossed hundreds of miles of open desert during daylight hours, day after day, without a single Iraqi aircraft taking any of them under attack. "If any proof of allied air supremacy were necessary," one Army historian wrote, "this was it."[54]

CENTAF's other major contribution to the shift west took the form of airlift. General Schwarzkopf's plan required 270,000 troops and their equipment to move across hundreds of miles of desert. Airlift would help move the XVIII Airborne Corps, which had approximately 21,000 wheeled vehicles and more than 4,300 tracked ones. Trucks would be needed to transport the VII Corps, which was heavier and had more equipment. The shift west also required establishing logistical bases with enough ammunition, spare parts, fuel, food, and other materiel to support combat operations for at least two months. The CENTCOM commander later explained that he "wanted to have enough supplies on hand so if we launched this [ground offensive], if we got into a slug-fest battle, which we very easily could have gotten into, we'd have enough supplies to last for sixty days."[55] Tactical airlift was essential for transporting the XVIII Airborne Corps and for keeping it and other Coalition forces in supply.

As it arrived from Europe, General Franks's VII Corps moved largely by truck from the ports to its assembly areas, but General Luck's XVIII Airborne Corps, with a longer distance to cover, had a greater need for tactical airlift. Every C–130 unit that was deployed to a provisional wing in the theater contributed to this effort, moving personnel and equipment.[56] Stymied on January 18 by bad weather, the Hercules aircraft began the next day transporting the XVIII Airborne Corps from King Fahd Air Base, near Dhahran, to Rafha, along an air corridor about 500 miles to the northwest.[57] King Fahd was a forward operating location (FOL) established by tactical airlifters from their main station at Al Ain Air Base in the United Arab Emirates.[58] The C–130 transports operating from this FOL eventually developed a pattern of double shuttles that typically took a load of airborne troops and some of their rolling stock from King Fahd to Rafha, returned to King Fahd (or to nearby Abqaiq), picked up a second load, and flew again to Rafha. These cargo aircraft usually made their inbound flights to Rafha at approximately 7,000 feet and returned at approximately 8,000.[59] Other missions originated at the Al Ain home base and then flew the King Fahd/Abqaiq-to-Rafha shuttle. In addition to these operations, in early February, the airlifters also moved XVIII Airborne Corps personnel and equipment to Landing Zone 37 near Arar, Saudi Arabia, west of Rafha.[60]

However, CENTAF's airlift support of ARCENT's shift west was not without problems. Rafha airfield was not instrumented, which aggravated the initial problem of bad weather. Saudi personnel made the meteorological observations for the field, and MAC ground controllers quickly discovered that their reports were overly optimistic. Pilots got their C–130s airborne, only to encounter bad weather and be forced to abort. This situation improved after a subordinate unit of the XVIII Airborne Corps, the 101st Airborne Division, quickly deployed three of its own experts to Rafha. On January 19, this ARCENT team began making weather observations and reporting them through MAC channels, whose controllers then reduced the number of air aborts and, when better visibility returned, developed the optimum timing for the C–130 launches.[61]

With the exception of a few veterans of the Vietnam War, the aircrews found themselves flying corridor operations for the first time, and the wing took roughly three days to develop an effective aircraft flow. Frequent fog and low ceilings put an end to the early, ambitious hope for a five-minute interval between takeoffs. Eventually, the wing settled into a more realistic flow, sometimes as brief as ten minutes,[62] but the flight interval increased to thirty minutes during poor flying conditions. The airlifters received their weather information immediately, over high-frequency radio, and they slowed their pace of operations or stopped them altogether when fog and low ceilings set in.[63]

Two C–130s, probably from the 1670th TAG(P), fly over Al Kharj, Saudi Arabia.

The C–130 personnel who transported the XVIII Airborne Corps and its equipment worked under demanding conditions. The aircrews at the main base at Al Ain put in fifteen- to sixteen-hour days, and those at the FOL, when they began moving the ARCENT airborne troops, worked for even longer periods.[64]

The more than 300 transporters at King Fahd lived in a particularly austere setting. When the airlifters first arrived at the FOL, their new home left much to be desired. Too few tents were erected to accommodate the new arrivals, and, at first, crews coming off missions had to raise their own shelters before they could sleep in them.[65] The showers and latrines of this large but Spartan facility stood unfinished, and the galvanized water pipes needed for their completion had to be brought in from Al Ain, approximately 390 miles away.[66] King Fahd Air Base was less than 200 miles from the Iraqi border, and its personnel were constantly alert to the threat of Scuds with chemical warheads. Officers and airmen wore their protective suits most of the time; they slept in them and often carried them to the showers to ensure that they were close at hand. Long hours of working in this heavy gear rendered the crews more vulnerable to the desert menace of dehydration, and Al Ain accordingly had to ship daily one or two pallets of water to the FOL.[67] Scud alerts, sometimes several a night, disrupted sleep and forced everyone on the base to take shelter. An officer who visited the Al Ain FOL reported on January 22 that the aircrews and others were "tired, frazzled, and in their suits most of the time."[68]

The C–130 crews overcame these hardships and accomplished their mission. "Positioning of Army units going well," General Tenoso, Commander, Airlift Forces (COMALF), reported to General Horner on January 28. "Crews flying hard with heavy flow. Maintainers keeping aircraft in excellent shape." Maintenance crews of the 1650th TAW(P) illustrated the COMALF's point on February 19 when the departure of one of their C–130Es set a remarkable record: the takeoff represented one hundred consecutive, on-time launches by the aircraft, an unprecedented number in the theater. The 1630th and 1675th TAW(P)s also compiled a dramatic record by their support to the XVIII Airborne Corps. In their operations from King Fahd and Al Ain, the two wings flew nearly 2,000 sorties and moved almost 11,000 troops and more than 9,600 tons of cargo. The total movement of units to the west was completed in three weeks.[69]

After the XVIII Airborne Corps had moved to its new position, tactical airlift units took on the vital mission of sustaining it and other Coalition forces. On February 8, senior officers of General Luck's corps, acknowledging the "superb" work of the C–130 crews in transporting their unit, stated the requirements to supply it at its current location. The airlifters would have to carry 100 pallets of supplies a day from the Dhahran port to Rafha and to Log Base C (or Charlie), which was the supply depot for the XVIII Airborne Corps. This logistical center, the westernmost of ARCENT's five theater bases, was located southeast of Rafha along the Trans-Arabian Pipeline roadway. The "Tapline" road was a desolate, but paved, two-lane route that crossed northern Saudi Arabia, paralleling one of the country's most important crude-oil pipelines. Although this highway would support some of Log Base Charlie's transportation needs, the supply flights, which were to begin on February 11, proved essential as well. In addition to the flights from Dhahran, the C–130s also would transport enormous quantities of fuel from King Fahd and elsewhere into this western logistics center.[70]

The airlifters readily accepted this challenge. Beginning in early February, the 1630th devoted most of its efforts to transporting supplies from the Dhahran port to Army and Marine landing zones. "Herky birds" landed along a mile-long stretch of the thirty-eight-foot wide Tapline road southeast of Rafha, bringing fuel and other supplies to the XVIII Airborne Corps.[71] Several days before the opening of the ground campaign, C–130s began making tactical resupply airdrops. In the first of these, they conveyed eight container-delivery-system pallets of water and meals-ready-to-eat (MREs) to Marines dug in near the Saddam Line.[72]

In addition to the airlift that moved and sustained the troops during and after the shift west, CENTAF also helped prepare for the ground campaign with B–52 breachings of the Iraqi frontline defenses. These bomber missions contributed, if only modestly, to the Coalition's successful land attack.

During the Desert Shield deployment, General Schwarzkopf asked if SAC heavy bombers would be able to help ARCENT with the task of clearing the Iraqi minefields along the Saddam Line. In late November, Air Force liaison officers at the U.S. Army Engineer Center at Fort Leonard Wood, Missouri, contacted operations officers at Headquarters SAC and raised preliminary questions about the B–52's capabilities to deliver general-purpose bombs against such defenses and to clear lanes for the advancing Coalition troops. On December 3, the Army Engineer Center formally requested SAC's help with breaching the Iraqi lines, candidly acknowledging that pitting the Army's current doctrine and equipment unassisted against the sophisticated Iraqi landmines and other obstacles probably would "achieve marginal success at best and…result in significant losses to the breaching force." Nor was there time to train with new theory or to develop improved hardware. Given the crisis that Iraq had created, the Army would have to use the resources that were presently available, so it turned to the Air Force.[73]

SAC conducted B–52 breaching tests, and, after General Schwarzkopf received the results, he directed the heavy bombers to attack the Iraqi defenses in the MARCENT sector. A STRATFOR aircrew did so on February 7, but General Horner regarded the results as inconclusive because the targeted area was so large. The BUFFs made further efforts from February 17 through 23.[74] The sorties on the seventeenth were disappointing, with seven of eight bomb trains falling short. Mixed results were produced the following day and successful ones from the twentieth through the twenty-third, when in most cases the B–52s cut the lines of concertina wire and other defensive barriers.[75]

The B–52 crews had reason to be satisfied with the results of their breaching sorties. At the opening of the ground offensive, some Coalition forces advanced through lanes cleared by the bombers. General Caruana's evaluation was that, after the initial adjustment, the ground campaign breachings were "outstanding." "The B–52 proved to have an effective breaching capability," a STRATFOR afteraction report contended, "against mines, barriers, and other blocks."[76]

The breaches contributed to the ground campaign, but CENTAF's senior leaders believed their significance was modest. General Horner, while praising the SAC crews for being "good soldiers" and wanting "to help," remained unpersuaded of the value of the breaching operations. "They tried it in the Marine sector and they tried it in the Army sector," the CENTAF commander candidly reflected after the war, "but I'm not sure it did any good at all." General Glosson suggested that the Coalition troops could advance through the same lanes that the Iraqis used to gain access to their own defenses, eliminating much of the need for B–52 breachings. Commenting on the operations a year later, General Olsen pointed out that, at the time, the Coalition leaders did not know in detail the composition of the Iraqi defenses, that ARCENT officers had been "rightly" concerned about their strength, and that STRATFOR sorties were "just another effort" to reduce them before the allied soldiers advanced. One CENTAF KTO planner offered the opinion that the breaching sorties "probably didn't make that much difference…. Obviously [the Coalition ground forces] went through very fast and very easily, with minimal losses,…but I'm not so sure that was because of B–52 strikes."[77]

In addition to the B–52 breachings, MC–130E Combat Talons, special operations variants of the C–130 transport, contributed to the same mission by carrying BLU–82s against the Iraqi frontline defenses. This colossal 15,000-pound bomb had gained the nickname "Daisy Cutter" during the Vietnam War, when it was used to clear landing zones by leveling areas with 260-foot diameters. The BLU–82 was so huge that it had to be mounted on a cargo pallet and delivered by opening the back of its MC–130, which went into a slow climb until the enormous

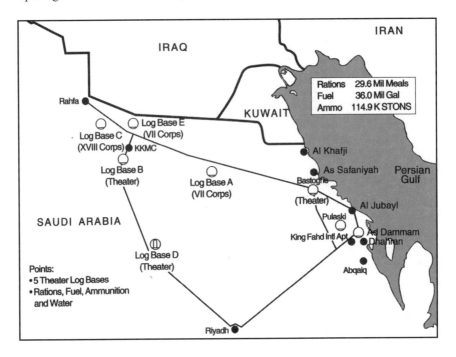

G-day logistical posture.

bomb rolled out of the aircraft. Briefed on the capabilities of these titanic weapons on January 28, General Schwarzkopf evidenced interest in using them to clear the minefields of the Saddam Line. In Vietnam, however, the Daisy Cutters sometimes had proved a dangerous liability: their huge blasts turned trees into large splinters, and American airborne troops sometimes impaled themselves on these hazards. In the treeless KTO, CENTCOM officers had no such concern. They were confident that the BLU–82s would inflict extensive damage on the Iraqi defenses and would also have a staggering psychological effect on the enemy.[78]

They were not disappointed. On February 3, two MC–130Es of the 8th Special Operations Squadron, operating from King Fahd International Airport, delivered the first two BLU–82s of the air campaign. The initial bomb blasted a passage through a minefield, which Marine units used on the opening morning of the ground campaign. The second bomb was targeted against a battalion headquarters; it resulted in the desertion of the battalion commander, two officers, and a noncommissioned officer, who brought with them maps of the mine defenses in their sector. This detonation was so loud that the Iraqis believed it represented the beginning of a ground offensive, and they turned on all their radars, thus revealing their locations to CENTAF fighters. The Combat Talons flew other BLU–82 missions against Iraqi defenses: on February 14 across from ARCENT troops in the tri-border area, on February 18 against Faylaka Island, on February 20 against two logistics areas behind the Saddam Line, and on February 22 in front of the MARCENT sector.[79]

Although ARCENT liked the BLU–82 sorties so well it submitted many requests for them to CENTAF,[80] in other areas the two commands experienced tensions as the ground offensive approached. ARCENT and MARCENT commanders understandably directed their first concern to their own units and to the enemy troops in their immediate front. These officers wanted more air attacks made on the Iraqi forces directly across from their own positions, and they wanted greater control over the prioritizing of targets. On February 9, Colonel Deptula wrote that Army colonels frequently wanted to know when the Air Force "will start giving them air for Army use only. 'When will we get our air?' is a familiar quote. People keep on talking about Army targets, Navy targets, and Marine targets." A few days later, General Schwarzkopf's ground campaign planning group expressed ARCENT's point of view on the air preparations for the land offensive. "The group's analysis of the ATO," one member reported, "indicates that even when kill boxes are included, battlefield [preparation] sorties account for less than 40% of the total. The concern with kill boxes is that they may not be where they can best support the ground scheme and pilots may not be going after the right targets." "Too few sorties are made available to VII and XVIII [Airborne] Corps," a Headquarters ARCENT message of February 18 stated. "And while air support missions are being flown against 1st echelon enemy divisions, Army-nominated targets are not being serviced." After February 20, with the ground campaign closely approaching, the ARCENT corps commanders strongly contended that not enough assets were being allocated to attacking the frontline Iraqi divisions and to breaching operations.[81]

CENTAF officers differed with these points of view. They acknowledged the ground commanders' understandable concern with the enemy units closest to them, but the air planners also saw the significance of other targets farther from the front. The Iraqi Mi–8 Hip and Mi–24 Hind helicopters, for example, although based 250 miles from the Saddam Line, posed a threat as dangerous as that of the enemy's frontline forces because they could deliver chemical weapons against the Coalition troops in Saudi Arabia. "Interdiction of these assets," General Glosson pointed out on February 15, "is just as important to shaping the battlefield as is destroying an artillery piece 10 km [kilometers] inside the anticipated [Forward Line of Own Troops]." "Corps people don't think deep," another CENTAF officer asserted, "airmen do."[82]

The air planners also replied to the criticism that too few attacks had been directed against the frontline Iraqi units, and their answer harkened back to CENT-

Lucrative Targets

AF's lack of confidence in ARCENT's BDA effort. "They couldn't keep track of anything," one KTO air planner complained, "and yet they were using [these BDA statistics] as a basis for [making] the decision on which units to hit." CENT-AF officers firmly believed that Coalition aircraft were attacking the enemy's KTO forces more often, and more effectively, than the G–2 assessments credited. They contended, for example, that allied air strikes on February 22 had eliminated more than one hundred artillery pieces of the Iraqi 47th Division, which opposed the VII Corps, but that ARCENT evaluators had failed to count these destroyed weapons. In another instance, the CENTAF planners challenged a MARCENT evaluation of February 23 that frontline Iraqi units had been reduced to only 78 percent of their initial strength. The air officers believed this assessment was far too high, and they contended that the Marines had arrived at it without using mission reports from A–6s, because the Navy had refused to submit reports from this aircraft.[83]

CENTAF officers also held strong points of view on the issues of controlling and prioritizing sorties. The control of air assets, they believed, was the responsibility of the JFACC, and they favored leaving all of these resources under his centralized authority, rather than dividing them among several commanders. Some CENTAF officers believed that the issue of prioritizing sorties was related to the Black Hole planners' concept of bombing to achieve broad effects rather than specific, quantifiable results. They favored having the JFACC determine how to use all of the available air assets to achieve the desired result: the expulsion of the Iraqis from Kuwait. The alternative, as these planners saw it, was to have individual ground commanders use their fraction of the total sorties to work sequentially through a prioritized list of targets across from their immediate front.[84]

Some air officers concluded that their ARCENT and MARCENT counterparts were too narrow in their views of how air power should be used in the theater. On January 30, General Hall, Headquarters CENTAF air liaison officer, convened a meeting at which the command's five "customers,"—ARCENT, MARCENT, NAVCENT, JFC–N, and JFC–E—spent four hours briefing their requirements. "The land components appeared overly focused on their individual maneuver, timing, and objectives," General Hall later reported to General Corder. "There was little expression of their role in the big picture." Writing in early February, Colonel Deptula expressed concern that the land campaign planners had a "[sequential] target list mentality" that created a "tactical level mindset" and caused them to "miss the big picture." He argued that the ground commanders should identify their "desired effects" and then let "the JFACC use air assets in a manner to best achieve those effects…. I keep on telling folks not to get hung up on who nominated what target or…[whose] list it's on, but rather [on] how to achieve the best effect given the wide array of weapons system we have." General Horner commented after the war that the Army "wanted to load their [target] list up because they thought they would get more air; there would be more destruction in their corps sector.... That drove the Marine Corps to have a similar attitude, and of course they didn't want to lose any of the Marine air."[85]

In addition to the views of the ground component commanders and of CENT-AF on target priorities, the CENTCOM commander had his own opinions on the subject. While the ARCENT and MARCENT planners focused on the Iraqi forces in their fronts, General Schwarzkopf continued to emphasize the importance of the Republican Guard, as he had from the time of the Desert Shield deployment. Whereas the component commanders were concerned about the infantry divisions holding the Saddam Line, the CENTCOM commander stressed the significance of the enemy's elite troops, his theater reserve units that stretched across a long semicircle north of the front. Deployed widely apart, the Iraqi frontline infantry divisions and the Republican Guard competed for CENTAF's attention. "One of the most frustrating things in [the KTO cell]," an air planner said shortly after Desert Storm, was that the CINC's guidance "very frequently didn't translate" into that of his component commanders, "so we had an immediate conflict." When General Hall addressed the conference on requirements held January 30, he discussed Phase III of the air campaign as two distinct parts, just as Checkmate planners had done earlier: the first was an attack on the Republican Guard, and the second was "shaping the battlefield." "The CINC['s] focus on Republican Guards as a separate part of phase III," he commented later the same day, "did not seem to be well understood by the land components. Once explained, their concern that current battlefield target nominations were not being serviced at a high rate disappeared."[86]

Analogous to the competition among corps commanders for aircraft to strike against the Iraqis in their fronts was one for the J–STARS aircraft to look at the enemy units there. "The 18th Corps on one flank," an Air Force colonel who served as an ACE later recalled, "and the Marines over on the eastern side...each thought that their particular part of the battle was absolutely crucial—and it was to [them]." While each corps rightfully pressed its own case, the E–8A officer concluded, "We couldn't do both because of the distance between them.... There was a little bit of competition for the amount of time that we spent serving each corps commander." Another senior officer recalled, "You know, the VII Corps [commander] wanted to run it his way, and MARCENT wanted to run it their way, and every night we'd get into a battle. CENTCOM would tell us where we were supposed to be because we only flew one airplane." This situation improved in mid-February, when Lt. Gen. Calvin A. H. Waller, CENTCOM Deputy Commander in Chief (DCINC), instituted daily meetings to schedule the priorities for J–STARS.[87]

The prioritizing of targets for the "shooters" remained an issue. Each of the services nominated targets at the 1230 daily meetings of the JTCB at Headquarters CENTAF.[88] General Schwarzkopf held the authority to apportion sorties among the component commands, and, on January 31, he delegated that responsibility to General Waller. "He and the JFACC," General Schwarzkopf directed, "will consult on [sortie] apportionment allocation, developed by the JFACC prior to each ATO cycle (H-72). Subsequent to that consultation, ground commanders…can expect to receive a sortie allocation for planning purposes only. The DCINC and JFACC will revise the apportionment recommendation as necessary and get it to me NLT [no later than] H-48." Following this directive, the JTCB meetings convened at Headquarters CENTCOM.[89]

On February 15, General Waller offered CENTAF and the other component commands his guidance on apportioning air sorties. Iraqi divisions that had been reduced to below 50 percent strength would not be targeted further, but an artillery unit within such a formation might be, if it retained more than one-half of its capability and if its pieces were deployed within range of one of the planned breach sites. "As the campaign approaches Phase IV," General Waller also directed, "we will begin employment of close air support to exercise CAS command and control, hone CAS procedures and train personnel." The CENTCOM deputy commander also advised that three days before the start of the ground offensive he would provide the component commanders with his guidance on CAS distribution, "for planning purposes only," and he asked CENTAF to create two new kill boxes and reorient a third.[90]

General Schwarzkopf's delegation of his apportionment role to General Waller had relatively little effect on Headquarters CENTAF. General Horner, who of course retained his JFACC authority of tasking sorties through the ATO process, was unconcerned by the change. He described how the process worked: "Rather than resolving [target priorities] at our [CENTAF] staff, I would wind up with a priority list from ARCENT, MARCENT,…the two Islamic corps—Northern and Eastern Corps, VII Corps, and XVIII Corps. So I had five different 'priority ones,' for example, or six. What we tried to do, we tried to get the DCINC, [General] Cal Waller, to be the focal point to resolve it." The CENTAF commander had no qualms about the arrangement: "I didn't care. I had 'X' amount of airpower, 'X' amount of enemy. You tell me where you want it first; that's fine with me." General Glosson believed that CENTAF's successful use of the kill-box system overshadowed General Waller's role in the prioritizing process. The chief air planner recalled that he and the CENTCOM deputy commander had agreed that the DCINC's daily prioritized target list would consist of sixty to seventy targets, but, in General Glosson's opinion, the success of his aircrews against their kill boxes soon rendered this accounting largely "irrelevant." In the course of working their assigned grid areas, CENTAF aircraft destroyed many of the targets on General Waller's list. Sometimes, General Glosson recalled, the CENTCOM deputy commander "would give me seventy targets and I would…only hit fifteen. And then…he couldn't understand why I wasn't doing what he said. The reason was either they were already hit, or the targets were not valid as verified by intelligence." Working at a level below General Glosson's position, Colonel Baptiste indicated that neither the role of General Waller nor the location of the JTCB meeting made any great difference to the KTO cell planners. "As long as I got the end product," he said, "which was that Prioritized Target List, I didn't care where the meeting was held, when in fact the same representatives that did it at CENT-AF at combat plans just moved over to CENTCOM and [the Ministry of Defense building] and did it over there, and General Waller put his stamp of approval on it, and I got the same product. So to me, it was very transparent."[91]

Regardless of where the target prioritizing was done, some ground officers remained convinced that CENTAF was not giving their particular units enough support. The tension over this issue was clearly strongest at corps commander level. At one end of the chain of command, the CENTAF and ARCENT commanders worked closely together, shared quarters in the U.S. Military Training Mission apartments, and had long opportunities to discuss air-ground subjects. After Desert Storm, General Horner spoke very favorably of General Yeosock and of their relations during the war.[92] Further down the command spectrum were approximately 2,200 air liaison officers, forward air controllers, and liaison personnel serving in the DASC, the Air Support Operations Centers, Tactical Air Control Parties, Control and Reporting Centers, and other liaison assignments all across the theater. These officers faced immediate, day-to-day problems and, working with their counterparts in the other services, nearly always found ways to resolve them.[93] It was between these two poles in the chain of authority, at the corps command level, that officers voiced the most disaffection with CENTAF's operations before the ground campaign.

As Air Force officers observed during Desert Storm, Army doctrine assigned a significant role to the corps and their commanders. General Horner concluded from his experience that "the Army is designed around the corps" and that "Army doctrine tells the corps commander he is supposed to be the guy to run this war."[94] Colonel Reavey expanded on this same point: "The Army's focus in their training is predicated on giving a corps commander all the assets he needs to train and letting him train his corps as hard as he can…. They don't pay very much attention to the echelon above corps training where you have one or two corps or three corps lined up side by side and how you interface those corps." He went on to contrast this philosophy with that of the Air Force: "We don't care if you have one corps or five corps. You are all going to get a little piece of the [air] action. If there are five, you are going to get a little less than if there were two corps." Tensions between CENTAF planners and the corps commanders inevitably followed from these contrasting points of view.[95]

During February, the corps commanders pressed CENTAF for more sorties against the Iraqi units immediately in their front. General Corder emphasized that these leaders, and division ones as well, "always wanted to have stuff done right in front of them. They didn't care about the Republican Guard. They didn't care about the units just south of the Republican Guard. They wanted stuff done in front of them." The corps commanders "have to understand that they get a slice of air [support] that is available based on the theater CINC's guidance," a TACC colonel pointed out, "and if they chose to move that air around in their corps from one target to another, they are not going to get a backfill to replace air that they moved off a target to hit that target again…. And that became kind of tough to explain a couple of times to those corps commanders." The corps leaders pressed their case strongly, particularly during the last four days before the ground campaign began.[96]

A U.S. camp situated in the typically flat, desolate Saudi terrain.

General Schwarzkopf intervened on CENTAF's side of one particular air-ground issue: the CENTCOM commander agreed with the leaders of his air component command that, once an Iraqi division fell below 50 percent strength, Coalition aircrews should not attack it again, but direct their efforts elsewhere. On February 20, General Schwarzkopf criticized the practice of accepting nominations from the land component commanders of targets in enemy units that air strikes had already reduced to less than half strength. General Glosson recalled, "General Schwarzkopf told me, 'Buster, once you get a division below 50 percent, don't use any assets against it until you get everybody else below 50 percent.'… When he said don't hit divisions below 50 percent, I didn't care how many targets [the DCINC and corps commanders] gave me in those divisions, I wasn't going to hit them."[97]

One certainty in this issue was that, despite the enormous forces available in the AOR and the potential to deploy yet more, CENTAF never would have enough resources to support all the requests of every ground commander. "There is an abundance of airframes and munitions in [the] theater," General Hall pointed out on January 30, "but CENTAF does not have the capability to meet all land component requirements simultaneously." General Schwarzkopf himself made the same point, about two weeks later. "The closer we get to G-Day," he told his senior officers, "each sortie becomes more significant…. There will never be enough assets to satisfy all requirements." Shortly after Desert Storm, Maj. John Sweeney held fresh memories of his "discussions" of the use of sorties with Army, Marine, and Navy representatives. He recalled that these officers would ask, "'Why didn't you hit this or that? How come he got this many airplanes?'" Then the KTO planner added, with a certain amount of resignation: "It's kind of like being a referee. No matter what you call, somebody thinks it's wrong."[98]

Another certainty was that General Schwarzkopf held the final authority within the theater over how air resources would cooperate with ground forces before and during the land campaign. When he asked the DCINC to represent him in planning the apportionment of sorties, the CENTCOM commander also stated that he himself would "approve or modify the final apportionment recommendation for each ATO cycle." General Glosson believed that General Schwarzkopf "had his own vision of how he wanted that battlefield 'prepped' and…he controlled everything in that respect." General Horner recounted with good humor a meeting held shortly before the opening of the ground campaign, when the MARCENT commander and the ARCENT corps commanders had both contended that they needed air forces under their own control. The CENTAF commander recalled that General Schwarzkopf had "summarized [the issue] by saying, 'Guys, it's all mine, and I will put it where it needs to be put.'"[99]

Although the air apportionment issue could not be resolved to everyone's satisfaction, CENTAF did arrive at a CAS arrangement that General Schwarzkopf and the ground commanders readily accepted.[100] During exercises conducted before Desert Shield, General Horner and his Headquarters Ninth Air Force planners had refined a concept for employing support called "Push CAS." This name came about because the concept was based on the CENTAF commander's strong belief in a "push" system, in which his component would push a flow of CAS sorties to the ground commands, as opposed to a "pull" process, in which the land units requested—or pulled—these sorties from a pool of aircraft held on ground alert. A CENTAF colonel contrasted the two concepts: "Pull CAS is essentially close air support where, when [an Army unit] wants air power to support ground action, they call up and get airplanes airborne in order to take out a target…. We wanted to use Push CAS, where we always had some airborne assets available for them instantaneously, and it's flowed out."[101]

General Horner urged that the advantages of Push CAS were obvious. It was reasonable to assume that the ground campaign would produce fluid battles between armored units. Under these circumstances, the Marine Corps and Army corps commanders could not know in advance when and where they would need CAS. "I did not want airplanes sitting on the ground [on] alert," General Horner emphasized, "… because that is just a waste." With the Push CAS arrangement, squadrons would put a predetermined, per-hour flow of sorties over the battlefield. Aircraft other than A–10s usually received a specific tasking in the ATO, making them available for a predetermined period of time to support the requirements of a specified Army corps, whereas the Warthogs generally were directed to report to a particular ABCCC to get their CAS assignments. The CENTAF "shooters" then had their CAS taskings, but, until an armor-on-armor battle developed or they otherwise were needed, they could attack other available targets.[102]

Lucrative Targets

This arrangement continuously put Coalition strike aircraft over the battlefield, without their losing idle time on ground alert. The command's CAS concept of operations provided, "Ground alert will normally not be used except to meet extraordinary requirements which cannot be met by the normal push flow of air."[103]

During the day, O/A–10s and OV–10s would serve as airborne FACs, and ground FACs usually would advance with MARCENT's and ARCENT's forward elements, although they might operate from helicopters when CENTAF fighters and ARCENT attack helicopters conducted joint air attacks.[104] At night, no O/A–10s would be up, and the FACs would operate from the ground and from helicopters, working with IR-equipped A–10s; LANTIRN-capable F–15Es and F–16s; and F–111s.[105] Although the ATO tasked CENTAF aircraft to provide CAS for a specific corps or to fulfill this mission through an ABCCC, these shooters were not required to answer unquestioningly every request for support. Colonel Sawyer reminded his A–10 wing that it was to respond when Coalition troops were "in contact" with the enemy's forces—but not necessarily when they were "involved" with them. The Warthogs need not fly a CAS mission, for example, when ARCENT or MARCENT units engaged the Iraqis in an artillery duel. Colonel Sawyer advised, "Flight leads—get a clear picture, use good judgment and don't needlessly expose your flight. Adding an A–10 [search and rescue mission] to an already critical situation will not help."[106]

CENTAF officers professed strong confidence in the Push CAS arrangement that was in place on the eve of the ground campaign. Colonel Baptiste pointed to the large number of air liaison personnel—more than 2,000 of them—and to the amount of practicing they had done, and he wholeheartedly endorsed the effort. "The push flow of air support," General Corder emphasized, "is designed to make air readily available, in near real time, for support of land forces.... We believe the [CAS concept of operations] provides sufficient flexibility to support either preplanned or immediate battlefield-generated Army schemes of maneuver." General Horner contended after the conflict that the Army "liked Push CAS.... In fact, it probably gave them more than they could handle."[107]

The eve of the ground campaign saw nearly 536,700 CENTCOM personnel in the theater, with roughly 54,600 of them assigned to CENTAF. Unknown to the Iraqis, the XVIII Airborne Corps stood poised on its line of departure, far west of the Saddam Line, ready for its strategic envelopment of the enemy's forces in the KTO. To its right was the VII Corps, which would advance northeast to engage the elements of the Republican Guard that had survived the air campaign. Farther east was the JFC–N command (including Egyptian, Saudi Arabian, Syrian, and Kuwaiti forces) and confronting the Saddam Line to their right was General Boomer's I MEF. Beyond the Marines, the Saudi Arabian and Qatari units that composed the JFC–E command stood ready to advance up the coast to Kuwait City.[108] NAVCENT maintained its six carriers and their escorts on station in the theater. By the eve of the ground campaign, the *America* had left the *Kennedy* and the *Saratoga* in the Red Sea and had joined the *Ranger*, the *Midway*, and the *Theodore Roosevelt* in the Persian Gulf.[109]

On the eve of the war, CENTAF had had 1,125 combat and support aircraft; on February 20, it had 1,218.[110] The command's ability to bring aircraft into the theater, its successful maintenance of them, and its relatively light losses during the air campaign combined to give the command a larger number of combat-ready airplanes on G-day than it had had at the opening of the Gulf War. On February 20, it had 515 fighters, which was 23 more than it had had on January 17.[111]

With the success of the air campaign and the approach of the ground offensive, Coalition morale remained high. "People perceive that we're getting the job done in grand fashion," wrote one fighter wing commander on February 12, "and everyone is doing their part to do it well." After hearing President Bush's announcement of the ground campaign, a maintenance officer commented that "the mood upswing is like it was when the air campaign started." Reporting on the initial Saudi reaction to the start of land operations, the American Embassy in Riyadh reported the allies were "jubilant, strongly supportive, [and] relieved that the final phase is underway and hopeful that it will mean the end of Saddam Husayn [Hussein] as well as his occupation of Kuwait."[112]

Although the mood of the Coalition was buoyant as the ground campaign began, concerns remained regarding the strength of the Iraqis still in the KTO. Some analysts either underestimated the results of the air campaign or overestimated the enemy's initial numbers—or both—and they offered overly conservative assessments of the opponent's condition. One officer who served in the TACC during the war afterward acknowledged, "Our intel may have overestimated in gross numbers. They were talking about 500,000 Iraqis in Kuwait or [the] KTO, and it was only 250,000 or something.... I don't know what the real truth is." More than a year after the war, General Schwarzkopf wrote that "on the eve of the ground war, [the CIA] was still telling the President that we were grossly exaggerating the damage inflicted on the Iraqis. If we'd waited to convince the CIA, we'd still be in Saudi Arabia." The CINC's own intelligence officers also continued to credit the enemy with large numbers. On February 23, they believed that the Iraqis still had nearly 2,600 tanks in the KTO (more than 60 percent of their number at the beginning of the air campaign), more than 1,900 APCs (68 percent of their original number), and more than 1,650 artillery pieces (53 percent). On the same day, DIA analysts offered a guarded evaluation: "While morale in frontline infantry units has been severely eroded, morale in the regular army's heavy divisions and the Republican Guard is probably better. Iraq's army is not ready to collapse, although cracks in its capability and cohesion are appearing."[113]

A great deal of information about the enemy's condition remained in doubt until after the start of the ground campaign. As General Olsen pointed out after the war, the Coalition leaders were not entirely certain of the strength of the defenses along the Saddam Line until after the ground forces had advanced into them. After the war, General Schwarzkopf characterized his assessment of the situation as of mid-February: "I knew we'd defeat them—but I didn't know how bloody the ground war might be." The CENTCOM commander and his subordinates continued to base their plans on worst-case assumptions. If General Schwarzkopf had been certain in advance of a rapidly successful land offensive, he would not, for example, have positioned the enormous quantities of ammunition and supplies required for sixty days of combat. On February 27—after the outcome of the ground campaign was known—the CENTCOM commander told reporters that he had believed his troops "very easily could have gotten into" a "slug-fest battle."[114]

Despite these uncertainties, the Coalition leaders had considerable evidence that the enemy was not in good condition for battle. Except for the few units that had participated in the Battle of Khafji, their formations suffered from weeks of inactivity. Moreover, the Coalition air campaign had greatly reduced the enemy's morale. Early in the war, it virtually had eliminated the Iraqi Air Force from the conflict. For fourteen straight days before G-day, the enemy's aircraft did not even attempt to fly. After gaining air superiority, CENTAF had battered the Iraqis in the KTO and damaged their will to fight. On February 11, CENTCOM intelligence officers reported that the "vast majority" of enemy prisoners and deserters they questioned "had told stories of short rations, poor leadership, bad morale, and some summary executions of personnel by roving [Republican Guard] 'morale squads.'" The DIA, despite its concerns about the numbers of Iraqi troops and equipment in the KTO, was confident that the enemy's will had deteriorated. "Individual morale has hit rock bottom in many frontline infantry units," the agency reported on February 18, "which has seriously affected unit cohesion and unit willingness to resist a Coalition offensive…. Most [enemy prisoners of war] report that those who are staying with their units will probably surrender." Two days later, General Horner told his staff, "The [Iraqi] forces in the KTO are just not in very good shape. They are not very happy, and it's time for them to go home."[115]

Following Secretary Cheney's and General Powell's visit to the theater from February 8 to 10 to discuss the ground campaign, the chairman of the JCS had called General Schwarzkopf on February 12. "You can go anytime after twenty-one February," General Powell told the CENTCOM commander. "It'll be your call." General Schwarzkopf selected February 24 as G-day, the day that the Coalition would begin its land offensive against the Iraqis in Kuwait.[116] On February 22, President Bush, giving Saddam Hussein a final chance to leave Kuwait without a ground campaign, stated a deadline of noon, February 23 (Washington, D.C., time) for the Iraqis to withdraw. The Baghdad leader ignored this ultimatum, and that night the president announced, "I have…directed General H. Norman Schwarzkopf, in conjunction with the Coalition forces, to use all force available, including ground forces, to eject the Iraqi Army from Kuwait." At 1050 on February 23 (Riyadh time) General Schwarzkopf alerted General Horner and his other component commanders that H-hour, G-day would be 0400, February 24.[117]

General Schwarzkopf's order to execute the Desert Storm ground offensive reflected his satisfaction with the air campaign and other operations to date, as well as his confidence in victory. "The ground offensive must be conducted," he said, "with the same speed and efficiency that Coalition forces have exhibited so far in Desert Shield and Desert Storm operations.... We will soundly defeat the enemy and restore the sovereignty of Kuwait."[118]

Chapter Seven

Tanks Abandoned:
Phase IV, the Ground Campaign

At 0400 on Sunday, February 24, 1991, the Coalition forces opened the ground campaign on schedule, but in dismal weather. On the eve of the offensive, the high-pressure system that had provided excellent flying conditions (particularly over the northeastern part of the theater) gave way to a low-pressure one that slowly moved eastward along the Saudi-Iraqi border.[1] During the first morning of the ground campaign, extensive cloud cover, gusty winds, and rain set in across the KTO. Ceilings of 8,000 feet—and in a few places as low as 2,500 feet—prevailed until 0800, and isolated showers fell for another hour. The rains at times reduced visibility to approximately three miles, and, from noon until midnight, dust storms added to this problem. Dense smoke from the Kuwaiti oilfield fires,[2] by now rising as high as 10,000 feet in places, blew toward the northwest into the Euphrates River valley and across the area south of Baghdad. By the end of the day, the thick smoke hovered over the region around Arar, in northern Saudi Arabia. The smoke prevented some pilots operating over the northern KTO from seeing their targets.[3]

With the ground campaign underway, CENTAF aircrews made every effort to operate through the bad weather. On the first afternoon of the offensive, General Horner told his staff, "The weather considerations that were valid last week are no longer valid. There are people's lives depending on our ability to help them if help is required…. Up over the battlefield, it's time to go to work." "Close Air Support and Air Interdiction missions are not [to be] weather canceled," General Glosson directed CENTAF's wing operations centers the same day, "by some decision-maker removed from the scene. The time has come for the flight lead to make every reasonable effort to attack the target and get his flight back home." When the ground campaign opened, pilots countered the low ceilings by flying under them—"farther down than they wanted to," as General Olsen pointed out—and operating in some cases through the rain. General Corder recounted: "We lost airplanes under there doing that. But our guys went down under and did it anyway. So, weather is something you have to learn to take care of. That's part of your job."[4]

An Astros II multiple rocket launcher in action; both the Iraqi and Saudi armies were equipped with this Brazilian-made launcher.

The CENTCOM forces began the ground campaign at 0400, penetrating the Iraqi defenses in so many places that the enemy could not distinguish the main attacks from the secondary ones and react effectively. NAVCENT had opened the operation earlier that morning, with battleship fire and amphibious feints to keep the defenders' attention focused on the Kuwaiti coast and away from the crucial areas farther west.[5] At 0400, I MEF attacked into the barrier system of the Saddam Line at the heel of Kuwait, defended by the Iraqi III Corps. East of them, Saudi units of the JFC–E began their advance north against the enemy defenses.[6]

The opening of the ground offensive brought compelling evidence of the achievements of the air campaign. As soon as the MARCENT and JFC–E troops passed through the obstacle belts in their fronts, they began accepting the surrenders of enormous numbers of enemy soldiers. "We captured 5,000 Iraqi prisoners the first day," Lt. Gen. William M. Keys, commander of the 2d Marine Division, said later. "They would take us under fire. We would return fire with effect—killing a few—and then they would just quit." The large number of Iraqi III Corps infantrymen who surrendered that first morning supported what some Coalition members had concluded before the ground offensive began: that many of the defenders had lost their will to fight. "On more than one occasion," a military police unit reported, "the [enemy prisoners of war] were so eager to reach the EPW camps that they volunteered to drive." During the entire war, no escape attempt was made from any of these camps.[7]

Also at 0400, at the same time as the I MEF and JFC–E advances, units of the XVIII Airborne Corps left their line of departure and began moving northeast across the open desert. During the shift west, CENTAF airlifters had brought into position many of the supplies and personnel of this corps, which now began its strategic envelopment of the Iraqis. By 0800, the 101st Airborne Division of the

M1A1 main battle tanks of the 3d Armored Division (VII Corps) move from the assembly area in eastern Saudi Arabia to their attack position—Forward Assembly Area Garcia, west of Wadi al Batin—on February 14, 1991. In the background, trucks and other support vehicles can also be seen moving forward.

XVIII Airborne Corps, although somewhat delayed by the morning's bad weather, had begun establishing Forward Operating Base (FOB) Cobra, halfway to the Euphrates from the division's jump-off point for this air assault.[8]

The Coalition forces sustained their advances that afternoon. The two MAR-CENT divisions moved north into Kuwait, and the JFC–E units made progress up the coast. On the left of the Marines, Egyptian and Saudi units of the JFC–N and supported by a Syrian division penetrated the Saddam Line in their front, held by the Iraqi IV Corps. General Schwarzkopf did not plan to have General Franks's VII Corps, on the left of the JFC–N, advance until February 25, but, after the Coalition's early successes, he directed the heavy corps to attack that first afternoon.[9] The 1st Infantry Division, the "Big Red One," cleared the obstacle belt and minefield in its front, opening a breach for the British 1st Armored Division. Coalition forces now had broken through the entire Saddam Line.[10] Beyond the Iraqi defenses to the west, the 101st Airborne Division, with the French 6th Armored Division covering its left, refueled its helicopters at FOB Cobra and prepared to continue north. By evening, the spearhead units of the Screaming Eagles had reached the Euphrates and cut Highway 8, a main link between the KTO and Baghdad. Headquarters CENTCOM intelligence officers characterized the opposition encountered on the first day of the offensive: "Iraqi resistance to the Coalition ground campaign has been generally light thus far, marked by sporadic ground and artillery fire. Large groups of Iraqis are surrendering before being seriously pressed."[11]

On the first day of the ground campaign, as they had since the opening of the war, Coalition aircrews held air superiority over the KTO. They flew more than 1,200 combat sorties over the theater; in stark contrast, their opponents were virtually inactive, save for two MiG–23 Floggers that fled to Iran.[12] Preliminary BDA estimates credited the Coalition aircrews with destroying nearly 180 tanks, almost 100 APCs, more than 200 artillery pieces or multiple-rocket launchers (MRLs), and more than 200 trucks and other vehicles.[13] No Coalition aircraft were lost, and no Air Force ones reported damaged on February 24.[14]

Throughout the day, the TACC received reports of the ground campaign's initial progress. General Moore called the center at 0935 to report that, given the lack of Iraqi resistance, General Schwarzkopf already was considering accelerating the offensive, and again at 1238 to announce that the CINC indeed had given the "go ahead" to the VII Corps.[15] At 1010, General Hall telephoned the TACC from the XVIII Airborne Corps Air Support Operations Center with the good news that the corps so far had experienced "no problems" with its advance and "little contact" with the Iraqis. Later in the day, General Hall made an exciting helicopter ride east through a sandstorm to the VII Corps, and, at 1825, he was able to phone in an optimistic report from there, as well.[16]

The start of the land campaign increased the premium on flexible air operations, as the rapid moves of the ground units made it difficult to tell where aircrews might find their best opportunities. A little after 1000, for example, a Marine FAC in front of the JFC–E forces began turning back Coalition aircraft because there were no targets available. Late in the night of the twenty-fourth, on the other hand, TACC officers diverted some F–15Es from an attack against Al Asad Airfield in west-central Iraq to kill box AE6, which was in the line of advance of the VII Corps and offered what one of them called "mucho targets." In addition to demonstrating flexibility, striking aircraft had to take every measure to prevent fratricide, an even greater danger now that Coalition ground forces were advancing quickly. Late in the afternoon of the first day of the offensive, General Glosson emphasized to the aircrews that the unexpectedly rapid progress of the Coalition troops "meant increased potential for dropping on friendlies, if all air players don't keep up with FSCL changes or fail to get target and friendly location updates from controlling agencies. If you have any doubt about friendly locations in the vicinity of your target, do not drop."[17]

On the second day of the offensive—Monday, February 25—the Coalition forces sustained their momentum, advancing in places ahead of schedule. The Iraqi defenders, pummeled by the air campaign, offered so little resistance that allied units did less fighting and maneuvering than anticipated, and they ended the day with more ammunition and fuel than expected.[18] While the JFC–E units

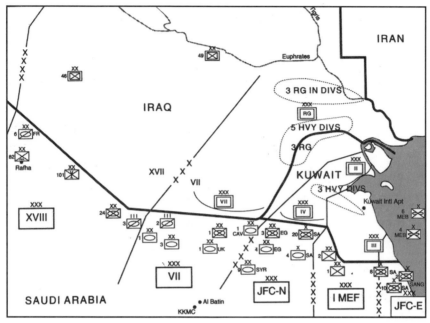

Coalition ground campaign:
H-hour/0400, February 24, 1991 (*above*).
Key to units (*below*).

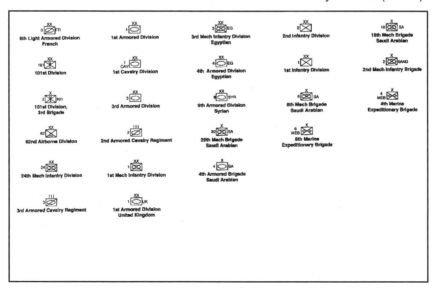

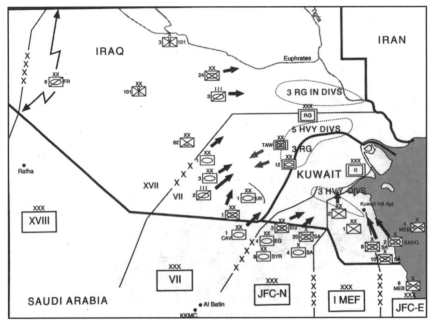

Coalition ground campaign:
H+64/2000, February 26, 1991 (*above*).
H+86/1800, February 27, 1991 (*below*).

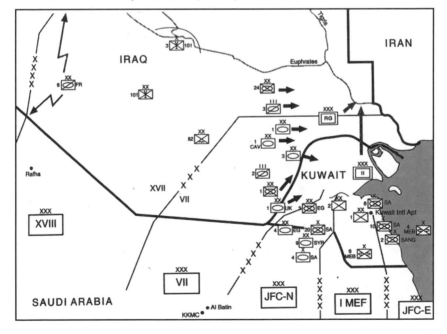

moved up the coast, the 1st Marine Division made more dramatic progress. Supported by A–10s, the Marines repulsed an armored brigade that made the first Iraqi counterattack of the campaign, consolidated their hold on Al Jaber Airfield, and captured Al Burgan oilfield, the largest in Kuwait, with 684 of the country's

A burned-out Iraqi tank sits amid the rubble of an Iraqi storage facility that was destroyed by the French 6th Armored Division.

950 wells.[19] Farther west, the 2d Marine Division reached its objective south of Al Jahra, the western suburb of Kuwait City and the central road intersection of the country.[20] The Iraqi III Corps retreated in disarray, without any effort to hold even a few strong points, and apparently without any plan for the defense of Kuwait City.[21]

West of the Marines, the JFC–N forces made enough progress against the Iraqi IV Corps to allow General Franks's VII Corps to advance without undue concern for its right flank.[22] Until the third day of the campaign, General Schwarzkopf remained dissatisfied with the progress of this corps,[23] but, during the afternoon of February 25, the unit's tanks pressed into Iraq and captured large numbers of the enemy. Nearly 300 prisoners surrendered to the 1st Armored Division near Makhfar al Busayyah, and another 700 to the 3d Armored Division.[24] One prisoner told his captors that his division and another in its vicinity had been unable to shell the U.S. 1st Infantry Division during its breaching, because the air campaign had destroyed their artillery. The air liaison officer with the Big Red One reported that some of enemy prisoners questioned why the Coalition had not attacked sooner; they claimed they had been trying to surrender for two weeks.[25]

While the Coalition forces advanced, most, although not all, of the Republican Guard remained in their reserve positions. During the morning of the twenty-fifth, some of the artillery from the elite units moved south to bolster the crumpling regular infantry divisions. The air campaign against the bridges then paid a dividend: the battlefield coordination element (BCE) (the Army liaison in the TACC) and the ABCCC both reported that these Republican Guard field pieces were backing up behind a dropped span, and the TACC directed Killer Scouts into the area.[26] In addition to the artillery, other Republican Guard units became active later in the day, when the mechanized Tawakalna Division moved to make contact with the VII Corps.[27]

On the left of General Franks's corps, the XVIII Airborne Corps continued its strategic envelopment. By 1600, the French 6th Armored Division, the western-most of the Coalition forces, had surrounded the village of Al Salman and secured the airfield there. The 197th Mechanized Infantry Brigade, 24th Mechanized Infantry Division, and 3d Armored Cavalry Regiment advanced northeast along lines parallel to that taken by the 101st Airborne Division, which already was on the Euphrates.[28] The second day of ground operations ended with ARCENT, MARCENT, and Arab forces occupying half of the KTO.[29]

The poor flying weather continued on February 25, when 279 sorties were canceled,[30] yet Coalition aircrews still flew more combat sorties over the KTO than they had on the first day of the ground campaign.[31] They dominated the air over the theater: the Iraqi Air Force did not fly that day, nor would it for the remainder of the war.[32] Early BDA credited the air attackers with destroying more than 75 tanks; almost 60 APCs; roughly 245 vehicles; nearly 130 artillery pieces or MRLs; more than 50 revetments, buildings, and bunkers; and some SAMs and AAA guns as well.[33] CENTAF crews also claimed the destruction of thirteen helicopters at Al Amara Airport, north of the KTO.[34] Given the volume of the air operations, Coalition losses remained relatively light. Two Marine aircraft were lost on February 25. The Iraqis hit an AV–8B near Al Jaber Airfield during the 1st Marine Division's operations there, and its pilot was rescued off the Kuwaiti coast. The enemy also downed an OV–10 FAC early in the afternoon near Kuwait City and captured its crew.[35]

Success on the ground had a direct relationship with success in the air. The Tawakalna Division gave the VII Corps little resistance, in part because of the preceding night's F–15E operations over kill box AE6. By 0400 on February 25, F–111s had destroyed approximately sixty Iraqi tanks within that square, and, with the daylight, Killer Scouts and A–10s would arrive to continue their work.[36] After talking to the 1st Infantry Division's air liaison officer during the afternoon of the twenty-fifth, General Horner noted in the TACC log, "The enemy troops shoot and then when air shows up, they surrender."[37]

Colonel Sawyer had predicted in mid-February that, after the ground campaign began, the A–10s would "strafe up a storm and get in as close as we need to get the job done. No A–10 pilot should ever have to buy a drink at any Army bar in the future."[38] The Warthogs made good on these words, recording a number of dramatic successes on the afternoon of February 25. In one instance, Capt. Eric Salomonson and 1st Lt. John Marks of the 76th TFS each flew their A–10s three times, carrying four Mavericks apiece. Twenty-three of their twenty-four missiles scored confirmed kills of Iraqi tanks. The commander of the 354th TFW sent the TACC a brief message summarizing an exploit of two other Warthogs. "Covered surrender of 10 or so tanks in column," reported Col. Ervin C. "Sandy" Sharpe. "Hatches opened. White flags waved. Tanks abandoned. Having a nice day."[39]

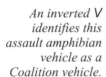

An inverted V identifies this assault amphibian vehicle as a Coalition vehicle.

After the A–10s had done their work that afternoon, the J–STARS came to the fore during the night of February 25/26, when the enemy began to abandon Kuwait City. Hammered from the air and pressed on the ground, the disorganized remnants of the Iraqi III Corps hastily prepared to retreat from the capital that evening. Soldiers sacked the city and piled their loot into any conveyance at hand. "They took every bus, car, jeep, armored personnel carrier, tank," one F–15E pilot recalled, "anything with four wheels on it."[40] Hoping that the night, rain, and smoke that covered the area would protect them from air strikes, the Iraqis began to withdraw from Kuwait City. The long convoys of disparate vehicles moved west through Al Jahra and then turned north toward the Iraqi border. Secretary of Defense Cheney, mocking Saddam Hussein's earlier boast that he would wage "the mother of all battles" against the Coalition, called this flight "the mother of all retreats."[41]

The eastern-orbit J–STARS came down briefly that night with a radar problem but soon returned on station. During the middle of the night, the aircraft, and other intelligence sources, reported the massive retreat north from Kuwait City. "We began to see convoys develop," recounted Col. George W. Cox, the ACE on the J–STARS that night, "and we hadn't seen anything bigger than fifteen to twenty vehicles in a convoy for quite a while…. Then we saw another main support route fill up with convoys. Of course, it was obvious to all of us that this was a mass withdrawal."[42]

Several factors now combined to give CENTAF aircrews one of their best opportunities of the war: the chance to attack these retreating convoys. The earlier success of the air campaign and the rapid advance of the ground forces had put the Iraqi III Corps into headlong retreat. J–STARS and other sources quickly had detected the withdrawal, and the Coalition enjoyed the communications to convey this information rapidly to its flying units. Technology also contributed to the opportunity, giving CENTAF its systems that could make air-to-ground attacks at night and in bad weather. Finally, the earlier successes of the air campaign against

An Abrams main battle tank during Desert Shield.

the bridges now proved their full value. The retreating convoys reached the Euphrates River crossings only to find many of their escape routes blocked, the spans having been dropped by air strikes and the approaches mined from the air.[43]

As the Iraqis fled Kuwait City, CENTAF had aircraft available that were capable of intercepting them. "We did have airplanes up that night that could fly and strike in bad weather," Colonel Cox pointed out. "You need F–16 LANTIRN aircraft or F–15Es to work in that kind of environment." The road north from the capital ran through a kill box that the ATO had assigned to A–6Es, and these Navy Intruders also could operate in all weather, at night. Around midnight, the TACC adjusted the kill-box assignments to put night-operating, moving target indicator-capable F–16Ls on the section of the road just above that covered by the A–6s. At about the same time, the mining of the bridge approaches began.[44]

CENTAF planners deliberately permitted the retreating enemy to put some distance between themselves and the capital. "We could have hit them initially right on the outskirts of Kuwait City," Colonel Cox noted, "but what the TACC decided was that, if we did that, it would do nothing but bottle them up in Kuwait City and we wanted them to get out of there. So we didn't hit those convoys as hard as we could have initially until we let them get out of Kuwait City and almost up to the Iraqi border, and then we stopped them."[45] One senior Air Force officer later recounted how an F–111 closed one of the bridges over the Euphrates. The J–STARS radar had shown a causeway that "was reasonably non-trafficable," he said, but the Iraqis managed to open it. After "they started to get movers across it," he continued, "we had two F–111s that were actually orbiting in the area and we figure one vehicle got across it. And we got the Pave Tack scene of the second vehicle as he was trying to cross it when we dropped the bomb on it, and it shows the vehicle disappearing."[46]

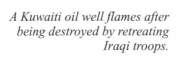

A Kuwaiti oil well flames after being destroyed by retreating Iraqi troops.

General Glosson began directing F–15Es, F–111s, F/A–18s, F–16Ls, and A–6s against the convoys, shifting some aircraft from targets over Iraq.[47] Although the bad weather prevented some of these attackers from finding the retreating column, the Strike Eagles had excellent success. Beginning at about midnight, two-ship cells of F–15Es began attacking the convoys every fifteen minutes. After 0300, the 4th TFW began turning Strike Eagles from Al Kharj with combined-effects munitions (CEMs), while armorers began preparing F–16Cs at Al Minhad with CBUs, readying them for operations after daylight. At 0400, the TACC directed three B–52s against a marshalling area just north of the Euphrates. At the same hour, twelve more F–15Es also joined the attack, keeping pressure on the Iraqis in northwestern Kuwait and southern Iraq until 0700, when the F–16 Killer Scouts would arrive for their daytime work.[48] Even though most of the Strike Eagle crews already had flown five- or six-hour missions that night, they stepped up to the job. One officer recalled, "Every jet that could fly, every guy that could walk went to an airplane, basically, went on that mission, out of crew rest."[49]

The Coalition attackers capitalized on the night's opportunity. "We hit them at the top [of their column] just south of the Euphrates river," Colonel Cox recounted, "blocked them off there, and started working our way down the convoys that were scattered up and down the road." That night and into the next day, the campaign against the bridges culminated in the destruction of hundreds of vehicles. Another Air Force officer recalled, "They get to where the bridges were out and they can't go anywhere. They can't go to the side because of the mines, and then we call in the F–16s, F–18s, and A–10s." An F–15E pilot described the end of many of the Iraqi convoys: "We found the lead guys on both roads that ran north out of Kuwait City and northeast.... And it was a thirty-mile traffic jam on

Aerial view of the Highway of Death leading from Kuwait City to Basra: retreating Iraqi troops, driving every kind of vehicle imaginable and carrying looted goods, were caught on February 25/26, by U.S. Air Force F–15Es, which bottled up the convoy. It was then virtually destroyed by U.S. Air Force, Navy, and Marine Corps aircraft.

both roads. And then the E models went in and, basically, destroyed everything on both roads for thirty miles."[50]

While CENTAF aircrews continued these shattering attacks into the morning of Tuesday, February 26, the Coalition ground forces sustained their advance. The French 6th Armored Division of the XVIII Airborne Corps captured Al Salman by 0930 and then set up a flank-guard position, to prevent Iraqi reinforcements from entering the theater from the northwest and interfering with ARCENT's operations. The 101st Airborne Division remained along Highway 8 and planned to move farther east the next day to cut the enemy's escape routes from Kuwait to Basra.[51] The 24th Mechanized Infantry Division—the "Victory Division"—completed its long advance into the Euphrates Valley and confronted the Republican Guard divisions to the east.[52]

First the devastating air campaign and then the rapid ground one had thoroughly convinced many Iraqis that resistance was useless. A single episode soon after midnight of the twenty-sixth dramatically illustrates the point. An XVIII Airborne Corps "Humvee," an Army vehicle blending the features of a jeep with those of a three-quarter-ton truck, became stuck in the mud. An Iraqi T–72 happened along, and its crew offered a chain, pulled the Humvee out of the mud, and then promptly surrendered.[53]

To the right of the XVIII Airborne Corps, the VII Corps closed in against Saddam Hussein's elite units. During General Horner's 1700 meeting with his staff on February 26, the CENTAF commander commented that the Iraqis were "trying to salvage what they can of the Republican Guard. We are attempting to close with the Republican Guard and annihilate it. The challenge for air will be to keep the pressure on the Republican Guard right up to the moment when the Army closes, and then get out of there so we don't damage the Army." During the twenty-sixth, the Tawakalna Division continued the advance it had begun the day before, perhaps intending to outflank the VII Corps or, as intercepted Iraqi radio messages suggested, fight a delaying action to cover the retreat of the Medina and Hammurabi Divisions.[54] Whatever the movement's intent, General Franks's heavy units quashed it. The 1st Armored Division, on the corps' left flank, attacked to the northeast and at 2230 struck a battalion of the Tawakalna Division, destroying thirty to thirty-five tanks. Southeast of this engagement, the 2d Armored Cavalry Regiment fought against elements of the same Republican Guard division and small units of Iraqi regulars, until it was relieved by the 1st Infantry Division at 2030. At 0143, on the twenty-seventh, the VII Corps BCE reported to the TACC that the Tawakalna Division no longer existed.[55] With this unit out of the fight, the Hammurabi and Medina Divisions tried to speed their retreat to Basra.[56]

Farther to the right, the British 1st Armored Division attacked the Iraqi 12th Armored Division during the afternoon of the twenty-sixth. The defenders were protected by revetments, but the allied tankers attacked them in the flank, brigade by brigade, and destroyed forty of their tanks. By 2100, the allied tankers claimed the capture of 200 APCs and more than 1,000 prisoners.[57] (It was during this engagement that a flight of two A–10s, controlled by a British FAC, mistakenly attacked two Warrior infantry fighting vehicles, killing nine British soldiers and wounding seven others.[58])

On the right flank of the VII Corps, the 1st Cavalry Division passed through the U.S. 1st Armored Division and attacked the armored Hammurabi Division, destroying more than forty of its T–72 tanks. The Army's M1A1 tank outranged the best Iraqi armor and, as General Schwarzkopf pointed out, the American 120-mm gun "would blow the turret 20–30 yards beyond the tank's position."[59] The VII Corps reported that it had captured 5,000 prisoners in three days.[60]

By February 26, the two MARCENT divisions had outrun the JFC–N forces on their left and the JFC–E on their right. General Schwarzkopf concluded that these allied units had moved slowly, partly because they preferred a methodical style of fighting and partly because their national leaders had directed them "to keep casualties to an absolute minimum" in this combat against fellow Arabs. Leaving these JFC forces behind, the 1st Marine Division advanced on Kuwait International Airport, at the southern edge of Kuwait City, moving through the dense smoke from the oilfield fires. "It was like three total eclipses," General Myatt, the division commander, said. "We had to use flashlights to be able to read the maps at noon."[61] That evening, the Marines made heavy contact with the Iraqi 3d Armored Division, as it attempted to defend the airport. The Americans identified the opposing unit by its T–72 tanks, sealed off the air facility, and, later that night, encircled it.[62]

On the morning of February 26, General Boomer cleared the 2d Marine Division, accompanied by the Tiger Brigade of the 2d Armored Division, to drive on Kuwait City. Jumping off at 1200, the Army unit seized Al Jahra, which cut the enemy's retreat route west from the capital. By the early afternoon, the last of the Iraqis had abandoned Kuwait City, leaving behind weapons and ammunition in their haste. One Headquarters CENTAF officer later characterized the Iraqi "order of the day" as "Turn and run for Basrah."[63] Kuwaiti resistance leaders advised the residents of the capital that they would be safest indoors and that they should not shoot at any aircraft or helicopters—any they saw now belonged to the Coalition. The 2d Marine Division pressed up on the right of the Tiger Brigade the same afternoon, and by evening it stood poised to enter Kuwait City.[64]

The advancing Army armor cut the road west from the capital; it also blocked the southern escape route of the enemy convoys, which now had been under CENTAF's attacks since the preceding night. The Tiger Brigade deployed its tanks onto Mutla Ridge, which, although only twenty-five feet high, represented the highest piece of terrain for hundreds of miles in any direction. The Army tanks now added their fire to that of the A–10s, F–16s, F–18s, and other aircraft attacking the long traffic jam of enemy vehicles. Later, journalists labeled the four-lane roadway north to Basra the "Highway of Death."[65] After the war, visitors to the region found that one building along this road, a mosque, stood undamaged—a monument to the precision of CENTAF's bombing. After the war, the Kuwaitis displayed an enormous "museum" of charred Iraqi tanks, APCs, and artillery pieces on the fairgrounds of Kuwait City, dramatic reminders of how allied air attacks had helped liberate their country.[66]

The first three days of the ground campaign had far exceeded expectations, and General Yeosock's largest concern on the night of the twenty-sixth seemed to be the continuing bad weather. He reported that the impressive advances of the VII and XVIII Airborne Corps had been accompanied by rain, low ceilings, and dense morning fog, which limited the CAS sorties flown against Iraqi artillery and tanks. General Yeosock emphasized, however, that these conditions would not significantly hinder his units from attacking the Republican Guard.[67]

The ARCENT commander's point was well made, for intermittent thunderstorms and rain showers fell throughout the twenty-sixth. From the central Tigris-Euphrates Valley south into Kuwait, fog and oilfield smoke reduced visibility to approximately a mile and a quarter. This distance was cut in half in the areas where heavy rains fell through the soot-blackened air.[68]

156

Tanks Abandoned: Phase IV, the Ground Campaign

Despite the persistently bad weather, CENTAF aircrews flew roughly 1,550 sorties over the KTO on February 26, the largest number of any day during the Gulf War.[69] Preliminary BDA credited them with destroying more than 75 tanks; more than 65 APCs; more than 150 vehicles; nearly 100 artillery pieces and MRLs; approximately 60 revetments, buildings, or bunkers; and 8 SAM or AAA sites.[70] No CENTAF aircraft were lost that day, and only one, an F–16A from the 174th TFW, was damaged when it was hit by an Iraqi SA–13 SAM.[71]

The Coalition continued the air assault against the Iraqi convoys retreating toward the border. The daylight of the twenty-sixth brought A–10s, F–16s, and other aircraft into action, and the crews of the night-capable strikers extended themselves to sustain the attack. The F–15Es operated through the night and well into the next morning. The LANTIRN-equipped F–16Ls flew continually for thirty-six hours, with General Glosson restricting individual aircrews to a maximum of three sorties and a duty day of sixteen hours. He also directed that twelve of these fighters, which operated from Al Minhad, in the Emirates, were to be back on the ground by 1200. The aircrews could sustain this pace against the convoys for another twenty-four hours, he advised General Horner at 0600 on February 26, and then they would have to reduce it slightly.[72]

The ground campaign had progressed so expeditiously that one of CENTAF's largest problems developed with the FSCL, which was moving so rapidly that nearly every target had to be "deconflicted" with ARCENT or MARCENT units.[73] Before G-day, planners had established a successive series of lines that could serve as the FSCL as the Coalition ground forces advanced through the KTO.[74] Difficulties arose as early as February 24, when the allied units advanced quickly and the line changed rapidly.

Ground commanders could establish their FSCLs, and this authority usually was exercised at the corps level. The lines were to follow well-defined terrain features: the Euphrates River, for example, made an excellent boundary line because, as one TACC officer pointed out, "fighter pilots going 600 knots can discern [it]. It's easy for any Army guy in a tank because it's got water, and he's gotta cross."[75] As units advanced and ground commanders moved the FSCL, they were to coordinate its changes with "the appropriate tactical air commander and other supporting elements." Each rapid move of the FSCL "had to be passed to those assets already airborne," Colonel Baptiste explained, "so that they would get an update."[76]

Aircrews also needed adequate notice of these changes. Two days before G-day, Headquarters CENTCOM advised that the location of the line had to be communicated at least three hours before it took effect. CENTAF officers were not satisfied that this guidance always was met. Colonel Baptiste commented after Desert Storm, "We had some problems with [the timeliness of] when the Combat Ops floor [the TACC] was notified of the FSCL change." One instance occurred very early in the ground campaign, when TACC officers did not learn about a new boundary line for the XVIII Airborne Corps until after it had been in effect for three hours.[77]

Lucrative Targets

The rapid success of the ground campaign exacerbated these issues. By late in the night of February 26, the 101st Airborne Division had moved in front of the XVIII Airborne Corps's FSCL, and the TACC had to alert the F–15Es working the kill box over the area to the location of the Screaming Eagles.[78] Another incident in which the FSCL became an issue began during the early morning hours of the twenty-seventh. F–111s delivered GBU–24s against a causeway over the Euphrates River crossing and backed up Iraqi vehicles for miles, well behind the XVIII Airborne Corps's fire-support boundary. Shortly after 0500 on February 27, the Army unit's BCE offered CENTAF permission to attack this traffic jam, but a TACC duty officer declined, prudently suggesting instead that the corps move its FSCL back five to six miles. The BCE rejected this idea, indicating that ARCENT assets would deal with the convoy.[79]

Perhaps the sharpest FSCL controversy developed during the night of February 26/27, while CENTAF aircraft were making their second night of CEM attacks on the Iraqi convoys retreating from Kuwait to the north and northwest. Having advanced rapidly, the XVIII Airborne Corps proposed moving its FSCL far north of the Euphrates River. The TACC's night-operations officer demurred, because such a move would bring to an end the F–15E and F–16L attacks against the enemy vehicles fleeing northwest on the road to An Nasiriyah. After the corps liaison indicated that ARCENT Apaches would begin operating against those convoys in the morning, the two officers agreed that the XVIII Airborne Corps would advance its FSCL, but not until the morning, when the Army helicopters could assume the efforts of the CENTAF fighters. This arrangement broke down when no Apaches arrived on the scene.[80] "I came in one morning at the end of the war [February 27]," General Horner later recalled, "and instead of putting the FSCL on the…Euphrates river,…they had put it way north of there. I hit the ceiling because that meant that I had to put FACs over the river, for all practical purposes, that's dumb because there weren't any friendlies over there." At the 0900 CENTAF briefing that morning, General Horner directed the Army BCE to get the FSCL moved back to the line of the Euphrates and Hawr al Hammar, the large lake south of it. General Schwarzkopf agreed with the CENTAF commander on this issue, and the boundary was shifted south, to the line of the river and the lake.[81]

The Coalition ground offensive culminated on February 27, still in bad weather. The rain and thunderstorms continued that Wednesday morning, and a dense fog left visibility near zero along the Tigris and Euphrates Valleys. Smoke, blowing dust, ground fog, rain, and haze obscured other areas of the theater. With the ground campaign approaching its end, the day also offered the first signs of improving weather: cloud ceilings climbed, and, early in the day, the dust storms west of Kuwait cleared.[82]

On the morning of the twenty-seventh, the XVIII Airborne Corps prepared to advance on Basra. While the French 6th Armored Division still held its screening position and the 101st Airborne Division remained in the Euphrates Valley astride

Highway 8, the 24th Mechanized Infantry Division captured Tallil Airfield, southwest of An Nasiriyah, and, beyond it to the southeast, Jalibah Southeast Airfield.[83] With these two facilities secured, the Victory Division and the 3d Armored Cavalry Regiment pressed east toward Basra into the night, passing south of Hawr al Hammar. After 2000, the 24th Mechanized Infantry Division exhausted

An F–16C of the 4th TFS (388th TFW) flies over the Saudi desert after the war.

its fuel, but it would again be underway at 0400 on the twenty-eight.[84] By dawn that day, its lead elements had reached a point only thirty miles west of Basra.[85]

On the right of the XVIII Airborne Corps, the VII Corps moved east to close with the remaining Iraqi elite units. While the Iraqi II Corps fled north from Kuwait and most of the Republican Guard retreated northeast, the armored Medina and Hammurabi Divisions tried to defend Basra.[86] For the first time during the campaign, all of the major subordinate units of the VII Corps advanced on a continuous front, rolling eastward with some 1,500 tanks, 1,500 M2 Bradley fighting vehicles and other APCs, 650 artillery pieces, and hundreds of supply trucks. The dust storms in this area had cleared early that morning, and these ARCENT vehicles presented an intimidating sight, stretching across the desert from horizon to horizon and closing with the enemy. "To Iraqi units depleted and demoralized by 41 days of continuous air assault," wrote one Army historian, "the VII Corps advance appeared irresistible." The heavy corps destroyed hundreds of enemy tanks and APCs and accepted the surrenders of thousands of enemy prisoners of war. At 1700 on February 27, General Franks alerted his divisions that a ceasefire was imminent; then he continued his advance until 1940, when all of the corps, except one Apache battalion, halted operations for the night.[87]

To the southeast, MARCENT units had encircled Kuwait City and stood poised to enter the capital. "In the morning [of February 27]," General Keys related, "the word came down: 'Don't go.' The Coalition forces from the region had been selected to enter Kuwait City." The capital has a series of concentric roads, beginning with the First Ring Road, which lies the farthest downtown, and rippling out to the Sixth Ring Road, which encircles the city's perimeter. The 1st Marine Division held Kuwait Airport and the 2d Marine Division at a position along the Sixth Ring Road, where it arranged for a JFC–N force to pass through its lines. At about 1400, these units—two Kuwaiti brigades, two Saudi brigades, and one Egyptian—entered Kuwait City.[88]

At 2100 on the evening of February 27, 1300 Eastern Standard Time, General Schwarzkopf met the theater press corps in Riyadh's Hyatt Hotel and briefed them on the culmination of Desert Storm. That afternoon in the United States, the public learned for the first time some of the details of the plan for the land offensive and how the air campaign, the shift west, and the rapid advance of the ground forces had defeated the Iraqis and liberated Kuwait. Some tensions had arisen between the military and the press during the Gulf War, and the journalists had asked some contentious questions after this presentation, as they had after others during the conflict, but the briefing ended with a positive incident, one unprecedented during the Vietnam War. As General Schwarzkopf left this last news conference, several reporters called their thanks and congratulations to the departing commander.[89]

General Schwarzkopf had commended the air campaign to the press, and the day's operations well merited his praise. As the fast-paced ground operations continued, sorties over the KTO decreased only slightly from the record-setting number flown on February 26.[90] Working with helicopter- or ground-based FACs,[91] CENTAF aircrews flew more than 500 CAS sorties on the twenty-seventh. The early BDA estimates credited them with approximately 170 tank kills (the largest number since G-day), more than 60 APCs, roughly 155 trucks and other vehicles, more than 100 artillery pieces and MRLs, and 2 AAA or SAM sites.[92] The twenty-seventh also proved the costliest day of the ground campaign for Coalition aircrews. The first loss came at about 0700, when a Marine AV–8B was shot down.[93] Later in the morning, an Iraqi infrared SAM hit an O/A–10, completely destroying its hydraulics. At approximately 0900, the pilot attempted to land at King Khalid Military City, but his aircraft crashed and was engulfed in flames.[94] The enemy also downed an F–16C of the 363d TFW on February and captured its pilot, returning him after the war.[95] Two Army OV–1D Mohawks had a noncombat mishap the same day; their crews were rescued.[96] It was also on the twenty-seventh that four B–52s and an F–16C from the 388th TFW suffered battle damage.[97]

During the early morning hours of February 28, CENTAF officers and airmen knew that a ceasefire was approaching. After midnight, TACC officers discussed the option of keeping the B–52s armed but on hold, while maintaining the F–111s, F–15Es, and A–6s over their kill boxes until hostilities ended.[98] At 0202, General Corder alerted all of CENTAF's field commanders that a ceasefire might be ordered as early as 0500, indicating that the units would receive at least two hours' notice of the event.[99] At 0530, Brig. Gen. Richard Neal, Headquarters CENTCOM/J–3's Director of Operations, called the TACC to advise that hostilities would end at 0800. Consistent with General Schwarzkopf's long-running emphasis on the Republican Guard, he directed that Coalition aircraft continue to cover the remaining Iraqi tank routes out of the KTO until 0745, a task that F–16s and Navy aircraft performed with EF–111 support.[100] The CENTCOM commander asked CENTAF also to continue until 0745 its coverage against Scud launches from western Iraq. All other combat flights would cease at 0600.[101]

The ground forces knew equally well that the end was approaching. During the night of February 27/28, the 24th Mechanized Infantry Division stood prepared to continue its attack east against the Republican Guard units still retreating across the Euphrates.[102] At 2300 on the twenty-seventh, General Schwarzkopf had called General Yeosock and told him that President Bush and his senior military advisers were considering a ceasefire, which might take effect as soon as 0500 on the twenty-eighth. The 24th Infantry Division's attack was put on hold.[103]

At 0300 on February 28, General Schwarzkopf called General Yeosock again, updating him that the ceasefire probably would become effective at 0800. At 0330, the ARCENT commander ordered the VII Corps to continue its attack east. The British 1st Armored Division closed on the Egyptian division to its right, thus connecting the VII Corps with JFC–N and MARCENT forces south of it. The U.S. 1st Armored Division remained in contact with retreating Republican Guard and Iraqi regular units, until the ceasefire began at 0800.[104]

The final air operations of the Gulf War were conducted after daylight arrived on February 28. The same low ceilings that had limited visibility throughout the ground campaign stubbornly remained during its final hours, forcing CENTAF aircrews to employ radar bombing. The poor weather did not significantly reduce the number of CAS sorties, and Coalition strike aircraft continued to score heavily against tanks, APCs, artillery, and vehicles until the end of the war.[105]

Forcefully aided by Phases III and IV of the air campaign, the Coalition ground units had conducted remarkable operations. The armor-heavy VII Corps had advanced 100 miles into Iraq and another 55 miles east. The lead elements of the XVIII Airborne Corps had penetrated 190 miles into Iraq and then 70 miles east.[106] The Marines had made an important contribution to the campaign as well, encircling Kuwait City and passing through their lines the Arab units that captured the capital. The air campaign had been so successful that the ground units were delayed far more by massive Iraqi surrenders than by stout enemy resistance. One TACC officer later commented, "We absolutely decimated them with airpower…. So at the time we decided to kick off the ground war, there were not very many Republican Guard guys who were interested in fighting." The advancing troops accepted more than 65,000 surrenders within 100 hours. During the entire course of the war, Coalition forces captured a staggering total of 86,743 prisoners.[107]

CENTAF's remaining task was to bring its operations to an orderly end. During the morning of February 28, the command gained more details about the approaching ceasefire. At 0350, shortly after General Yeosock had directed the VII Corps to continue its advance east, the TACC learned that General Schwarzkopf wanted the J–STARS aircraft to maintain their coverage until 0830. Just after 0540, General Neal followed up on his earlier call to the air command center, indicating that General Schwarzkopf intended to have all reconnaissance missions, including RF–4 and Navy F–14 flights, continue after the impending ceasefire.[108]

Many hours before General Neal's telephone call to the TACC, on the afternoon of the twenty-seventh in Washington, D.C., President Bush, General Powell, Secretary Cheney, and other senior military advisers had met at the White House to discuss a Gulf War ceasefire. The chairman of the JCS gave a thorough briefing on the course of the war, which concluded that its main military objectives had been achieved. After a telephone conversation between Generals Powell and Schwarzkopf at 1430 Eastern Standard Time (2230 in the theater), the conferees agreed that the time had come to end the conflict.[109]

In Riyadh at 0800 on February 28, Headquarters CENTCOM sent a message welcomed by the Air Force, the other services, the Coalition allies, and others around the world. "The President of the United States," General Schwarzkopf informed his command, "has directed a cessation of offensive operations for US-CENTCOM forces involved in Operation Desert Storm." The order took effect with the transmission of the message, at 0800: all units stopped offensive operations and remained in place. Just as General Neal earlier had advised the TACC, CENTAF aircrews continued to fly electronic surveillance and other reconnaissance missions. The command maintained the air supremacy it had won during the war and remained ready for the possibility of future operations. Aircraft remained on ground and air alert and continued to fly defensive CAPs and Scud-response missions.[110]

Although the United States had declared a ceasefire, the Gulf War had not ended. Just as Headquarters CENTCOM was transmitting the 0800 message, the XVIII Airborne Corps Air Support Operations Center (ASOC) sent a report through the ABCCC aircraft to the TACC that a large number of T–72 tanks, enough to equip a division, were moving west. If they continued their advance, they would encounter the 24th Mechanized Infantry Division, which had halted for the ceasefire just west of a causeway across the Euphrates. Six A–10s quickly flew to the area, but, when no threat developed, they returned to base that afternoon, with all of their ordnance.[111] Two days later, at 0450 on the morning of March 2, the XVIII Airborne Corps ASOC issued a similar alert. About twenty-four T–52s and approximately fifteen T–72s were moving in the vicinity of the 24th Infantry Division. The TACC responded again, sending four A–10s to the scene and alerting the 354th TFW's operations officer of this second possible confrontation.[112]

The advance of these Iraqi tanks and other vehicles, a larger force than at first reported, created the final confrontation of the Gulf War. At 0720, these enemy units approached the Euphrates, initially heading for the causeway as if hoping to escape over the river into Iraq, but then turning to confront the 24th Infantry Division. The CENTCOM message declaring the ceasefire also had reminded commanders of their duty of self-defense.[113] When the Iraqis fired on the Victory Division, the unit vigorously replied. Learning of this encounter, the TACC directed four F–16s to join the four A–10s already dispatched, and a tanker to support them. None of these aircraft proved needed:[114] the 24th Infantry Division destroyed more than 80 Iraqi tanks, approximately 95 APCs, and a number of other vehicles, and captured 3,000 prisoners, without a single casualty of its own.[115] An entry in the TACC logbook made at 1045 on March 2 provided an understated, yet fitting, epitaph to this last engagement of the ground campaign: "Shut off A–10/F–16 flow," Colonel Doman reported. "Tank battle appears to be over."[116]

This incident, General Schwarzkopf said, "underscored the urgency of setting ceasefire terms that would definitely separate the two sides."[117] The CENTCOM commander met with Iraqi representatives for that purpose at Safwan Airfield, Iraq, just north of the Kuwaiti border on the main road to Basra. Early on the morning of February 28, General Schwarzkopf had directed the 1st Infantry Division to capture this asphalt strip, but the infantrymen did not secure the location until 1800 on March 1.[118] The meeting was originally scheduled for March 2,[119] but ARCENT logisticians had to prepare the site, and the conference was postponed until the following day.[120] That afternoon, General Schwarzkopf, Prince Khalid, and other Coalition leaders met for ninety minutes with Lt. Gen. Sultan Hashim Ahmad al-Jabburi, Deputy Chief of Staff of the Iraqi Ministry of Defense, and ten other senior officers of the enemy army. General Schwarzkopf and Prince Khalid set the terms for a military ceasefire, and the Iraqi delegation agreed to them.[121]

It appeared on March 3 that the Coalition could be well satisfied with the conclusion of the Gulf War, but it was not long before some analysts contended that President Bush had declared the ceasefire too soon. Although General Schwarzkopf had agreed to the proposal to end hostilities during a telephone conversation with General Powell at 2230 on February 27, earlier on the same day the CENT-COM commander had advised the JCS chairman: "I want the Air Force to keep bombing those convoys backed up at the Euphrates where the bridges are blown. I want to continue the ground attack tomorrow, drive to the sea, and totally destroy everything in our path." The public learned of this initial recommendation shortly after the war, when General Schwarzkopf gave a March 27 interview to journalist David Frost. During this session, the CENTCOM commander stated, "Frankly, my recommendation had been…, continue the march—I mean, we had had them in a rout, and we could have continued to…wreak great destruction upon them. We could have completely closed the door and made it in fact a battle of annihilation."[122] Saddam Hussein remained in power after the war, brutally repressed the Kurds and Shiites within Iraq, rebuilt his army, and continued to defy the resolutions of the United Nations, all of which added weight to the contention that the Coalition should have prosecuted the war longer.[123]

Closely related to the issue of the conflict's termination was that of the escape of many Republican Guard units. During General Schwarzkopf's interview with David Frost, the general commented that the president's ceasefire decision had left "some escape routes open" for the Iraqis to retreat from Kuwait, and that "there were obviously a lot of people who escaped who wouldn't have escaped if the decision hadn't been made…to stop us where we were at that time." One post-war study found that the Republican Guards had been able to bring large amounts of their combat equipment out of the theater. "Many surviving [Iraqi] units," another report stated, "including those from the Republican Guard, managed to reach Basra."[124]

President Bush and Secretary Cheney did not comment specifically on the escape of the Republican Guards, but they immediately contradicted some of General Schwarzkopf's interview with David Frost. The president told reporters, "There was total agreement concerning when this war should end." Presidential press secretary Marlin Fitzwater contended that the CENTCOM commander's statements "contradict what happened at the time." Secretary Cheney provided journalists with a written statement that said that the decision for a ceasefire had been "coordinated with and concurred in" by General Schwarzkopf, who had "raised no objections to terminating hostilities."[125]

CENTAF's senior leaders did not criticize the timing of the ceasefire. General Olsen later recalled that his opinion at the time had been "the sooner, the better, because that meant fewer casualties…. We had accomplished our mission." General Horner pointed out that the Coalition's military effort had reached a point "where some people felt we were beating a tethered goat."[126] Answering the suggestion that the ground forces should have captured the Iraqi capital, the CENTAF commander said, "I don't agree with that. My point there is, 'You want the 82d Airborne still doing street duty in Baghdad?'" General Tenoso, the COMALF, expressed the feeling of many airmen: "Like everyone, we felt we had more to give, but damn glad it wasn't required."[127]

CENTAF's leaders had good reason to be satisfied with Phase IV of the air campaign, which had culminated in victory, more rapidly than Coalition members had dared hope. One F–16 pilot tersely summarized the last phase of the air effort: "Basically, [the Iraqis] got out of their holes and got pounded." First Lt. John Marks, who with Capt. Eric Salomonson had killed twenty-three Iraqi tanks with twenty-four Mavericks, made much the same assessment of the Phase IV operations. "It was exactly what we had hoped," Lieutenant Marks said, "that the Army advance would do exactly what it did, that is, force the Republican Guard out of their prepared positions, out in the open and onto the roads." The aircrews could receive no higher compliment than the one implied by the rapid progress and low casualties of the Coalition ground forces. As Colonel Reavey summarized it: "Basically they went, 'ready, ready, go,' cranked up the tanks, went as fast as they could for 96 hours, got as far as they could go in 96 hours without very much in the way of resistance."[128]

Epilogue

A Success Story and a Cautionary Tale

The Coalition defeated a large enemy force, although exactly how large remained a matter of dispute. On the eve of Desert Storm, CENTCOM intelligence officers had credited the Iraqis with forty-three divisions in the KTO, comprising roughly 546,700 personnel, approximately 4,280 tanks, 2,880 APCs, and 3,100 pieces of artillery. Postwar studies gave lower numbers, and the precise figures will probably never be known.[1]

The Coalition could only estimate Iraqi losses but believed they were high. CENTCOM assessments, adjusted after the war, estimated that the air campaign had destroyed 1,388 tanks (another 1,245 had been destroyed or abandoned during the ground campaign), 929 APCs (739 during the ground campaign), and 1,152 artillery pieces (1,044 during the ground campaign). The Coalition forces captured more than 86,000 prisoners of war.[2] The numbers of Iraqi military personnel killed and wounded were unknown and are likely to remain so. During General Schwarzkopf's press conference on the evening of February 27, he predicted that there would never be an "exact count" of the enemy dead, and several months later the CENTCOM commander told a congressional committee that he did not have enough information to make even a "reasonable estimate" of that statistic. General Behery, the RSAF commander, estimated the enemy's military dead at 70,000 to 100,000,[3] but the absence of mass graves in the KTO argued for a lower figure. The aggregate casualties among Iraqi civilians were another controversial issue. During the war, the Baghdad government accused the Coalition of targeting residential districts, and the American press speculated about the number of nonmilitary fatalities.[4] As with the case of battle losses, these statistics probably never would be known, but it was certain that the Coalition's use of PGMs greatly reduced the casualties among civilians, and that the enemy's AAA barrages over Baghdad and elsewhere increased them.[5]

Although Iraqi numbers and losses remained in dispute, the Coalition could establish more reliable statistics for its own forces. On the last day of the Gulf

Lucrative Targets

War, approximately 795,400 allied personnel were in the theater (539,300 from the United States, 100,300 from Saudi Arabia, and 45,000 from the United Kingdom). CENTCOM's exact strength on February 28 totaled 539,321, of whom 54,531 were assigned to CENTAF.[6]

Soldiers of the 62d Engineering Battalion, 20th Engineer Brigade, salute the Saudi leader, King Fahd, as he reviews the Coalition forces on March 8, 1991.

   Whereas these numbers represented only dry statistics, CENTCOM's casualty figures could not be separated from the suffering they represented. "To the trooper who has lost a buddy," an air cavalryman wrote during the Vietnam War, "no amount of figures will be able to make it appear that the battle was a success." This statement applied equally well to those who lost a friend or relative in the Gulf, or any other war. Yet it was also true that, given the large number of personnel engaged and the intensity of contemporary warfare, CENTCOM's losses were remarkably low, and far fewer than most Americans dared hope before the conflict began. Perhaps underestimating what an air campaign might achieve, some analysts predicted that ground operations would result in as many as 20,000 allied casualties.[7] The reality proved far lower: an accounting in June 1991 put Coalition losses at 390 killed in action and 776 wounded in action, and U.S. casualties at 148 killed in action and 458 wounded in action.[8] The Air Force reported a total of 35 fatalities, which included battle and nonbattle deaths.[9] Eight CENTAF officers were held as prisoners during the conflict.[10] While destroying 41 Iraqi aircraft in air-to-air combat and driving almost 140 others to Iran, the Coalition lost none of its own airplanes.[11] Over the course of the war, the allies lost a total of 41 fixed-wing aircraft; the enemy lost more than 100.[12]

   These statistics could not define the Coalition's accomplishment, but they suggest its dimensions. The Gulf War allowed the United States to bring to bear many of its military strengths: its high-technology weapons; its well-trained and motivated personnel; its air refueling and cargo capabilities which, given time, could move enormous amounts of materiel; its space-based and other advanced communications; and its ability to use computers for planning highly complex operations. The United States led an international alliance to a remarkable triumph and had every reason to be proud of its achievement. A crowd of about 800,000 cheered a parade of 8,800 Desert Storm veterans in Washington, D.C., on June 8, 1991, the first such event since 1945.[13] In this celebration and others, the Gulf War triumph offered a counterweight to America's tragic experience during its preceding war in Vietnam.[14]

The air campaign contributed the centerpiece of the victory. Retired Air Force General Bryce Poe II, commenting in October 1992, underscored his service's historic achievement. "The Air Force had been waiting for three generations," General Poe said, "for the opportunity it got in the Gulf War. And when the chance came, God bless 'em, they did a great job. And it would have been the only chance; had they blown it, no one would have ever given us another chance. But they didn't. It was magnificent."[15]

The success of the air campaign depended on a synergy among its four phases. Phase IV's rapidly triumphant ground campaign was based on Phase III's destruction of the tanks, armored vehicles, and field artillery of the Republican Guard and Iraqi regulars. During the KTO phase, Coalition aircraft flew more than 35,000 sorties, including approximately 5,600 against the elite Guard units.[16] The allies gave a larger effort to Phase III targets in the KTO than to Phase I targets in Iraq, and, in fact, they devoted more sorties to this theater—more than 30 percent—than they did to any other portion of the air campaign.[17]

The success of Phase III in turn depended on Phase II, the defeat of the Iraqi air defenses in the KTO. Writing a year before the Gulf War, two military analysts predicted, "It is also likely that sophisticated Western forces like USCENTCOM can exploit the technical advantages they will gain from superior C^3I organization and technology and could use a combination of electronic warfare, targeting, and strike systems that [will] massively degrade the C^3I assets in Third World forces. The experience of [the] Iran-Iraq [War] indicates such strikes might cripple many Third World air forces and critically weaken their regular armies, particularly if they hit at both military and civil C^3 links." This prediction well described the achievements of the Coalition's Phase II SEAD sorties over the KTO and its Phase I attacks against air defenses in Iraq. The fundamental importance of these operations was immediately obvious to professional airmen. When General Schwarzkopf had asked Colonel Warden on August 17, 1990, "What would you have to do if we wanted our airplanes to operate freely over the battlefield in Kuwait?" the Air Staff planner had replied, "Immediately destroy their air defenses."[18] That exchange harbored the origin of Phases I and II, the attacks against the enemy's air defenses in Iraq and the KTO. These operations won the Coalition's air supremacy and made possible all of its successes that followed: the strategic strikes against nuclear, biological, chemical, and other targets in Iraq; the damage to the Republican Guard and other enemy forces in the KTO; and the rapid victory during the ground campaign.

Lucrative Targets

These were remarkable achievements, and it does not detract from them to recognize that the history of the Gulf War was both a success story and a cautionary tale. Senior Air Force leaders knew that this was true, and they recognized not only that their service should be proud of its achievement, but also that it should study cautiously the lessons of the conflict. Shortly after the ceasefire began, General Horner admonished his staff against a prideful reaction to the victory, warning them not to "become puffed up like a toad." General McPeak reminded a gathering of Air Force officers soon after Desert Storm that the past offered many examples of victorious nations that took for granted their success in combat, while their opponents soberly studied their defeat, improved their military forces, and triumphed in their next war. History, the chief of staff said, advised that the United States should not become complacent about its success in the Gulf. After he had underscored the Air Force's achievements during Desert Storm, General Poe, a veteran of 90 Korean War missions as well as of 213 in Vietnam, then added this caution: "But we should also remember that they had five months to get ready, and an incompetent leader on the other side. If Saddam Hussein had been smarter, the first F–15s might have gotten over there and found what I found at Kimpo—enemy tanks on the runway."[19]

Senior Air Force leaders offered these cautions at a time when the end of the Cold War and a recession in the national economy had brought deep cuts in military spending. Given this setting, the country's defense leaders were anxious to reduce the force structures of all of the services and were tempted to emphasize the triumphs, rather than the difficulties, of the Gulf War. Television had encouraged the same tendency among the public, by creating the illusion that the United States had technologies readily at hand that had won the war easily. Videotapes played without informed commentary left the impression that the air campaign succeeded without difficulties or risks to personnel. Although Stealth, PGMs, IR, and other advanced technologies did indeed contribute enormously to the victory, television presentations failed to emphasize the expenditures made years before the war to develop these weapons, or the long investment in training the personnel who operated them under the stress of combat. The war, General Horner commented soon after its close, "made great television…. But I did sense from some of the questions I'd get asked [by the press] that people were thinking of war in sterile, mechanical, technological terms, when I was thinking of the guys going through this hail of lead, having surface-to-air missiles shot at them, and having the sweat running down their necks."[20]

Air Force leaders knew that it would be foolish to predicate defense budgets and force structures on the assumption that all of the nation's future conflicts would be waged against opponents like Saddam Hussein's Iraq. In the Gulf War, the Coalition defeated an opponent who deployed a powerful order of battle, but who also carried some harsh liabilities. Iraq's 1980–1989 war against Iran left it ill prepared for a conflict with the United States. During most of the eight years of fighting, it waged static ground campaigns that were characterized by bloody, protracted battles of attrition.[21] Western military analysts estimated Iraq's losses in this war at 150,000 to 340,000 killed, and 400,000 to 700,000 wounded. This conflict had ended only about two years before Saddam Hussein challenged the military forces of the United States, and his army had not yet recovered from its enormous casualties against Iran. After questioning dozens of prisoners captured during Desert Storm, officers at the Joint Debriefing Center concluded that the Iran-Iraq War had rendered Saddam's units "war weary," rather than "battle-hardened."[22] If even the lowest estimates of the number of dead and wounded during that eight-year war were correct, thousands of the Iraqi army's best small-unit leaders had been killed and wounded. As for its senior officers, including Saddam Hussein, they had gained long experience with positional fighting but only limited practice with maneuver warfare,[23] the style of combat that the Gulf War air campaign allowed General Schwarzkopf to impose on them.

Moreover, Iraqi air operations during its war with Iran strongly suggested that Saddam's air force would prove no match for the advanced-technology systems and highly trained personnel of the USAF and its allies. Two thorough students of the Iran-Iraq War concluded that the conflict proved that "Iraq had no real concept of air power." Nor did this wartime experience in any way prepare Saddam's airmen for combat against the large number of high-quality aircraft that the Coalition put into the skies. As Colonel Christon remarked, the Iraqis "had never seen more than about thirty aircraft at a time, and we [threw] four hundred and some at them, the first night." General Horner expanded on this point, emphasizing that the Iraqis "had no idea what airpower is. We flew in one day as many sorties as [Saddam] faced in eight years of war with Iran. He had no air experience."[24]

Saddam Hussein was Iraq's worst liability, and it would be dangerous to assume that America's future opponents will have his weaknesses. The Iraqi autocrat precipitously enraged public opinion in the United States and around the world, which actively helped President Bush build an international alliance against him. Saddam gave the Department of Defense five months to mobilize its resources; America's next opponent might not be so accommodating. "I don't think we can count on being so lucky in the future," General Pagonis said of the dictator's decision to halt at the Saudi border. "Most aggressors are more determined." After stopping in Kuwait and voluntarily taking up the defensive, the Iraqi dictator failed to mount a single effective counteroffensive against the Coalition. His air force never undertook any initiative on a scale that might have stressed CENTAF's three-day ATO process. Saddam launched only one ground offensive, which U.S. Air Force and Marine Corps units promptly squelched during the Battle of Khafji, an effort so feeble that General Schwarzkopf dismissed it as "a mosquito on an elephant." Later, when a journalist asked the CENTCOM commander for his assessment of the Iraqi dictator as a military leader, General Schwarzkopf replied, "As far as Saddam Hussein being a great military strategist, he is neither a strategist, nor is he schooled in the operational arts, nor is he a tactician, nor is he a general, nor is he a soldier. Other than that, he's a great military man. I want you to know that." General Horner skewered Saddam equally well: "He is obviously a very sorry soldier. He doesn't have a clue."[25]

For all of Saddam Hussein's military incompetence, however, he survived the Gulf War, remained in power, and disdained the UN's resolutions. During the summer of 1992, he delayed for nearly a month a UN inspection of facilities that the United States believed were used to develop weapons of mass destruction.[26] Saddam's resilience pointed up another way in which the Gulf War was both a success story and a cautionary tale. Without question, it was the story of a resounding victory: the Air Force and the other services decisively drove the Iraqis from Kuwait, with considerable losses to the enemy and relatively low ones to themselves. Yet it was also a cautionary tale: Saddam's longevity demonstrated the durability of dictators and America's continuing need for an Air Force able to deal with that Iraqi leader, or a similar autocrat, in the future.

Long after the Gulf War ended, visitors to the region found persisting evidence of Saddam Hussein's menacing policies and their tragic results. In October 1991, more than eighty oil fires still burned across Kuwait, lakes of petroleum polluted the desert around the damaged wells, and hundreds of miles of the Saudi coast remained heavily contaminated. Before the Gulf War, Kuwaitis had camped in the desert for recreation, but, after the conflict, fearful of the many landmines planted by Saddam's invaders, they abandoned this old custom. In addition to leaving these hazards, the occupying troops also had mined the shores of the small kingdom. By the summer of 1992, Kuwaitis again began swimming from their country's beaches, but American visitors—still wary of Saddam's lingering treachery—refused to enter the waters.

Glossary

AAA	Antiaircraft artillery
ABCCC	Airborne Battlefield Command and Control Center
ACE	Airborne command element
AI	Air interdiction
ANGLICO	Air Naval Gunfire Liaison Company
AOR	Area of responsibility
APC	Armored personnel carrier
ARCENT	Army Central Command
ASOC	Air Support Operations Center
ATO	Air tasking order
AWACS	Airborne Warning and Control System
BAI	Battlefield air interdiction
BCE	Battlefield coordination element
BDA	Bomb damage assessment
BMW(P)	Bombardment Medium Wing (Provisional)
BUFF	Slang for a B–52 (Big, ugly, fat fellow)
BW(P)	Bombardment Wing (Provisional)
C^2	Command and control
C^3	Command, control, and communications
C^3I	Command, control, communications, and intelligence
CAFMS	Computer Assisted Force Management System
CAP	Combat air patrol
CAS	Close air support
CEM	Combined-effects munition
CENTAF	U.S. Air Force, Central Command
CENTCOM	U.S. Central Command
CEP	Circular error probable
CINCSAC	Commander in Chief, Strategic Air Command
COMALF	Commander, Airlift Forces
COMUSCENTAF	Commander, U.S. Air Force, Central Command
COPS	Combat Operations Planning Staff

Lucrative Targets

DASC	Direct Air Support Center
DCINC	Deputy Commander in Chief
DIA	Defense Intelligence Agency
DSP	Defense Support Program
ECM	Electronic countermeasures
EW	Electronic warfare
I MEF	I Marine Expeditionary Force
IN	Intelligence
FAC	Forward Air Controller
FLIR	Forward-looking infrared
FOB	Forward operating base
FOL	Forward operating location
FSCL	Fire support coordination line
G–2	Army Intelligence Directorate
GAT	Guidance, Apportionment, and Targeting
GWAPS	Gulf War Air Power Survey
HARM	High-speed antiradiation missile
IFF	Identification–friend-or-foe
IN	Intelligence
IOC	Interceptor Operations Center
IR	Infrared
JCS	Joint Chiefs of Staff
JFACC	Joint Force Air Component Commander
JFC	Joint Force Commander
JFC–E	Joint Forces Command–East
JFC–N	Joint Forces Command–North
JTCB	Joint Target Coordination Board
JTF	Joint Task Force
J–2	Joint Intelligence Directorate
J–3	Joint Operations Directorate
J–5	Joint Strategic Plans and Policy Directorate
J–STARS	Joint Surveillance Target Attack Radar System
KTO	Kuwaiti Theater of Operations
LAI	Light Armored Infantry
LANTIRN	Low-altitude navigation and targeting infrared for night
LAV	Light armored vehicle
LGB	Laser-guided bomb
MAC	Military Airlift Command
MAP	Master attack plan
MARCENT	Marine Corps Central Command
MEF	Marine Expeditionary Force
MRE	Meals-ready-to-eat

MRL	Multiple-rocket launcher
NAVCENT	Naval Central Command
OP–1	Outpost 1
OP–4	Outpost 4
PGM	Precision-guided munition
RSAF	Royal Saudi Air Force
SAC	Strategic Air Command
SAM	Surface-to-air missile
SANG	Saudi Arabian National Guard
SAR	Synthetic aperture radar
SEAD	Suppression of enemy air defenses
SOC	Sector Operations Center
SPACECOM	Space Command
SPINS	Special instructions
SRBM	Short-range ballistic missile
STRATFOR	Strategic Air Command Strategic Force
TAC	Tactical Air Command
TACC	Tactical Air Control Center
TAS	Tactical Airlift Squadron
TAW(P)	Provisional Tactical Airlift Wing
TFS	Tactical Fighter Squadron
TFW	Tactical Fighter Wing
TFW(P)	Provisional Tactical Fighter Wing
TLAM	Tomahawk land attack missile
TOT	Time over target
UN	United Nations
USAF	U.S. Air Force
USAFE	United States Air Forces in Europe
USCENTCOM	United States Central Command
USTRANSCOM	United States Transportation Command

Essay on Sources

This work was based on two groups of primary sources: documents created by members of U.S. Air Force, Central Command (CENTAF) and other organizations that planned and conducted the Gulf War, and oral history interviews with participants. I completed nearly all of the research for it within a year, beginning in the spring of 1991, and I finished writing the initial manuscript in November 1992.

Any discussion of primary sources about the Air Force in the Gulf War must begin with the Air Force History Program's enlisted historians, who did their jobs well during Desert Shield and Storm. They collected thousands of feet of documents, which were microfilmed by the Air Force Historical Research Agency (AFHRA) at Maxwell AFB, Alabama. A copy of the film was sent promptly after the war to the Center for Air Force History (CAFH) at Bolling AFB, Washington, D.C. I used this film in April and May 1991 and cite it as the "CAFH Desert Shield/Desert Storm microfilm collection" although the present Headquarters Air Force History Office is now designated "AFHO" and its functional support unit, the Air Force History Support Office, "AFHSO." The original documents are now held by AFHRA.

During the spring and summer of 1991, I also conducted research at the Checkmate office in two major collections of documents. The first was a group of papers that Checkmate either created or received between August 1990 and April 1991. Dr. Wayne Thompson, a CAFH historian detailed to Checkmate early in the Kuwaiti crisis, did an excellent job of collecting and organizing these documents. I cite them as "Checkmate files." In August 1991, Secretary of the Air Force Donald B. Rice commissioned the Gulf War Air Power Survey (GWAPS) to review all aspects of air warfare during that conflict and report on them to the Air Force. Dr. Thompson became the senior historical advisor to the GWAPS personnel, and he and the Checkmate files moved from the basement of the Pentagon to the Survey's office in Crystal City, Virginia. The GWAPS team prepared a five-volume report, and, in April 1993, it transferred its records, including the documents that Dr. Thompson had assembled at Checkmate, to AFHRA, which began the process of microfilming them.

Lucrative Targets

The second group of documents that I researched at the Checkmate office during the spring of 1991 consisted of papers from the "Black Hole" files of Lt. Col. David A. Deptula and Brig. Gen. Buster C. Glosson. Colonel Deptula gathered these records and sent them to the Pentagon during and after the war. I cite this collection as "CENTAF records." Like the Checkmate documents, the great bulk of these CENTAF materials went with Dr. Thompson to the GWAPS site and then to AFHRA. Colonel Deptula allowed the CAFH to photocopy nearly all of them; therefore, the CAFH collection closely matches the one at Maxwell.

After reviewing these sources, I pursued my research at the headquarters of three Air Force major commands. In late July and early August, I reviewed the Desert Storm holdings of the history office at Headquarters Military Airlift Command (MAC) at Scott AFB, Illinois, where I collected many valuable items, including the official unit histories of the organizations that supported the XVIII Airborne Corps' shift west and a particularly useful special study, "History of Airlift in the Desert: Circumventing the Iraqis," written by SMSgt. James R. Ciborski, the historian of the 1630th Tactical Airlift Wing (Provisional). I cite the source of these items as the "HQ MAC/HO Archives." During the late spring of 1992, about a year after my research at the Headquarters MAC History Office, the Air Force underwent a major reorganization. MAC deactivated and was succeeded on June 1, 1992, by the Air Mobility Command (AMC). Gulf War–related and all other documents held by the Headquarters MAC History Office are now retained by its successor, the Headquarters AMC History Office. These holdings include the official histories of the tactical airlift units that served during Desert Shield and Storm, which are also available at AFHRA.

After my research at Headquarters MAC, I traveled to the Headquarters Strategic Air Command (SAC) History Office in late August 1991. The materials I gathered there came from two sources. The first was a Desert Storm working archive that the Headquarters SAC History Office had built during the war. Its staff historians had collected SAC Support Battle Staff briefings, daily intelligence briefings and other intelligence sources, newspaper clippings, and other documents, assigned them decimal file numbers, and maintained them in a single file cabinet. I cite this collection as the "HQ SAC/HO Desert Storm working archives." After the Air Force reorganization of 1992, AFHRA gained these materials. The second group of Headquarters SAC documents was the one that the staff historians had gathered and maintained in their own files. At the time of my research, the historians were using some of these sources to write their 1990 history of SAC, and they were holding others to use the following year. I cite these as "historians' working files, HQ SAC/HO." Many of these materials appear as supporting documents in the 1990 and 1991 SAC annual histories. With the Air Force reorganization of 1992, some of these documents were transferred to the Headquarters Air Combat Command (ACC) History Office at Langley AFB, Virginia; other records, pertaining to air refueling operations, were sent to AMC.

In late September 1991, I visited the Headquarters Tactical Air Command (TAC) History Office at Langley AFB, which had the largest Desert Storm holdings of any office in the Air Force History Program. The Headquarters TAC materials fell into three groups: documents sent to Langley by the CENTAF historian CMSgt. John Burton and the field historians he supervised, the Headquarters TAC History Office's own collection of messages and other documents its staff historians had gathered from within the headquarters, and a sizeable number of unit histories. I cite this large and valuable source as the "Desert Storm collection, HQ TAC/HO." With the 1992 reorganization, these TAC documents, like the SAC History Office holdings, became the responsibility of the Headquarters Air Combat Command (ACC) History Office. AFHRA also holds copies of nearly all of these items.

In December 1991, I did research at the history office of Headquarters United States Central Command (USCENTCOM) at MacDill AFB, Florida. During Desert Shield and Storm, representatives of the Air Force, Army, and Marine Corps History Programs were temporarily assigned there, and while there these individuals gathered and filed many valuable sources. They included briefings and other summary papers compiled by J–2 officers into the HQ CENTCOM battle staff's "war room" reference book, Desert Storm operations orders, division-level maps of the ground campaign, State Department message traffic, and J–5 planning documents. I cite this collection as the "HQ USCENTCOM/CCHO working files." In 1993, the National Archives began transferring some of these documents to their classified holdings and digitizing them for storage on optical disks.

In early March and late April 1992, another CAFH historian, Dr. Richard G. Davis, and I made a research trip to Headquarters Ninth Air Force, Shaw AFB, South Carolina. Its history office had developed a Desert Storm collection that included some useful items such as CENTAF/DO's classified "Concept of Operations for Command and Control of TacAir in Support of Land Forces" and Col. Randy Witt's paper, "Air Force Tactical Communications in War: The Desert Shield/Desert Storm Comm Story." I cite these as the "HQ 9 AF/HO working files." On March 4, 1992, Dr. Davis, Dr. Barry Barlow of the Headquarters Ninth Air Force History Office, and I conducted an oral history interview with Lt. Gen. Charles A. Horner. Following this session, the CENTAF commander made available to us several feet of records that he had brought back with him from the Gulf. They included, for example, the notes General Horner had made on legal pads during the seven o'clock meetings each evening at Headquarters CENTCOM. I cite this collection as "Lt. Gen. Horner's Desert Storm files, HQ 9 AF/CC." General Horner retains these documents to help him write his own account of the Gulf War.

The history offices of other military services also contributed many useful sources, particularly on the ground campaign. During the summer of 1991, I visited the Center for Military History (CMH), then located in its Southeast Federal

Lucrative Targets

Center offices in Washington, D.C., where I collected a number of valuable items. Among them were several helpful ARCENT documents and a draft of "The Whirlwind War," CMH's official history of the Army's role in Desert Shield and Desert Storm, which Drs. Frank N. "Mickey" Schubert and Theresa L. Kraus were then editing. At the time I wrote this essay, this fine draft remained unpublished. I cite it and the other items I collected at the Southeast Federal Center as "CMH draft." Also during the summer of 1991, I visited the Marine Corps Historical Center, which made available many official unit histories and chronologies. Capt. David A. "Scotty" Dawson gave me transcripts of the twice-daily briefings to Lt. Gen. Walter E. Boomer at Headquarters I Marine Expeditionary Force. These and other Marine Corps sources improved my understanding of MARCENT operations during the Battle of Khafji and the ground campaign. I cite these items as being held by the USMC Historical Center. Among my sources from the Navy, Dr. Edward J. Marolda's paper, "A Host of Nations: Coalition Naval Operations in the Persian Gulf," was especially useful.

This work also depended on oral history interviews conducted by historians from the CAFH and elsewhere. All were done within roughly a year after the Gulf War, while the participants' memories remained fresh. Getting the interviews done promptly was not nearly as difficult as preparing useful transcripts of them. In some fortunate cases, GWAPS or the Air University's College of Aerospace Doctrine, Research, and Education (CADRE) personnel prepared transcripts, which the CAFH holds. In other instances, no transcription has been done and the Center holds only a tape recording of the interview. Among the oral histories most helpful to my topic were a classified interview of Lt. Gen. Charles A. Horner conducted by Drs. Davis and Barlow and myself on March 4, 1992 (transcript held by CAFH); a classified interview of Maj. Gen. Thomas R. Olsen by Drs. Davis and Barlow and myself on March 5, 1992 (tape recording held by CAFH); a classified interview of Maj. Gen. Buster C. Glosson by Drs. Davis and Diane Putney (a CAFH historian) and myself on December 12, 1991 (tape recording held by CAFH); a classified interview of Lt. Col. David A. Deptula by Dr. Davis on November 20, 1991 (tape recording held by CAFH); a classified interview of Colonel Deptula by Drs. Davis and Putney and myself on November 27, 1991 (tape recording and transcript held by CAFH); a classified interview of Colonel Deptula by Drs. Davis and Putney and myself on January 8, 1992 (tape recording held by CAFH); and a classified interview of Lt. Col. Sam Baptiste by Dr. Barlow and myself on March 2, 1992 (tape recording held by CAFH). I made use of several other oral history interviews; most appear in the list of short citations and all are cited in the endnotes.

Nearly all of this work was based on oral histories or primary documents. It made use of few published sources, for only a handful were available when the manuscript was completed. Three books that appeared very soon after the Gulf War were James Blackwell's *Thunder in the Desert* (1991), a brief survey history that offered more on ground than air operations; Norman Friedman's *Desert Vic-*

tory (1991), which suffered from a heavy bias in favor of the U.S. Navy; and Bob Woodward's *The Commanders* (1991), which focused on the decision-making by the senior defense leaders during the crises in Panama and Southwest Asia.

After these initial postwar books, a few others appeared within a year or so after Desert Storm. *On Strategy II* (1992) by Harry G. Summers, Jr., took a thesis that the author had developed in a previous book on the Vietnam War and extended it to the Gulf War. *On Strategy II* deserved the attention that it received in military circles, but, because it focused on larger questions of policy and strategy, rather than the details of operations, it did not offer much help to my project. Similarly, Lawrence Freedman and Efraim Karsh's *The Gulf Conflict 1990–1991* (1993) was stronger on the diplomatic history of the Gulf War than on the military aspects of the confrontation. Among the general works that appeared within a year or two of the war, the *U.S. News & World Report*'s *Triumph Without Victory* (1992) was perhaps the most helpful to my efforts, particularly in providing background material on prewar diplomacy and on the ground campaign.

A few memoirs appeared before I completed my initial manuscript. The most useful, of course, was General H. Norman Schwarzkopf's *The Autobiography: It Doesn't Take a Hero* (1992), published a month before I finished my first draft. Two other memoirs deserve mention: Lt. Gen. William G. "Gus" Pagonis's *Moving Mountains* (1992), which in some ways is less a military memoir than a business school primer, and General Sir Peter de la Billiere's *Storm Command* (1992), which, at least during the earliest months after its publication, was difficult to find outside the United Kingdom.

Among the books specifically addressing the air campaign, James P. Coyne's *Airpower in the Gulf* (1992) became available while I was working on this monograph, but Richard P. Hallion's *Storm over Iraq* (1992) was not published until just after I had finished. The five-volume final report of the GWAPS group was not in print until 1993, but my research drew on many of the same primary sources used by the GWAPS team. After working in the CAFH's Air Staff Division in the Pentagon throughout 1993, I then returned to my November 1992 manuscript and made some revisions, which in a few cases drew on the work of the GWAPS researchers.

Two books that appeared too late for me to use deserve mention here. The first, William L. Smallwood's *Warthog* (1993) offers a lively account of A–10 operations over the Kuwaiti theater. The second book, Rick Atkinson's *Crusade* (1993), is a valuable survey history of the Gulf War. The broad patterns in Atkinson's work, if not always the precise details, match up well with the evidence in official sources.

List of Short Citations

1st LAI Battalion chronol—Command chronol, 1st Light Armored Infantry Battalion, Jan 1–Feb 28, 1991, USMC Historical Center.

2d LAI Battalion chronol—Command chronol, 2d Light Armored Infantry Battalion, Jan 1–Mar 31, 1991, USMC Historical Center.

2d Marine Division chronol—Command chronol, 2d Marine Division, Jan 1–Apr 13, 1991, USMC Historical Center.

3d Marine chronol—Command chronol, 3d Marine Regt, Jan 1–Feb 28, 1991, USMC Historical Center.

"3d Marines in Desert Storm"—Brig. Gen. John H. Admire, "The 3d Marines in Desert Storm," *Marine Corps Gazette*, Sep 1991.

4 TFW msg—Msg, 4 TFW Deployed/CC to HQ TAC/DR/DO and 9 AF/DO, "F–15E Performance in Desert Storm," 1630Z Mar 16, 1991, "Lessons Learned" file, Box 25, HQ TAC/HO archives.

9 AF chart—Chart, HQ 9 AF, "Deputy Chief of Staff, Operations," n.d., HQ 9 AF/HO working files.

33 TFW Weather—Summary paper, "Operation Desert Storm [Weather] History, 22 Feb 91–28 Feb 91," atch to hist, 33 TFW (Provisional), Feb 24–Mar 2, 1991, Unit Histories Collection, HQ TAC/HO.

"100-Hour Ground War"—Brfg, HQ CENTCOM/CCDCS, "The 100-Hour Ground War," n.d., HQ USCENTCOM/CCHO working files.

A–10 recap—Brfg, "Operation Desert Storm A–10 Combat Recap," n.d., Unit Histories Collection, HQ TAC/HO.

"Air Defense and Airspace Control Procedures"—Rpt, COMUSCENTAF, "Air Defense and Airspace Control Procedures for Operation Desert Shield," Jan 8, 1991, Box 13, CENTAF Records.

"Air Support" paper—Summary paper, HQ USAFE/XPPF, "Corps Air Support at Desert Storm," Jul 3, 1991.

"Air Weather Service Contribution"—Rpt, HQ Air Weather Service, "Air Weather Service Contribution to Winning the War—the Value of Weather Support: Operation Desert Storm/Desert Shield Report 1," May 23, 1991.

ARCENT BDA msg—Msg, COMUSARCENT/G2 to VII Corps Main Fwd/CG, et al., "ARCENT Battle Damage Assessment Process," 0600Z Feb 17, 1991, "KTO/Republican Guards" file, Checkmate files.

ARCENT hist—Hist, Col. Richard M. Swain, ARCENT Historian, "Operational Narrative: Operations Desert Shield–Desert Storm," Sep 24, 1991.

ATO brfg—Brfg, HQ 9 AF/DOOW, "Air Tasking Order (ATO) Preparation and Composite Force Packaging," Jan 1992.

Baptiste, Lt. Col., intvw—Intvw, Lt. Col. Sam Baptiste with Drs. Perry Jamieson and Barry Barlow, Mar 2, 1992, tape recording held by CAFH.

BDA Jan 28, 1991—Point paper, AF/XOXWF, "BDA—Desert Storm—Operator's Look (As of 28 Jan 91/0900L Baghdad)," Jan 28, 1991, Folder 2, Box 11C, CENTAF Records.

Bergeron hist—Draft hist, SSgt. Randy G. Bergeron, "Air Force Special Operations Command in Operations Desert Shield and Desert Storm," n.d.

"Bomb Damage"—Memo, to "See Distribution," "Bomb Damage to Military Forces and Facilities," Jan 30, 1991, Checkmate files.

"Bomber Story"—Draft rpt, HQ SAC, "Operations Desert Shield & Desert Storm: 'The Bomber Story,'" n.d., historians' working files, HQ SAC/HO.

Boyd chronol—Chronol, SSgt. Gary W. Boyd, "Combat Chronology, 23/354 TFW(P): Operation Desert Storm, 17 Jan 1991–28 Feb 1991."

Brfg to Gen. Khalid—Brfg, CENTAF/CV, "Air Forces Briefings to His Royal Highness Lt. Gen. Khalid," Nov 27, 1990, MSgt. Theodore J. Turner files, HQ CENTAF/HO.

"Bridge Interdiction"—Memo, Lt. Comdr. Muir to Brig. Gen. Glosson, "Bridge Interdiction," Feb 20, 1991, "RR & Bridges History" file, Box 13, CENTAF records.

Burton notes—Notes, CMSgt. John Burton, CENTAF/HO, "Notes Taken During the 0700 to 1230L Shift in the Tactical Air Control Center (TACC) During Operation Desert Storm, 17 January–28 February 1991," Burton file, Box 84, CENTAF collection, HQ TAC/HO.

"Camp David" memo—Memo for Record, Col. Douglas C. Roach, Dep Asst Dir for Joint and NSC Matters, DCS/Plans and Operations, "Camp David Discussions Re: Iraq, Saturday, 4 Aug 90," Aug 4, 1990, atch to memo, Col. Theodore R. Coberly, Secretary, Joint Staff, to Chairman, Joint Chiefs of Staff, et al., "NSD–54," Jan 23, 1991.

"Campaign Plan Chronology"—Chronol, HQ USCENTCOM/J5, "Chronology of Theater Campaign Plan," n.d., HQ USCENTCOM/CCHO working files.

Caruana, Brig. Gen., intvw—Intvw, Brig. Gen. Patrick P. Caruana, STRAT-FOR/CC, with Lt. Col. Edward C. Mann III, AU CADRE/RI, Aug 19 and 23, 1991, tape recording held by HQ SAC/HO.

CENTCOM OpPlan, Jan 17, 1991—Operation Plan, HQ USCENTCOM and HQ JF/Theater of Operations, "Combined Operation Desert Storm," Jan 17, 1991, file 0269608, Roll 10261, CAFH Desert Shield/Desert Storm micro-film collection.

Checkmate files—HQ USAF Checkmate Planning Office files, HQ USAF/XOXW.

Christon, Col., intvw—Intvw, Col. Christopher Christon with Drs. Richard Davis and Barry Barlow, Mar 4, 1992, tape recording held by CAFH.

Ciborski study—Special study, SMSgt. James R. Ciborski, 1630 TAW(P)/HO, "History of Airlift in the Desert: Circumventing the Iraqis," May 23, 1991, HQ MAC/HO archives.

CINC's War Book—List, "Threat Ranges of Iraqi Systems," Aug 10, 1990, in HQ USCENTCOM/CCJ2, U.S. Central Command Battle Staff Operation Desert Storm War Room Book, n.d. [compiled Aug 1990–Apr 1991], HQ USCENTCOM/CCHO working files.

CINC's War Book input—Brfg slide, HQ USCENTCOM/CCJ2, in CINC's War Book inputs, [dates and times vary], HQ USCENTCOM/CCHO working files.

CMH draft—Draft monogr, U.S. Army Center of Military History, [untitled monogr on the U.S. Army in Operations Desert Shield and Storm], n.d., U.S. Army Center of Military History.

COMUSCENTAF OpOrd—Operations Order, HQ COMUSCENTAF, "COM-USCENTAF Operations Order: Offensive Campaign—Phase I," Sep 2, 1990, Box 12, CENTAF Records.

ConOps for C²—Concept of Operations, CENTAF/DO, "Concept of Operations for Command and Control of TacAir in Support of Land Forces," Feb 22, 1991, HQ 9 AF/HO working files.

Corder, Maj. Gen., intvw—Intvw, Maj. Gen. John Corder with Robert L. Mandler, USAFAWC/HO, Dec 21, 1991, published transcript held by CAFH.

Cox, Col., intvw—Intvw, Col. George W. Cox, Commandant, USAF Air Ground Operations School, USAF Air Warfare Center, with Robert L. Mandler, USAFAWC/HO, Dec 21, 1991.

Crigger, Col., intvw—Intvw, Col. James Crigger with Drs. Richard Davis and Barry Barlow, Mar 5 1992, tape recording held by CAFH.

CSAF brief—Brfg slide, in brfgs, "Desert Storm CSAF Brief," [dates vary], Checkmate files.

Daily Aircraft Losses chart—Chart, "Daily Aircraft Losses," "26 Feb 91" file, Lt. Gen. Horner's Desert Storm files, HQ 9 AF/CC.

"Daily Notes"—"Daily Notes from Desert Storm," Jan 17, 1991, Tab A to hist, 363 TFW(P), Jan 27–Feb 2, 1991, Vol 1, Desert Storm collection, HQ TAC/HO.

Damaged Aircraft chart—Chart, USAFTAWC/INS, "Details on Damaged USAF Aircraft," Aug 6, 1991, Lt. Gen. Horner's Desert Storm files, HQ 9 AF/CC.

DD/TWP brfg—Brfg slide, "Summary of Attacks on Iraqi Ground Forces: Key Ground Equipment," in brfg, Steven L. Head, DD/TWP, "The Conduct and Performance of the Air Campaign in Operation Desert Storm," Mar 21, 1991, DD/TWP working files.

Deptula, Lt. Col., brfg—Brfg, Lt. Col. David A. Deptula, "Air Power in the Gulf War: The View from the Black Hole," CAFH Symposium, Jan 8, 1992.

Deptula, Lt. Col., intvw, Nov 1, 1990—Intvw, Lt. Col. David A. Deptula with TSgt. Theodore J. Turner, Nov 1, 1990, transcript held by AF/CAFH.

Deptula, Lt. Col., intvw, Nov 20, 1991—Intvw, Lt. Col. David A. Deptula, AF/OSX, with Dr. Richard Davis, CAFH, Nov 20, 1991, tape recording held by CAFH.

Deptula, Lt. Col., intvw, Nov 27, 1991—Intvw, Drs. Richard Davis, Perry Jamieson, and Diane Putney, CAFH, with Lt. Col. David A. Deptula, AF/OSX, Nov 27, 1991, tape recording held by CAFH.

Deptula, Lt. Col., intvw, Nov 29, 1991—Intvw, Drs. Richard Davis, Perry Jamieson, and Diane Putney, CAFH, with Lt. Col. David A. Deptula, AF/OSX, Nov 29, 1991, tape recording held by CAFH.

Deptula, Lt. Col., intvw, Jan 8, 1992—Intvw, Drs. Richard Davis, Perry Jamieson, and Diane Putney, CAFH, with Lt. Col. David A. Deptula, AF/OSX, Jan 8, 1992, tape recording held by CAFH.

Devino's, MSgt., intvws—Interviews with MSgt. Robert S. Devino, 416th Wing Historian, SAC, transcripts atch to ltr, Col. Michael F. Loughran, 416 Wg (SAC)/CC, to Dr. Dick Hallion, AF/HO, Nov 18, 1991.

DIM 59–91—Memo, DIA, DIM 59–91, Feb 1991.

"Directorate of Campaign Plans"—Talking paper, Lt. Col. David A. Deptula, JFACC Special Planning Group, "JFACC Directorate of Campaign Plans," Nov 4, 1991.

"DISum 149"—Msg, TAC/TACOPS/INO to AIG 621, et al., "CENTAF Rear DISum 149," 2300Z Jan 30, 1991, "Khafji" file, Checkmate files.

"F–16 Effectiveness"—Rpt, 57 FWW Tactics Team, "F–16 Effectiveness in the Gulf War," Feb 14, 1991, "F–16" file, Checkmate files.

"F–111 Chart"—Chart, Dr. Barry Watts, GWAPS, "F–111E/F Summary Data," Aug 12, 1992, GWAPS working files.

"Feedback from SecDef/CJCS Meeting"—Memo, Lt. Col. David A. Deptula, HQ CENTAF/DCP, to [no addressee], "Feedback from SecDef/CJCS Meeting with CINC and Component Commanders," Feb 9, 1991, "KTO/Republican Guards" file, Checkmate files.

Feinstein, Lt. Col., intvw—Intvw, Lt. Col. Jeffrey S. Feinstein with Drs. Richard Davis, Barry Barlow, and Perry Jamieson, Mar 3, 1992, tape recording held by CAFH.

Final Report—Rpt, DoD, "Conduct of the Persian Gulf War: Final Report to Congress," Apr 1992.

Glosson, Brig. Gen., intvw, Mar 13, 1991—Intvw, Brig. Gen. Buster C. Glosson, CENTAF/DCP, with MSgt. Theodore J. Turner, CENTAF/HO, Mar 13, 1991, transcript held by CAFH.

Glosson, Maj. Gen., intvw, Dec 12, 1991—Intvw, Maj. Gen. Buster C. Glosson, with Drs. Richard Davis, Perry Jamieson, and Diane Putney, Dec 12, 1991, tape recording held by CAFH.

"Gulf War Weather"—Rpt, USAF Environmental Technical Applications Center, "Gulf War Weather," Mar 1992.

GWAPS—*Gulf War Air Power Survey*, Washington, D.C., 1993.

Hall, Brig. Gen., memo—Memo, Brig. Gen. Mike Hall to Maj. Gen. John Corder, "Memo for the Record, 30 Jan Air/Gnd Ops Planning Mtg," Jan 30,

1991, file 0269617, Roll 10264, CAFH Desert Shield/Desert Storm microfilm collection.

Hawkins, Capt., intvw—Intvw, Capt. James R. Hawkins, HQ SAC/DOOQ, with Dr. Kent M. Beck, HQ SAC/HOL, Apr 30, 1991, transcript in historians' working files, HQ SAC/HO.

Horner, Lt. Gen., intvw, Mar 1991—Intvw, Lt. Gen. Charles A. Horner, COMUSCENTAF, commenting on questions prepared earlier by CMSgt. Burton, CENTAF/HO, Mar 1991, tape recording held by CAFH.

Horner, Lt. Gen., intvw, Dec 3, 1991—Intvw, Lt. Gen. Charles A. Horner, COMUSCENTAF, with Lt. Cols. Suzanne Gehri and Richard Reynolds, CADRE/RIR, Dec 3, 1991, tape recording held by CAFH.

Horner, Lt. Gen., intvw, Mar 4, 1992—Intvw, Lt. Gen. Charles Horner, with Drs. Richard Davis, Barry Barlow, and Perry Jamieson, Mar 4, 1992.

Horner, Lt. Gen., testimony—Hearings, Senate Committee on Armed Services, 102d Cong., 1st Sess., May 21, 1991.

Horner's, Lt. Gen., CINCCENT notes—Notes, Lt. Gen. Horner, CINCCENT Meeting, [dates vary], Lt. Gen. Horner's Desert Storm files, HQ 9 AF/CC.

Horner's, Lt. Gen., daily comments—Transcript, HQ CENTAF Office of History, "Daily Comments of Lieutenant General Charles A. Horner, Commander, United States Central Command Air Forces during Operation Desert Storm, 17 January through 28 February 1991," Mar 20, 1991.

Hosterman notes—Notes, TSgt. Frederick Hosterman, CENTAF/HO, "CENTAF TACC Notes," Hosterman file, Box 84, CENTAF collection, HQ TAC/HO.

"How-Goes-It"—Memo, Brig. Gen. Buster C. Glosson, 14 AD/CC, to CENTAF/CC, "Wing 'How-Goes-It,'" Feb 6, 1990, Lt. Gen. Horner's Desert Storm files, HQ 9 AF/CC.

HQ TAC Lessons Learned—Brfg, HQ TAC/DO, "Desert Storm Lessons Learned," Jul 12, 1991, "Title V Report Inputs" file, Checkmate files.

"I Marine Expeditionary Force"—Summary paper, HQ USMC/Current Ops Br, "I Marine Expeditionary Force," n.d., USMC Historical Center.

I MEF Command brfg—Transcript, I MEF Comd Brfgs, Jan 30, 1991 A.M., Jan 31, 1991 A.M, "28–31 Jan 91 file," USMC Historical Center, copy held by CAFH.

"Instant Thunder"—Brfg, JCS/J–36, "Iraqi Air Campaign Instant Thunder," Aug 17, 1990, "Threat Data Targeting Info; CSAF Briefing Book," Box 7, CENTAF Records.

"Intelligence Summary 91–035"—Msg, CENTAF/IN to AIG 12929, et al., "CENTAF Desert Storm Intelligence Summary 91–035 as of 02/2200Z Feb 91," 0329Z Feb 3, 1991, "Khafji" file, Checkmate files.

Interim Report—Rpt, Department of Defense, "Conduct of the Persian Gulf Conflict: An Interim Report to Congress," Jul 1991.

"Iraqi Generals Perspective"—Memo for Record, 513th Military Intelligence Brigade, Joint Debriefing Center, "The Gulf War: An Iraqi General Officer's Perspective," Mar 11, 1991, "Iraqi POW Debriefs" file, Checkmate files.

"Iraqi Situation"—Brfg, AF/XOXW, "Iraqi Situation: Checkmate Strategic Assessment," Jan 30, 1991, "Checkmate BDA" file, Checkmate files.

"J5 After Action Report"—Exec summary, HQ USCENTCOM/CCJ5–P, "J5 Plans After Action Report," Mar 5, 1991, HQ USCENTCOM/CCHO working files.

Joint STARS brfg—Notes, Dr. Perry Jamieson, CAFH, on videotape of brfg, Maj. Jim Coates, 12 TIS, "Joint STARS," USAF Intelligence Conference at Goodfellow AFB, Texas, Oct 31–Nov 1, 1991.

Killer Scout brfg—Brfg, Lt. Col. Mark Welch, 4 TFS, "Warrior Briefings to the Air Staff: Killer Scout—Kill Zone Procedures in Desert Storm," Oct 15, 1991.

Loh, Gen., speech—Speech, General Michael Loh, Commander TAC, to Virginia American Legion, Norfolk, Va., Jul 13, 1991, historians' working files, HQ TAC/HO.

Magaw's, Lt. Col., trip rpt—Trip rpt, Lt. Col. Milton A. Magaw, 8 AF/DOTN, Mar 26, 1991, historians' working files, HQ SAC/HO.

MAP Jan 16, 1991—Plan, CENTAF/DCP, Master Attack Plan, Jan 16, 1991, Box 25, CENTAF collection, HQ TAC/HO.

"Master Target List"—Chart, HQ CENTAF/DCP, "Master Target List," Feb 5, 1991, file 029616, Roll 10264, CAFH Desert Shield/Desert Storm microfilm collection.

McPeak, Gen., brfg—Brfg, General Merrill A. McPeak, CSAF, Mar 15, 1991.

Msg, 0652Z, Mar 1, 1991—msg, 513 MIBdeFwd/JDC to DIA/OC–4A/ DC–1 (CCP), 0652Z Mar 1, 1991, "Iraqi POW Debriefs" file, Checkmate files.

Muellner, Brig. Gen., intvw—Intvw, Brig. Gen. George K. Muellner, HQ TAC/DR, with Thomas C. Hone, Anne Leary, and Mark Mandeles, Apr 16, 1992, copy of transcript held by CAFH.

NGB Feb 15 msg—Msg, NGB/CSS to AIG 7303/CC/DO, et al., 0020Z Feb 15, 1991, "Lessons Learned" file, Box 25, HQ TAC/HO Archives.

Olsen, Maj. Gen., intvw—Intvw, Maj. Gen. Thomas Olsen (USAF Ret.) with Drs. Richard Davis, Barry Barlow, and Perry Jamieson, Mar 5, 1992.

Reavey, Col., intvw—Intvw, Col. Michael F. Reavey with Robert L. Mandler, USAFAWC/HO, May 29, 1991, published transcript held by CAFH/HO.

"Reports of progress"—Memo for Record, AF/XOXW, "Reports of progress in theater," 2330L Feb 26, 1991, "KTO/Republican Guards" file, Checkmate files.

"Response to Navy/Marine Study"—Summary paper, AF/XOXWD, "Response to Navy/Marine Lessons Learned Study," Apr 29, 1991, "Navy/Marine" file, Checkmate files.

"SAC Bomber and Tanker Operations"—Draft RAND study, "Strategic Air Command Bomber and Tanker Operations in Desert Storm," Sep 1991.

SAC/XPA rpt—Rpt, SAC/XPA, "Air Staff/Desert Shield Planning," Apr–May 1991, historians' working files, HQ SAC.

Sawyer, Col., ltr—Letter, Col. David A. Sawyer, 23 TFW/CC, to Lt. Gen. Charles A. Horner, CENTAF/CC, "Yr 15/1930Z Msg, Aircraft Losses," Feb 16, 1991, supporting document to hist, 354 TFW, HQ TAC/HO.

Schwarzkopf, Gen., brfg—Brfg, Gen. H. Norman Schwarzkopf, USCENTCOM, Feb 27, 1991, "KTO/Republican Guards" file, Checkmate files.

Schwarzkopf, Gen., intvw—Notes, Dr. Diane Putney of telephone intvw with Gen. H. Norman Schwarzkopf, May 5, 1992.

Schwarzkopf, Gen., testimony—Hearings before the Committee on Armed Services, United States Senate, 102d Congress, 1st Session, Jun 12, 1991.

"Significant Operations Events"—Chronol, HQ USCENTCOM/ CCJ2,"Significant Operations Events" [compilation of inputs to CINC's War Book], HQ USCENTCOM/CCHO working files.

Smith-McSwain paper—Summary paper, Comdrs. Smith and McSwain, "Operation Desert Storm," "Riyadh Perspective" file, Comdr. Duck Mc-Swain working files.

STRATFOR rpt—Rpt, HQ CENTAF/STRATFOR, "Desert Shield/Storm After Action Report," n.d., historians' working files, HQ SAC/HO.

Support Battle Staff brfg—Brfg slides, in Brfgs, SAC/INCT, file 2.1, "Intelligence Portion of Support Battle Briefings," HQ SAC/HO Desert Storm working archives.

Sweeney, Maj., intvw, Mar 3, 1991—Intvw, Maj. John D. Sweeney with MSgt. Theodore J. Turner, Mar 3, 1991.

Sweeney, Maj., intvw, Mar 4, 1991—Intvw, Maj. John D. Sweeney with MSgt. Theodore J. Turner, Mar 4, 1991.

TACC log—Tactical Air Control Center CC/DO Current Operations Log, Box 81, CENTAF collection, HQ TAC/HO.

"Targets Attacked"—Chart, HQ CENTAF/DCP, "Targets Attacked by Day by Aircraft," Feb 26, 1991, file 029616, Roll 10264, CAFH Desert Shield/Desert Storm microfilm collection.

Thompson memo—Memo, Dr. Wayne Thompson, GWAPS, to Mr. Kurt Guthe, GWAPS, "Phase III," Apr 6, 1992, GWAPS working files.

Thompson's, Dr., trip rpt—Trip rpt, Dr. Wayne Thompson, GWAPS, Visit to Saudi Arabia and Kuwait, Jul 8–16, 1992.

Turner notes—Notes, MSgt. Theodore J. Turner, CENTAF/HO, "USCENTAF/ TACC Notes: Operation Desert Storm," Turner file, Box 84, CENTAF collection, HQ TAC/HO.

"Unexpected in the Campaign"—Brfg, AF/XOXW to the Secretary of Defense, "The Unexpected in the Campaign," Feb 6, 1991, Folder 2, Box 11C, CENTAF Records.

"USAF Forces"—Summary paper, "Desert Storm Fact Sheet: USAF Forces," Mar 19, 1991, historians' working files, HQ TAC/HO.

Vinas special study—Gustave Vinas, "Desert Shield/Desert Storm and the 405th Tactical Training Wing," Jul 24, 1991.

Walker notes—Notes, TSgt. Marcus R. Walker, CENTAF/HO, "Tactical Air Control Center Notes for Desert Storm, 0100–0700, 17 Jan–28 Feb 1991," Walker file, Box 4, CENTAF collection, HQ TAC/HO.

Warden, Col., brfg—Brfg, Col. John A. Warden III, "Instant Thunder: A Strategic Air Campaign Proposal for CINCCENT/Desert Storm," Feb 6, 1992.

Warden, Col., intvw—Intvw, Col. John A. Warden III, AF/XOXW, with Drs. Richard Davis, Perry Jamieson, and Diane Putney, CAFH, Feb 6, 1992.

Waterstreet, Lt. Col., intvw—Intvw, Lt. Col. David L. Waterstreet with Drs. Richard Davis and Barry Barlow, Mar 6, 1992, tape recording held by CAFH.

Lucrative Targets

Winstel, Col., intvw—Intvw, Col. Mark A. Winstel with Robert L. Mandler, US-AFAWC/HO, Dec 21, 1991, published transcript held by CAFH.

Notes

Chapter One

1. H. Norman Schwarzkopf with Peter Petre, *The Autobiography: It Doesn't Take a Hero* (New York: Bantam Books, 1992), 293; rpt, DoD, "Conduct of the Persian Gulf War: Final Report to Congress," Apr 1992, 1, 4 (hereafter, Final Report); memo, HQ USCENTAF FWD/IN, "Republican Guards Forces Command," Nov 5, 1990, "Planning Material from XOXW" file, Box 13, HQ USCENTAF Campaign Planning Records, AF/XOXW (hereafter, CENTAF records); "Iraq's Advantage Limits U.S. Options," *New York Times*, Aug 3, 1990.

2. "The Trouble Zone at a Glance," *New York Times*, Aug 3, 1990; James Blackwell, *Thunder in the Desert: The Strategy and Tactics of the Persian Gulf War* (New York: Bantam Books, 1991), 71; "Kuwaitis Recall Invasion's Horrors," *New York Times*, Aug 3, 1991.

3. "Iraq Army Invades Capital of Kuwait in Fierce Fighting," *New York Times*, Aug 2, 1990.

4. "Invading Iraqis Seize Kuwait and Its Oil," *New York Times*, Aug 3, 1990; "Iraqi Threatens U.S. Interests, CIA Says," *Washington Post*, Aug 6, 1990.

5. Blackwell, *Thunder in the Desert*, 29; "Trouble Zone," *New York Times*, Aug 3, 1990.

6. "A New Gulf Alignment," *New York Times*, Aug 3, 1990; Samir al-Khalil, *Republic of Fear: The Politics of Modern Iraq* (Berkeley & Los Angeles: University of California Press, 1989).

7. "Iraq Declares Kuwait Annexed; Arab Summit Set," *Washington Post*, Aug 9, 1990.

8. "Ill Equipped for the Crises of the 90's," *New York Times*, Aug 7, 1990; "Invading Iraqis," *New York Times*, Aug 3, 1990. On the diplomatic issues in Southwest Asia before and during the Gulf War, see Lawrence Freedman and Efraim Karsh, *The Gulf Conflict 1990–1991: Diplomacy in the New World Order* (Princeton, N.J.: Princeton University Press, 1993).

9. "Iraq Marches, Kuwait Crumbles, and the Markets Convulse," *New York Times*, Aug 5, 1990; intvw, Brig. Gen. Patrick P. Caruana, STRATFOR/CC, with Lt. Col. Edward C. Mann III, AU CADRE/RI, Aug 19 and 23, 1991, tape recording held by HQ SAC/HO (hereafter, Brig. Gen. Caruana intvw); intvw, Capt. David R. Ross, 668 Bom Sq, with MSgt. Robert S. Devino, 416 Wg Historian, Oct 29, 1991, transcript attached to ltr, Col. Michael F. Loughran, 416 Wg (SAC)/CC, to Dr. Dick Hallion, AF/HO, Nov 18, 1991 (hereafter, MSgt. Devino's intvws).

10. Schwarzkopf, *Autobiography*, 310; intvw, Lt. Gen. Charles A. Horner, COMUSCENTAF, commenting on questions prepared earlier by CMSgt. John R. Burton, USCENTAF/HO, Mar 1991, tape recording held by CAFH (hereafter, Lt. Gen. Horner intvw, Mar 1991); intvw, Maj. Gen. Thomas Olsen (USAF, Ret.) with Drs. Richard Davis, Barry Barlow, and Perry Jamieson, Mar 5, 1992 (hereafter, Maj. Gen. Olsen intvw).

11. "Iraq Declares Kuwait An-

nexed," *Washington Post*, Aug 9, 1990; msg, USCINCCENT to CINCPACFLT et al., "Commander's Call on Operations in Southwest Asia," 1100Z Aug 10, 1990, CENTAF collection, HQ TAC/HO; Anthony H. Cordesman and Abraham R. Wagner, *The Lessons of Modern War,* Vol 2*, The Iran-Iraq War* (Boulder & San Francisco: Westview Press; London: Mansell Publishing Company, 1991); "U.S. Military Facing Terror of Chemical War," *Los Angeles Times*, Aug 9, 1990.

12. MR, Col. Douglas C. Roach, Dep Asst Dir for Joint and NSC Matters, DCS/Plans and Ops, "Camp David Discussions Re: Iraq, Saturday, 4 Aug 1990," Aug 4, 1990, atch to memo, Col. Theodore R. Coberly, Secy, Joint Staff, to Chmn, JCS et al., "NSD–54," Jan 23, 1991 (hereafter, "Camp David" memo); Lt. Gen. Horner intvw, Mar 1991. On the Camp David meeting on Aug 4, see also Schwarzkopf, *Autobiography*, 299–300.

13. "Camp David" memo; "U.S. Sends Troops, Jets to Saudi Arabia As Iraqi Forces Pose 'Imminent Threat,'" *Washington Post*, Aug 8, 1990. On the Cheney-Fahd meeting, see also Schwarzkopf, *Autobiography*, 302–305.

14. "U.N. Security Council Votes Embargo on Iraq; Saddam Says Seizure of Kuwait Is Permanent," *Washington Post*, Aug 7, 1990.

15. "Egyptian Troops, British Planes Join Persian Gulf Military Buildup," *Philadelphia Inquirer*, Aug 13, 1990; "Sanctions Starting to Pinch Iraq Economy, U.S. Aides Say; U.N.'s Diplomacy Welcomed," *New York Times*, Aug 27, 1990; rpt, DoD, "Conduct of the Persian Gulf Conflict: An Interim Report to Congress," Jul 1991, App A (hereafter, Interim Report).

16. Msg, 513 MIBdeFwd/JDC to CMO ARCENT/G2 et al., "IIR 6 072 0054 91/Source Debriefing," 0635Z Mar 13, 1991, "Iraqi POW Debriefs" file, HQ USAF Checkmate Planning Office files, HQ USAF/XOXW (hereafter, Checkmate files).

17. "U.S. Sends Troops," *Washington Post*, Aug 8, 1990; monogr, William T. Y'Blood, *The Eagle and the Scorpion: The USAF and the Desert Shield First-Phase Deployment, 7 August–8 November, 1990* (Center for Air Force History, 1992), 38; speech, Gen. Michael Loh, Comdr TAC, to Virginia American Legion, Norfolk, Va., Jul 13, 1991, historians' working files, HQ TAC/HO (hereafter, Gen. Loh speech); draft RAND study, "Strategic Air Command Bomber and Tanker Operations in Desert Storm," Sep 1991, 1 (hereafter, "SAC Bomber and Tanker Operations").

18. Y'Blood, *Eagle and Scorpion*, 9; hist, USCENTCOM, 1988, chap I, 5.

19. Hist, USCENTCOM, 1988, chap I, 1; bio, SAF/PA, Lt. Gen. Charles A. Horner, Jan 1989; Lt. Gen. Horner intvw, Mar 1991. See also Schwarzkopf, *Autobiography*, 306.

20. Maj. Gen. Olsen intvw. Charles J. Gross has explored this development in a series of oral history interviews with senior defense officials. See, for example, intvw, Gen. Larry D. Welch with Dr. Charles J. Gross, AF/HOX, Jul 12, 1991, transcript held by CAFH. See also "Saudis to Let U.S. Use Bases in Crisis," *New York Times*, Sep 5, 1985.

21. Draft, USTRANSCOM/TCHO, "Operation Desert Shield/Desert Storm," chapter in hist, USTRANS-COM, 1990, HQ USTRANSCOM Office of History; Gen. Loh speech.

22. Draft, USTRANSCOM/TCHO, "Operation Desert Shield/Desert Storm," chapter in hist, USTRANSCOM, 1990, HQ USTRANSCOM Office of History. On Operation Desert Shield, see also Y'Blood, *Eagle and Scorpion*, and

draft, HQ MAC/HO, "Chapter III: Operation Desert Shield," in hist, MAC, 1990, HQ MAC/HO.

23. "U.S. to Rely on Air Strikes If War Erupts," *Washington Post*, Sep 16, 1990; "Chief of Air Staff Fired by Cheney," *Washington Post*, Sep 18, 1990; hist, HQ USAF, 1990, 10; Lt. Gen. Horner intvw, Mar 1991.

24. Y'Blood, *Eagle and Scorpion*, 103; memo, Lt. Gen. Charles A. Horner, Comdr, USCENTCOM (Fwd), to All U.S. Commanders in Saudi Arabia, "Awareness of Host-Nation Sensibilities," Aug 15, 1990, File 0269451, "General Order #1," Roll 10204, CAFH Desert Shield/Desert Storm microfilm collection; General Order (GO)–1, HQ USCENTCOM, Operation Desert Shield, Aug 30, 1990, CAFH Desert Shield/Desert Storm microfilm collection.

25. [Classified source]; "U.S. Troops' Biggest Fight So Far Is with 115-Degree Desert Heat," *New York Times*, Aug 15, 1990; "After Months of Heat, Saudi Desert Turns Frigid," *Philadelphia Inquirer*, Nov 15, 1990; OpPlan, HQ USCENTCOM and HQ JF/Theater of Operations, "Combined Operation Desert Storm," Jan 17, 1991, Sec B, 2–4, File 0269608, Roll 10261, CAFH Desert Shield/Desert Storm microfilm collection (hereafter, CENTCOM OpPlan, Jan 17, 1991); brfg slide, "Weather Trends in Kuwait," n.d., "The Kuwait Air Campaign CSAF Information Book," Box 7, CENTAF records.

26. [Classified source]; CENTCOM OpPlan, Jan 17, 1991, Sec B, 2–4.

27. "Camp David" memo; "Air Option Will Save U.S. Lives," *Miami Herald*, Dec 17, 1990. The historian was Richard P. Hallion, who later became the Air Force Historian.

28. "U.S. Decides to Add As Many As 100,000 to Its Gulf Forces," *New York Times*, Oct 26, 1990; "Bush Sends New Units to Gulf to Provide 'Offensive' Option; U.S. Force Could Reach 380,000," *New York Times*, Nov 9, 1990; brfg, Gen. H. Norman Schwarzkopf, USCENTCOM, Feb 27, 1991, "KTO/Republican Guards" file, Checkmate files (hereafter, Gen. Schwarzkopf brfg).

29. Gen. Schwarzkopf brfg; draft monogr, U.S. Army Center of Military History, [untitled, on the U.S. Army in Operations Desert Shield and Storm], n.d., U.S. Army Center of Military History (hereafter, CMH draft), 98, 100, 181.

30. Gen. Schwarzkopf brfg; CMH draft, 181–182.

31. Gen. Schwarzkopf brfg.

32. "Bush Wants Jan. 1 Deadline on Saddam," *Washington Times*, Nov 26, 1990; "PLO Move Imperils U.N. Vote on Use of Force Against Iraq," *Washington Post*, Nov 28, 1990; msg, US Mission US UN New York to SecState, "SC Adopts Resolution Authorizing Use of Force," 0047Z Nov 30, 1990, "War Termination—Emergency Strike Plan" file, Checkmate files; "U.N. Vote Authorizes Use of Force Against Iraq," *Washington Post*, Nov 30, 1990; Lt. Gen. Horner intvw, Mar 1991.

33. "Bush Asks Congress to Back Force Against Iraq," *Washington Post*, Jan 9, 1991; H.J. Res 77, "Authorization for Use of Military Force Against Iraq Resolution," n.d., "War Termination—Emergency Strike Plan" file, Checkmate files; Donald R. Hickey, *The War of 1812: A Forgotten Conflict* (Urbana & Chicago: University of Illinois Press, 1989), 46; "Saddam Orders the Release of All Hostages," *Washington Post*, Dec 7, 1990; "Congress Acts to Authorize War in Gulf; Margins Are 5 Votes in Senate, 67 in House," *New York Times*, Jan 13, 1991.

34. "Congress Acts to Authorize War," *New York Times*, Jan 13, 1991.

See also President George Bush to Robert C. Byrd, President pro Tempore of the Senate et al., Jan 16, 1991, and President George Bush to Thomas S. Foley, Speaker, House of Representatives, Jan 18, 1991, "War Termination—Emergency Strike Plan" file, Checkmate files.

35. Final Report, 118; CENTCOM OpPlan, Jan 17, 1991, 1.

36. Brfg slide, HQ USCENT-COM/CCJ2, "Overall KTO Ground Summary," CINC's War Book input, Jan 17, 1991 [A.M.], HQ USCENT-COM/CCHO working files (hereafter, CINC's War Book input); Final Report, 203.

Primary sources give various figures for the numbers of Iraqi personnel, tanks, APCs, and artillery in the KTO. See also brfg slide, "Enemy Ground Situation," [Jan 17, 1991], File 0269537, "CENTAF/DOO Daily Slides for General Horner and TACC Briefing," Roll 10227, CAFH Desert Shield/Desert Storm microfilm collection; brfg slide, "Ground Forces in Theater," Jan 16, 1991, in brfg, SAC/INCT, "Support Battle Staff Briefing: Intelligence Portion," 0600L Jan 17, 1991, File 2.1 "Intelligence Portion of Support Battle Briefings," HQ SAC/HO Desert Storm working archives (hereafter, Support Battle Staff brfg); brfg slide, "Summary of Attacks on Iraqi Ground Forces: Key Ground Equipment," in brfg, Steven L. Head, DD/TWP, "The Conduct and Performance of the Air Campaign in Operation Desert Storm," Mar 21, 1991, DD/TWP working files (hereafter, DD/TWP brfg), which cites Gen. Schwarzkopf's press brfg of Feb 27, 1991; brfg slide, "Equipment Degradation in KTO," in brfg, JCS-J2, "J-2 Daily BDA Assessment," Feb 13, 1991, "JCS BDA" file, Checkmate files; brfg slide, "Major Equipment in KTO," in

brfg, "Desert Storm CSAF Brief" (hereafter, CSAF brief), Feb 25, 1991, Checkmate files. Postwar studies gave lower numbers. Rick Atkinson, *Crusade: The Untold Story of the Persian Gulf War* (Boston & New York: Houghton Mifflin, 1993), 340–343.

37. Final Report, 3.

38. MR, 513 Mil Intel Brig, Joint Debriefing Ctr, "The Gulf War: An Iraqi General Officer's Perspective," Mar 11, 1991, "Iraqi POW Debriefs" file, Checkmate files (hereafter, "Iraqi Generals Perspective"). On the accuracy of intelligence estimates of Iraqi numbers, see also intvw, Col. Michael F. Reavey with Robert L. Mandler, US-AFAWC/HO, May 29, 1991, published transcript held by CAFH/HO (hereafter, Col. Reavey intvw).

39. Intvw, Lt. Col. David A. Deptula, AF/OSX, with Drs. Richard Davis, Perry Jamieson, and Diane Putney, CAFH, Nov 27, 1991, tape recording held by CAFH (hereafter, Lt. Col. Deptula intvw, Nov 27, 1991); "Iraqis Setting Up Strong Defensive Line, U.S. Says," *Washington Post*, Aug 10, 1990.

40. Diagram, "Example of Complex Obstacle," in memo, HQ SAC SBS/DOO to 17 ADP/Bom Ops, "Joint Obstacle Breach," Jan 28, 1991, historians' working files, HQ SAC/HO; msg, 513 MIBdeFwd/JDC to DIA/OC-4A/DC-1 (CCP), 0652Z Mar 1, 1991, "Iraqi POW Debriefs" file, Checkmate files (hereafter, msg, 0652Z Mar 1, 1991).

41. Brfg, Col. John A. Warden III, "Instant Thunder: A Strategic Air Campaign Proposal for CINCCENT/Desert Storm," Feb 6, 1992 (hereafter, Col. Warden brfg); Gen. Schwarzkopf brfg; speech, Saddam Hussein, Jan 20, 1991, quoted in Micah L. Sifry and Christopher Cerf, eds., *The Gulf War Reader: History, Documents, Opinions* (New

York: Random House, 1991), 316.

42. Gustave Vinas, "Desert Shield/ Desert Storm and the 405th Tactical Training Wing," Jul 24, 1991, 37 (hereafter, Vinas special study); brfg slide, HQ CENTAF/DOO, "Iraqi Air Order of Battle," [Jan 17, 1991], File 0269537, "CENTAF/DOO Daily Slides for General Horner and TACC Briefing," Roll 10227, CAFH Desert Shield/Desert Storm microfilm collection; Cordesman and Wagner, *Iran-Iraq War*, 50; Lt. Col. Deptula intvw, Nov 29, 1991.

43. DD/TWP brfg; msg, 99 SWW/INIA to AIG 9471 et al., "Iraqi Tactics Analysis Team Report," 1800Z Jan 16, 1991, File 9.0 "Intelligence," HQ SAC/HO Desert Storm working archives.

44. [Classified source]; Interim Report, ch 2, p 3; point paper, AF/ XOXWD, "Iraqi Nuclear Weapon Threat," Oct 24, 1990, "The Kuwait Air Campaign CSAF Information Book," Box 7, CENTAF records.

45. [Classified source]; Def Intel memo 3–91, Jan 1991, "Nuclear, Biological, Chemical" file, Box 4, CENTAF records.

46. Def Intel memo 3–91, Jan 1991, "Nuclear, Biological, Chemical" file, Box 4, CENTAF records; CMH draft, 256; notes, TSgt. Marcus R. Walker, USCENTAF/HO, "Tactical Air Control Center Notes for Desert Storm, 0100– 0700, 17 Jan–28 Feb 1991," entry for 0235 Feb 24, 1991, "Walker file," Box 4, CENTAF collection, HQ TAC/HO (hereafter, Walker notes); notes, Lt. Gen. Horner, [on CENTCOM staff meeting], 0900 Feb 24, 1991, "24 Feb 91" file, Lt. Gen. Horner's Desert Storm files, HQ 9 AF/CC; Gen. Schwarzkopf brfg.

47. Maj. Gen. Olsen intvw; [Classified source]; transcript, HQ USCENT-AF Office of History, "Daily Comments of Lieutenant General Charles A. Horner, Commander, United States Central Command Air Forces during Operation Desert Storm, 17 January through 28 February 1991," Mar 20, 1991, 11 (hereafter, Lt. Gen. Horner's daily comments).

48. Intvw, Lt. Gen. Charles Horner with Drs. Richard Davis, Barry Barlow, and Perry Jamieson, Mar 4, 1992 (hereafter, Lt. Gen. Horner intvw, Mar 4, 1992); Maj. Gen. Olsen intvw.

49. Interim Report, ch 13, p 1; msg, USCINCCENT/CCJ3 to COMUS-CENTAF et al., "FragOrd 007 to Desert Storm OpOrd 001–91," 2000Z Jan 25, 1991, HQ USCENTCOM/CCHO working files; OpOrd, USCINCCENT, "FragOrd 008 to Desert Storm OpOrd 001–91," Jan 27, 1991, HQ USCENT-COM/CCHO working files; msg, US-CINCCENT/CCJ3 to COMUSNAV-CENT et al., "FragOrd 009 to Desert Storm OpOrd 001–91," 2045Z Jan 27, 1991, HQ USCENTCOM/CCHO working files; Final Report, App T, 81.

50. Msg, Am Emb Riyadh to US-CINCCENT, "Saddam's Oil Slick— U.S. Coordination and Offer of Technical Assistance," 0646Z Jan 26, 1991, "State Department Message" file, HQ USCENTCOM/CCHO working files; Interim Report, ch 13, p 1; msg, Am Emb Riyadh to SecState et al., "Saddam's War: Kuwaiti Oil Fires Update," 1345Z Feb 25, 1991, "State Department Message" file, HQ USCENTCOM/ CCHO working files; msg, Am Emb Riyadh to SecState et al., "Saddam's Slicks: Initial Cost Estimates," 1442Z Feb 23, 1991, HQ USCENTCOM/ CCHO working files. See also msg, Am Emb Riyadh to SecState et al., "Saddam's War: Kuwaiti Oil Fires Update," 1312Z Feb 24, 1991, "State Department Message" file, HQ USCENTCOM/ CCHO working files.

51. Hearings, Senate Committee on Armed Services, 102d Cong., 1st Sess., May 21, 1991, 235 (hereafter, Lt. Gen. Horner testimony); memo, HQ SAC/DOO, [untitled], n.d., historians' working files, HQ SAC/HO; [classified source]; Interim Report, ch 2, p 4; brfg slide, HQ CENTAF/DOO, "Iraqi Air Order of Battle," [Jan 17, 1991], File 0269537, "CENTAF/DOO Daily Slides for General Horner and TACC Briefing," Roll 10227, CAFH Desert Shield/Desert Storm microfilm collection.

52. DD/TWP brfg; [Classified source].

53. Interim Report, ch 2, p 4; Col. Warden brfg; OpOrd, HQ COMUS-CENTAF, "COMUSCENTAF Operations Order: Offensive Campaign—Phase I," Sep 2, 1990, Box 12, CENT-AF records (hereafter, COMUSCENT-AF OpOrd); intvw, Lt. Col. David A. Deptula with Drs. Richard Davis, Perry Jamieson, and Diane Putney, Jan 8, 1992, tape recording held by CAFH (hereafter, Lt. Col. Deptula intvw, Jan 8, 1992).

54. [Classified source]. On Iraqi EW capabilities, see also msg, HQ US-CENTAF FWD HQS ELEMENT/EC to 1 TFW/WOC et al., "Iraq Electronic Support Measures (ESM), Direction Finding (DF), and Passive Detection (PD) Capabilities," 1100Z Oct 14, 1990, File 0269522, Roll 10215, CAFH Desert Shield/Desert Storm microfilm collection.

55. Draft rpt, HQ SAC, "Operations Desert Shield & Desert Storm: 'The Bomber Story,'" n.d., 23, historians' working files, HQ SAC/HO (hereafter, "Bomber Story").

56. Msg, USCINCCENT to AIG 904 et al., "SitRep," 2115Z Jan 16, 1991, Box 23, CENTAF collection, HQ TAC/HO; CMH draft, 100, 195, 196. The VII Corps began entering the the-

ater in November, and its units were still arriving from Europe into February. CMH draft, 269.

57. Gen. Schwarzkopf brfg; CMH draft, 297–298; map, situation as of G–40, Jan 15, 1991, in brfg, HQ CENT-COM/CCDCS, "The 100-Hour Ground War," n.d., HQ USCENTCOM/CCHO working files (hereafter, "100-Hour Ground War").

58. "US Gulf Commanders," *Saudi Gazette*, Feb 26, 1991, in TACC CC/DO Current Ops Log, Box 81, CENT-AF collection, HQ TAC/HO (hereafter, TACC log); Interim Report, ch 4, p 6; map, situation as of G-40, Jan 15, 1991, in "100-Hour Ground War."

59. Y'Blood, *Eagle and Scorpion*, 27–28; "US Gulf Commanders," *Saudi Gazette*, Feb 26, 1991, in TACC log; USCINCCENT to AIG 904 et al., "SitRep," 2115Z Jan 16, 1991, CENT-AF collection.

60. Maj. Gen. Olsen intvw; Steven B. Michael, *The Persian Gulf War: An Air Staff Chronology of Operation Desert Shield/Desert Storm*, 1992, 235; point paper, AF/XOXW, "Proven Force," n.d. [early Feb 1991], "Proven Force" file, Checkmate files; SSS, AF/XOXWF, "'Proven Force' Trip Report," Feb 21, 1991, with atch (1) trip rpt from observation of JTF "Proven Force" and 7440 Cmbt Wg, and (2) draft point paper on 7440th Concept of Operations, Checkmate files. See also point paper, AF/CSS, "Deployment of Fighter Aircraft to Turkey (SOA #1273)," Jan 16, 1991, "16–17 Jan 91 (Day 1)" file, Checkmate files.

61. Michael, *Chronology*, 235.

62. Point paper, AF/XOOSO, "Space Support to Desert Shield," Jan 16, 1991, "16–17 Jan 91 (Day 1)" file, Checkmate files; chronol, AFSPACE-COM/HO, "A Chronology of Space and Missile Warning Systems Support to the

Allied Coalition in the Gulf War," Aug 27, 1991.

63. Allan R. Millett, *Semper Fidelis: The History of the United States Marine Corps*, rev. ed. (New York: Free Press, 1991), 638; Maj. Gen. Olsen intvw.

Chapter Two

1. Hist, 9 AF, 1980, 13–15; intvw, Lt. Col. Jeffrey S. Feinstein with Drs. Richard Davis, Barry Barlow, and Perry Jamieson, Mar 3, 1992, tape recording held by CAFH (hereafter, Lt. Col. Feinstein intvw).

2. Brfg, HQ 9 AF/DOOW, "Air Tasking Order (ATO) Preparation and Composite Force Packaging," Jan 1992 (hereafter, ATO brfg); intvw, Lt. Col. Sam Baptiste with Drs. Perry Jamieson and Barry Barlow, Mar 2, 1992, tape recording held by CAFH (hereafter, Lt. Col. Baptiste intvw); Maj. Gen. Olsen intvw.

3. ATO brfg; Lt. Col. Baptiste intvw.

4. Hist, TAC, 1988, 589; Lt. Col. Feinstein intvw.

5. Y'Blood, *Eagle and Scorpion*, 25; Lt. Col. Baptiste intvw; intvw, Col. Chris- topher Christon with Drs. Richard Davis and Barry Barlow, Mar 4, 1992, tape recording held by CAFH (hereafter, Col. Christon intvw); intvw, Lt. Col. David L. Waterstreet with Drs. Richard Davis and Barry Barlow, Mar 6, 1992, tape recording held by CAFH (hereafter, Lt. Col. Waterstreet intvw); intvw, Lt. Gen. Charles A. Horner, COMUSCENTAF, with Lt. Cols. Suzanne Gehri and Richard Reynolds, CADRE/RIR, Dec 3, 1991, tape recording held by CAFH (hereafter, Lt. Gen. Horner intvw, Dec 3, 1991); Lt. Gen. Horner intvw, Mar 4, 1992.

6. Bio, SAF/PA, Lt. Gen. Charles A. Horner, Jan 1989; Col. Reavey intvw; Lt. Col. Feinstein intvw.

7. Lt. Gen. Horner intvw, Mar 1991; Lt. Gen. Horner intvw, Dec 3, 1991; exec summary, HQ USCENT-COM/CCJ5-P, "J5 Plans After Action Report," Mar 5, 1991, 4, HQ USCENT-COM/CCHO working files (hereafter, "J5 After Action Report"); Y'Blood, *Eagle and Scorpion*, 22. See also brfg, HQ USCENTCOM, OpPlan 1002–90, n.d., "Preliminary Planning Documents" file, HQ USCENTCOM/CCHO working files.

8. "J5 After Action Report," 4; Lt. Gen. Horner intvw, Mar 1991; Lt. Gen. Horner intvw, Dec 3, 1991.

9. Lt. Gen. Horner intvw, Dec 3, 1991; Lt. Col. Waterstreet intvw; Lt. Gen. Horner intvw, Mar 4, 1992. On Lt. Gen. Horner's trips to MacDill AFB, Fla., and Camp David, Md., see also *U.S. News & World Report, Triumph Without Victory: The Unreported History of the Persian Gulf War* (New York: Random House, 1992), 55–56, 69.

10. Lt. Gen. Horner intvw, Mar 4, 1992; Y'Blood, *Eagle and Scorpion*, 41, 67; Col. Reavey intvw; Maj. Gen. Olsen intvw.

11. ATO brfg; intvw, Col. James Crigger with Drs. Richard Davis and Barry Barlow, Mar 5, 1992, tape recording held by CAFH (hereafter, Col. Crigger intvw); Lt. Gen. Horner intvw, Dec 3, 1991.

12. ATO brfg; Lt. Col. Baptiste intvw; Lt. Col. Waterstreet intvw; Lt. Col. Feinstein intvw.

13. Lt. Gen. Horner intvw, Mar 4, 1992; Maj. Gen. Olsen intvw. See also intvw, Maj. Gen. John Corder with Robert L. Mandler, USAFAWC/HO, Dec 21, 1991, published transcript held by CAFH (hereafter, Maj. Gen. Corder intvw).

14. Atchmt 8, "Doctrinal and Interoperability," to rpt, "Air Force Inputs to the Conduct of the Persian Gulf Conflict, Final Title V Report to Congress," Sep 6, 1991, "Title V Report Inputs" file, Checkmate files; intvw, Lt. Col. David A. Deptula, AF/OSX, with Dr. Richard Davis, CAFH, Nov 20, 1991, tape recording held by CAFH (hereafter, Lt. Col. Deptula intvw, Nov 20, 1991); msg, CINCSAC to CJCS, "Preliminary Report on Lessons Learned in Operation Desert Shield and Desert Storm," 1500Z Apr 1, 1991, atch to SSS, HQ SAC/DOOG, "Preliminary Report on Lessons Learned in Operation Desert Shield/Storm," Mar 28, 1991, historians' working files, HQ SAC/HO; Lt. Gen. Horner intvw, Mar 4, 1992. See also intvw, Col. Mark A. Winstel with Robert L. Mandler, USAFAWC/HO, Dec 21, 1991, published transcript held by CAFH (hereafter, Col. Winstel intvw). For the formal definition of the JFACC, see Atchmt 8, "Glossary: Definition of Terms," to Concept of Ops, USCENTAF/DO, "Concept of Operations for Command and Control of TacAir in Support of Land Forces," Feb 22, 1991 (hereafter, ConOps for C²), citing JCS Pub 1–02, Dec 1, 1989, HQ 9 AF/HO working files, and see also brfg slides on the JFACC, atch to memo, 9 AF/DO to CC, [no subject], Nov 4 [1991], in Lt. Gen. Horner's Desert Storm files, HQ 9 AF/CC. On the Navy and the ATO, see also summary paper, Comdrs. Smith and McSwain, "Operation Desert Storm," "Riyadh Perspective" file, Comdr. Duck McSwain working files (hereafter, Smith-McSwain paper).

15. Notes, Dr. Diane Putney, telephone intvw with Gen. H. Norman Schwarzkopf, May 5, 1992 (hereafter, Gen. Schwarzkopf intvw). General Schwarzkopf gave Dr. Putney one of the few interviews he granted between the end of the Gulf War and the publication of his memoirs.

16. Schwarzkopf, *Autobiography*, 313. On the CENTCOM commander's decision to request help from the Air Staff, see also Schwarzkopf, *Autobiography*, 320.

17. Gen. Schwarzkopf intvw. General Schwarzkopf's memoirs indicate that he made this telephone call to General Powell on August 10. Schwarzkopf, *Autobiography*, 313. Doubtless he called General Powell about this issue earlier than that, because there is overwhelming evidence that the CENTCOM commander telephoned the Air Staff on August 8. General Schwarzkopf's memoirs no doubt telescope a series of phone calls between himself and the chairman, made during days of intense crisis, to simplify the sequence of events for a general audience.

18. Gen. Schwarzkopf intvw; Lt. Col. Deptula intvw, Jan 8, 1992; Col. Warden brfg; intvw, Col. John A. Warden III, AF/XOXW, with Drs. Richard Davis, Perry Jamieson, and Diane Putney, CAFH, Feb 6, 1992 (hereafter, Col. Warden intvw).

19. Col. Warden brfg; John A. Warden III, *The Air Campaign: Planning for Combat* (Washington, D.C.: National Defense University Press, 1988).

20. Col. Warden intvw; rpt, SAC/XPA, "Air Staff/Desert Shield Planning," Apr–May 1991, historians' working files, HQ SAC (hereafter, SAC/XPA rpt); memo, Wayne Thompson to Perry Jamieson, [comments on draft of

Lucrative Targets], Jun 15, 1993, copy in possession of P. D. Jamieson.

21. Warden, Air Campaign, 9–10, passim; brfg, Lt. Col. David A. Deptula, CENTAF Special Planning Group and Strategic Target Planning Cell, "The Air Campaign: Planning & Execution," n.d.; brfg, JCS/J–36, "Iraqi Air Campaign Instant Thunder," Aug 17 1990, "Threat Data Targeting Info; CSAF Briefing Book," Box 7, CENTAF records (hereafter, "Instant Thunder"); intvw, Lt. Col. David A. Deptula with TSgt. Theodore J. Turner, Nov 1, 1990, transcript held by AF/CAFH (hereafter, Lt. Col. Deptula intvw, Nov 1, 1990).

22. Col. Warden brfg; Lt. Col. Deptula intvw, Jan 8, 1992; "Instant Thunder." On Rolling Thunder, see Larry E. Cable, "Evaluating the Air War, 1964–1968," paper presented at the Fourteenth Military History Symposium, United States Air Force Academy, Oct 18, 1990, and Mark Clodfelter, *The Limits of Air Power: The American Bombing of North Vietnam* (New York & London: Macmillan, 1989), 39–146. On the designation "Instant Thunder," see also Lt. Col. Deptula intvw, Nov 1, 1990.

23. SAC/XPA rpt.

24. Lt. Col. Deptula intvw, Jan 8, 1992; Schwarzkopf, *Autobiography*, 318; SAC/XPA rpt; Lt. Col. Deptula intvw, Nov 27, 1991; paper, Dr. Diane Putney, CAFH/HOH, "Gulf War Air Campaign: Developing and Merging the Phases," 2, presented at Eglin AFB, Fla., Mar 1, 1994, copy held by CAFH. General Schwarzkopf's *Autobiography* describes a single briefing by Colonel Warden on August 16 whereas Air Force sources make it certain that there were two, on August 10 and 17. This is doubtless another case, like that of the CENTCOM commander's telephone conversations with General Powell, in which General Schwarzkopf's memoirs

telescope events, perhaps to simplify them for the benefit of general readers.

25. Col. Warden intvw; draft End of Tour Report, Lt. Gen. Jimmie V. Adams, AF/XO, with Mr. Jacob Neufeld and Dr. Walton Moody, AF/HOA, Dec 27, 1990, 22; org chart, J–3 Air, Aug 13, 1990, Lt. Col. Ron Stanfill notes, Gulf War Air Power Study files; "Instant Thunder"; Lt. Col. Deptula intvw, Jan 8, 1992.

26. Col. Warden intvw; SAC/XPA rpt; Lt. Col. Deptula intvw, Jan 8, 1992; Lt. Col. Deptula intvw, Nov 27, 1991.

27. SAC/XPA rpt; Putney, "Gulf War Air Campaign"; Col. Warden intvw.

28. Lt. Col. Deptula intvw, Jan 8, 1992; SAC/XPA rpt.

29. Schwarzkopf, *Autobiography*, 319; *Gulf War Air Power Survey*, Vol I, Part 1, "Planning" (Washington, D.C., 1993), 170 (hereafter, *GWAPS*); Field Manual 34–3, HQ Dept Army, "Intelligence Analysis," Mar 1990, Sec 3, 28 (hereafter, FM 34–3); intvw, Col. Gary R. Ware (USAF, Ret.) with Dr. Diane Putney, CAFH, Mar 28, 1994. (Colonel Ware was the chief of the CENTCOM Combat Analysis Group.) See also CMH draft, 288, and hist, Col. Richard M. Swain, ARCENT Historian, "Operational Narrative: Operations Desert Shield–Desert Storm," Sep 24, 1991, 39 (hereafter, ARCENT hist).

30. Gen. Schwarzkopf intvw.

31. Col. Warden intvw.

32. Schwarzkopf, *Autobiography*, 320; Gen. Schwarzkopf intvw. The narration of what happened on August 17 given in General Schwarzkopf's memoirs represents another case of this book's telescoping of events. The account presented here is based on the work of Dr. Diane Putney, who interviewed both General Schwarzkopf and Colonel Warden and made a thorough

study of the primary sources on the planning of the air campaign.

33. Col. Warden intvw; intvw, Lt. Col. David A. Deptula, AF/OSX, with Dr. Richard Davis, CAFH, Nov 20, 1991, tape recording held by CAFH (hereafter, Lt. Col. Deptula intvw, Nov 20, 1991); Lt. Gen. Horner intvw, Mar 1991; Maj. Gen. Olsen intvw; Col. Crigger intvw.

34. Lt. Gen. Horner intvw, Mar 1991; Col. Warden intvw; Brig. Gen. Caruana intvw.

35. Talking paper, Lt. Col. David A. Deptula, JFACC Special Planning Group, "JFACC Directorate of Campaign Plans," Nov 4, 1991 (hereafter, "Directorate of Campaign Plans"); intvw, Maj. Gen. Buster C. Glosson with Drs. Richard Davis, Perry Jamieson, and Diane Putney, Dec 12, 1991, tape recording held by CAFH (hereafter, Maj. Gen. Glosson intvw, Dec 12, 1991).

36. Col. Warden intvw; Lt. Gen. Horner intvw, Mar 4, 1992.

37. Col. Crigger intvw; Lt. Col. Waterstreet intvw. See also Schwarzkopf, *Autobiography*, 320.

38. Lt. Col. Waterstreet intvw; Lt. Col. Feinstein intvw; Col. Crigger intvw.

39. Lt. Col. Deptula intvw, Nov 27, 1991; Lt. Col. Deptula intvw, Nov 20, 1991; Col. Warden intvw; memo, Wayne Thompson to Perry Jamieson, [comments on draft of *Lucrative Targets*], Jun 15, 1993, copy in possession of P. D. Jamieson.

40. Col. Warden brfg; Col. Warden intvw; meeting notes, Drs. Wayne Thompson and Perry Jamieson, AF/CAFH, with Dr. Dana Johnson, RAND Corporation, at the Checkmate Office, Aug 22, 1991, P. D. Jamieson personal files; Lt. Col. Feinstein intvw; Lt. Col. Deptula intvw, Nov 27, 1991; brfg, Lt.

Col. David A. Deptula, "Air Power in the Gulf War: The View from the Black Hole," CAFH Symposium, Jan 8, 1992 (hereafter, Lt. Col. Deptula brfg); Maj. Gen. Glosson intvw, Dec 12, 1991. See also MR, Dr. Wayne Thompson, AF/HO, "Notes of a telephone conversation with Lt. Col. Deptula [paraphrased]," Sep 13, 1991, copy in possession of P. D. Jamieson.

41. Lt. Col. Deptula brfg; intvw, Rear Adm. J. M. McConnell with Drs. Ron Cole and Diane Putney, Feb 5, 1992, tape recording held by CAFH; Maj. Gen. Glosson intvw, Dec 12, 1991. See also MR, Dr. Wayne Thompson, AF/HO, "Notes of a telephone conversation with Lt. Col. Deptula [paraphrased]," Sep 13, 1991, copy in possession of P. D. Jamieson. On the resources available to Rear Adm. J. M. McConnell and his cooperation with Brig. Gen. Buster C. Glosson, see draft monogr, Dr. Diane Putney, "Planning the Gulf War Air Campaign," CAFH MS.

42. Maj. Gen. Glosson intvw, Dec 12, 1991; Lt. Gen. Horner intvw, Mar 1991.

43. Lt. Col. Deptula brfg; "Directorate of Campaign Plans"; Lt. Col. Waterstreet intvw; Col. Crigger intvw.

44. Manning Schedule, HQ CENTAF Special Planning Group, "Offensive Air Campaign Planning Cell Shifts," n.d., Folder 1, Box 11C, CENTAF records; Maj. Gen. Olsen intvw; Lt. Col. Waterstreet intvw.

45. Maj. Gen. Olsen intvw; Lt. Col. Waterstreet intvw.

46. Lt. Col. Deptula intvw, Nov 20, 1991; Lt. Col. Waterstreet intvw.

47. Lt. Col. Deptula intvw, Nov 27, 1991.

48. Lt. Col. Deptula intvw, Jan 8, 1992; Lt. Gen. Horner intvw, Mar 4, 1992.

49. Lt. Col. Deptula intvw, Nov 27, 1991.

50. Ibid., Nov 20, 1991.

51. Ibid., Jan 8, 1992.

52. Ibid., Nov 27, 1991.

53. This controversy became public when Gen. Schwarzkopf acknowledged it during open congressional testimony, shortly after the war. Hearings, Senate Committee on Armed Services, 102d Cong., 1st Sess., Jun 12, 1991, 320 (hereafter, Gen. Schwarzkopf testimony). The CENTCOM commander also discussed the subject in his memoirs. Schwarzkopf, *Autobiography*, 430–432. For representative points of view on each side of this issue, see Lt. Col. Deptula intvw, Nov 27, 1991; Col. Christon intvw.

54. Col. Christon intvw.

55. Maj. Gen. Olsen intvw.

56. Col. Christon intvw.

57. Lt. Gen. Horner intvw, Mar 1991.

58. Ibid.

59. See, for example, Lt. Gen. Horner intvw, Mar 1991; Maj. Gen. Olsen intvw; and intvw, Maj. John D. Sweeney with MSgt. Theodore J. Turner, Mar 4, 1991 (hereafter, Maj. Sweeney intvw, Mar 4, 1991).

60. Lt. Col. Deptula intvw, Jan 8, 1992.

61. Gen. Schwarzkopf testimony, 342; Maj. Gen. Glosson intvw, Dec 12, 1991; Lt. Col. Deptula intvw, Nov 27, 1991. See also Schwarzkopf, *Autobiography*, 430.

62. Lt. Col. Deptula intvw, Nov 20, 1991. Col. John Warden used a similar term, "parallel warfare," to mean attacking all of the enemy's target sets within a matter of days, as opposed to "serial warfare," attacking his targets in sequence, with pauses that allowed him to reconstitute his forces and "work around" the damage inflicted from the air. Col. Warden brfg.

63. Col. Warden brfg.

64. Lt. Col. Deptula intvw, Nov 27, 1991; plan, CENTAF/DCP, Master Attack Plan, Jan 16, 1991, Box 25, CENTAF collection, HQ TAC/HO (hereafter, MAP Jan 16, 1991).

65. "Directorate of Campaign Plans."

66. Lt. Gen. Horner intvw, Mar 4, 1992; Maj. Gen. Olsen intvw.

67. Lt. Col. Deptula intvw, Nov 27, 1991; Lt. Gen. Horner intvw, Mar 1991; Lt. Col. Deptula intvw, Nov 1, 1990; Maj. Gen. Glosson intvw, Dec 12, 1991.

68. Lt. Gen. Horner intvw, Dec 3, 1991; Lt. Col. Deptula intvw, Nov 27, 1991.

69. Brfg, HQ CENTAF, "Theater Air Campaign," [Dec 1990], [untitled], brfg book, Box 11B, CENTAF records. The multiple versions of this briefing give the phases various labels.

70. Lt. Gen. Horner intvw, Dec 3, 1991; Lt. Gen. Horner intvw, Mar 4, 1992.

71. Brfg, AF/XOXW, "Kuwait Offensive Air Campaign: Phases II & III," Oct 26, 1990, "Plan—Phases 2/3" file, Checkmate files; Tab 2, AF/XOXWF, to rpt, AF/XOX, "The Kuwait Air Campaign," Oct 30, 1990, Checkmate files.

72. Lt. Gen. Horner intvw, Mar 1991; Lt. Col. Deptula intvw, Nov 1, 1990; Schwarzkopf, *Autobiography*, 353–354; Maj. Gen. Glosson intvw, Dec 12, 1991.

73. CMH draft, 142–143; Maj. Gen. Olsen intvw; Lt. Gen. Horner intvw, Mar 4, 1992; Maj. Gen. Glosson intvw, Dec 12, 1991.

74. Lt. Col. Deptula intvw, Nov 29, 1991; Col. Warden intvw.

75. Maj. Gen. Glosson intvw, Dec 12, 1991; Schwarzkopf, *Autobiography*, 320.

76. Maj. Gen. Glosson intvw, Dec 12, 1991; Lt. Col. Deptula intvw, Nov 20, 1991.

77. Brfg, HQ USAF/SA, "Operation Desert Shield: Contingency Plan Phase 3 Analysis," Oct 1990, "Plan—Phases 2/3" file, Checkmate files.

78. Memo, Dr. Wayne Thompson, Gulf War Air Power Survey (GWAPS), to Mr. Kurt Guthe, GWAPS, "Phase III," Apr 6, 1992, GWAPS working files (hereafter, Thompson memo); memo, Ted Parker to Natalie Crawford, "10/30/90 Visit to AF/XOXWF (Checkmate)," Oct 31, 1990, "Plan—Phases 2/3" file, Checkmate files. Neighboring documents in this file identify this memo as a RAND document.

79. Thompson memo; brfg, AF/XOXWF, "Phase III Air Operations in Kuwait," n.d., "The Kuwait Air Campaign CSAF Info" notebook, Box 7, CENTAF records; point paper, AF/XOXWF, Oct 15, 1990, "Plan—Phases 2/3" file, Checkmate files. See also brfg, AF/XOXWF, "Kuwait Offensive Air Campaign Phases II & III," Oct 26, 1990, and brfg, AF/XOXWF, "Instant Thunder Phase II: An Operational Air Campaign Against Iraqi Forces in Kuwait," n.d., Checkmate files. On Lt. Gen. Adams's interest in particular, see the series of handwritten memos attached to summary paper, AF/XOXWF, n.d., Checkmate files.

80. Thompson memo; Maj. Gen. Glosson intvw, Dec 12, 1991. See also memo, Col. Warden, AF/XOXW, to Gen. Loh, AF/CV, [no subject], Nov 1, 1990, "Plan—Phases 2/3" file, Checkmate files.

81. Thompson memo; brfg, AF/XOXW, "Offensive Air Campaign: Phases II & III," Nov 6, 1990, Checkmate files. See also memo, Col. Warden, AF/XOXW, to Gen. Loh, AF/CV, [no subject], Nov 1, 1990; memo, Col. Warden, AF/XOXW, to Lt. Gen. Adams, AF/XO, "Reference Our Conversation This Morning, Some Addition-

al Thoughts," Nov 8, 1990, CENTAF records; and brfg, AF/XOXW, "Offensive Air Campaign: Phases II & III," Nov 2, 1990, "Plan—Phases 2/3" file, Checkmate files.

82. Thompson memo. See also brfg, AF/XOXW, "Offensive Air Campaign: Phases II & III," Nov 2, 1990, which includes this marginalia: "2 Nov 90 Faxed to CENTAF Riyadh (Glosson)."

83. ARCENT hist, 41; CMH draft, 188; chronol, HQ USCENTCOM/J5, "Chronology of Theater Campaign Plan," n.d., HQ USCENTCOM/CCHO working files (hereafter, "Campaign Plan Chronology"). See also MR, Brig. Gen. Buster C. Glosson, "Q&A During Presidential Briefing," [n.d], Box 12, CENTAF records; MR, Brig. Gen. Buster C. Glosson, "Presidential Briefing Slides," n.d., with atch slides, n.d., CENTAF records; Lt. Gen. Horner intvw, Mar 4, 1992; and Lt. Gen. Horner intvw, Dec 3, 1991.

84. Lt. Gen. Horner intvw, Dec 3, 1991; Col. Warden brfg; Thompson memo.

85. Col. Warden brfg; Thompson memo.

86. Maj. Gen. Glosson intvw, Dec 12, 1991; Lt. Col. Deptula intvw, Jan 8, 1992.

87. Intvw, Brig. Gen. Buster C. Glosson, USCENTAF/DCP, with MSgt. Theodore J. Turner, USCENTAF/HO, Mar 13, 1991, transcript held by CAFH (hereafter, Brig. Gen. Glosson intvw, Mar 13, 1991); Lt. Gen. Horner intvw, Mar 4, 1992.

88. Maj. Gen. Glosson intvw, Dec 12, 1991; brfg slide, "BDA—Railroad Hwy Bridge," CSAF brief, Feb 28, 1991.

89. Brfg, Lt. Col. David A. Deptula, CENTAF Special Planning Group and Strategic Target Planning Cell, "The Air Campaign: Planning & Execution,"

n.d.; memo, Lt. Col. David A. Deptula, "Observations on the Air Campaign against Iraq, Aug 90–Mar 91," Mar 29, 1991, 4.

90. ATO brfg; "Directorate of Campaign Plans"; org charts, HQ USCENT-AF, [Mar 1, 1991], HQ 9 AF/HO working files; Lt. Col. Baptiste intvw; Lt. Col. Waterstreet intvw.

91. Lt. Gen. Horner intvw, Mar 4, 1992; Lt. Col. Feinstein intvw; Maj. Gen. Olsen intvw. For a Navy perspective on this reorganization, see Smith-McSwain paper.

92. Rpt, HQ USCENTAF/STRATFOR, "Desert Shield/Storm After Action Report," n.d., historians' working files, HQ SAC/HO (hereafter, STRATFOR rpt); Y'Blood, *Eagle and Scorpion*, 123–125, 124n; msg, USCENTAF/CV to USCENTAF Rear/BS–XP et al., "Establishment of Provisional Air Divisions for Desert Shield," 0930Z Nov 22, 1990; msg, COMUSCENTAF to AIG 10322/CC et al., "USCENTAF Organization Structure," 0600Z Dec 12, 1990. Also useful are SO GB–14, HQ TAC, Dec 5, 1990; Lt. Gen. Horner intvw, Mar 4, 1992; and Maj. Gen. Olsen intvw.

93. Schwarzkopf, *Autobiography*, 407; "Baker-Aziz Talks on Gulf Fail; Fears of War Rise; Bush Is Firm; Diplomatic Effort to Continue," *New York Times*, Jan 10, 1991; "U.N. Chief's Talks with Iraqis Bring No Sign of Change," *New York Times*, Jan 14, 1991; ltr, President George Bush to Speaker of the House Thomas S. Foley, [War Powers Notification Letter], Jan 18, 1991, "War Termination—Emergency Strike Plan" file, Check- mate files. See also msg, USCINCCENT/CCJ3 to JCS/Joint Staff et al., "Follow-Up Execute Order—USCINCCENT Opord 001 for Desert Storm," 0001Z Jan 17, 1991, and msg, Joint Staff to OCSA et al., "Commencement of Hostilities," 0015Z Jan 17, 1991, "16–17 Jan 91 (Day 1)" file, Checkmate files.

94. "Daily Notes from Desert Storm," Jan 17, 1991, Tab A to hist, 363 TFW(P), Jan 27–Feb 2, 1991, Vol 1, Desert Storm collection, HQ TAC/HO (hereafter, "Daily Notes"); intvw, Lt. Col. Henry L. Taylor, Comdr, 1702 Consol AMS, Oct 25, 1991, MSgt. Devino's intvws; intvw, 1st Lt. Peter J. Bloom, nav, 416 Bom Wg, Apr 24, 1991, MSgt. Devino's intvws.

Chapter Three

1. Lt. Gen. Horner testimony, 238; MAP Jan 16, 1991; Lt. Col. Deptula intvw, Nov 20, 1991.

2. Brfg, Gen. Merrill A. McPeak, CSAF, Mar 15, 1991 (hereafter, Gen. McPeak brfg); MAP Jan 16, 1991; Walker notes, entry for 0317 Jan 17, 1991; Lt. Col. Deptula intvw, Jan 8, 1992; CMH draft, 264–265.

3. MAP Jan 16, 1991; Lt. Col. Deptula intvw, Jan 8, 1992; point paper, AF/XOXOC, "Executive Summary:

Desert Storm," Jan 17, 1991, "16–17 Jan 1991 (Day 1)" file, Checkmate files.

4. Lt. Col. Deptula intvw, Jan 8, 1992; memo, Lt. Col. David A. Deptula to Brig. Gen. Glosson, "Initial Statistics," 0600 Jan 17, 1991, Folder 1, Box 11C, CENTAF records; Gen. McPeak brfg.

5. MAP Jan 16, 1991; Lt. Col. Deptula intvw, Jan 8, 1992; summary paper, AF/XOXWF, "Target Summary—By Day," Jan 18, 1991, "17–18 Jan 91 (Day 2)" file, Checkmate files;

Brig. Gen. Caruana intvw.

6. Brig. Gen. Glosson intvw, Mar 13, 1991; Gen. McPeak brfg; Walker notes, Jan 17, 1991, 5–6; Gen. Loh speech; MR, AF/XOXWF, *"Washington Post* Articles, Monday, 11 Feb 91," Feb 11, 1991, "10–11 Feb 91 (Day 26)" file, Checkmate files.

7. Brfg, AF/XOXW to SecDef, "The Unexpected in the Campaign," Feb 6, 1991, Folder 2, Box 11C, CENT-AF records (hereafter, "Unexpected in the Campaign"); Col. Warden brfg.

8. Brig. Gen. Glosson intvw, Mar 13, 1991; Lt. Col. Baptiste intvw.

9. Brig. Gen. Glosson intvw, Mar 13, 1991; DD/TWP brfg.

10. Lt. Col. Baptiste intvw. See also Col. Crigger intvw.

11. General Horner, quoted in "Desert Storm Highlights Need for Rapid Tactical Intelligence," *Aviation Week & Space Technology*, Feb 11, 1991, 18.

12. Blackwell, *Thunder in the Desert*, 118–119; Norman Friedman, *Desert Victory: The War for Kuwait* (Annapolis, Md.: Naval Institute Press, 1991), 171; James P. Coyne, *Airpower in the Gulf* (Arlington, Va.: Air Force Association, 1992), 61–62.

13. Brig. Gen. Glosson intvw, Mar 13, 1991; Col. Crigger intvw; Lt. Gen. Horner intvw, Dec 3, 1991.

14. Brig. Gen. Glosson intvw; Lt. Col. Baptiste intvw; memo, Lt. Col. David A. Deptula, "Observations on the Air Campaign against Iraq, Aug 90–Mar 91," Mar 29, 1991, 2; Lt. Gen. Horner testimony, 234.

15. MAP Jan 16, 1991; Brig. Gen. Glosson intvw, Mar 13, 1991; Lt. Col. Deptula intvw, Jan 8, 1992. On the overlapping phases, see also Lt. Gen. Royal N. Moore, Jr., "Marine Air: There When Needed," *U.S. Naval Institute Proceedings*, Nov 1991, 64.

16. MAP Jan 16, 1991; memo,

"Bomb Damage to Military Forces and Facilities," Jan 30, 1991, Checkmate files.

17. MAP Jan 16, 1991; Maj. Gen. Glosson intvw, Dec 12, 1991; "Bomber Story," 29; Lt. Col. Deptula intvw, Jan 8, 1992.

18. Lt. Col. Waterstreet intvw.

19. Lt. Col. Deptula intvw, Nov 20, 1991; Lt. Col. Waterstreet intvw; Lt. Gen. Horner testimony.

20. Brfg slide, "Daily Aircraft Losses," [Jan 17–Feb 5, 1991], File 0269535, "CENTAF/DOO Daily Slides for General Horner and TACC Briefing," Roll 10227, CAFH Desert Shield/Desert Storm microfilm collection; CINC's War Book input, "Overall KTO Ground Summary," Jan 17, 1991 evening; brfg slide, HQ USCENTCOM/CCJ2, "Aircraft Losses (Last 12 Hours)," Jan 31, 1991 P.M., "CENTAF/DOO Daily Slides for General Horner and TACC Briefing," Roll 10227, CAFH Desert Shield/Desert Storm microfilm collection.

21. Lt. Gen. Horner's daily comments, Jan 17, 1991, 1; "Daily Notes."

22. Lt. Gen. Horner's daily comments, Jan 17, 1991, 1.

23. "Directorate of Campaign Plans"; brfg, Lt. Col. David A. Deptula, CENT-AF Special Planning Group and Strategic Target Planning Cell, "The Air Campaign: Planning & Execution," n.d.; Lt. Col. Deptula intvw, Nov 20, 1991.

24. "Directorate of Campaign Plans."

25. Brfg, AF/XOXW, "Iraqi Situation: Checkmate Strategic Assessment," Jan 30, 1991, "Checkmate BDA" file, Checkmate files (hereafter, "Iraqi Situation"); point paper, AF/XOXWF, "BDA—Desert Storm—Operator's Look (As of 28 Jan 1991/0900L Baghdad)," Jan 28, 1991, Folder 2, Box 11C, CENTAF records (hereafter, BDA Jan

28, 1991); Col. Warden brfg.

26. Lt. Gen. Horner's daily comments, Jan 26, 1991, 15; Gen. McPeak brfg.

27. Rpt, USAF Environmental Technical Applications Center, "Gulf War Weather," Mar 1992, Sec 3, 2 (hereafter, "Gulf War Weather"); Lt. Col. Deptula intvw, Nov 20, 1991; Blackwell, *Thunder in the Desert*, 146.

28. Maj. Gen. Glosson intvw, Dec 12, 1991; Blackwell, *Thunder in the Desert*, 146; notes, CMSgt. John Burton, USCENTAF/HO, "Notes Taken During the 0700 to 1230L Shift in the Tactical Air Control Center (TACC) During Operation Desert Storm, 17 January–28 February 1991," entry for 1700 Jan 29, 1991, Burton file, Box 84, CENTAF collection, HQ TAC/HO (hereafter, Burton notes); Gen. McPeak brfg.

29. Burton notes, entry for 1700 Jan 28, 1991; notes, TSgt. Frederick Hosterman, USCENTAF/HO, "CENTAF TACC notes," entry for 1930 Jan 28, 1991, Hosterman file, Box 84, CENTAF collection, HQ TAC/HO (hereafter, Hosterman notes).

30. "Unexpected in the Campaign"; list, "Threat Ranges of Iraqi Systems," Aug 10, 1990, in HQ USCENTCOM/CCJ2, U.S. Central Command Battle Staff Operation Desert Storm War Room Book, n.d. [compiled Aug 1990–Apr 1991], HQ USCENTCOM/CCHO working files (hereafter, CINC's War Book); msg, TAC/TACOPS/INO to AIG 621 et al., "CENTAF Rear DISum 149," 2300Z Jan 30, 1991, "Khafji" file, Checkmate files (hereafter, "DISum 149").

31. ARCENT hist, 116–117.

32. DD/TWP brfg; Maj. Gen. Olsen intvw.

33. "Unexpected in the Campaign"; brfg slide, "Special Capabilities," CINC's

War Book. For a postwar source, see DD/TWP brfg.

34. Final Report, 248; DD/TWP brfg.

35. Maj. Gen. Glosson intvw, Dec 12, 1991; Gen. McPeak brfg.

36. DD/TWP brfg; CMH draft, 266; speech, Lt. Gen. Thomas S. Moorman, Jr., "Military Space Systems Utility," Twenty-Eighth Space Congress, Cocoa Beach, Fla., Apr 24, 1991. For examples of SPACECOM operations, see chronol, HQ USCENTCOM/CCJ2, "Significant Operations Events" [compilation of inputs to CINC's War Book], Jan 17–Apr 18, 1991, 10, 29, 34, HQ USCENTCOM/CCHO working files (hereafter, "Significant Operations Events").

37. Gen. McPeak brfg; Lt. Gen. Horner's daily comments, Jan 20, 1991, 5; point paper, SAF/AQPC, "Joint Surveillance Target Attack Radar System (Joint STARS)," Dec 14, 1990, and exec summary, atch to memo, Col. Ronald T. Sconyers, HQ TAC/Dir Public Affairs, to HQ TAC/DR, [no subject], Jan 13, 1991, "JSTARS Background" file, historians' working files, HQ TAC/HO; msg, AF News/IIB to AIG 9333/PA et al., "Tracking Radar System," 2200Z Feb 25, 1991, historians' working files, HQ TAC/HO; draft, "Joint Surveillance Target Attack Radar System," excerpt from Chapter III, "Requirements," in hist, TAC, 1990, historians' working files, HQ TAC/HO. On J–STARS, see also Lt. Gen. Horner intvw, Mar 4, 1992, and intvw, Brig. Gen. George K. Muellner, HQ TAC/DR, with Thomas C. Hone, Anne Leary, and Mark Mandeles, Apr 16, 1992, copy of transcript held by CAFH (hereafter, Brig. Gen. Muellner intvw).

38. Lt. Gen. Horner's daily comments, Jan 20, 1991, 5; Col. Warden brfg; Gen. McPeak brfg.

39. Gen. McPeak brfg. On CENT-AF's overcoming the Scud diversions and weather delays, see also Schwarz-kopf, *Autobiography*, 421.

40. Gen. McPeak brfg; msg, 0652Z Mar 1, 1991; msg, USCENTAF/IN to AIG 12929 et al., "CENTAF Desert Storm Intelligence Summary 91–029," 0407Z Jan 31, 1991, "Khafji" file, Checkmate files.

41. *GWAPS*, Vol V, Part 1, "A Statistical Compendium," 653.

42. *GWAPS*, Vol V, Part 1, "A Statistical Compendium," 653–654.

43. Final Report, 238; chart, "Air-to-Air Kills," "26 Feb 91" file, Lt. Gen. Horner's Desert Storm files.

44. Col. Christon intvw; Lt. Col. Baptiste intvw; Lt. Gen. Horner intvw, Dec 3, 1991.

45. Vinas special study; Maj. Gen. Glosson intvw, Dec 12, 1991; Lt. Col. Baptiste intvw.

46. Brfg, "The Backbone of Air Power in Operation Desert Storm: The F–15 Eagle," [May 1991], "F–15" file, Checkmate files; Final Report, App T, 65–67; summary paper, "Desert Storm Fact Sheet: USAF Forces," Mar 19, 1991, historians' working files, HQ TAC/HO (hereafter, "USAF Forces").

47. CINC's War Book input, "Iraqi Air Assets (As of 0300L 27 Feb 91)," Feb 27, 1991 P.M.; BDA Jan 28, 1991; Gen. McPeak brfg.

48. Col. Warden brfg; msg, US-CENTAF/IN to AIG 12929 et al., "CENTAF Desert Storm Intelligence Summary 91–025," 0821Z Jan 29, 1991, "Khafji" file, Checkmate files.

49. "Allies Claim to Bomb Iraqi Targets at Will," *Washington Post*, Jan 31, 1991; CINC's War Book input, "Iraqi Air Assets," Feb 27, 1991 P.M.; brfg, AF/XOXW–G, "Strategic Assessment Team," May 8, 1991.

50. Col. Christon intvw; msg, US Mission US NATO to SecState et al., "February 6 NAC: PermReps' Discussion of the Gulf," 1827Z Feb 7, 1991, "State Department Message" file, HQ USCENTCOM/CCHO working files; Gen. McPeak brfg; brfg slide, "Air Campaign Summary: Cumulative Results as of 0300L 31 Jan 91," HQ US-CENTCOM/CCJ2, CINC's War Book Input, "Air Campaign Summary: Cumulative Results as of 0300L 31 Jan 91," Jan 31, 1991 A.M.; "Iraqi Situation."

51. Gen. McPeak brfg; Support Battle Staff brfg, Jan 29, 1991; msg, CINC-CENT to [unknown], [subject unknown], 2330Z Jan 24, 1991, photocopy found in Folder 2, Box 11C, CENTAF records; msg, USCENT-AF/IN to AIG 12929 et al., "CENTAF Desert Storm Intelligence Summary 91–025," 0821Z Jan 29, 1991, "Khafji" file, Checkmate files. See also msg, DIA/DI-6B to USCENTCOM Rear/CCJ2 et al., "Military Situation Summary as of 28/1900Z Jan 91," 0201Z Jan 29, 1991, "DIA Jan 91" file, HQ USCENTCOM/CCHO working files.

52. Final Report, App T, 65; Walker notes, entry for 0505 Jan 29, 1991; Gen. McPeak brfg; "Iraq Trying to Shelter Jets in Iran, U.S. Says," *Washington Post*, Jan 29, 1991; DD/TWP brfg; "Wham Bam—Where's Saddam?," *Washington Post Magazine*, Dec 29, 1991.

53. Maj. Gen. Olsen intvw; Lt. Col. Baptiste intvw; Final Report, 143.

54. Maj. Gen. Olsen intvw; Lt. Col. Baptiste intvw; Final Report, 143.

55. Lt. Gen. Horner intvw, Mar 4, 1992; Final Report, 384.

56. Schwarzkopf, *Autobiography*, 430; Lt. Gen. Horner's daily comments, Jan 20, 1991, 6; TACC log, entries for Feb 4, 1991.

57. Chart, HQ 9 AF, "Deputy Chief of Staff, Operations," n.d., HQ 9 AF/

HO working files (hereafter, 9 AF chart); Lt. Col. Baptiste intvw; intvw, Maj. Sanford S. Terry with Dr. Richard Davis, Apr 9, 1992, tape recording held by CAFH; Col. Crigger intvw.

58. ATO brfg; Lt. Col. Baptiste intvw; Maj. Sweeney intvw, Mar 4, 1991; Lt. Col. Feinstein intvw; Smith-McSwain paper; Final Report, 145. On ingress, attack, and airspace deconfliction options, see rpt, HQ 9 AF, "Mission Commander Ops Orders," n.d., HQ 9 AF/HO working files. On communications SPINS, see After Action Report, Airborne Communications Planning Cell, "Airborne Communications for Tactical Operations," n.d., atch to SSS, 1850 ACSQ/SCO to 1 ACOMMW/CV et al., "Operation Desert Shield/Storm After Action Reports," Apr 8, 1991, historians' working files, HQ SAC/HO.

59. ATO brfg; summary paper, Capt. Lee Patton, "Getting the Air Tasking Order (ATO) to the Navy," in Col. Randy Witt, ed., "Air Force Tactical Communications in War: The Desert Shield/Desert Storm Comm Story," Mar 1991, HQ 9 AF/HO working files; Final Report, 147–148.

60. ATO brfg; Lt. Col. Baptiste intvw.

61. Lt. Col. Baptiste intvw; ATO brfg; 9 AF chart; Lt. Col. Deptula brfg.

62. Final Report, 375; notes, Lt. Gen. Horner, on CINCCENT mtg, 1900L Feb 15, 1991, Lt. Gen. Horner's Desert Storm files, HQ 9 AF/CC (hereafter, Lt. Gen. Horner's CINCCENT notes); log, Brig. Gen. Glosson, "CINCCENT Daily Priorities," entry for Feb 15, 1991, Campaign Plans ("Black Hole") file, Box 58, CENTAF collection, HQ TAC/HO; Lt. Col. Baptiste intvw.

63. Lt. Gen. Horner intvw, Mar 4, 1992; ATO brfg; Lt. Col. Baptiste intvw.

64. For three examples among many, see ltrs, USCENTAF/DCP, "COMUSCENTAF Air Guidance Letter," D+31–D+33 [Feb 17–19, 1991], File 0269524, Roll 10217, CAFH Desert Shield/Desert Storm microfilm collection.

65. Brfg, USCENTAF/CV, "Air Forces Briefings to His Royal Highness Lt. Gen. Khalid," Nov 27, 1990, MSgt. Theodore J. Turner files, HQ USCENTAF/HO (hereafter, brfg to Gen. Khalid); summary, KTO planning cell, "KTO Cell Summary: D+29 (15 Feb 91)," [Feb 15, 1991], "KTO Summaries 7–23 Feb 91" file, Box 6A, CENTAF records; Lt. Col. Baptiste intvw.

66. Final Report, 144–145; ATO brfg; Lt. Col. Baptiste intvw.

67. ATO brfg; summary paper, AF/XOXWD, "Response to Navy/Marine Lessons Learned Study," Apr 29, 1991, "Navy/Marine" file, Checkmate files (hereafter, "Response to Navy/Marine Study"); Smith-McSwain paper; brfg to Gen. Khalid; Lt. Col. Baptiste intvw; Final Report, 375. For an example of the joint combined prioritized target list for Desert Shield, see list, HQ USCENTAF, "Combined/Joint Integrated/Prioritized Target List for C+56," Oct 2, 1990, Lt. Gen. Horner's Desert Storm files, HQ 9 AF/CC.

68. COMUSCENTAF OpOrd; Lt. Gen. Horner intvw, Dec 3, 1991; Final Report, 140–141; brfg, AF/XOXWF to SecAF and CSAF, "Day 1 Master Attack Plan," Jan 16, 1991, "16–17 Jan 91 (Day 1)" file, Checkmate files; msg, USCINCCENT/CCJ3/CCJ2 to COMUSCENTAF et al., "USCINCCENT Joint No-Fire Target List (JNFTL) for Operation Desert Storm," 1605Z Feb 11, 1991, Folder 2, Box 11C, CENTAF records. On strictures on operations against Kuwait City, see also notes, Lt. Col. David A. Deptula, on brfg by Brig.

Gen. Glosson to Maj. Gen. Moore, 1530 Aug 27, 1990, Box 12, CENTAF records. For an example of a potential target that required close review, see memo, CENTAF/JAO to USCINC-CENT/CCJA/CCJ3, Feb 18, 1991, with two ends and atch msg, DIA/ITF to CENTAF, "Response to RII 2359," 0320Z Feb 16, 1991, Folder 3, Box 11C, CENTAF records; and memo, Lt. Comdr. Muir to Brig. Gen. Glosson, "Bridge Interdiction," Feb 20, 1991, "RR & Bridges History" file, Box 13, CENTAF records (hereafter, "Bridge Interdiction").

69. Brfg to Gen. Khalid; ATO brfg; Lt. Col. Baptiste intvw.

70. 9 AF chart; ATO brfg; Lt. Col. Baptiste intvw.

71. ATO brfg; Lt. Col. Baptiste intvw; chart, HQ CENTAF, "Daily Sortie Recap: 29 Jan 91, D+12," rev Mar 15, 1991, File 0269588, Roll 10254, CAFH Desert Shield/Desert Storm microfilm collection; Col. Reavey intvw; minutes, HQ SAC/DOTN to "See Distribution," "High Altitude Bombing Conference," Mar 12, 1991, historians' working files, HQ SAC/HO. On the enormous length of the ATO, see also Maj. Gen. Corder intvw and Col. Winstel intvw.

72. ATO brfg; Lt. Col. Baptiste

intvw. On the work cycle during a typical day in the KTO planning cell, see also intvw, Maj. John D. Sweeney with MSgt. Theodore J. Turner, Mar 3, 1991 (hereafter, Maj. Sweeney intvw, Mar 3, 1991), which gives a concise but useful summary of a representative twenty-four hours' work.

73. ATO brfg; point paper, AF/XOOTC, "Tactical Command and Control Forces," Jan 30, 1991, "29–30 Jan 91 (Day 14)" file, Checkmate files; intvw, Maj. Gen. John A. Corder with Robert L. Mandler, USAFAWC/HO, Dec 21, 1991, published transcript held by CAFH (hereafter, Maj. Gen. Corder intvw).

74. Maj. Gen. Corder intvw; Col. Winstel intvw.

75. Maj. Gen. Corder intvw.

76. ATO brfg; Lt. Col. Baptiste intvw.

77. Brfg slide, CENTAF/DOO, "Iraqi Air Order of Battle," [Jan 17, 1991], File 0269537, "CENTAF/DOO Daily Slides for General Horner and TACC Briefing," Roll 10227, CAFH Desert Shield/Desert Storm microfilm collection; CINC's War Book input, "Iraqi Air Assets (As of 0300L Jan 31, 1991)," Jan 31, 1991 A.M.; Col. Warden brfg.

Chapter Four

1. CINC's War Book input, intel summary, Jan 31, 1991 A.M. The numbers of Iraqi tanks, APCs, and artillery pieces in the KTO on the first of February were calculated from Final Report, 203. Other primary sources, including the CINC's War Book input, give other figures. On this subject, see the extension to note 36 to Chapter 1. On the sta-

tus of Iraqi forces in late January and early February, see also point paper, AF/XOXWF, "BDA—Desert Storm—Operator's Look (As of 31 Jan 91/0600L Baghdad)," Jan 31, 1991, "30–31 Jan 91 (Day 15)" file, Checkmate files, and brfg, JCS/J–2, "J–2 Daily Assessment: Operation Desert Storm," Feb 13, 1991, "JCS BDA" file,

Checkmate files.

2. [Classified source]; CINC's War Book input, "Republican Guards in the KTO (As of 0300L 31 Jan 91)," Jan 31, 1991 A.M.

3. [Classified source]; point paper, CENTAF/IN, "Republican Guard Forces Command," n.d., Lt. Gen. Horner's Desert Storm files, 9 AF/CC; memo, HQ USCENTAF FWD/IN, "Republican Guards Forces Command," Nov 5, 1990, "Planning Material from XOXW" file, Box 13, CENTAF records. See also Friedman, *Desert Victory*, 20–21; Blackwell, *Thunder in the Desert*, 25, 52, 54–55; and Cordesman and Wagner, *Lessons of Modern War*, 2:354–355.

4. Cordesman and Wagner, *Lessons of Modern War*, 2:373–375; Sydney Nettleton Fisher, *The Middle East: A History* (New York: Knopf, 1979), 10; Trevor Mostyn and Albert Hourani, eds., *The Cambridge Encyclopedia of the Middle East and North Africa* (Cambridge: Cambridge University Press, 1988), 42.

5. Chester G. Starr, *A History of the Ancient World* (New York: Oxford University Press, 1983), 139.

6. Mostyn and Hourani, *Cambridge Encyclopedia of the Middle East*, 58.

7. Blackwell, *Thunder in the Desert*, 54.

8. CINC's War Book input, "Republican Guards as of 0300L 31 Jan 91," Jan 31, 1991 A.M.; CSAF brief, Feb 25, 1991. Other useful maps of the positions of the Republican Guards and regular divisions were found in Final Report, 385, and brfg slide, COMUS-ARCENT, "Battle Damage Assessment," Feb 16, 1991, "Desert Shield/ Storm USN Ops" file, Comdr. Duck McSwain's working files.

9. Memo, HQ CENTAF/CS to HQ CENTAF/CC, [no subject], n.d., "Iraq Order of Battle" file, Lt. Gen. Horner's Desert Storm files, HQ 9 AF/CC; Blackwell, *Thunder in the Desert*, 42.

10. Lt. Col. Deptula intvw, Nov 27, 1991; Col. Warden intvw, Feb 6, 1992; Maj. Gen. Glosson intvw, Dec 12, 1991; brfg, AF/XOXW, "Offensive Air Campaign: Phases II & III," Nov 2, 1990, "Plan–Phases 2/3" file, Checkmate files.

11. Lt. Gen. Horner intvw, Mar 4, 1992; Final Report, 347; Schwarzkopf, *Autobiography*, 381.

12. Charts, HQ USCENTAF/DCP, "Targets Attacked by Day by Aircraft," Feb 26, 1991, and "Master Target List," Feb 5, 1991, both in File 029616, Roll 10264, CAFH Desert Shield/Desert Storm microfilm collection (hereafter, "Targets Attacked" and "Master Target List"); Maj. Gen. Glosson intvw, Dec 12, 1991; "Bomber Story"; Lt. Col. Deptula intvw, Jan 8, 1992; chart, "US-CENTAF B–52 Operations: Missions/ Sorties Against Target Types," in summary paper, "SAC Bombers," n.d., "Title V Inputs" file, Checkmate files. See also "SAC Bomber and Tanker Operations," 8.

13. *GWAPS*, Vol II, Part 1, "Operations," 138, 347, 348.

14. "Targets Attacked"; "Master Target List."

15. DD/TWP brfg. For the numbers of sorties planned for a sample of three days in mid-February, see summaries, KTO planning cell, Feb 11–13, 1991, "KTO Summaries, 7–23 Feb 91" file, Box 6A, CENTAF records.

16. Lt. Gen. Horner's CINCCENT notes, 1900L Feb 15, 1991. See also TACC log, entry for 1712Z Feb 15, 1991.

17. Final Report, 375.

18. Hist, 363 TFW(P), Jan 27–Feb 2, 1991, Vol 1, Desert Storm collection, HQ TAC/HO.

19. Vinas special study, 25, 26.

20. "SAC Bomber and Tanker Operations," 8; memo, to "See Distribution," "Bomb Damage to Military Forces and Facilities," Jan 30, 1991, Checkmate files (hereafter, "Bomb Damage"); Support Battle Staff brfg, Jan 29, 1991.

21. "Bomb Damage"; msg, CENTAF/IN to AIG 12929 et al., "CENTAF Desert Storm Intelligence Summary 91–029 as of 30/2200Z Jan 91," 0407Z Jan 31, 1991, "Khafji" file, Checkmate files. To "translate" the coordinates in this message, see "DISum 149."

22. Msg, USCINCCENT/CCJ2 to AIG 7861 et al., "USCENTCOM Collateral Intelligence DISUM No. 177 for the Period 02/1500Z to 03/1459Z Feb 91," "Khafji" file, Checkmate files.

23. Lt. Col. Baptiste intvw; Maj. Gen. Corder intvw.

24. Lt. Gen. Horner intvw, Mar 4, 1992; MAP Jan 16, 1991; Col. Christon intvw; Brig. Gen. Glosson intvw, Mar 13, 1991; memo, [Lt. Comdr.] Dan [Muir] to [Maj.] Gary [Green], "Daily Passdown," Feb 22, 1991, "RR & Bridges History" file, Box 13, CENTAF records.

25. Marginalia on memo, Brig. Gen. Buster C. Glosson, Dir Plans, for CENTCOM J3 Plans, "Theater Campaign Strategy Assessment," Feb 15, 1991, "War Termination—Emergency Strike Plan" file, Checkmate files; summary paper, AF/LRC and JCS/J4 SMD, "Strategic Resupply between Baghdad and Southern Iraq," Feb 20, 1991, "KTO/Republican Guards" file, Checkmate files; brfg, AF/LRC and JCS/J4 SMD, "LRC Assessment: Strategic Resupply between Baghdad and Southern Iraq," Feb 20, 1991, "Khafji" file, Checkmate files.

26. Memo, DIA, DIM 59–91, Feb 1991 (hereafter, DIM 59–91).

27. Maj. Gen. Olsen intvw; Maj.

Gen. Glosson intvw, Dec 12, 1991.

28. Charts, "Bridges Fragged," Jan 29–Feb 24, 1991, "RR & Bridges History" file, Box 13, CENTAF records; Final Report, App T, 79–81.

29. Chart, Dr. Barry Watts, GWAPS, "F–111E/F Summary Data," Aug 12, 1992, GWAPS working files (hereafter, "F–111 chart"). This is a particularly valuable statistical compilation.

30. Memo, Brig. Gen. Buster C. Glosson, 14 AD/CC, to USCENTAF/CC, "Wing 'How-Goes-It,'" Feb 6, 1990, Lt. Gen. Horner's Desert Storm files, HQ 9 AF/CC (hereafter, "How-Goes-It"); charts, "Bridges Fragged," Jan 29–Feb 24, 1991, "RR & Bridges History" file, Box 13, CENTAF records.

31. Final Report, App T, 80–81; "How-Goes-It"; Lt. Col. Deptula intvw, Jan 8, 1992.

32. Lt. Col. Waterstreet intvw; Maj. Gen. Olsen intvw; Lt. Gen. Horner intvw, Mar 4, 1992.

33. Lt. Gen. Horner intvw, Mar 4, 1992; Maj. Gen. Olsen intvw; list, "Prioritized Bridges Targets List," Feb 24, 1991, "RR & Bridges History" file, Box 13, CENTAF records.

34. Lt. Gen. Horner intvw, Mar 4, 1992; Maj. Gen. Olsen intvw; "Bridge Interdiction."

35. Lt. Gen. Horner intvw, Mar 4, 1992; "Bridge Interdiction"; list, "Prioritized Bridges Targets List," Feb 24, 1991, "RR & Bridges History" file, Box 13, CENTAF records.

36. DIM 59–91; Lt. Gen. Horner intvw, Mar 4, 1992; Maj. Gen. Olsen intvw.

37. BDA Jan 28, 1991; Final Report, 230; point paper, AF/CSS Exec, "Desert Storm SitRep Summary: Day 14/30 Jan 91," "29–30 Jan 91 (Day 14)," file, Checkmate files.

38. "Unexpected in the Campaign";

MR, Dr. Wayne Thompson, AF/CHO, "Briefing of Secretary of Defense Cheney," 1100–1210 Feb 6, 1991, Folder 2, Box 11C, CENTAF records.

39. Support Battle Staff brfg, Feb 19, 1991.

40. Final Report, 231; CSAF brief, Feb 28, 1991.

41. Final Report, 194. See also graph, R. Hallion, AF/HO, "Effectiveness of Iraqi Command Structure, Air Defenses, KTO Resupply, and Tank-APC-Artillery," n.d., AF/HO working files.

42. Vinas special study, 32.

43. Lt. Gen. Horner intvw, Mar 4, 1992; Maj. Gen. Olsen intvw; memo, Lt. Col. David A. Deptula for SAF Rice, "PGM/Stealth Effectiveness," Feb 17, 1991, "F–117A" file, Checkmate files.

44. Maj. Gen. Olsen intvw; Final Report, 231; A.J.C. Lavalle, ed., *The Tale of Two Bridges*, Monogr 1, Vol I, USAF Southeast Asia Monograph Series (Washington, D.C.: Government Printing Office, 1976).

45. CINC's War Book input, "Non-Republican Guard Heavy Divisions in the KTO as of 0300L 31 Jan 91," Jan 31, 1991 A.M.; msg, USCENTAF/IN to AIG 12929 et al., "CENTAF Desert Storm Intelligence Summary 91–035 as of 02/2200Z Feb 91," 0329Z Feb 3, 1991, "Khafji" file, Checkmate files (hereafter, "Intelligence Summary 91–035"). For the corps order of battle of the Iraqi divisions, see CSAF brief, Feb 25, 1991.

46. "Iraqi Generals Perspective."

47. CSAF brief, Feb 25, 1991. Other useful maps of the Iraqi regular divisions and Republican Guards were found in Final Report, 384, and brfg slide, COMUSARCENT, "Battle Damage Assessment," Feb 16, 1991, "Desert Shield/Storm USN Ops" file, Comdr.

Duck McSwain's working files.

48. Summary, KTO planning cell, "KTO Cell Summary: D+21 (7 Feb)," "KTO Summaries, 7–23 Feb 91" file, Box 6A, CENTAF records.

49. Summaries, KTO planning cell, "KTO Cell Summary: D+21 (7 Feb)," "KTO Cell Summary: D+24 (10 Feb)," and "KTO Cell Summary: D+37 (23 Feb)," all in "KTO Summaries, 7–23 Feb 91" file, Box 6A, CENTAF records.

50. "DISum 149"; CINC's War Book input, "Non-Republican Guard Heavy Divisions in the KTO ," Jan 31, 1991 A.M.; "Intelligence Summary 91–035"; Support Battle Staff brfg, Feb 15, 1991.

51. "Iraqi Generals Perspective."

52. Vinas special study, 14. Statistics on Iraqi materiel calculated from chart, Final Report, 203. For the ARCENT origin of these numbers, see ibid., 202. Postwar studies gave lower numbers. Atkinson, *Crusade*, 340–343.

53. FM 34–3.

54. Final Report, 202; ARCENT hist, 74; Lt. Gen. Horner intvw, Mar 4, 1992.

55. FM 34–3; Schwarzkopf, *Autobiography*, 319; intvw, Col. Gary R. Ware (USAF, Ret.), with Dr. Diane Putney, CAFH, Mar 28, 1994; CMH draft, 288; ARCENT hist, 38–39. See also Lt. Gen. Horner intvw, Mar 4, 1992, and Lt. Col. Baptiste intvw.

56. Lt. Gen. Horner, quoted in *Air Force Magazine*, Jun 1991, 57; Walker notes, entry for 0540 Feb 15, 1991. See also Walker notes, entries for 0429 Feb 12, 1991, and 0042 Feb 20, 1991.

57. On artillery in the Iran-Iraq War, see Support Battle Staff brfg, Feb 24, 1991. On the resilience of artillery to air attacks, see Hosterman notes, entry for 1930 Feb 13, 1991, and Walker notes, entry for 0445 Feb 15, 1991.

58. Although various sources credit

the F–16 with different numbers of total sorties, they agree that it flew the most combat missions of the war. See Final Report, App T, 78; chart, USAFTAWC/ECER, "USAF Combat Forces," Aug 5, 1991, in Lt. Gen. Horner's Desert Storm files, HQ 9 AF/CC; brfg slide, "Total Sorties Flown by USAF Combat A/C," Feb 28, 1991, in DD/TWP brfg.

59. Final Report, App T, 75–76; point paper, CSS–Fighter Desk, "Fighter Status and Issues," Feb 15, 1991, "15–16 Feb 91 (Day 31)" file, Checkmate files.

60. Michael, *Chronology*, 451; Final Report, App T, 77.

61. "How-Goes-It"; Final Report, App T, 76.

62. Final Report, 196, App T, 76; "USAF Forces"; brfg, Lt. Col. Mark Welch, 4 TFS, "Warrior Briefings to the Air Staff: Killer Scout—Kill Zone Procedures in Desert Storm," Oct 15, 1991 (hereafter, Killer Scout brfg).

63. Jerry Scutts, *Wolfpack: Hunting MiGs over Vietnam* (Osceola, Wisc.: Motorbooks Int., 1988), 96; msg, NGB/CSS to AIG 7303/CC/DO et al., 0020Z Feb 15, 1991, "Lessons Learned" file, Box 25, HQ TAC/HO archives (hereafter, NGB Feb 15 msg).

64. Lt. Col. Baptiste intvw; ConOps for C^2; intvw, Capt. Timothy W. Mers, Apr 24, 1991, MSgt. Devino's intvws.

65. Lt. Col. Baptiste intvw; Maj. Gen. Corder intvw; Killer Scout brfg.

66. Killer Scout brfg; Brig. Gen. Glosson intvw, Dec 12, 1991.

67. Brfg, HQ TAC/DO, "Desert Storm Lessons Learned," Jul 12, 1991, "Title V Report Inputs" file, Checkmate files (hereafter, HQ TAC Lessons Learned); Walker notes, entry for 0255 Feb 8, 1991; Killer Scout brfg; msg, CENTAF/DO to All Unit Commanders, "Desert Storm Bombing Halt ROE Update," [Feb 28, 1991], in TACC log.

68. Final Report, App T, 76; NGB Feb 15 msg.

69. Lt. Col. Baptiste intvw; Final Report, 196; rpt, HQ Air Weather Service, "Air Weather Service Contribution to Winning the War—the Value of Weather Support: Operation Desert Storm/Desert Shield Report 1," May 23, 1991 (hereafter, "Air Weather Service Contribution").

70. Brig. Gen. Muellner intvw; notes, Dr. Perry D. Jamieson, CAFH, on videotape of brfg, Maj. Jim Coates, 12 TIS, "Joint STARS," USAF Intelligence Conference at Goodfellow AFB, Tex., Oct 31–Nov 1, 1991 (hereafter, Joint STARS brfg).

71. Intvw, Col. George W. Cox, Comdt, USAF Air Gnd Ops School, USAF Air Warfare Center, with Robert L. Mandler, USAFAWC/HO, Dec 21, 1991 (hereafter, Col. Cox intvw); Maj. Gen. Corder intvw.

72. Brig. Gen. Muellner intvw; Col. Cox intvw.

73. Maj. Gen. Corder intvw.

74. Ltr, USCENTAF/DCP, "COMUSCENTAF Air Guidance Letter," D+31 [Feb 17, 1991]; Battle Staff Directive, 354/23 TFW(P), Battle Staff Directive 35: "Killer Scouts," n.d., both in CENTAF collection, HQ TAC/HO archives.

75. "How-Goes-It"; rpt, 57 FWW Tactics Team, "F–16 Effectiveness in the Gulf War," Feb 14, 1991, "F–16" file, Checkmate files (hereafter, "F–16 Effectiveness"); marginalia on memo, Brig. Gen. Buster C. Glosson, Dir Plans, for CENTCOM J3 Plans, "Theater Campaign Strategy Assessment," Feb 15, 1991, "War Termination—Emergency Strike Plan" file, Checkmate files; HQ TAC Lessons Learned.

76. Lt. Gen. Horner, quoted in *Air Force Magazine*, Jun 1991, 60; Final Report, App T, 8; "Air Force Plan En-

counters Army Flak," *Washington Post*, Dec 28, 1990.

77. Final Report, App T, 9; chronol, SSgt. Gary W. Boyd, "Combat Chronology, 23/354 TFW(P): Operation Desert Storm, 17 Jan 1991–28 Feb 1991," entry for Jan 17, 1991 (hereafter, Boyd chronol).

78. Point paper, CSS–Fighter Desk, "Fighter Status and Issues," Feb 15, 1991, "15–16 Feb 91 (Day 31)" file, Checkmate files; Final Report, App T, 9; DD/TWP brfg.

79. Final Report, App T, 11.

80. Lt. Col. Baptiste intvw; Boyd chronol, entry for Jan 18, 1991; brfg, "Operation Desert Storm A–10 Combat Recap," n.d., Unit Histories collection, HQ TAC/HO (hereafter, A–10 recap).

81. Boyd chronol, entry for Jan 18, 1991.

82. Ibid.; *Airman*, Apr 1991, 3–4; Final Report, App T, 10.

83. Boyd chronol, entry for Jan 17, 1991; "Air Weather Service Contribution."

84. Boyd chronol, entry for Jan 22, 1991; TACC log, entry for Jan 28, 1991.

85. Boyd chronol, entries for Jan 29, Feb 8, and Feb 14, 1991; Lt. Col. Baptiste intvw.

86. Boyd chronol, entry for Jan 22, 1991.

87. "Essay on the A–10", in ibid.; Final Report, App T, 10; A–10 recap.

88. *Aviation Week and Space Technology*, Aug 5, 1991, 42–43; A–10 recap.

89. *Aviation Week and Space Technology*, Aug 5, 1991, 42–43; Boyd chronol, entry for Feb 22, 1991.

90. *Aviation Week and Space Technology*, Aug 5, 1991, 43; A–10 recap.

91. Boyd chronol, entry for Feb 15, 1991; ltr, Col. David A. Sawyer, 23 TFW/CC, to Lt. Gen. Charles A. Horner, CENTAF/CC, "Yr 15/1930Z Msg, Aircraft Losses," Feb 16, 1991, support- ing doc to hist, 354 TFW, HQ TAC/HO (hereafter, Col. Sawyer ltr); TACC log, entry for 0820Z Feb 15, 1991.

92. Final Report, 198; Maj. Gen. Corder intvw; Vinas special study, 31.

93. Maj. Gen. Corder intvw.

94. Lt. Gen. Horner intvw, Mar 4, 1992; TACC log, entry for Feb 7, 1991; "F–111 chart."

95. "F–111 chart"; see also log, "F–111 Stuff: Williford/Snyder," entry for Feb 19/20, 1991, F–111 Logbook, Box 13, CENTAF records.

96. TACC log, entry for Feb 11, 1991; Final Report, App T, 69; msg, 4 TFW Deployed/CC to HQ TAC/DR/ DO and 9 AF/DO, "F–15E Performance in Desert Storm," 1630Z Mar 16, 1991, "Lessons Learned" file, Box 25, HQ TAC/HO archives (hereafter, 4 TFW msg). See also draft summary paper, "F–15E 72 Hour Surge Schedule," "Priority Target Information Book" file, Box 11C, CENTAF records.

97. Walker notes, entry for 0428 Feb 13, 1991; TACC log, entry for Feb 11, 1991; 4 TFW msg.

98. Lt. Gen. Horner intvw, Mar 4, 1992; Walker notes, entry for 0443 Feb 13, 1991. On the prewar thinking about the 500-pound bomb, see also Maj. Gen. Glosson intvw, Dec 12, 1991.

99. TACC log, entry for Feb 8, 1991; Lt. Gen. Horner, quoted in *Air Force Magazine*, Jun 1991, 60.

100. Brfg, "The Backbone of Air Power in Operation Desert Storm: The F–15 Eagle," [May 1991], "F–15" file, Checkmate files; Final Report, App T, 69–70; Burton log, entry for 0900, Feb 15, 1991; Vinas special study, 38; "USAF Forces."

101. Final Report, App T, 72; Col. Warden brfg; A–10 recap.

102. HQ TAC Lessons Learned.

103. Special study, 37 FW/HO, "Nighthawks over Iraq," Jan 9, 1992, 8.

104. Contingency hist rpt, 37 TFW(P), Feb 10–16, 1991, 15, Unit Histories collection, HQ TAC/HO; Brig. Gen. Glosson intvw, Mar 13, 1991. See also Lt. Gen. Horner intvw, Mar 4, 1992.

105. Special study, 37 FW/HO, "Nighthawks over Iraq," Jan 9, 1992, 33; memo, Wayne Thompson to Perry Jamieson, [comments on draft of *Lucrative Targets*], Jun 15, 1993, copy in possession of P. D. Jamieson.

106. Vinas special study, 12.

107. Final Report, App T, 9, 10; Boyd chronol, entry for Jan 17, 1991.

108. Msg, USCENTAF/IN to AIG 12929 et al., "CENTAF Desert Storm Intelligence Summary 91–029," 0407Z Jan 31, 1991, "Khafji" file, Checkmate files; Final Report, App T, 82.

109. "DISum 149"; Burton log,

entry for 1700 Feb 15, 1991; chart, "48 TFW Tank Busting BDA," Feb 24, 1991, Folder 2, Box 11C, CENTAF records. Not surprisingly, the unit claimed a higher number of kills than ARCENT verified.

110. Calculated from Final Report, 203. See also point paper, AF/XOXWF, "Checkmate Strategic Assessment (As of 22 Feb 91/1600L Washington time)," Feb 22, 1991, "23–24 Feb 91 (Day 39)" file, Checkmate files.

111. Paraphrase of Lt. Gen. Behery's comments in trip rpt, Dr. Wayne Thompson, GWAPS, Visit to Saudi Arabia and Kuwait, Jul 8–16, 1992, 5 (hereafter, Dr. Thompson's trip rpt); Col. Reavey intvw; brfg slide, HQ US-CENTAF/DCP, Jan 29, 1991, in "KTO/Republican Guards" file, Checkmate files; Vinas special study, 33.

Chapter Five

1. Anatol Rapoport, ed., Carl von Clausewitz, *On War* (Middlesex, England: Penguin Books, 1982), 164.

2. "SAC Bomber and Tanker Operations," 16.

3. Ibid.

4. STRATFOR rpt.

5. "SAC Bomber and Tanker Operations," 1; STRATFOR rpt.

6. STRATFOR rpt; point paper, AF/XOXW, "Bomber Operations," Jan 23, 1991, "22–23 Jan (Day 7)" file, Checkmate files; msg, 3909 SAES/CC to HQ SAC/DO/DOO et al., "SAC Participation in Desert Storm," 1400Z Apr 1, 1991, historians' working files, HQ SAC/HO; Colonel Randall E. Wooten, quoted in *New York Times*, Mar 8, 1991; intvw, Capt. Brooks R. Lieske, Apr 23, 1991, MSgt. Devino's intvws. See also msg, 1708 PBW/DO/IN to USCENT-

AF/DO/IN et al., "Improved Accuracy of Iraqi Heavy AAA," 0100Z Feb 4, 1991, historians' working files, HQ SAC/HO; and Brig. Gen. Caruana intvw.

7. Intvw, 1st Lt. Peter J. Bloom, Apr 23, 1991, MSgt. Devino's intvws; intvw, Brig. Gen. Patrick P. Caruana, STRATFOR/CC and 17 AD(P)/CC, with TSgt. Frederick Hosterman, Feb 17, 1991; trip rpt, Lt. Col. Milton A. Magaw, 8 AF/DOTN, Mar 26, 1991, historians' working files, HQ SAC/HO (hereafter, Lt. Col. Magaw's trip rpt). On the coordinates error, see also Lt. Gen. Horner intvw, Mar 4, 1992, and transcript, intvw, Capt. James R. Hawkins, HQ SAC/DOOQ, with Dr. Kent M. Beck, HQ SAC/HOL, Apr 30, 1991, historians' working files, HQ SAC/HO (hereafter, Capt. Hawkins

intvw). On other factors, see intvw, Lt. Col. James A. Thomits, HQ SAC/DOOB, with Dr. Kent M. Beck, HQ SAC/HOL, May 15, 1991, transcript in historians' working files, HQ SAC/HO. (These transcripts are Dr. Beck's notes of his interviews with HQ SAC personnel, revised by the interviewees.)

8. "SAC Bomber and Tanker Operations," 14; "Bomber Story," 34.

9. Lt. Col. Magaw's trip rpt; "SAC Bomber and Tanker Operations," 11, 14.

10. "SAC Bomber and Tanker Operations," 13.

11. Ibid., 14.

12. Lt. Col. Magaw's trip rpt; Capt. Hawkins intvw. See also msg, 801 BMW(P)/CC to 17 AD(P)/CC et al., "Bombing Review," 1402Z Feb 19, 1991, historians' working files, HQ SAC/HO; and msg, HQ SAC/SBS to 8 AF/DO/DOO et al., "B–52 Conventional Bombing Ballistics," 0500Z Feb 19, 1991, historians' working files, HQ SAC/HO.

13. Capt. Hawkins intvw; Lt. Col. Baptiste intvw. On postwar studies of the problem, see After Action Report, HQ SAC, "Desert Storm Bombing and Navigation Conference," Apr 22–24, 1991, historians' working files, HQ SAC/HO; memo, SAC/DOTN to "See Distribution," "High Altitude Bombing Conference," Mar 12, 1991, historians' working files, HQ SAC/HO; and memo, SAC/DOO to 8 AF/DOO and 15 AF/DOO, "Operation Desert Storm Bombing and Navigation Conference After-Action Report," Jun 19, 1991, historians' working files, HQ SAC/HO.

14. Summary paper, HQ SAC/SBS, "SAC Desert Shield/Desert Storm Summary Data," Mar 20, 1991, historians' working files, HQ SAC/HO; Coyne, *Airpower in the Gulf*, 89; Capt. Hawkins intvw; Lt. Col. Baptiste intvw.

15. "SAC Bomber and Tanker Operations," 9; msg, USCINCCENT to AIG 904 et al., "SITREP USCINCCENT 179," 2115Z Feb 4, 1991; msg, 513 MIBdeFwd/JDC to CMO ARCENT/G2 et al., [no subject], 0441Z Mar 10, 1991, both in "Iraqi POW Debriefs" file, Checkmate files.

16. Maj. Gen. Corder intvw; "Iraqi Generals Perspective."

17. "Iraqi Generals Perspective." The Coalition did not mount a general psychological-operations campaign beyond these B–52 missions, a deficiency that troubled Colonel Warden and other officers. See Col. Warden intvw; msg, AF/XOXW to USCENTAF Fwd Hqs/DO, 0125Z Sep 8, 1990, MSgt. Turner files; memo, Col. Warden to Gen. Loh, [no subject], Nov 1, 1990, "Plan—Phases 2/3" file, Checkmate files.

18. "F–16 Effectiveness"; Vinas special study, 31; HQ TAC Lessons Learned; STRATFOR After Action Report. See also brfg, Lt. Gen. Horner, 9 AF Comdr and COMUSCENTAF, "Hot Wash," Maxwell AFB, Jul 12, 1991, Checkmate files; and Lt. Col. Waterstreet intvw.

19. Maj. Gen. Glosson intvw, Dec 12, 1991; remarks, Gen. Merrill A. McPeak at HQ USAF "Hot Wash" Desert Storm debriefing, Apr 17, 1991; Lt. Col. Baptiste intvw. See also Maj. Gen. Corder intvw.

20. Lt. Col. Waterstreet intvw; "Air Weather Service Contribution"; Vinas special study; bio, SAF/PA, Maj. Gen. John A. Corder, May 1989; Maj. Corder intvw. Colonel Maidh Ayed Al-Lehaibi, commander of the RSAF 3d Flying Wing, commented that the Saudis did little prewar training at medium altitudes. Dr. Thompson's trip rpt. On the shift to medium altitudes, see also HQ TAC Lessons Learned.

21. Vinas special study, 16; msg, 97

BMW/DO to 15 AF/DO et al., "Tactics After-Action Report," 1300Z Apr 16, 1991, historians' working files, HQ SAC/HO; msg, 0652Z Mar 1, 1991.

22. Ltr, Col. Ervin C. Sharpe, 354 TFW/CC, and Col. David A. Sawyer, 23 TFW/CC, to Brig. Gen. Buster Glosson, 14 AD(P) Comdr, [no subject], Feb 3, 1991, "Kill Box" file, Box 76, HQ TAC/HO collection; "How-Goes-It"; Col. Sawyer ltr.

23. Col. Sawyer ltr; "How-Goes-It"; ltr, Col. Ervin C. Sharpe, 354 TFW/CC, and Col. David A. Sawyer, 23 TFW/CC, to Brig. Gen. Buster Glosson, 14 AD(P) Comdr, [no subject], Feb 3, 1991, "Kill Box" file, Box 76, HQ TAC/HO collection.

24. Col. Sawyer ltr.

25. A–10 recap; Boyd chronol, entry for Feb 15, 1991.

26. Col. Sawyer ltr; HQ TAC Lessons Learned.

27. Col. Sawyer ltr; list, CENTAF/DP, "Operation Desert Storm Reported USAF Casualties as of 6 Mar 91," File 0269629, "CENTAF/DP Casualty Statistics," Roll 10265, CAFH Desert Shield/Desert Storm microfilm collection; Final Report, App A, 8.

28. "USAF Forces"; Lt. Gen. Horner, quoted in *Air Force Magazine*, Jun 1991, 61; TACC log, entries for 1720Z Feb 15, 1991, and 1215Z Feb 16, 1991. See also Hosterman notes, entry for 1840Z Feb 15, 1991.

29. Col. Sawyer ltr; Lt. Gen. Horner, quoted in *Air Force Magazine*, Jun 1991, 61. On pulling back the A–10s, see also Lt. Col. Baptiste intvw.

30. Brig. Gen. Caruana intvw; Lt. Gen. Horner intvw, Mar 4, 1992. The Vietnam War practice of body-counting fell into total discredit. Similar to thousands of other field-grade officers during the Vietnam War, General Schwarz kopf believed this procedure was "a bureau-

cratic sham," and his experience during the Grenada operation reinforced this opinion. Schwarzkopf, *Autobiography*, 119, 252–253. It is a telling indictment of body-counting that two other Vietnam veterans, who took divergent positions on many issues raised by the Southeast Asian conflict, agreed in criticizing this practice: William C. Westmoreland, *A Soldier Reports* (Garden City, N.Y.: Doubleday & Company, 1976), 273, and David H. Hackworth and Julie Sherman, *About Face* (New York: Simon & Schuster, 1989), 467, 572–573, 667–668, 778–779.

31. Msg, COMUSARCENT/G2 to VII Corps Main Fwd/CG et al., "ARCENT Battle Damage Assessment Process," 0600Z Feb 17, 1991, "KTO/Republican Guards" file, Checkmate files (hereafter, ARCENT BDA msg); Lt. Gen. Horner intvw, Mar 4, 1992; summary paper, HQ USAFE/XPPF, "Corps Air Support at Desert Storm," Jul 3, 1991 (hereafter, "Air Support" paper).

32. "Air Support" paper; CINC's War Book input, "Republican Guards in the KTO (As of 0300L 31 Jan 1991)," Jan 31, 1991 A.M.

33. ARCENT hist, 38–39; FM 34–3; "Air Support" paper.

34. Lt. Gen. Horner intvw, Mar 4, 1992; "Air Support" paper. The A–10 is a single-seat aircraft.

35. "Air Support" paper; Maj. Gen. Glosson intvw, Dec 12, 1991; ARCENT BDA msg.

36. ARCENT BDA msg; "Air Support" paper.

37. ARCENT BDA msg; brfg, "Battle Damage Assessment," Feb 19, 1991, File 0269536, "CENT-AF/DOO Daily Slides for General Horner and TACC Briefing," Roll 10226, CAFH Desert Shield/Desert Storm microfilm collection; CINC's War Book input, "Overall Iraqi Ground Summary (As of

0300L 25 Feb 91)," Feb 25, 1991 P.M.; CINC's War Book input, "Overall Iraqi Ground Summary (As of 0300L 26 Feb 91)," Feb 26, 1991 P.M.

38. Maj. Sweeney intvw, Mar 3, 1991; Lt. Col. Baptiste intvw; Lt. Gen. Horner intvw, Mar 4, 1992. See also Col. Christon intvw.

39. Air Support paper. For AR-CENT's perspective on the BDA issue, see rpt, Brig. Gen. John F. Stewart, Jr., G–2, Third Army, "Operation Desert Storm, The Military Intelligence Story: A View from the G–2 3d U.S. Army," Apr 1991; ARCENT BDA msg; AR-CENT hist, 74; CMH draft, 288–290.

40. Maj. Gen. Corder intvw; Lt. Col. Baptiste intvw.

41. Col. Warden brfg; Support Battle Staff brfg, Jan 31, 1991. See also Support Battle Staff brfg, Feb 1, 1991; "Iraqi Situation"; and msg, Am Emb Riyadh to SecState et al., "Saddam's War: Riyadh SitRep No. 26 (As of 1800L 1/30)," 1539Z Jan 30, 1991, "State Department Message" file, HQ USCENTCOM/CCHO archives.

42. CINC's War Book input, intel summary, Jan 31, 1991 A.M.; "Iraqi Generals Perspective." For additional ideas about the origins of the Battle of Khafji, see Brig. Gen. John H. Admire, "The 3d Marines in Desert Storm," *Marine Corps Gazette*, Sep 1991, 68 (hereafter, "3d Marines in Desert Storm"), and Lt. Gen. Horner intvw, Mar 4, 1992. These generals both offered plausible alternatives to the conventional explanation of the causes of the engagement, reinforcing the fact that, without Iraqi sources, there can be no definitive explanation of the origin of the Battle of Khafji.

43. Blackwell, *Thunder in the Desert*, 160; Friedman, *Desert Victory*, 197–198; "DISum 149."

44. ARCENT hist, 97, 98; maps, situations as of G–40, Jan 15, 1991, and H-Hour/0400, Feb 24, 1991, in "100-Hour Ground War"; command chronol, 2d Marine Div, Jan 1–Apr 13, 1991, p II-9, USMC Historical Center (hereafter, 2d Marine Division chronol).

45. 2d Marine Division chronol; "3d Marines in Desert Storm"; command chronol, 1st Lt Armd Inf Bn, Jan 1–Feb 28, 1991, p II-2, USMC Historical Center (hereafter, 1st LAI Battalion chronol).

46. Summary paper, HQ USMC/ Current Ops Br, "I Marine Expeditionary Force," n.d., USMC Historical Center (hereafter, "I Marine Expeditionary Force"); command chronol, 3d Marine Regt, Jan 1–Feb 28, 1991, [unpaginated], USMC Historical Center (hereafter, 3d Marine chronol); "3d Marines in Desert Storm," 68.

47. "I Marine Expeditionary Force"; command chronol, 2d Lt Armd Inf Bn, Jan 1–Mar 31, 1991, [unpaginated], USMC Historical Center (hereafter, 2d LAI Battalion chronol); 2d Marine Division chronol, p II-9.

48. "I Marine Expeditionary Force"; 1st LAI Battalion chronol, p II-2; Capt. Roger L. Pollard, "The Battle for OP–4: Start of the Ground War," *Marine Corps Gazette*, Mar 1992, 48 (hereafter, "Battle for OP–4"). Two letters should be read with Captain Pollard's article: Capt. William H. Weber IV, "More on OP–4," *Marine Corps Gazette*, Jun 1992, 64, and Capt. Steven A. Ross and SSgt. G. L. Gillispie, "OP–4 Once More," *Marine Corps Gazette*, Jul 1992, 11–12.

49. Final Report, 189; msg, DIA/ J21–6C to AIG 962 et al., 1959Z Feb 15, 1991, "DIA Intelligence" file, Checkmate files; CSAF brief, Feb 25, 1991; transcript, I MEF Comd Brfgs, Jan 30, 1991 A.M., Jan 31, 1991 A.M., "28–31 Jan 91" file, USMC Historical

Center, copy held by CAFH (hereafter, I MEF Command brfg). The Khafji naval operation is treated in Edward J. Marolda, "A Host of Nations: Coalition Naval Operations in the Persian Gulf," 1–2, paper presented at the fifty-ninth annual meeting of the Society for Military History, Apr 12, 1992. A few postwar sources state that elements of a third Iraqi division, the 1st Mechanized, also participated in the Khafji operation. This unit, however, was deployed farther north of the Saudi border than either the 5th Mechanized or the 3d Armored Division. *GWAPS*, Vol II, Part 1, "Operations," 252. Moreover, it is known that the units that suffered casualties during the Battle of Khafji belonged to either the 5th Mechanized or the 3d Armored Division. [Classified source].

50. I MEF Command brfg, Jan 31, 1991 A.M.; "Battle for OP–4," 48.

51. TACC log, entry for 1940Z Jan 29, 1991; 2d Marine Division chronol; excerpt, from IntRep 91–168, 2027Z Jan 30, 1991, Box 17, CENTAF collection, HQ TAC/HO archives; "DISum 149."

52. Excerpt, from IntRep 91–168, 2027Z Jan 30, 1991, Box 17, CENTAF collection, HQ TAC/HO archives; I MEF Command brfg, Jan 30, 1991 A.M.; "3d Marines in Desert Storm," 68. On the Iraqis' gaining strength, see also 2d LAI Battalion chronol.

53. TACC log, entry for 1940Z Jan 29, 1991; I MEF Command brfg, Jan 30, 1991 A.M.

54. Msg, USCINCCENT/CCJ2 to AIG 7861 et al., "USCENTCOM Collateral Intelligence DISum No. 175 for the Period 31/1500Z Jan to 01/1459Z Feb 91," 2330Z Feb 1, 1991, "Khafji" file, Checkmate files.

55. I MEF Command brfg, Jan 30, 1991 A.M.; "Battle for OP–4."

56. Msg, USCENTAF/DO to USCINCCENT/CCJ2 et al., "Joint STAR[S] End of Mission Report, 29 Jan 1991," 1600Z Jan 29, 1991, File 0269566, "J–STARS Support of Desert Storm," Roll 10238, CAFH Desert Shield/Desert Storm microfilm collection; Col. Warden brfg. For a later Checkmate alert to the planners in the AOR, see memo, [AF/XOXW] to [USCENTAF/DCP], "Hot for Desert Dave & Buck!!!," 1900Z Jan 31, 1991, "30–31 Jan 91 (Day 15)" file, Checkmate files.

57. "Significant Operations Events," 1930 Jan 29, 1991; Col. Warden brfg.

58. 1st LAI Battalion chronol, p II-2; "Battle for OP–4," 49–50; TACC log, entry for 1940Z Jan 29, 1991.

59. "Significant Operations Events," 2305 Jan 29, 1991; TACC log, entry for 2024Z Jan 29, 1991; Final Report, 189.

60. Final Report, 189; "Significant Operations Events," 2305 Jan 29, 1991; TACC log, entries for 2024Z and 2046Z Jan 29, 1991.

61. "Battle for OP–4," 50; command chronol, 1st Marine Div, Jan 1–Feb 28, 1991, p II-3, USMC Historical Center. The Saudis wisely had abandoned the Umm Hjul police post, which was near the Saddam Line. "Battle for OP–4," 48.

62. I MEF Command brfg, Jan 31, 1991 A.M.; Capt. William H. Weber IV, "More on OP–4," *Marine Corps Gazette*, Jun 1992, 64.

63. Memo, Maj. Robertson to Lt. Gen. Horner, "Maverick Firing on LAV," Feb 3 [1991], with atch Friendly Casualty Report; "Battle for OP–4," 50.

64. TACC log, entry for 1940Z Jan 29, 1991; Hosterman notes, entries for 1931Z and 1957Z Jan 29, 1991; Joint STARS brfg; msg, USCENTAF/DO to USCINCCENT/CCJ2 et al., "Joint STAR[S] End of Mission Report 30 Jan

91," 1200Z Jan 30, 1991, File 0269566, "J–STARS Support of Desert Storm," Roll 10238, CAFH Desert Shield/Desert Storm microfilm collection. See also TACC log, entry for 0040Z Jan 30, 1991.

65. 2d Marine Division chronol, p II-9; TACC log, entry for 1940Z Jan 29, 1991; 2d LAI Battalion chronol.

66. 2d Marine Division chronol, p II-9; 2d LAI Battalion chronol.

67. 2d Marine Division chronol, p II-9; "Significant Operations Events," 1000 Jan 30, 1991.

68. "Significant Operations Events," 0235 and 0350 Jan 30, 1991.

69. "Attacks at Saudi Border Kill 12 U.S. Marines: Iraqis Lose 24 Tanks, Suffer 'Heavy' Casualties," *Washington Post*, Jan 31, 1991. See also TACC log, entry for 1055Z Jan 30, 1991.

70. I MEF Command brfg, Jan 31, 1991 A.M.

71. Dr. Thompson's trip rpt; TACC log, entries for 2230Z and 2240Z Jan 29, 1991, and 0310L, 0115Z, and 1055Z Jan 30, 1991. Brig. Gen. Sudairy died of cancer two years after the Gulf War. Memo, SAF/IA to SAF/OS et al., "Death of BGen. Ahmed M. Al-Sudairy," Feb 1, 1993.

72. TACC log, entry for 0115Z Jan 30, 1991; "3d Marines in Desert Storm," 68; Schwarzkopf, *Autobiography*, 425. See also Friedman, *Desert Victory*, 200.

73. "Significant Operations Events," 0830, 0930, and 1000 Jan 30, 1991.

74. Ibid., 0730, 1000, and 1020 Jan 30, 1991; TACC log, entry for 1055Z Jan 30, 1991.

75. TACC log, entry for 1055Z Jan 30, 1991; "Significant Operations Events," 1330 and 1645 Jan 30, 1991.

76. TACC log, 1900Z Jan 30, 1991; Hosterman notes, entry for 1900L Jan 30, 1991. See also notes, MSgt.

Theodore J. Turner, USCENTAF/HO, "USCENTAF/TACC Notes: Operation Desert Storm," entries for 1905L and 1909L Jan 31, 1991, Turner file, Box 84, CENTAF collection, HQ TAC/HO archives (hereafter, Turner notes).

77. Hosterman notes, entry for 2148L/1848Z Jan 30, 1991; Lt. Gen. Horner intvw, Mar 4, 1992.

78. Hosterman notes, entry for 2010L/1710Z Jan 30, 1991.

79. Schwarzkopf, *Autobiography*, 424; Hosterman notes, entry for 2222L/ 1922Z Jan 30, 1991; Lt. Gen. Horner intvw, Mar 4, 1992.

80. TACC log, entry for 1900Z Jan 30, 1991.

81. Hosterman notes, entries for 2010L/1710Z, 2222L/1922Z, and 2253L/ 1956Z Jan 30, 1991, and 0026L/ 2126Z Jan 30/31, 1991. See also TACC log, entry for 2045Z Jan 30, 1991, and "SAC Bomber and Tanker Operations," 11.

82. TACC log, entries for 1900Z and 2003Z Jan 30, 1991, with accompanying sketch map; Hosterman notes, entry for 2222L/1922Z Jan 30, 1991.

83. TACC log, entry for 2036Z Jan 30, 1991.

84. Ibid., entries for 1900Z and 2003Z Jan 30, 1991.

85. Ibid., entry for 2048Z Jan 30, 1991; Hosterman notes, entries for 2346L/2046Z Jan 30, 1991 and 0040L/ 2140Z Jan 31/30, 1991; Lt. Gen. Horner intvw, Mar 4, 1992.

86. "Significant Operations Events," 0230 and 0445 Jan 31, 1991; Burton notes, entry for 0730 Jan 31, 1991.

87. Draft hist, SSgt. Randy G. Bergeron, "Air Force Special Operations Command in Operations Desert Shield and Desert Storm," n.d., 31 (hereafter, Bergeron hist); "Significant Operations Events," 0643 Jan 31, 1991.

88. Col. Winstel intvw; Hosterman

notes, entry for 1930 Jan 31, 1991; Bergeron hist, 31. See also Col. Reavey intvw.

89. 3d Marine chronol; Turner notes, entry for 1305L Jan 31, 1991; "Significant Operations Events," 1500 Jan 31, 1991; Burton notes, entry for 0730 Jan 31, 1991.

90. "Significant Operations Events," 1500 and 1415 Jan 31, 1991; "3d Marines in Desert Storm," 68.

91. "Significant Operations Events," 1800 Jan 31, 1991; Schwarzkopf, *Autobiography*, 426; "3d Marines in Desert Storm," 68. On other small actions, see "Significant Operations Events," 2015 Jan 31, 1991 and 0030, 0100, and 1610 Feb 1, 1991; and Schwarzkopf, *Autobiography*, 429.

92. Lt. Gen. Horner intvw, Mar 4, 1992; Hosterman notes, entry for 2148L/1848Z Jan 30, 1991; Walker notes, [time group not specified] Jan 31, 1991.

93. "Allies Claim to Bomb Iraqi Targets at Will," *Washington Post*, Jan 31, 1991; I MEF Command brfgs, Jan 30, 1991 A.M., Jan 31, 1991 A.M.

94. Walker notes, entry for 0525 Jan 30, 1991; TACC log, entry for 2046Z Jan 29, 1991; "3d Marines in Desert Storm," 69; Schwarzkopf, *Autobiography*, 427.

95. Msg, USCINCCENT/CCJ2 to AIG 7861 et al., "USCENTCOM Collateral Intelligence DISum No. 175 for the Period 31/1500Z Jan to 01/1459Z Feb 91," 2330Z Feb 1, 1991, "Khafji" file, Checkmate files; Col. Warden brfg; Lt. Gen. Horner intvw, Mar 4, 1992. See also Lt. Gen. Horner testimony and Schwarzkopf, *Autobiography*, 424.

96. J. F. C. Fuller, *A Military History of the Western World*, 3 vols (New York: Funk & Wagnalls, 1954–1956), 1:141; Howard H. Peckham, *The War for Independence* (Chicago & London:

University of Chicago Press, 1958), 72; Douglas Southall Freeman, *Lee's Lieutenants: A Study in Command*, 3 vols (New York: Charles Scribner's Sons, 1942– 1944), 2:567. On the U.S. Army's transition from nineteenth-century linear tactics to more flexible, small-unit ones, see Perry D. Jamieson, *Crossing the Deadly Ground: United States Army Tactics, 1865–1899* (Tuscaloosa & London: University of Alabama Press, 1994).

97. Final Report, App M, 2; *U.S. News & World Report, Triumph Without Victory*, 293.

98. Final Report, App M, 3; msg, OSD/PA to AIG 8798 et al., "DoD News Briefing," 1336Z Aug 15, 1991.

99. Rpts, CENTAF Friendly Casualty Report, Incidents Number 1, 2148C Jan 29, 1991, and Number 9, 1520L Feb 26, 1991, both in "Fratricide" file, Box 76, CENTAF collection, HQ TAC/HO archives. (Other CENTAF friendly casualty reports are compiled in the same file.) See also "Human Error Blamed for 2 'Friendly Fire' Incidents," *Air Force Times*, Mar 18, 1991, 8.

100. Msg, USCENTAF/CV to AIG 10322/CC/SE et al., 1800Z Feb 3, 1991, File 00269321, "Outgoing CENTAF Messages," Roll 10161, CAFH Desert Shield/Desert Storm microfilm collection; msg, USCINCCENT/CCJ3 to COMUSARCENT/G3 et al., "Anti-Fratricide Measures for Coalition Forces," 1304Z Feb 13, 1991, File 1, Box 8, CENTAF collection, HQ TAC/HO archives; excerpt, from msg, "IntRep 91–295: Anti-Fratricide Measures for Coalition Forces," 2350Z Feb 23, 1991, Box 17, CENTAF collection, HQ TAC/HO archives. For the quantities of identification materials available in the theater on the eve of the ground campaign, see brfg slide, USARCENT, "Anti-Fratricide Marking Material:

Theater Requirements," 0001 Feb 22, 1991, in brfg, COMUSCENTAF, "Air Support for the Ground Campaign," n.d., Box 4, CENTAF records.

101. Msg, USCINCCENT/CCJ3 to COMUSARCENT/G3 et al., "Anti-Fratricide Measures for Coalition Forces," 1304Z Feb 13, 1991, File 1, Box 8, CENTAF collection, HQ TAC/HO archives; *GWAPS*, Vol II, Part 1, "Operations," 313.

102. Gen. McPeak brfg; Maj. Gen. J. M. Myatt, "The 1st Marine Division in the Attack," *U.S. Naval Institute Proceedings*, Nov 1991, 74.

103. Gen. McPeak brfg; Maj. Gen. Corder intvw; Interim Report, ch 17, p 1.

104. Maj. Gen. Olsen intvw; Cordesman and Wagner, *Lessons of Modern War*, 2:583. On fratricide, see also Schwarzkopf, *Autobiography*, 500–501.

105. Msg, NGB/CSS to AIG 7303/CC/DO et al., "Desert Storm Lessons Learned by the ANG Fighter/Recce Units," 2100Z Feb 12, 1991, "Lessons Learned" file, Box 25, CENTAF collection, HQ TAC/HO archives; "Gulf War Weather," Sec 3, 64; Walker notes, entry for 0148 Feb 13, 1991.

106. "Gulf War Weather," Sec 3, 66; DD/TWP brfg.

107. "Gulf War Weather," Sec 3, 72; Walker notes, entry for 0100 Feb 18, 1991.

108. Lt. Col. Baptiste intvw; TACC log, entry for 0500Z Feb 20, 1991.

109. Lt. Col. Baptiste intvw.

110. Col. Winstel intvw; "Directorate of Campaign Plans"; Lt. Gen. Horner's daily comments, Jan 25, 1991, 12; Lt. Col. Deptula intvw, Nov 20, 1991.

111. Maj. Gen. Olsen intvw; Lt. Col. Deptula intvw, Nov 20, 1991.

112. Lt. Col. Baptiste intvw; Lt. Gen. Horner's daily comments, Feb 6,

1991, 29; Maj. Gen. Olsen intvw; Lt. Col. Deptula intvw, Jan 8, 1992.

113. Lt. Gen. Horner's daily comments, Feb 4, 1991, 26.

114. Ibid., Jan 19, 1991, 4; Maj. Gen. Corder intvw; Lt. Col. Baptiste intvw; Maj. Sweeney intvw, Mar 3, 1991; Col. Christon intvw; Lt. Col. Waterstreet intvw. On the issue of retargeting based on new intelligence, see also Smith-McSwain paper.

115. Lt. Col. Waterstreet intvw; Lt. Col. Baptiste intvw. See also Lt. Col. Feinstein intvw and Maj. Sweeney intvw, Mar 4, 1991.

116. Lt. Col. Baptiste intvw; Col. Winstel intvw; Lt. Gen. Horner's daily comments, Jan 19, 1991, 4.

117. Lt. Col. Baptiste intvw.

118. Col. Reavey intvw; Moore, "Marine Air," 63; point paper, AF/XOXWP, "Navy & Marine Lessons Learned: Desert Shield/Storm," Apr 29, 1991, "Navy/Marine" file, Checkmate files.

119. Smith-McSwain paper; "Response to Navy/Marine Study." On Marine Corps "gaming" of the ATO process, see also Moore, "Marine Air," 63, and Lt. Col. Deptula intvw, Nov 20, 1991.

120. "Response to Navy/Marine Study." For another criticism of the ATO process from a Navy perspective, see Friedman, *Desert Victory*, 172–180.

121. Lt. Col. Baptiste intvw; msg, CINCCENT to CG I MEF/Info CENTAF Fwd, "Marine Aviation," 1330Z Feb 1, 1991, copy in TACC log.

122. "Response to Navy/Marine Study"; Smith-McSwain paper.

123. ATO brfg; summary paper, Capt. Lee Patton, "Getting the Air Tasking Order (ATO) to the Navy," in Col. Randy Witt, ed., "Air Force Tactical Communications in War: The Desert Shield/Desert Storm Comm Story,"

Mar 1991, HQ 9 AF/HO working files.

124. ATO brfg.

125. Address, Gen. Merrill H. Mc-Peak, Air Force Historical Foundation Association Symposium, Andrews AFB, D.C., Sep 17, 1992; memo, Brig. Gen. Mike Hall to Maj. Gen. John Corder, "Memo for the Record, 30 Jan Air/Gnd Ops Planning Mtg," Jan 30, 1991, File 0269617, Roll 10264, CAFH Desert Shield/Desert Storm microfilm collection (hereafter, Brig. Gen. Hall memo); Maj. Gen. Corder intvw.

126. Lt. Col. Baptiste intvw; Maj.

Gen. Corder intvw. For an Air Force officer's reply to an ATO critic, see MR, Lt. Col. Al Howey, AF/XOXW-G, "Review of *Desert Victory: The War for Kuwait* by Norman Friedman, Chapter 9, 'The Air Campaign,'" Sep 12, 1991.

127. Moore, "Marine Air," 63–64; Col. Reavey intvw. See also Dr. Thompson's trip rpt, 4.

128. Lt. Gen. Horner intvw, Mar 4, 1992.

129. Quoted in J. Christopher Herold, *The Mind of Napoleon* (New York: Columbia University Press, 1955), 223.

Chapter Six

1. Maj. Gen. Corder intvw; Lt. Gen. Horner intvw, Mar 4, 1992.

2. Point paper, AF/XOXWD, "Surging Air Campaign in Desert Storm," Feb 11, 1991, "War Termination—Emergency Strike Plan" file, Checkmate files; brfg, AF/XOXWF, "Big Week II: Winning Desert Storm," Feb 16, 1991, Checkmate files. On the merits of continuing the air campaign, see also Maj. Gen. Glosson intvw, Dec 12, 1991, and Lt. Col. Deptula intvw, Jan 8, 1992. On Big Week, see Wesley Frank Craven and James Lea Cate, *The Army Air Forces in World War II*, 7 vols (Washington, D.C.: Government Printing Office, 1983), 3:30–48.

3. Col. Warden brfg. See also Lt. Col. Deptula intvw, Jan 8, 1992.

4. Maj. Gen. Glosson intvw, Dec 12, 1991; memo, Comdr. Duck McSwain to Lt. Col. Deptula, [no subject], 0730 Feb 3, 1991, Folder 2, Box 11C, CENTAF records.

5. "Bush 'Skeptical' Air Power Alone Can Prevail in Gulf," *Washington Post*, Feb 6, 1991; Gen. Schwarzkopf intvw; Lt. Col. Deptula intvw, Jan 8,

1992; Lt. Col. Deptula intvw, Nov 27, 1991.

6. Summary paper, AF/XOXWS, "Significant News—4 Feb 91," Feb 4, 1991, "3–4 Feb 91 (Day 19)" file, Checkmate files; summary paper, AF/XOXWS, "Significant News—21 Feb 91," Feb 21, 1991, "20–21 Feb 91 (Day 36)" file, Checkmate files.

7. "Bush 'Skeptical' Air Power Alone Can Prevail in Gulf," *Washington Post*, Feb 6, 1991; "600 Iraqi Tanks Ruined, Allies Say," *Washington Post*, Feb 9, 1991.

8. Memo, Lt. Col. David A. Deptula, HQ USCENTAF/DCP, to [no addressee], "Feedback from SecDef/CJCS Meeting with CINC and Component Commanders," Feb 9, 1991, "KTO/Republican Guards" file, Checkmate files (hereafter, "Feedback from SecDef/CJCS Meeting"); Schwarzkopf, *Autobiography*, 434.

9. Maj. Gen. Glosson intvw, Dec 12, 1991; "Iraq Rebuffs Iran on Peace Initiative; Cheney Returns to Report on Ground War," *Washington Post*, Feb 11, 1991.

10. Lt. Gen. Horner, quoted in *Air Force Magazine*, Jun 1991, 57; CMH draft, 142–143; Maj. Gen. Olsen intvw; Lt. Gen. Horner intvw, Mar 4, 1992; Maj. Gen. Glosson intvw, Dec 12, 1991.

11. ARCENT hist, 26.

12. Lt. Col. Deptula intvw, Nov 27, 1991; COMUSCENTAF OpOrd; summary paper, AF/XOXW for CSAF, "CINCCENT Campaign Plan Options," Nov 30, 1990, "The Kuwait Air Campaign CSAF Information Book," Box 7, CENTAF records.

13. CMH draft, 182; Schwarzkopf, *Autobiography*, 356; ARCENT hist, 36–38; "J5 After Action Report," 10; "Campaign Plan Chronology." On the School of Advanced Military Studies, see Sean D. Taylor, "Revenge of the 'Jedi,'" *Army Times*, Apr 22, 1991, 12–14.

14. Schwarzkopf, *Autobiography*, 319; "Campaign Plan Chronology"; ARCENT hist, 39.

15. CMH draft, 187; "Campaign Plan Chronology"; ARCENT hist, 40–41.

16. "Campaign Plan Chronology"; ARCENT hist, 40–41.

17. Schwarzkopf, *Autobiography*, 356; Lt. Gen. Horner intvw, Mar 4, 1992. See also Lt. Gen. Horner intvw, Dec 3, 1991.

18. ARCENT hist, 41; Schwarzkopf, *Autobiography*, 361; CMH draft, 188; "Campaign Plan Chronology." See also MR, Brig. Gen. Buster C. Glosson, "Q&A During Presidential Briefing," n.d., Box 12, CENTAF records; MR, Brig. Gen. Buster C. Glosson, "Presidential Briefing Slides," n.d., with atch slides, n.d., CENTAF records; Lt. Gen. Horner intvw, Mar 4, 1992; and Lt. Gen. Horner intvw, Dec 3, 1991. On Maj. Gen. Johnston's briefings, see also *U.S. News & World Report*, *Triumph Without Victory*, 156, 166; and Schwarzkopf, *Autobiography*, 358–361.

19. Schwarzkopf, *Autobiography*, 362; CMH draft, 188–189; ARCENT hist, 42; "Campaign Plan Chronology."

20. "Campaign Plan Chronology"; ARCENT hist, 43.

21. "Campaign Plan Chronology"; CMH draft, 189; Schwarzkopf, *Autobiography*, 367.

22. ARCENT hist, 45–49; CMH draft, 231.

23. ARCENT hist, 45, 57. See also "Campaign Plan Chronology."

24. ARCENT hist, 59; "Campaign Plan Chronology."

25. "Campaign Plan Chronology"; ARCENT hist, 59–60.

26. "Bush Sends New Units to Gulf to Provide 'Offensive' Option: U.S. Force Could Reach 380,000," *New York Times*, Oct 26, 1990. For some Air Staff perspectives on the force increase, see memo, Maj. Gen. Robert M. Alexander to Gen. Loh, [no subject], n.d. [Oct 25, 1990], "Plan—Phases 2/3" file, Checkmate files; memo, Col. John Warden to Lt. Gen. Adams, "Reference Our Conversation This Morning, Some Additional Thoughts," Nov 8, 1990, [unboxed], CENTAF records.

27. CMH draft, 268; ARCENT hist, 66.

28. CMH draft, 204.

29. ARCENT hist, 68–69; "Campaign Plan Chronology."

30. "Campaign Plan Chronology."

31. Maj. Gen. Glosson intvw, Dec 12, 1991.

32. See, among many examples, Lt. Col. Baptiste intvw; msg, USAEUR to 9 AF/CC, "Army/Air Force Doctrinal Issues," 1445Z Nov 5, 1991, Lt. Gen. Horner's Desert Storm files, HQ 9 AF/CC; and SSS, HQ 9 AF/DOXR, Oct 21, 1991, with atch summary papers and memos, Lt. Gen. Horner's Desert Storm files, HQ 9 AF/CC.

33. ARCENT hist, 75–76; "Cam-

paign Plan Chronology"; CMH draft, 250. On General Schwarzkopf's meeting on November 14 with his corps and division commanders, see also Schwarzkopf, *Autobiography*, 380–384.

34. ARCENT hist, 76; Schwarzkopf, *Autobiography*, 355.

35. ARCENT hist, 76.

36. Col. Warden brfg; Thompson memo; Lt. Gen. Horner intvw, Mar 3, 1991.

37. "Campaign Plan Chronology." See also ARCENT hist, 81.

38. "Campaign Plan Chronology"; ARCENT hist, 82.

39. CMH draft, 252; ARCENT hist, 86.

40. Brig. Gen. Hall memo, with atch note, "30 Jan KTO Planning Meeting," Jan 28, 1991.

41. Brfg, CENTAF/CC, "Theater Air Campaign," Feb 9, 1991, "Theater Campaign Slide/Brief" notebook, Box 7, CENTAF records; Lt. Gen. Horner intvw, Mar 4, 1992. In this interview, General Horner emphasized the "Push CAS" portion of his briefing.

42. ARCENT hist, 94–95; msg, US-CINCCENT/CCCC to COMUSCENT-AF/CC et al., "Preparing the Battlefield for Ground Operations," 0655Z Feb 12, 1991, "KTO/Republican Guards" file, Checkmate files.

43. Rpt, CENTAF/ADO to CENT-AF/DO, "After Action Report—Exercise Imminent Thunder," n.d., and msg, USCINCCENT to COMUSARCENT et al., "Exercise Imminent Thunder," 0001Z Nov 25, 1990, both in File 0882499, "Exercise Imminent Thunder," Roll 23993, CAFH Desert Shield/Desert Storm microfilm collection; Gen. Schwarzkopf brfg; Friedman, *Desert Victory*, 208. See also brfg, HQ COMUSCENTAF, "Exercise Imminent Thunder," n.d., File 0882499, "Exercise Imminent Thunder," Roll 23993, CAFH

Desert Shield/Desert Storm microfilm collection.

44. "Marines to Hold Mock Raid on Saudi Beaches," *Los Angeles Times*, Nov 14, 1991; Gen. Schwarzkopf brfg.

45. CSAF brief, Feb 25, 1991; Friedman, *Desert Victory*, photograph of battle map and accompanying cutline located between pp 216 and 217. In February 1991, a major news magazine published an accurate description of the general features of the actual attack plan, but by then there had been much speculation about the offensive, and this prediction fell among a jumble of other, inaccurate conjectures offered by the Western press. Schwarzkopf, *Autobiography*, 440.

46. CMH draft, 270, 271; William G. Pagonis, *Moving Mountains: Lessons in Leadership and Logistics from the Gulf War* (Boston: Harvard Business School Press, 1992), 146.

47. ARCENT hist, 97. The number given here for the distance covered by the XVIII Airborne Corps follows the CMH draft, 271, and Pagonis, *Moving Mountains*, 146.

48. Pagonis, *Moving Mountains*, 136; Lt. Gen. Horner's CINCCENT notes, 1900L Feb 22, 1991; Lt. Gen. Horner's daily comments, Feb 24, 1991, 63. On the shift west, see also maps, situation as of G–33, Jan 22, 1991, and G–19, Feb 5, 1991, in "100-Hour Ground War."

49. Schwarzkopf, *Autobiography*, 392; Gen. Schwarzkopf brfg.

50. Lieutenant General Pagonis made this same point in *Moving Mountains*, 137.

51. Schwarzkopf, *Autobiography*, 416; Pagonis, *Moving Mountains*, 145; "Air Weather Service Contribution," 30; msg, CINCCENT to AIG 904 et al., "SITREP," 2115Z Jan 25, 1991, "CINCCENT SITREPs" file, Check-

mate files; msg, COMUSARCENT to AIG 11743 et al., "SITREP," 0300Z Jan 20, 1991, Box 22, CENTAF collection, HQ TAC/HO archives.

52. "Air Weather Service Contribution," 31; Pagonis, *Moving Mountains*, 146.

53. Pagonis, *Moving Mountains*, 146.

54. Gen. Schwarzkopf brfg; Col. Wingfield, quoted in special study, SMSgt. James R. Ciborski, 1630 TAW(P)/HO, "History of Airlift in the Desert: Circumventing the Iraqis," May 23, 1991, 26, HQ MAC/HO archives (hereafter, Ciborski Study); Col. William D. Peters, Jr., quoted in Ciborski study, 24; "Iraqi Generals Perspective"; CMH draft, 273.

55. CMH draft, 270; ARCENT hist, 97; Gen. Schwarzkopf brfg.

56. Memo, AF/XOXX (Capt. Montgomery) to AF/XOXWG (Lt. Col. Kuehl), "Air Force Historical Symposium, 'Two Years After: The Air Force in the Gulf War,'" Apr 30, 1993, CAFH historians' working files.

57. Ciborski study, xi; "Air Weather Service Contribution," 30–31.

58. Ciborski study, 22–24.

59. Ibid., 25, 112.

60. Ibid., 25, 129.

61. "Air Weather Service Contribution," 30–31.

62. Ciborski study, 24, 112.

63. Ibid., 25.

64. Ibid., 25, 112.

65. Contingency hist rpt, 1630 TAW(P), Feb 24–Mar 2, 1991, HQ MAC/HO archives; Ciborski study, 24, 112, 122.

66. Ciborski study, 24.

67. Ibid., 25, 112, 114–115.

68. Ibid., 112, 114–115, 116.

69. Msg, 1610 ALDP/COMALF to USCENTAF/CC et al., "Desert Shield COMALF SitRep 170," 1200Z Jan 28,

1991, "16/0001Z Jan–31/2359Z Jan 91" file, 1610 ALDP SitReps collection, HQ MAC/HO archives; msg, 1650 TAW(P)/CV to HQ AFRES/OC/DO et al., "First Combat Airdrop and Operating Milestone Reached," 1310Z Feb 20, 1991, "Incoming Messages 24546–25249, 15 Feb–22 Feb 91" file, Desert Shield/Desert Storm 1610 ALD(P) message collection, HQ MAC/HO archives; Ciborski study, App J, 173; Contingency hist rpt, 1630 TAW(P), Feb 24–Mar 2, 1991, HQ MAC/HO archives; Schwarzkopf, *Autobiography*, 434.

70. Msg, XVIII Airborne Corps/G3/G4 to COMUSARCENT/G3/G4 et al., "XVIII Abn Corps Intratheater Airlift Sustainment Requirements," 1050Z Feb 8, 1991, "Incoming Messages 23645–24545, 7 Feb–15 Feb 91" file, Desert Shield/Desert Storm 1610 ALD(P) message collection, HQ MAC/HO archives; ARCENT hist, map located between pp 97 and 98. On the Tapline Road, see also Schwarzkopf, *Autobiography*, 416, and Pagonis, *Moving Mountains*, 122.

71. Ciborski study, 129; Final Report, 372. See also Contingency hist rpt, 1630 TAW(P), Feb 10–Feb 16, 1991, HQ MAC/HO archives.

72. Msg, 1650 TAW(P)/CV to HQ AFRES/OC/DO et al., "First Combat Airdrop and Operating Milestone Reached," 1310Z Feb 20, 1991, "Incoming Messages 24546–25249, 15 Feb–22 Feb 91" file, Desert Shield/Desert Storm 1610 ALD(P) message collection, HQ MAC/HO archives.

73. Maj. Gen. Glosson intvw, Dec 12, 1991; point paper, HQ SAC/DOOB, Nov 30, 1990, historians' working files, HQ SAC/HO; msg, Comdr. USAEC/ATZT-SSO to HQ SAC/DO et al., "Joint Obstacle Breaching," 1121Z Dec 3, 1990, historians' working files, HQ SAC/HO. See also

msg, HQ SAC/DO to 8 AF/CV et al., 1900Z Dec 21, 1990, historians' working files, HQ SAC/HO, and SSS, HQ SAC/DOOB, n.d., historians' working files, HQ SAC/HO.

74. Msg, USCINCCENT/CCJ3 to COMUSCENTAF et al., 1817Z Feb 1, 1991, HQ USCENTCOM/CCHO working files; Turner notes, entries for 1700L Feb 6, 1991, 1700L Feb 7, 1991, and 1700L Feb 21, 1991; summary paper, HQ STRATFOR, "B–52 Breach Results," Feb 24, 1991, File 0882434, "B–52 Support of MARCENT Operations (Breaches)," Roll 23988, CAFH Desert Shield/Desert Storm microfilm collection. See also msg, COMUSMARCENT to COMUSCENTAF, "B–52 Support of MARCENT Operations," 1207Z Feb 19, 1991, CAFH Desert Shield/Desert Storm microfilm collection.

75. Summary paper, HQ STRATFOR, "B–52 Breach Results," Feb 24, 1991, File 0882434, "B–52 Support of MARCENT Operations (Breaches)," Roll 23988, CAFH Desert Shield/Desert Storm microfilm collection.

76. Capt. Hawkins intvw; intvw, Brig. Gen. Patrick P. Caruana, STRATFOR/CC and 17 AD(P)/CC, with TSgt. Frederick Hosterman, Mar 15, 1991; STRATFOR After Action Report.

77. Lt. Gen. Horner intvw, Mar 4, 1992; Maj. Gen. Glosson intvw, Dec 12, 1991; Maj. Gen. Olsen intvw; Lt. Col. Baptiste intvw.

78. Bergeron hist, 33; Ray Bowers, *Tactical Airlift* (Washington, D.C.: Office of Air Force History, 1983), 394; Walker notes, entry for 0102 Feb 7, 1991; msg, USCINCCENT/CCJ3 to COMUSCENTAF et al., 0815Z Feb 6, 1991, historian's working files, HQ CENTCOM/CCHO. See also memo, AF/XOOTM to AF/XOOT et al., "15,000 GP Bomb," Jan 25, 1991, "War Termi-

nation—Emergency Strike Plan" file, Checkmate files. During the late 1980s, General Larry D. Welch, Air Force Chief of Staff, 1986–1990, discussed the problems caused by the "Daisy Cutter" in Vietnam with Mr. Jacob Neufeld, Chief of the Office of Air Force History's Air Staff Branch.

79. Bergeron hist, 33, 34; Michael, *Chronology*, 348, 354; point paper, AF/XOOTU, "Air Force Special Operations Forces," Jan 30, 1991, "29–30 Jan 91 (Day 14)" file, Checkmate files.

80. Bergeron hist.

81. "Feedback from SecDef/CJCS Meeting"; "Campaign Plan Chronology"; msg, COMUSARCENT Main/DT to USCINCCENT/CCJ3/CCCC et al., "COMUSARCENT SitRep D+ 32," 0300Z Feb 18, 1991, "KTO/Republican Guards" file, Checkmate files; "Air Support" paper. For MARCENT's point of view on this issue, see, for example, msg, COMUSMARCENT to CINCCENT, "Marine Aviation," 1050Z Jan 28, 1991, MSgt. Theodore J. Turner files.

82. Lt. Col. Deptula intvw, Nov 29, 1991; memo, Brig. Gen. Buster C. Glosson, Dir Plans, to CENTCOM J3 Plans, "Theater Campaign Strategy Assessment," Feb 15, 1991, "War Termination—Emergency Strike Plan" file, Checkmate files; marginalia on "Air Support" paper.

83. Maj. Sweeney intvw, Mar 3, 1991; "Air Support" paper.

84. "Feedback from SecDef/CJCS Meeting." See also Lt. Col. Deptula intvw, Jan 8, 1992; Lt. Col. Baptiste intvw; and Lt. Gen. Horner intvw, Mar 4, 1992.

85. Brig. Gen. Hall memo; "Feedback from SecDef/CJCS Meeting"; Lt. Gen. Horner intvw, Mar 4, 1992.

86. "Air Support" paper; Maj. Sweeney intvw, Mar 3, 1991; Brig.

Gen. Hall memo.

87. Col. Cox intvw; Brig. Gen. Muellner intvw; Maj. Gen. Corder intvw.

88. ATO brfg; Lt. Col. Baptiste intvw; Final Report, 375.

89. Msg, USCINCCENT to COM-USCENTAF et al., "Air Apportionment Planning," 1650Z Jan 31, 1991, in TACC log; Lt. Col. Baptiste intvw.

90. Memo, Lt. Gen. C. A. H. Waller, CENTCOM Dep CINC, to COM-USARCENT et al., "Air Apportionment Guidance," Feb 15, 1991, "KTO/Republican Guards" file, Checkmate files.

91. Final Report, 375; Lt. Gen. Horner intvw, Mar 4, 1992; Maj. Gen. Glosson intvw, Dec 12, 1991; Lt. Col. Baptiste intvw.

92. Lt. Gen. Horner intvw, Mar 4, 1992; Dr. Thompson's trip rpt, 1. See also Maj. Gen. Olsen intvw and Lt. Gen. Horner testimony, 247.

93. Lt. Col. Baptiste intvw; Maj. Gen. Olsen intvw; Lt. Gen. Horner testimony, 240.

94. Lt. Gen. Horner intvw, Mar 4, 1992. The CENTAF commander also drew an interesting contrast between the VII and XVIII Corps in this interview.

95. Lt. Gen. Horner intvw, Mar 4, 1992; Col. Reavey intvw. See also Col. Cox intvw.

96. Maj. Gen. Corder intvw; Col. Reavey intvw; "Air Support" paper. See also Lt. Gen. Horner intvw, Dec 3, 1991.

97. "Air Support" paper; Maj. Gen. Glosson intvw, Dec 12, 1991.

98. Brig. Gen. Hall memo; msg, USCINCCENT/CCCC to COMUS-CENTAF/CC et al., "Preparing the Battlefield for Ground Operations," 0655Z Feb 12, 1991, "KTO/Republican Guards" file, Checkmate files; Maj. Sweeney intvw, Mar 3, 1991.

99. Msg, USCINCCENT to COM-USCENTAF et al., "Air Apportionment Planning," 1650Z Jan 31, 1991, in TACC log; Maj. Gen. Glosson intvw, Dec 12, 1991; Lt. Gen. Horner intvw, Mar 4, 1992.

100. Lt. Gen. Horner intvw, Mar 4, 1992.

101. Lt. Gen. Horner intvw, Dec 3, 1991; ConOps for C^2, 4, 9; Col. Winstel intvw.

102. Lt. Gen. Horner intvw, Mar 4, 1992; ConOps for C^2, 9; Lt. Gen. Horner intvw, Dec 3, 1991; msg, USCENT-AF/DO to 682 ASOC Deployed/CC/DO, "CAS and Command and Control," 1600Z Jan 13, 1991, Box 85, CENTAF collection, HQ TAC/HO archives.

103. ConOps for C^2, 4.

104. Brfg, "Air Support for the Ground Campaign," n.d., Box 4, CENTAF records. See also ConOps for C^2, 5-i and 5-in.

105. Brfg, "Air Support for the Ground Campaign," n.d., Box 4, CENTAF records; brfg, 23 TASS, "OA–10 Concept of Operations," n.d., Lt. Gen. Horner's Desert Storm files, HQ 9 AF/CC.

106. Rpt, Col. David A. Sawyer, 23 TFW/CC, "CAS Guidance," in Battle Staff Directives, 354/23 TFW, HQ TAC/HO archives.

107. Lt. Col. Baptiste intvw; msg, USCENTAF/DO to 682 ASOC Deployed/CC/DO, "CAS and Command and Control," 1600Z Jan 13, 1991, Box 85, CENTAF collection, HQ TAC/HO archives; Lt. Gen. Horner intvw, Mar 4, 1992.

108. CINC's War Book input, "CENTCOM Personnel Status: Daily, as of 0001L, 24 Feb 91," "JFC East Operations," "JFC North Operations," "I MEF Operations," "VII Corps Operations," and "XVIII Corps Operations," Feb 24, 1991 P.M.; map, H-Hour/0400, Feb 24, 1991, in "100-Hour Ground

War." For the composition of JFC–N and JFC–E and their status on the third day of the ground campaign, see CINC's War Book input, "JFC East" and "JFC North," Feb 26, 1991 A.M.

109. CINC's War Book input, "North Arabian Sea/Gulf 'Zulu' (TF 154)," and Red Sea BF 'Yankee' (TF 155)," Feb 24, 1991 P.M.

110. Michael, *Chronology*, 235; *GWAPS*, Vol V, Part 1, "A Statistical Compendium," 53, 55–56.

111. *GWAPS*, Vol V, Part 1, "A Statistical Compendium," 53; Michael, *Chronology*, 235.

112. Ltr, Col. Raymond Huot to Lt. Gen. Horner, [no subject], Feb 12, 1991; "Daily Notes"; msg, Am Embassy Riyadh to SecState, "Saddam's War: Riyadh Sit Rep No. 41," 1027Z Feb 24, 1991, "State Department Message" file, HQ USCENTCOM/CCHO working files.

113. Col. Reavey intvw; Schwarzkopf, *Autobiography*, 432; msg, USCINCCENT/CCJ2 to AIG 7861 et al., "USCENTCOM Collateral Intelligence DISum No. 197 for the Period 22/1500Z to 23/1459Z Feb 1991," 2330Z Feb 23, 1991, File 9.0, "Intelligence," Desert Storm working archives, HQ SAC/HO. On intelligence overestimates

of the Iraqi forces, see also Col. Winstel intvw.

114. Maj. Gen. Olsen intvw; Schwarzkopf, *Autobiography*, 439; Gen. Schwarzkopf brfg.

115. Msg, DIA/DI–6B to USCENTCOM Rear/CCJ2 et al., "Military Situation Summary as of 24/0700Z Feb 1991," 1401Z Feb 24, 1991, "DIA Feb 91" file, HQ USCENTCOM/CCHO working files; msg, CINCCENT/CCJ2–IW to ALTAX et al., "USCENTCOM I&W Wartime Indicator Report," 0800Z Feb 11, 1991, "KTO/Republican Guards" file, Checkmate files; msg, DIA/J2I–6C to AIG 92 et al., 21[third digit illegible]9Z Feb 18, 1991; Lt. Gen. Horner's daily comments, Feb 20, 1991, 54.

116. Schwarzkopf, *Autobiography*, 435; Lt. Gen. Horner intvw, Mar 4, 1992.

117. "'One Last Chance,' Now 'The Final Phase,'" *New York Times*, Feb 24, 1991; msg, USCINCCENT/CCCC to USCENTAF et al., 0750Z Feb 23, 1991, MSgt. Turner files.

118. USCINCCENT msg 0100Z Feb 24, 1991, quoted in brfg slide, "USCINCCENT Message," CSAF brief, Feb 24, 1991.

Chapter Seven

1. Summary paper, "Operation Desert Storm [Weather] History, 22 Feb 91–28 Feb 91," atch to History, 33 TFW (Provisional), Feb 24–Mar 2, 1991, Unit Histories collection, HQ TAC/HO (hereafter, 33 TFW Weather); "Gulf War Weather," Sec 3, 87.

2. 33 TFW Weather; "Gulf War Weather."

3. 33 TFW Weather.

4. Lt. Gen. Horner's daily comments, Feb 24, 1991, 64; msg, DCO to All WOCs, [no subject], 1827Z Feb 24, 1991, in TACC log; Maj. Gen. Olsen intvw; Maj. Gen. Corder intvw.

5. Gen. Schwarzkopf brfg; msg, USCINCCENT to AIG 904 et al., "SitRep USCINCCENT," 2115Z Feb 24, 1991, Box 23, CINCCENT SitRep collection, HQ TAC/HO archives.

6. Gen. Schwarzkopf brfg; map, H-Hour/0400, Feb 24, 1991, in "100-Hour Ground War"; Lt. Gen. William M. Keys, "Rolling With the 2d Marine Division," *U.S. Naval Institute Proceedings*, Nov 1991, 79.

7. Keys, "Rolling With the 2d Marine Division," 79; Final Report, 389, App L, 13; Pagonis, *Moving Mountains*, 153. As the United States forces captured prisoners, they registered them and then transferred them to Saudi custody. Final Report, App L, 3.

8. Gen. Schwarzkopf brfg; ARCENT hist, 107 and map on following unnumbered page.

9. Gen. Schwarzkopf brfg; map, H+12/1600, Feb 24, 1991, in "100-Hour Ground War"; ltr, Maj. Paul J. Jacobsmeyer to Col. K. Hamburger, Mar 7, 1991, historians' working files, CMH; CMH draft, 305–306. See also msg, CINCCENT/CCJ3 to COMUSARCENT et al., "FragO 021 to USCINCCENT OpOrd 91–001 for Operation Desert Storm," 1400Z Feb 24, 1991, historians' working files, USCENTCOM/CCHO archives.

10. Gen. Schwarzkopf brfg.

11. Gen. Schwarzkopf brfg; CMH draft, 301; msg, USCINCCENT/CCJ2 to AIG 7861 et al., "USCENTCOM Collateral Intelligence DISum No. 198 for the Period 23/1500Z to 24/1459Z Feb 91," 2330Z Feb 24, 1991, File 9.0, "Intelligence," Desert Storm working archives, HQ SAC/HO.

12. Final Report, 143; Gen. McPeak brfg; TACC log, Brig. Gen. Glosson's entry, Feb 25, 1991 [no date-time group specified].

13. CSAF brief, Feb 24, 1991.

14. Chart, USAFTAWC/INS, "Details on Damaged USAF Aircraft," Aug 6, 1991, Lt. Gen. Horner's Desert Storm files, HQ 9 AF/CC (hereafter, Damaged Aircraft chart).

15. TACC log, entries for 0635Z and 0938Z Feb 24, 1991. See also TACC log, entry for 0725Z Feb 24, 1991.

16. TACC log, entries for 0710Z and 1525Z Feb 24, 1991.

17. Ibid., entries for 0710Z and 2100Z Feb 24, 1991; msg, DCO to All WOCs, "Fratricide," 1410Z Feb 24, 1991, in TACC log. On the kill-box episode involving the VII Corps, see also TACC log, "Intel Debrief" entry, Feb 25, 1991.

18. TACC log, entry for 1200Z Feb 25, 1991; Lt. Gen. Horner's daily comments, Feb 25, 1991, 66.

19. Gen. Schwarzkopf brfg; TACC log, entry for 0800Z Feb 25, 1991; Myatt, "1st Marine Division in the Attack," 72; ARCENT hist, 117; "Burning Wells Turn Kuwait Into Land of Oily Blackness," *New York Times*, Mar 6, 1991.

20. ARCENT hist, 117. See also Keys, "Rolling With the 2d Marine Division," 79.

21. Lt. Gen. Horner's CINCCENT notes, 0900 Feb 25, 1991.

22. Map, H+36/1600 Feb 25, 1991, in "100-Hour Ground War"; CMH draft, 313.

23. Schwarzkopf, *Autobiography*, 455–456, 460–464.

24. CMH draft, 314; ARCENT hist, 115.

25. TACC log, entries for 1030Z and 1200Z Feb 25, 1991.

26. Msg, DIA/DI–6B to USCENTCOM Rear/CCJ2 et al., 1401Z Feb 25, 1991, "DIA Feb 91" file, historians' working files, HQ CENTCOM/CCHO; TACC log, entry for 0750Z Feb 25, 1991.

27. ARCENT hist, 115; TACC log, entry for 1013Z Feb 25, 1991; map, H+36/1600 Feb 25, 1991, in "100-Hour Ground War." See also Walker notes, first entry for Feb 25, 1991.

28. ARCENT hist, 113, 114; map, H+36/1600 Feb 25, 1991, in "100-Hour Ground War."

29. *U.S. News & World Report, Triumph Without Victory*, 327.

30. "Gulf War Weather," Sec 3, 90–91; Lt. Gen. Horner's CENTAF notes, [0730], Feb 26, 1991.

31. TACC log, entry for 1200Z Feb 25, 1991; Final Report, 143.

32. CINC's War Book input, intel summary, 26 Feb P.M.; Gen. McPeak brfg.

33. Point paper, AF/CSS-Exec, "SitRep Summary Operation Desert Storm: 25 Feb 91, Day 40," Feb 25, 1991, "24–25 Feb 91 (Day 40)" file, Checkmate files; CSAF brief, Feb 25, 1991.

34. CSAF brief, Feb 25, 1991.

35. Chart, "Daily Aircraft Losses," "26 Feb 91" file, Lt. Gen. Horner's Desert Storm files, HQ 9 AF/CC (hereafter, Daily Aircraft Losses chart); TACC log, entry for 1030Z Feb 25, 1991.

36. TACC log, "Intel Debrief" entry, Feb 25, 1991; Walker notes, entry for 0418 Feb 25, 1991.

37. TACC log, entry for 1200Z Feb 25, 1991.

38. Col. Sawyer ltr.

39. "A–10 Pilots Find Iraqi 'Hot Spot,' Get Record Tank Kill," *Air Force Times*, Mar 11, 1991; TACC log, "Intel Debrief" entry, Feb 25, 1991; msg, 354 TFW/CC to TACC, [no subject], 1334Z Feb 25, 1991, in TACC log, "Intel Debrief" entry, Feb 25, 1991.

40. TACC log, entry for 2100Z Feb 25, 1991; Vinas special study, 35. See also Maj. Gen. Olsen intvw.

41. Col. Cox intvw; Brig. Gen. Muellner intvw; Gen. McPeak brfg.

42. TACC log, entries for 2034Z, 2100Z, and 2235Z Feb 25, 1991; Col. Cox intvw.

43. On the mining, see TACC log, entry for 2100Z Feb 25, 1991; Vinas special study, 32.

44. Col. Cox intvw; TACC log, entry for 2100Z Feb 25, 1991.

45. Col. Cox intvw. See also Walker notes, entry for 0109 Feb 26, 1991.

46. Brig. Gen. Muellner intvw.

47. Maj. Gen. Olsen intvw; Vinas special study, 32, 35–36.

48. Vinas special study, 36; TACC log, entries for 0037Z and 0100Z Feb 26, 1991. See also Walker notes, entry for 0303 Feb 26, 1991.

49. Vinas special study, 36.

50. Col. Cox intvw; Vinas special study, 32, 36.

51. ARCENT hist, 122, 123; Gen. Schwarzkopf brfg. See also TACC log, entry for 0935L Feb 26, 1991.

52. ARCENT hist, 122; Gen. Schwarzkopf brfg; map, H+64/2000 Feb 26, 1991, in "100-Hour Ground War." After the conflict, General Schwarzkopf characterized the commander of the 24th Infantry Division (Mechanized) as "the most aggressive and successful ground commander of the war." Schwarzkopf, *Autobiography*, cutline with photograph located between pp 338 and 339.

53. MR, AF/XOXW, "Reports of progress in theater," 2330L Feb 26, 1991, "KTO/Republican Guards" file, Checkmate files (hereafter, "Reports of progress"); TACC log, entry for 2200Z Feb 26, 1991. The vehicle's nicknames derived from HMMWV, the acronym for its full designation: High-Mobility Multipurpose Wheeled Vehicle.

54. Lt. Gen. Horner's daily comments, Feb 26, 1991, 69; "Reports of progress"; Schwarzkopf, *Autobiography*, 462.

55. ARCENT hist, 119–120, 121; Lt. Gen. Horner's CENTAF notes, [0730] Feb 26, 1991; TACC log, entry for 2243[Z] Feb 26, 1991. On the end of

the Tawakalna Division, see also Walker notes, entry for 0144 Feb 27, 1991, and Schwarzkopf, *Autobiography*, 466.

56. Schwarzkopf, *Autobiography*, 466.

57. Summary paper, "Desert Sabre Operations Summary," n.d., historians' working files, CMH; ARCENT hist, 120.

58. Rpt, CENTAF Friendly Casualty Report, Incident 9, "Fratricide" file, Box 76, CENTAF collection, HQ TAC/HO archives; MR, n.d., CENTAF collection, HQ TAC/HO; "Human Error Blamed for 2 'Friendly Fire' Incidents," *Air Force Times*, Mar 18, 1991; Lt. Gen. Horner intvw, Mar 4, 1992. See also TACC log, entries for 1349Z and 2300Z Feb 26, 1991. For the British commander's account of this tragedy, see General Sir Peter de la Billiere, *Storm Command: A Personal Account of the Gulf War* (London: Harper Collins, 1992), 291–296.

59. ARCENT hist, 120; "Reports of progress"; Gen. Schwarzkopf testimony, 316.

60. ARCENT hist, 121.

61. Schwarzkopf, *Autobiography*, 457; ARCENT hist, 124; Myatt, "1st Marine Division in the Attack," 74.

62. ARCENT hist, 124; Myatt, "1st Marine Division in the Attack," 75.

63. Keys, "Rolling With the 2d Marine Division," 79–80; ARCENT hist, 124; TACC log, entry for 1127Z Feb 26, 1991; "Reports of progress."

64. TACC log, entry for 1127Z Feb 26, 1991; Keys, "Rolling With the 2d Marine Division," 80.

65. CMH draft, 321–322; Vinas special study, 32; Schwarzkopf, *Autobiography*, 468. See also Blackwell, *Thunder in the Desert*, 4.

66. Dr. Thompson's trip rpt.

67. ARCENT hist, 124–125.

68. "Gulf War Weather," Sec 3, 95.

69. Final Report, 143. The twenty-sixth also saw the largest daily total of sorties for the entire air campaign. Final Report, 143.

70. Point paper, AF/CSS-Exec, "SitRep Summary Operation Desert Storm: 26 Feb 91, Day 41," Feb 26, 1991, "25–26 Feb 91 (Day 41)" file, Checkmate files.

71. Damaged Aircraft chart.

72. TACC log, entry for 0300Z Feb 26, 1991.

73. "Reports of progress."

74. Lt. Gen. Horner intvw, Mar 4, 1992; Lt. Col. Baptiste intvw; map, "Forecast FSCLs," n.d. "24 Feb 91" file, Lt. Gen. Horner's Desert Storm files, HQ 9 AF/CC.

75. Rpt, COMUSCENTAF, "Air Defense and Airspace Control Procedures for Operation Desert Shield," Jan 8, 1991, Box 13, CENTAF records (hereafter, "Air Defense and Airspace Control Procedures"); Col. Reavy intvw. See also Lt. Gen. Horner intvw, Mar 4, 1992.

76. "Air Defense and Airspace Control Procedures"; Lt. Col. Baptiste intvw. See also Lt. Gen. Horner intvw, Mar 4, 1992, and Maj. Gen. Olsen intvw.

77. Msg, USCINCCENT/CCJ3 to COMUSMARCENT/G3 et al., "Fire Support Coordination Measures and Fratricide," 0001Z Feb 22, 1991; Lt. Col. Baptiste intvw; Walker notes, entry for 0506 Feb 24, 1991.

78. TACC log, entry for 1700[Z] Feb 26, 1991.

79. TACC log, entry for 0205Z Feb 27, 1991; Walker notes, entry for 0457 Feb 27, 1991.

80. Col. Reavey intvw; Lt. Gen. Horner intvw, Mar 4, 1992.

81. Lt. Gen. Horner intvw, Mar 4, 1992; Burton notes, entry for 0900 Feb 27, 1991; Turner notes, entry for 1645L

Feb 27, 1991. See also Col. Reavey intvw. Other references to the FSCL controversies can be found in TACC log, entry for 0250Z Feb 27, 1991, and in Walker notes, entry for 0352 Feb 26, 1991, and 255n.

82. "Gulf War Weather"; CMH draft, 327.

83. Map, H+86/1800 Feb 27, 1991, in "100-Hour Ground War"; CMH draft, 323–325.

84. Map, H+86/1800 Feb 27, 1991, in "100-Hour Ground War"; ARCENT hist, 129.

85. CMH draft, 326.

86. Map, H+86/1800 Feb 27, 1991, in "100-Hour Ground War"; ARCENT hist, 125–126.

87. CMH draft, 327–329; ARCENT hist, 129.

88. Keys, "Rolling With the 2d Marine Division," 80; ARCENT hist, 126.

89. Schwarzkopf, *Autobiography*, 469; Gen. Schwarzkopf brfg.

90. Gen. Schwarzkopf brfg; Final Report, 143.

91. Msg, NGB/CSS to AIG 7316/CC/DO et al., 2101Z Mar 1, 1991, "Lessons Learned" file, Box 25, HQ TAC/HO archives; Col. Winstel intvw.

92. Point paper, AF/CSS-Exec, "SitRep Summary Operation Desert Storm: 27 Feb 91, Day 42," Feb 27, 1991, "26–27 Feb 91 (Day 42)" file, Checkmate files.

93. Daily Aircraft Losses chart; TACC log, entry for 0357Z Feb 27, 1991.

94. TACC log, entry for 0600Z Feb 27, 1991; Daily Aircraft Losses chart; list, CENTAF/DP, "Operation Desert Storm Reported USAF Casualties as of 6 Mar 91," File 0269629, "CENTAF/DP Casualty Statistics," Roll 10265, CAFH Desert Shield/Desert Storm microfilm collection; Damaged Aircraft chart.

95. Daily Aircraft Losses chart; list, CENTAF/DP, "Operation Desert Storm Reported USAF Casualties as of 6 Mar 91," File 0269629, "CENTAF/DP Casualty Statistics," Roll 10265, CAFH Desert Shield/Desert Storm microfilm collection.

96. Daily Aircraft Losses chart.

97. Damaged Aircraft chart.

98. TACC log, entry for 2245Z Feb 27, 1991.

99. Msg, CENTAF/DO to All Unit Commanders, [no subject], 2302Z Feb 27, 1991, in TACC log.

100. TACC log, entry for 0230Z Feb 28, 1991. See also msg, USCINC-CENT to COMUSCENTAF et al., 0850Z Feb 13, 1991, Folder 3, Box 11C, CENTAF records. The overwhelming emphasis of the pre-ceasefire planning was on Phase I, rather than on Phase IV, targets. See summary paper, AF/XOXW, "Emergency Strike Plan," [Jan 27, 1991], "War Termination—Emergency Strike Plan" file, Checkmate files; memo, Lt. Col. David A. Deptula to Lt. Gen. Horner, "Air Strategy," Feb 21, 1991, Checkmate files; Lt. Gen. Horner intvw, Mar 4, 1992.

101. TACC log, entry for 0230Z Feb 28, 1991.

102. ARCENT hist, 131; map, H+100/0800 Feb 28, 1991, in "100-Hour Ground War."

103. ARCENT hist, 131. See also Schwarzkopf, *Autobiography*, 469.

104. ARCENT hist, 131–132. See also Schwarzkopf, *Autobiography*, 470.

105. "Gulf War Weather," Sec 3, 100; point paper, AF/CSS-Exec, "SitRep Summary Operation Desert Storm: 28 Feb 91, Day 43," Feb 28, 1991, "27–28 Feb 91 (Day 43)" file, Checkmate files.

106. CMH draft, 331.

107. Col. Reavey intvw; DD/TWP brfg; Final Report, App L, 2.

108. TACC log, entries for 0050Z and 0242 Feb 28, 1991.

109. "Bush, Cheney Dispute General on End of Fighting," *Washington Post*, Mar 28, 1991; Schwarzkopf, *Autobiography*, 469–470. See also "Bush Halts Offensive Combat; Kuwait Freed, Iraqis Crushed," *New York Times*, Feb 28, 1991.

110. Msg, USCINCCENT to COMUSARCENT et al., "FragO 028 to USCINCCENT OpOrd 91–001 for Operation Desert Storm," 0500Z Feb 28, 1991, historians' working files, HQ USCENTCOM/CCHO.

111. TACC log, entries for 0801L and 1635L Feb 28, 1991; ARCENT hist, 136–137.

112. TACC log, entry for 02/0450.

113. ARCENT hist, 136–137; msg, USCINCCENT to COMUSARCENT et al., "FragO 028 to USCINCCENT OpOrd 91–001 for Operation Desert Storm," 0500Z Feb 28, 1991, historians' working files, HQ USCENTCOM/ CCHO.

114. ARCENT hist, 137; TACC log, entries for 0530Z and 1425[Z] Mar 2, 1991.

115. ARCENT hist, 137; TACC log, entry for 1425[Z] Mar 2, 1991. See also excerpt, from msg, CENTAF/IN, 2310Z Mar 2, 1991, File 0882479, "2 Mar Tank Battle," Roll 23989, CAFH Desert Shield/Desert Storm microfilm collection; and Schwarzkopf, *Autobiography*, 478–479.

116. TACC log, entry for 0745Z Mar 2, 1991.

117. Schwarzkopf, *Autobiography*, 479.

118. Ibid., 472, 474–478; ARCENT hist, 136; TACC log, entry for 1520Z Mar 1, 1991.

119. Msg, USCINCCENT/CCJ3 to COMUSARCENT et al., 1500Z Mar 1, 1991, HQ USCENTCOM/CCHO working files; TACC log, entries for 1855Z and 2100Z Mar 1, 1991.

120. Pagonis, *Moving Mountains*, 155, 196; TACC log, entry for 2310Z Mar 1, 1991.

121. Interim Report, ch 4, pp 9–10; Schwarzkopf, *Autobiography*, 484–485, 488–490.

122. "Bush, Cheney Dispute General," *Washington Post*, Mar 28, 1991. General Schwarzkopf treated these and related issues from the perspective of more than a year later in his autobiography (*Autobiography*, pp 497–500).

123. *U.S. News & World Report*, *Triumph Without Victory*, 402–403, 412. On Saddam's continued resistance to the UN resolutions, see, for example, "U.S. Asks U.N. to Accelerate Weapons Inspections in Iraq," *Washington Post*, Jul 28, 1992, and "No Hint of Arms Found in Iraqi Ministry," *New York Times*, Jul 30, 1992.

124. "Bush, Cheney Dispute General," *Washington Post*, Mar 28, 1991; [Classified source]; *GWAPS*, Vol II, Part 1, "Operations," 310.

125. "Bush, Cheney Dispute General," *Washington Post*, Mar 28, 1991.

126. Maj. Gen. Olsen intvw; Lt. Gen. Horner intvw, Mar 4, 1992. See also Schwarzkopf, *Autobiography*, 468, and *U.S. News & World Report*, *Triumph Without Victory*, 395.

127. Lt. Gen. Horner intvw, Mar 4, 1992; speech, Brig. Gen. Edwin E. Tenoso, Desert Shield COMALF, to Air Force Association Briefing Session, Saint Louis, Mo., Aug 2, 1991, historians' working files, HQ MAC/HO.

128. Msg, NGB/CSS to AIG 7316/CC/DO et al., 2101Z Mar 1, 1991, "Lessons Learned" file, Box 25, HQ TAC/HO archives; "A–10 Pilots Find Iraqi 'Hot Spot,'" *Air Force Times*, Mar 11, 1991; Col. Reavey intvw.

Epilogue

1. CINC's War Book input, "Overall KTO Ground Summary," Jan 17, 1991 [A.M.]; Final Report, 118, 203; Atkinson, *Crusade*, 340–343. For other sources on Iraqi numbers and the intelligence controversy about them, see endnotes 36 and 38 to Chapter 1 of this book. See also John Heidenrich, "The Gulf War: How Many Iraqis Died?," *Foreign Policy* 90 (spring 1993): 108–125.

2. *GWAPS*, Vol II, Part 2, "Effects and Effectiveness," 261; Final Report, App L, 2.

3. Gen. Schwarzkopf brfg; Gen. Schwarzkopf testimony, 326; Dr. Thompson's trip rpt.

4. "Iraq Charges High Civilian Toll in Air Raids," *Washington Post*, Feb 7, 1991; "Iraqi Death Toll Remains Clouded," *Washington Post*, Jun 23, 1991.

5. Final Report, 265.

6. CINC's War Book input, "CENTCOM Personnel Status, Daily" and "Coalition Casualties," Feb 28, 1991 P.M.

7. Quoted in J. D. Coleman, *Incursion* (New York: St. Martin's Press, 1991), 156; Gen. Schwarzkopf testimony, 349.

8. Interim Report, ch 27, p 1.

9. Final Report, App A, 3–11. See also list, CENTAF/DP, "Operation Desert Storm Reported USAF Casualties as of 6 Mar 91," File 0269629, "CENTAF/DP Casualty Statistics," Roll 10265, CAFH Desert Shield/Desert Storm microfilm collection. This is an earlier and less complete accounting, but it distinguishes between battle and nonbattle casualties.

10. Final Report, App A, 13.

11. *GWAPS*, Vol V, Part 1, "A Statistical Compendium," 654; DD/TWP brfg.

12. *GWAPS*, Vol V, Part 1, "A Statistical Compendium," 641; "Allies Shoot Down 42 Iraqi Aircraft: 81 Others Destroyed on Ground," *Aviation Week and Space Technology*, Mar 11, 1991, 22.

13. "A Capital Thank-You: 800,000 Jam D.C. for Tribute to Troops," *Washington Post*, Jun 9, 1991.

14. Historians and others were quick to delineate the contrasts between the Gulf and Vietnam wars. For two examples, see Harry G. Summers, Jr., *On Strategy II: A Critical Analysis of the Gulf War* (New York: Dell Publishing, 1992), and Kenneth P. Werrell, "Air War Victorious: The Gulf War vs. Vietnam," *Parameters*, Summer 1992, 41–54.

15. Intvw, Gen. Bryce Poe II (USAF, Ret.), with Dr. Perry D. Jamieson, Center for Air Force History, Oct 27, 1992. See also ltr, Dr. Perry D. Jamieson, Center for Air Force History, to Gen. Bryce Poe II (USAF, Ret.), Oct 22, 1992, and notes, Dr. Perry D. Jamieson, telecon with Gen. Poe, Oct 21, 1992.

16. Final Report, 375.

17. Calculated from ibid., 244, 375.

18. Cordesman and Wagner, *Lessons of Modern War*, 2:421–422; Schwarzkopf, *Autobiography*, 319.

19. Lt. Gen. Horner's daily comments, Feb 28, 1991, 74; notes, Gen. Merrill A. McPeak comments at "Hot Wash" debriefing conference, Apr 17, 1991; bio, SAF/PA, Gen. Bryce Poe II, n.d.; Gen. Poe intvw, Oct 27, 1992. See also note 15, this chapter.

20. Lt. Gen. Horner, quoted in *Air Force Magazine*, Jun 1991, 64.

21. Cordesman and Wagner, *Lessons*

of Modern War, 2:76.

22. Ibid., 2:3; "Iraqi Generals Perspective."

23. Cordesman and Wagner, *Lessons of Modern War*, 2:76.

24. Ibid., 2:80; Col. Christon intvw; Lt. Gen. Horner quoted in *Air Force Magazine*, Jun 1991, 60. See also Brig. Gen. Prince Sudayri's comments in Dr. Thompson's trip rpt.

25. Pagonis, *Moving Mountains*, 210; General Schwarzkopf, quoted in "Allied Bombers Strike Shifting Iraqi Troops," *Washington Post*, Feb 1, 1991; Gen. Schwarzkopf brfg; Lt. Gen. Horner, quoted in *Air Force Magazine*, Jun 1991, 60.

26. "U.S. Asks U.N. to Accelerate," *Washington Post*, Jul 28, 1992; "No Hint of Arms Found," *New York Times*, Jul 30, 1992. The citations for the final paragraph are "Most Oil Fires Are Out in Kuwait, but Its Environment Is Devastated," *New York Times*, Oct 19, 1991; "Environmental Claims for Damage by Iraq Go Begging for Data," *New York Times*, Nov 12, 1991; and Dr. Thompson's trip rpt.

Index

Page numbers appearing in italic type indicate a photograph on that page.

Index

ISBN 0-16-050958-0